Memoirs of a 1000-Year-Old Woman
Berlin 1925 to 1945

by
Gisela R. McBride

Edited by: Patricia Scullin, Winter Park, FL
Cover design: 206 Design, Mechanicsburg, PA
Back cover photograph: Guy Freeman, Carlisle, PA

Published By:

1stBooks

2511 West Third Street, Suite 1

Bloomington, IN 47404

http://www.1stbooks.com

ISBN: 1-58820-074-4

1st Books-rev. 10/27/00

Memoirs of a 1000-Year-Old Woman

Berlin 1925 to 1945

To Kim
with my best wishes

Gisela R. McBride.

May 5, 2001

Foreword

Mine is an ordinary, yet extraordinary story because it happened at an extraordinary time and place. When viewed from today's perspective, it conjures up a different, indeed an unbelievably different world.

My memoirs are an accurate account of my personal experiences, feelings, thoughts and reactions about and in response to the events around me during my childhood and adolescence.

I have changed most names and identifying information of people in the book to ensure their privacy, with the exception of immediate family members. These changes in no way affect the content of the story. I have included details from the press and generally known historical facts, which I may or may not have known or been aware of at the time. Some explanations are simply used to illustrate and to clarify facts which influenced certain actions and situations.

My memoirs, I hope, will open a window through which today's readers, who are so far removed from that other and seemingly unreal world I lived in, can gain some understanding of the common but at the same time uncommon everyday life of a child and young adult in Nazi Germany.

Gisela R. McBride
September 2000

Preface

Key to Family Members

Mama - my mother
Papa - my father
Father - maternal grandfather
Mother - maternal grandmother
Opa - paternal grandfather
Oma - paternal grandmother
Kurt - my stepfather
Aunt Elsbeth - my father's second wife

My maternal grandparents were Ernst August and Bertha. I called them Father and Mother. Father was born on August 12, 1868, in Muencheberg/Mark, a small town approximately 40 kilometers east of Berlin. He had two younger sisters, Marie and Louise, and one younger brother, Wilhelm.

Father's family, originally Huguenots, had lived in Muencheberg since the early 1700s. His father died at only 42 or 43 years of age. I understand that my great-grandmother found it hard to bring up four fatherless children and making ends meet on what little she could earn. Father was of slight to medium build and explained this to me saying, "What can you expect? How can you grow strong bones when you are raised on herrings

1

and potatoes for most of the time? Children need more substantial nourishment in order to grow tall and strong."

Father was very intelligent and did extremely well at school. The local pastor and the doctor delighted in inviting him to be their chess partner and they advocated higher education. His mother, however, would not agree to send him to high school and the university even though he would have received scholarships and grants. She said she had two sons and would not favor one over the other. Consequently, Father was apprenticed at age 14 to a printer.

At that time, young men were required to serve a year in the armed forces and Father was no exception. However, by the time WWI broke out, Father was too old to be called up.

Father held a number of jobs in the printing and publishing business. He was fond of reading and continued his education on his own by learning English, French and Latin. He spent some time in Munich and later on was manager of the Scherl Publishing Company's branch in Frankfurt/Oder.

Good at drawing, he at one time, long before I was born, did wood carving and a type of decorative net knotting. He was well-read and took an interest in current events throughout his life. He also solved crossword puzzles every day to the day he died at 93.

Father and Mother were married on October 7, 1893 in the parish church in Muellrose and the young couple settled in Berlin.

Mother was born in Schlaubehammer on September 21, 1869. Her father was the bailiff on a large estate called Kaisermuehl. Her mother was an herbal specialist and collected herbs and wild plants that she took to market in Frankfurt. Botanists regularly commissioned her to find rare plant specimens for them. Mother's mother acquired extensive knowledge of how to use herbs for their medicinal powers.

2

Mother had three sisters: Adele, Auguste and Emily, who lived in Spandau. She had a brother, Ernst, who was killed in WWI, and a brother, Wilhelm, who lived in Schlaubehammer. Wilhelm died in the early 1930s as a result of injuries he sustained when he fell off his bicycle and the handlebar penetrated his abdomen.

Mother's father also died young, at age 41 or 42. Mother's mother was greatly beloved by her grandchildren. Father, Mother, Mama and my aunts spent their summer holidays with her. My aunts and Mama told me how much they enjoyed their stay with their grandmother.

Once, Father became very ill and lost weight rapidly. Doctors could not figure out what was wrong with him and informed Mother that there was nothing they could do, that Father was doomed to die young. Mother's mother told Mother to pack up the family and come to Schlaubehammer where she proceeded to take care of Father. She nursed him, treated him with her herbs and fed him delicacies, such as pigeon soup. Father recovered.

Mother was an excellent cook. She loved flowers and could knit very well. Mother and Father had five children, all girls, but two babies died.

My mother's name was Hertha and I called her Mama. Born on January 13, 1904 in Frankfurt/Oder, she was the youngest of three sisters. Her sisters were Martha, the eldest, and Margarethe, called Marga.

Aunt Martha was married to Uncle Gustav, who was a custom tailor by trade but worked for many years at the Government Printing Office. Aunt Martha was a custom dressmaker. She did not work after she married but she made clothes for all the female family members.

Aunt Marga lived with Aunt Martha and Uncle Gustav. She was an accountant, employed by the G'sellius Book and Rare Book Sellers, located in center city. G'sellius was owned and operated by the same family for 200 years and Aunt Marga was with G'sellius for more than 35 years. During WWII, the building was destroyed and there was no supply or demand for books in the aftermath of WWII. That came only much later. The immediate priorities were food, shelter and clothing. G'sellius struggled for a while and then went under.

Aunt Marga traveled extensively before WWII, alone or in the company of friends, sometimes by car and other times by train. She visited Austria, Switzerland, France and almost every part of Germany, as well as Belgium and Denmark. At one time, she had a boyfriend who was a well-known Danish actor.

My paternal grandfather, Gustav, was born in Berlin, as were his father and grandfather. My paternal great-grandfather I believe, emigrated to Berlin at a time when people had to pay a three thaler (a German silver coin used from the 15th to the 19th century) emigration fee. Gustav was a stuccoer, designing and making stucco ceiling and wall decorations. My paternal grandmother was Maria Helene and worked in a small firm that made silk designer ties. I called them Opa and Oma. Opa and Oma had four children but one died as a baby.

My father, Max, was born in Berlin on October 6, 1903 and I called him Papa. Papa had two sisters, Gertrud, his senior, and Frieda, his junior. Papa was a master precision tool and die maker, Gertrud was an accountant and Frieda was a furrier. Papa was a very versatile and industrious person with many interests and hobbies. He bred canaries and played the mandolin. He also enjoyed woodworking and made flower cribs, lamp shades, book ends and magazine racks. He was a photographer who developed, enlarged and colored his photographs. He gardened, smoked fish, baked fancy cakes, learned to fly gliders and was handy all around.

My grandparents, Father and Mother, changed their place of residence frequently during the first years of their marriage and had lived in different parts of Berlin, mostly in Charlottenburg. For a few years, they also lived in Frankfurt/Oder and Mama was born there. They returned to Berlin and eventually moved to a brand-new apartment house in the borough of Neukoelln, where they lived for more than 30 years. That is where I was born on December 21, 1925.

The Borough of Neukoelln became an administrative borough of the city of Berlin in 1920 and included the villages of Britz, Buckow and Rudow. Until 1912, Neukoelln was known as Rixdorf. Rixdorf was first mentioned in the chronicles of the year 1360 where it states that on June 26, 1360, the Friday before St. Thomas, Richardsdorf was incorporated with 100 inhabitants. The original estate was owned by the Templar Knights who also owned the above named villages and the Tempelhof.

1889-1924

April 20, 1889	Adolph Hitler is born in Braunau, Austria.
1912	Hitler moves to Munich.
1914-1918	Hitler serves in the German army as a Corporal in World War I (WWI).
1919-1920	Hitler develops National Socialist German Workers Party (NSDAP-*Nationalsozialistische Deutsche Arbeiter Partei*).
January 1923	French occupy Ruhr because of default in reparation payments by Germany. The German Government must pay so it prints millions of marks. The mark plummets and the exchange becomes 18,000 marks to $1 U.S. dollar.
June 9, 1923	1 pound of beef costs 8,500 - 12,000 Reichsmark. 1 pound of veal costs 6,800 - 10,000 Reichsmark. 1 pound of mutton costs 7,000 - 9,000 Reichsmark. 1 pound of pork costs 9,000 - 10,500 Reichsmark. 1 pound of butter costs 13,000 - 15,000 Reichsmark.

	1 pound of coffee costs 26,000 - 36,000 Reichsmark.
	1 pound of tea costs 30,000 - 48,000 Reichsmark.
	1 pound of potatoes costs 2,200 - 2,500 Reichsmark.
	1 pound of herring costs 2,500 Reichsmark.
	1 egg costs 800 - 810 Reichsmark.
July 1923	The exchange is 160,000 Reichsmark to $1 U.S.
August 1923	The exchange is 1 million Reichsmark to $1 U.S.
November 1923	The exchange is 4 billion Reichsmark to $1 U.S.
	2 pounds of potatoes cost 90 billion Reichsmark.
	1 loaf of bread costs 140 billion Reichsmark.
	1 pound of butter costs 2.8 billion Reichsmark.
November 8-9, 1923	Hitler and Ludendorff try to overthrow the Bavarian and German governments in Munich. Hitler fails and is arrested.
November 15, 1923	Hitler is sentenced to five years in prison at Landsberg. While in prison, Hitler writes *Mein Kampf* (*"My Struggle"*).
November 15, 1923	National Socialist German Labor Party banned in Prussia. The ban is strictly enforced in Berlin.

| November 19, 1923 | The camouflage organization of the NSDAP, the greater German Labor Party, is also banned. |
| December 1924 | Hitler is released from prison. |

Adolf Hitler was relatively inactive from 1925 until December 1932. He spent most of his time in the Bavarian mountains and had an affair with his niece, Feli Raubal. Meanwhile, the Weimar Republic was not doing well.

Years later Mother told me that, when Father came home with his pay, she immediately rushed with a laundry basket full of paper money to the grocery store and the bakery because during the time it took Father to get home, the prices could rise while the money value and its buying power dropped even further. Mother kept a beautiful box decorated with purple and yellow pansies in her bureau drawer. It was filled with paper currency in denominations of million and trillion mark bills as well as coins. The smallest coin was 500 marks. The coins were made of aluminum. Later on, Father drilled holes in them and strung them together with wire and I used them to play hopscotch.

1925

February 24	Hitler reestablishes the NSDAP.
April 26	Hindenburg is elected president of the Weimar Republic, following the death of Friedrich Ebert, the first president of the Weimar Republic. Hindenburg supports a return to the monarchy but promises to uphold the republican constitution.
May 6	Reich Republicans fear restoration of monarchy and protest Hindenburg's election.
June 20	Mr. Schaetzle demonstrates a wireless telephone for cars in Berlin.
July	Hitler's book, *"Mein Kampf"* ("My Struggle") is published. It includes a dedication to the memory of 23 of his followers who were killed during the 1923 abortive uprising in Munich.
November	The building of skyscrapers is banned in Berlin. They are declared "dangerous" and thought to be health hazards.
November 9	The SS (Schutz Staffel) is formed to protect Hitler during rallies and speeches from attack and becomes Hitler's personal guard for his protection.

| December 1 | 7,000 British troops are withdrawn from Cologne, which they had occupied since 1918. |
| December 21 | The author is born in Berlin. |

The SS, an elite paramilitary organization, was formed in 1923 and subsequently banned and reestablished in 1925. The SS was initially used as Hitler's bodyguards and later evolved into the party's police force. SS members had a number tattooed under their armpit. The SS insignia was Germanic runes signifying or symbolizing strength. Runes (from Goth runa, meaning secret) are the oldest written characters used by all Germanic tribes.

1926

January 6	The German airline "Lufthansa" is founded.
April 16	Unemployed Germans are granted 39 weeks of unemployment benefits.
July 4	The Nazi Party holds its First Party Congress since its reorganization.
November 1	Joseph Goebbels is appointed Head of the Berlin Nazi Party. The Berlin Nazis concentrate on provoking violent confrontations with their political opponents, primarily the Communists.
November 14	320 SA (Sturm Abteilung - Storm Troopers) men marched through the Berlin Borough of Neukoelln, one of the communist strongholds. The brown shirted SA men served as bodyguards to party leaders, distributed leaflets, collected donations and solicited votes for Hitler.
December 21	The author's first birthday.

On Sunday, May 23, 1926, I was baptized in the Martin Luther Church and was given the names Gisela Ruth Iris. It was quite usual for people to have three first names. The ceremony was followed by a small party for family and close friends. Mama had originally planned to name me Angela or Iris but both names were rejected by the family. Iris was the heroine in a novel Mama read but the family thought it was too theatrical a name. Mama's next selection was Gisela. Early on in WWI, Mother occasionally babysat for a couple who lived on the fourth floor in the house opposite hers. They had one child, a girl, named Gisela. The mother was German, the father a handsome Pole. As it turned out, some time later he was arrested as a spy.

1927

January 25	First major Nazi rally is held in Berlin-Spandau on Schuetzenstrasse.
February 11	Mass rally held at the Pharus Hall ends in bloodshed as Nazis fight with Communists, who considered the hall their territory.
March 10	Prussia lifts ban on Nazi Party and Hitler is allowed to speak in public.
March 20	The Station Lichterfelde-East is scene of first street fight between Nazis and Communists. Firearms are used by both sides and 20 are wounded.
May 1	Adolph Hitler speaks for the first time in Berlin.
May 13	Black Friday: the economic collapse of Germany.
December 21	The author's second birthday.

The Berlin Police Chief, President Zoergiebel, banned the NSDAP in Berlin due to their riotous activities, following an incident at a Nazi meeting. A man, a former pastor, interrupted the meeting at which Dr. Goebbels was the main speaker by shouting that "the keynote speaker is hardly the perfect embodiment and example of the ideal Aryan," whereupon the SA beat him up.

1928

March 5	Nazi Party wins majority in Bavarian elections.
May 20	In the Reichstag elections, Nazis have 810,000, or 2.6 percent, of the popular votes and 12 seats out of 491 in the Reichstag.
October 15	The dirigible "Graf Zeppelin" makes its first trip to New York and arrives at Lakehurst, NJ, a flight that took 111 hours.
November 1	The "Graf Zeppelin" arrives back in Germany, flying time is 69 hours.
December 21	The author's third birthday.

One evening, it was either early spring or early winter of 1928, I was sitting on a blanket on the floor in Mother's kitchen playing with my wooden painted duck on wheels and my painted wooden houses. The lights were on. I looked up and saw Papa and Mama sitting at the kitchen table facing each other. They were talking. Mama was crying. After a while, Mama got up and left the room, closing the door behind her. Papa immediately picked me up, took me into the hall and dressed me in my blue winter coat with the white fur trim. We left the apartment. Papa was carrying me. I recall very clearly looking down as we were about to walk out of the front door and seeing that I was still wearing my emerald green felt booties with black buckles, which were my house shoes. Papa took me to Oma's apartment. I remember Papa pacing the kitchen floor, carrying me, for some time. A small lamp with a rose colored shade was turned on. It made the room look warm and cozy. I have no idea how long I was there, a few hours or longer.

Papa and Mama were divorced a short time later. Mama and I moved in with Mother and Father. Mama went back to work.

I believe it was standard procedure in divorce cases at the time to appoint an official guardian for children of divorced parents, to act as an arbitrator between the parties in case of disputes, disagreements or complaints. It was decided by the court that I would visit Papa on the twelfth of each month from 5 p.m. to 7 p.m. and on every first and third Sunday from 10 a.m. to 1 p.m.

1929

February 15	The number of unemployed in Germany reaches 3.2 million.
April	In Paris, Hjalmar Schacht, the Reich Bank President, rejects new German debt total and states the Dawes Plan is preferable.
April 18	Schacht demands lower payments, as well as the return of the Saar and Upper Silesia.
May 1	Communists clash with police at a rally in Berlin, resulting in eight dead and 140 wounded.
May 29	The amount of $27 billion is agreed upon as the total figure of German reparations, as specified in the Young Plan. The Young Plan proposes payments totaling $7.8 billion in German reparations, with $488 million to be paid yearly from 1929 to 1966. Additional payments are to be made until the year 1988.
September 22	Communists and Nazis clash. There are gun fights in Berlin.
October 3	Gustav Stresemann dies.
October 26	Hitler and the Nationalist leader, Hugenberg, lead a large demonstration against the Young Plan.

October 29	Black Tuesday. The stock market collapses on Wall Street and has a disastrous effect on Germany.
November 29	Allies evacuate the second occupation zone in the Rhineland.
December 21	The author's fourth birthday.

In Berlin, a city at the time of about 4.5 million inhabitants, the majority of people lived in apartments. Generally, apartment houses were four stories high, counting the European way: ground floor, first, second, third and fourth floor. There were no high rise buildings in Berlin at that time. Skyscrapers were considered "hazardous and dangerous to health."

Every apartment house had janitors, usually a married couple, who occupied a ground floor apartment rent free and who received a small salary. The man held an outside job but was responsible for building maintenance. The woman cleaned the staircases and entrance hall. The couple saw to it that the house was locked in the evenings at 8 p.m. in the winter and at 9 p.m. in the summer, cleaned the pavement in front of the building, kept a log for booking the laundry room and took care of tenants' complaints and requests. It was in the janitors' apartment where the landlord's representative collected the rents once a month.

Each apartment house had a basement and an attic. The basement was divided into storage bins, one to each apartment. Here people stored coal, wood, potatoes, flower boxes, bicycles, tools and other odds and ends.

The attic consisted of two parts: the laundry room with its own entrance and the general attic with a separate entrance. One section of the general part was divided by wooden slats into storage cages and there was one for each apartment. The other section was used to dry clothes. Both the laundry room and the general attic were kept locked. Each tenant had a key to the general attic but the key to the laundry room was kept by the janitors.

There were two kinds of wash, large and small. Small laundry was washed in the apartment. The big wash–sheets, towels, table linens—was done once a month or every two months in the laundry room. The big wash was no small matter. It was done by hand, an arduous task that took two or three days. First, the laundry room was booked ahead of time. On the appointed date, the laundry was carried upstairs and buckets filled with cold water were poured into a large tub. Soap was added and the laundry was left to soak overnight. Early the following morning, coal was carried up six flights of stairs from the basement to the laundry room and a fire was built in the stove under the big built-in cauldron. The cauldron was filled with buckets of water and soap was added. Then the laundry was wrung out from its soak and transferred to the cauldron, covered and left to boil. All the while, the fire had to be tended. The laundry was stirred now and again with a big wooden paddle. The laundry room got quite warm and great clouds of steam issued from the cauldron, especially when the lid was lifted.

All the while this was going on, the big tub was emptied by pulling the plug and letting the water drain into buckets which were then emptied into a sink. After the laundry had been boiled long enough, a few pieces at a time were lifted with the paddle from the boiling water, swung over to the tub and each piece was washed by rubbing it with laundry soap and scrubbing it on the washboard. It was then wrung out and put into another tub filled with cold water for the first rinse. After everything was washed, wrung out, and rinsed, both tubs were drained and at least one of them was, again, filled with cold water for a second rinse.

This accomplished, the laundry was carried in baskets to the other part of the attic and hung on previously stretched lines to dry. The cauldron had to be emptied, the fire, which had been left to die while the rinsing took place, was extinguished properly, the ashes were taken out, the door of the attic and the laundry room were locked and the key returned to the custodians. By now the poor hausfrau was thoroughly exhausted.

Drying time varied, of course, depending on the weather and time of year. Once it was dry, the laundry was taken down, folded into a laundry basket and brought back to the apartment. The next step was to sprinkle each item with cold water and roll it up. Later on, they were ready to be ironed. In order to make this task easier, since these were large pieces, many of them linen, one took them to a "soap shop" and put them through a large rolling press one by one. Almost every block had a soap shop, dealing in laundry products such as soaps, soap flakes, starches, blues, clothes baskets, clothes lines, clothes pins, fine toilet soaps, brooms, mops, floor cloths, chamois leather, and other related items. The back part of the store had a large rolling press. I remember watching women perform this task many times.

Of course, there was a much easier way. If people were physically unable to do their own wash and/or could afford it, they had their laundry done by a professional laundry service that picked it up and returned it ready to be put away. They could choose to get their laundry back wet or dry, do their own ironing or take it to an ironing shop.

Father and Mother's apartment was located on the fourth floor. The only other apartment on the fourth floor was occupied by Mr. Riemann, a widower, and his two daughters, Gertrud and Charlotte. Gertrud was called "The Little Riemann" because she was not as tall as her older sister, Charlotte. I do not remember if Charlotte worked outside the house but Gertrud was a civil servant.

When I was born, Mr. Riemann was terminally ill and asked to see me. I was taken to visit him. Mother told me that he looked at me, the tiny newborn, smiled and shook his head as if to say, "Here is a new beginning and I am about to leave this world."

The apartment on the third floor was occupied by a childless elderly couple, the Winters. The Brehm family also lived on the third floor. The Brehms had fraternal twin boys, Willy and Werner, who were Mama's age. The Kaufmanns, on the first floor, had six children. I only remember two daughters clearly, Eva and Ursula, the youngest.

People were at all times considerate of their neighbors in those days and would soon hear about it if they were not. For instance, when people came home they changed from street shoes into house shoes or slippers to cut down on the noise when walking around, even though all floors, except corridors and kitchens, were carpeted.

Apartment living was quite restrictive and did not offer much space for a small child to romp and expend surplus energy. I used to race along our long corridor much to Mother's dismay. She was concerned the noise would disturb the Winters below us. However, the Winters were quite forbearing and understanding, assuring Mother that she should not worry, that it was natural for a small child to run and jump.

I was a popular visitor and was often invited to visit the Riemann sisters and the Brehms. Occasionally, we visited the Kaufmanns and Mama's schoolfriend, Ella, who lived with her widowed mother in a house around the corner.

One night when I walked into the Brehm's spacious kitchen, Werner scared me by picking up a large live lobster, which was crawling along on the kitchen floor. He came toward me bearing this huge crustacean with its big pinchers opening and closing, its legs waving in a most threatening way, or so I thought. I immediately took refuge behind Mama's skirt. From this vantage point, I watched Werner drop the lobster into a pot of boiling water on the stove and was amazed to see the creature turn bright red.

I was the only small child in the house and all the tenants liked me. I received little gifts from many of them at Christmas, Easter and on my birthday.

During the 1920s and 1930s, Gita Alpa and Richard Tauber reigned supreme in the operatic world. Tauber was famous for singing the romantic leads in Franz Lehar's operettas. Lehar wrote many of these roles specifically for him. One Saturday afternoon, Mama and I were riding on the top deck of a double decker bus along the Friedrichstrasse when I saw a huge crowd. I asked Mama what was going on. She explained, "Tauber is singing at the Metropole Theatre today."

My favorite was Gita Alpa, a coloratura soprano. I heard her on the radio and on records. At age 3, I knew exactly what I wanted to be when I grew up: I wanted to be a singer like Gita Alpa. However, I made up my mind that I would not sing any songs with lyrics that included the word "heart." I found this to be too personal and therefore too embarrassing to be mentioned in public. Every time we visited neighbors, they asked me to "do" Gita Alpa. I willingly obliged, provided I could do so sitting under the table or standing behind a door.

Other friends of Mama also appreciated my performances as Gita. I remember sitting many times under the table at the Hofer's apartment, warbling away. Vicki Hofer and Mama were school friends. She and her brother, Horst, lived with their mother, a WWI widow. I loved to visit them because they were fun. Horst often tried to frighten me by pretending to be a lion and jumping out unexpectedly from behind a door or cupboard with a great roar.

During this time, cigarette manufacturers, vying for business, included small novelties in each pack of cigarettes, such as silk embroidered appliques of flowers and leaves, pictures of film stars, pictures of fairy tales and, later on, pictures of SA men and of the Fuehrer. People purchased the appropriate albums, which supplied background information and pasted the pictures in them. Mama collected film stars. I collected silk flowers and fairy tales.

Skat, a card game, and Skat clubs were particularly popular in the 20's and early 30's. Father, Uncle Gustav, Emil and Karl Schaefer (friends of Father and Mother) and later on Kurt, my stepfather, played Skat. They formed their own club, "Club Harmless," and had a small green velvet standard with the club's name embroidered on it, which stood on the table when the club was in session. Once a week the club met, taking turns at the members' apartments. While the men played cards, the ladies sat in another room or on the balcony doing needlework. One of the ladies read aloud from a book or they conversed until it was time for refreshments.

Many other clubs met in pubs where they had their regular *Stammtisch*. The *Stammtisch* is an institution peculiar to Germany. It is a certain table in a café or pub reserved exclusively for a group or groups of regular customers or cronies. All or any number of members of the group may sit at it whenever they patronize the establishment. The *Stammtisch* is Dutch treat unless a member decides to foot the bill.

In February 1929, the number of unemployed in Germany reached 3.2 million.

These were very unsettled, difficult and even dangerous times caused by the precarious economic and political situation. Life was exceptionally difficult for the "little man," who had his back to the wall fighting for survival.

The Great Depression was as bad in Germany as it was elsewhere, if not worse. I did not really understand what it was all about; I was too young. I do recall seeing men standing on street corners and sitting on the pavement along the main streets begging or selling pencils, chocolate bars or cheap writing paper and greeting cards. Most of them were WWI veterans, amputees who had lost an arm or one or both legs and were confined to wheelchairs. Many were blind. For a while, some went door to door trying to sell their modest merchandise. Several times I witnessed Mama opening the door and buying something. After all these years, I still have not forgotten the terrible taste of the cheap chocolate bar she bought from one of these unfortunate men sitting on a blanket at a street corner.

As the depression deepened, families and couples became destitute. People who could no longer pay their rent were evicted from their apartments. Homeless people tried to find a place to spend the night under cover. One afternoon, Mother had the key to the laundry room and took me with her to check on her wash. When we reached the landing, a middle-aged, neatly dressed couple had settled there. It was obvious that they intended to spend the night sleeping on the floor. They wore coats and had two suitcases. They politely said "Good day" and moved out of our way. Later, Mother took them blankets, pillows and something to eat. They did not come back after the one night.

Berlin was a socialist and communist stronghold and held out against the Nazis until the takeover by Hitler in January 1933. I became aware of the frequent street fights that took place mainly in the blue collar working class districts of North Berlin, such as Moabit and Wedding, which were citadels of the Communists. Our borough, Neukoelln, was also socialist and communist. I saw lots of graffiti and posters on my daily walks with Father. I could not read but saw the writings, big white letters on fences and walls. I would ask, "Father, what letter is this? What letter is that?" Many spelled quite unpolitical words such as "Sports Grounds" or "Sports Club" or the name of a company or organization located behind the fence or wall. Many, however, were political slogans scrawled in white, untidy letters. I could soon make out German Social Democratic Party (SPD - *Sozialdemokratische Partei Deutschlands*) and German Communist Party (KPD - *Kommunistische Partei Deutschlands*).

In addition, swastikas and posters covered fences, walls and advertising pillars. Posters were more often than not defaced and torn, as rival factions tried to eliminate each other's propaganda. At an intersection on a street we frequently walked down was a long 8- or 10-foot high wooden fence, painted a dull reddish brown, somewhat like redwood garden furniture. It was a perfect background for political graffiti. Here the SPD and the KPD wrote their slogans. Even though the fence was repainted a number of times, the large white letters "KPD" kept bleeding through and remained visible for years.

One big political issue in Germany in 1929 was the WWI reparations. The Dawes Plan, named after the U.S. banker Charles G. Dawes, was an adjustment of the reparations demanded of Germany in the Versailles Peace Treaty.

On April 9, 1924, Dawes required stabilization of the German economy before further German payments would be made. The Dawes Plan called for yearly payments of 1 to 1.75 billion gold marks for four years, then 2.5 billion gold marks yearly. It was agreed to and passed by the Reichstag (German parliament) on August 29, 1924. The Young Plan later replaced the Dawes Plan and was vigorously opposed by the Nazis.

On June 7, 1929, the Young Plan was designed to adjust reparations demanded of Germany in the Versailles treaty. A conference was convened in Paris and Hjalmar Schacht represented Germany. Later, other meetings took place in The Hague on August 31, 1929 and on January 3 through 20, 1930.

The terms of the plan were retroactive as of September 1, 1929 and set the total reparations to be paid by Germany at 34.5 billion marks in 59 annual installments, ending in 1988.

The occupation of the Rhineland areas and the withdrawal of occupation troops were tied in with the plan. After Germany was forced to suspend payments on July 1, 1931, because of the world economic crisis, the Young Plan was formally canceled by the Lausanne Agreement of June 9, 1932.

As a small child, I repeatedly heard the names of Friedrich Ebert and Gustav Stresemann when family and friends talked about current events and the Weimar Republic. Friedrich Ebert (1817-1925) was the Leader of the Social Democrats and First President of the Weimar Republic. Stresemann (1878-1929) was Chancellor in 1923 and Foreign Minister of the Weimar Republic from 1923 to 1929. He was instrumental in ending the passive resistance in the fight over the Ruhr area and sought communication and agreement with France on the Dawes Plan of 1924. He was awarded the Nobel prize for peace in 1926 and accepted the Dawes Plan in 1929, thereby achieving the early evacuation of the Rhineland. Stresemann died on October 3, 1929. I listened at Aunt Martha's apartment to the live broadcast of his funeral.

During the holiday season, I went to a Christmas fair at a school with Father's friends, the Schaefers. It was fun. At different tables, one could purchase toys and items for dolls' houses. I left my doll in one section to have a new dress made for her while we walked around.

1930

January 3	The Second Conference on German War Reparations takes place in The Hague.
January 23	Wilhelm Frick becomes Minister of the Interior for Thuringia, the first Nazi to take office in Germany.
February 24	Horst Wessel, an SA man, dies after being shot by anti-Nazis.
June 30	French occupation troops are withdrawn from the Rhineland five years ahead of schedule. No German troops are to be stationed on the Left Bank of the Rhine, now a demilitarized zone.
September	The German government suffers a stunning setback in the elections and the NSDAP gains many seats.
October 6	The Reichstag is scandalized when Nazi delegates attend the Reichstag in uniform.
November	Nazis win victory in Bremen municipal elections.
December 12	The last Allied troops leave the Saar. Germany has 5 million unemployed.
December 21	The author's fifth birthday.

Shortly after Christmas 1929, Mama came down with a very severe case of jaundice brought on, so it was thought at the time, by overindulging in rich foods during the holidays. Mama did not look yellow. She looked orange. I invited everyone I met, "Do come and look at my mother. She has jaundice and looks like a canary. She is taking (the name of the medication escapes me) for the pancreas." The German word for pancreas is *Bauchspeicheldruese*, quite a mouthful for a child barely 4 years old. There were, of course, no antibiotics at the time. Our family physicians were Dr. Schmitz and his partner, Dr. Baumann. Dr. Baumann visited Mama and ordered strict bed rest. He put her on a diet of weak black tea and oatmeal cooked in water with no sugar or milk to be added to either.

We ate our main meal at noon. Aunt Marga came home to eat with us during her two hour lunch time. We took afternoon coffee immediately after the meal because she had to go back to work. Aunt Marga usually brought luscious pastries from a famous coffeehouse in the city. I thought that Mama was to blame for being sick and had brought this illness on herself. I am sorry to say that I once went into her bedroom gloating, "Look what we have for dessert. If you had not stuffed yourself at Christmas, you could have some, too."

Poor Mama. She lost a lot of weight. Her hands looked skeletal. She grew hungrier and hungrier. After three weeks on the diet, she was desperate for food and pleaded with Dr. Baumann to let her eat something besides oats. Dr. Baumann asked what we were having for lunch. She told him we were having spinach, potatoes and *Bouletten,* also known as German beefsteak. Dr. Baumann said, "All right, you may eat two tablespoons of spinach." As soon as he had left, Mama said she was allowed to eat lunch. Mama ate two helpings of everything and had a relapse. Poor Dr. Baumann, who was extremely conscientious, did not know what to think and blamed himself for the setback. Mama was sick for several more weeks before she recovered. No one ever knew what exactly caused her illness.

I think it was in 1930 that I was enrolled in a kindergarten. I had no contact with other children before this and was very shy. At the kindergarten, each child had a clothes and towel hook identified by a fruit or a flower. Mine was marked with a pair of cherries. Everything went well for a time. We learned songs, played games and colored. We all had a box or tin with crayons. One day, however, when we were coloring, a boisterous boy at my table grabbed my finger and deliberately cut it by pushing it down on the sharp edge of the metal box he used for his crayons. My finger was bleeding and I screamed. I refused to go back. That was the end of my kindergarten days.

Politically, the situation in Berlin was not peaceful. The various factions warred against each other and the Nazis tried very hard to make inroads into strongly social democratic and communist Berlin. I heard about Horst Wessel, an SA man who was shot when he opened his apartment door. I remember hearing reports that he was in the hospital for several days before he died. His funeral received extensive news coverage. The event became the scene of a violent clash between Nazis and Communists.

Papa was unemployed for a while and also contracted a slight case of tuberculosis, which is extremely contagious. The Health Department was very thorough in taking preventive measures. Everybody who had been in close contact with or was related to an infected person was screened and checked. As a precaution, I was X-rayed, my first experience with X-rays, and was checked a number of times afterwards.

Tuberculosis was a fearful disease. It killed one of Mama's friends, Annie. Annie lived with her parents in a suburb of Berlin, Hoppegarten, which was famous for horse racing. Mama and I visited her not long before she died and visited her mother after Annie's death. Annie was quite young when she died, I think only 25 or 26 years old.

We take it for granted now that everybody has a telephone. In prewar Berlin, few people had telephones. Mail service in Berlin was excellent with three or even four deliveries a day. The majority of apartment houses did not have elevators, neither did they have mailboxes downstairs in their entrance halls. Mailmen had to climb the stairs to every floor in every building several times a day. Most people communicated by postcard or by letter with friends, or dropped by in person. Dropping in on people was the thing to do and a friend or relative's home was often the destination when out for a Sunday walk.

We generally celebrated birthdays with an open house in the afternoon and evening. Family and friends were expected to call. If someone sent a birthday card it meant that the person could not visit. The table, covered with a fine cloth, was laid with bone china sets of matching medium size plate, cup and saucer, each of a different pattern, one or more platters of assorted fancy pastries and/or a gateau and whipped cream. Guests arrived and stayed however long they wanted, many of them until evening. For supper, open garnished sandwiches, long Vienna sausages, potato or herring salad, smoked shrimp or pork chops in aspic were served.

Special birthdays such as the 30th, 40th, 50th and 60th, as well as the 65th, 70th and 75th warranted special celebrations.

Aunt Marga lived with Aunt Martha and Uncle Gustav. On March 2 of this year, she celebrated her 30th birthday. The living room ceiling was decorated with garlands of pink paper flowers.

34

The ladies wore silk kimonos, that were the rage, and were given a Japanese sun umbrella as a memento.

When I was school-age, Aunt Marga often took me on day trips into the surrounding countryside. This way I became familiar with many parts of the fascinating Mark Brandenburg.

I was in for a special treat: Uncle Gustav and Aunt Martha took me to the famous Circus Krone, which had come to Berlin. I was very excited. It was thrilling to sit under the huge tent, hear the music, watch trapeze and high wire artists perform, clowns clown, jugglers juggle and to breathe in the atmosphere and the smells of the arena, the horses, camels and elephants. I was spellbound when a ballet was performed by dancers dressed in white Rococo costumes. It ended with a tableau, in which the dancers posed and purple spotlights transformed the group, giving it the appearance of delicate Dresden or Meissen porcelain figurines. I was enchanted.

But most exciting by far was the lion tamer. One of his tigers was young and, at one point during the act, he picked up the tiger, laid it across his shoulders and walked around the cage while the audience applauded. I was most impressed.

Aunt Martha owned a cat. It was black and had a little white bib. Its name was *Mohrchen* (little Moor). On my first visit to Aunt Martha, following our evening at the circus, I went straight for the cat. I picked him up and tried to drape him around my shoulders just as I had seen the lion tamer do with the tiger. *Mohrchen*, however, being up in years, did not appreciate this at all. He escaped my grasp and made a beeline for the highest kitchen cabinet where he retreated into the farthest corner. He sat there and kept a wary eye on me. No matter how much I pleaded with him to come down, he did not budge. Finally I got mad, stamped my foot and cried, "Come down, you silly old cat! Don't you know that all I want to do is play tiger tamer with you? Come down at once!" But *Mohrchen* turned a deaf ear, sat like a statue until, much chagrined, I had to leave. My tiger taming ambitions remained unfulfilled, for from then on *Mohrchen* withdrew to his retreat as soon as he heard me come in the front door. To my disgust, he always stayed there for the duration of my visits.

Two of Mama's friends, George and Ludwig, shared an apartment. They also had a cat, a big yellow tabby named Sunny Boy. Sunny Boy was a character. Every room in every apartment had a door, even the kitchen. All the interior doors had door handles and only the outside apartment door had a door knob. Doors were always kept closed. But Sunny Boy was independent. Often, when we sat in the living room, the door would suddenly and very quietly swing open, revealing Sunny Boy hanging on the door handle by his front paws.

Sunny Boy had all sorts of tricks. One evening, George was preparing a dinner of fried calf's liver. The frying pan was on the stove and the liver was on a plate on the kitchen table, next to another plate with flour. Sunny Boy sat on the kitchen chair next to the table. George coated each slice of liver with flour prior to transferring it to the frying pan on the opposite side of the kitchen. George put a couple of slices into the pan and was ready to coat additional slices when he stopped short. "Funny," he mused, "I thought I had more than this." He counted, turned, counted the slices in the pan, turned again to the table, checked the wrapping paper. No matter, one slice was missing. Sunny Boy sat there, very proper, tail tucked around, looking so innocent, like butter would not melt in his mouth. Finally, George chased Sunny Boy off the chair. Lo and behold, the mystery of the missing slice of liver was solved: Sunny Boy had been sitting on it all the time. He had neatly swiped the slice and was waiting patiently for a chance to remove himself and his "prey," unobservedly, to feast on it in some dark corner.

Frankfurt/Oder received its city charter in 1253, was a member of the Hanseatic League and once boasted of a University which was founded in 1506, but which was relocated to Breslau in Silesia in 1811. Frankfurt/Oder is situated about sixty miles east of Berlin, really no distance at all by today's standards. But in those days, taking a trip even to Frankfurt was a big undertaking. We would not dream of going just for the day, although it could easily have been done since there was frequent daily train service.

Two of Mother's sisters lived in Frankfurt, Adele and Auguste (called Aunt Klinger). Adele was Mother's favorite sister and Mother visited her, sometimes alone, sometimes with me and sometimes all of us went. Aunt Adele came to Berlin but infrequently. I eagerly anticipated guests. It was very exciting for me especially if they stayed overnight. On one of Aunt Adele's visits, she and Mother sat in the living room talking while I played. I overheard their conversation. I remember it as plainly as if it had happened yesterday. Aunt Adele was recounting a dream she had the previous night. In her dream, she was walking down the last flight of stairs leading into the entrance hall of an apartment house. The front door was wide open and as she approached she saw a black draped hearse with two black horses standing outside. (These hearses were still in use at that time.) The hearse contained a black coffin. Not only did Aunt Adele see the coffin but to her horror a glass leg was sticking out of the coffin.

It must have been almost time for afternoon coffee because Mother asked me if I would like to go downstairs to the bakery, which was just around the corner in the same apartment building, to get Danish pastries. I loved to do this and tripped happily downstairs, made the purchase and started back up the stairs. When I reached the landing between the second and third floors, I remembered Aunt Adele's dream. I was scared and for some unknown reason I suddenly saw, in color, the face of a man in front of me. The face was not ugly, evil or menacing, just middle-aged and ruddy with a mustache. I only saw the head, which was turned slightly sideways so that he was not looking directly at me but it appeared so suddenly and was so real that I screamed. Dear Mr. Winter came rushing out of his apartment carrying a stick, thinking someone in the staircase was being attacked. Mother was beside herself for allowing me to go to the bakery. Everyone calmed down when I explained what happened but that dream of Aunt Adele's haunted me for a long time.

When I was a small child, Berlin still had *Droschken,* horse drawn carriages, that served as taxis, although by now they were mainly used around the Tiergarten, the large heavily wooded park adjacent to the Brandenburg Gate, and Unter den Linden, Berlin's most famous boulevard lined with linden trees, cafés and elegant stores. Still, I saw a number of them, less and less as time went by, in Neukoelln. *Droschken* drivers were known to be real Berlin characters. Eventually, the carriages were all replaced by taxis.

I believe the only chain restaurant in Berlin, in my younger days, was Aschinger of which there were several in Neukoelln. Most Aschinger restaurants, but not all, consisted of two parts. One was open to the street for "fast food," with a few tall round tables where customers could stand and eat, the other was a proper dining room. The former served Aschinger's famous yellow pea soup with or without hot dogs. A large bowl of this thick, hot, delicious soup cost only 50 pfennig. Baskets of fresh rolls stood on the tables and customers could consume as many as they liked. Students, in particular, took advantage of this offer. The restaurant part was carpeted and tables were set with snow-white table linen and napkins, along with good flatware. The chairs were upholstered in a red plush material. Once in a while, we ate there or at the Schultheiss Restaurant or restaurants near the Funkturm and at the Kurfuersten Damm.

When I awoke on my fifth birthday, I ran into Father and Mother's bedroom and climbed onto Father's bed. I was too excited to eat breakfast and my birthday surprises were not long in arriving. Father and Mother entered the bedroom bearing a doll's kitchen, complete with pots, pans and dishes. There were games, a silver ring with a cloisonne ladybird from Mama's friend Vicki, a new dress, a beautiful book of fairy tales and a book called "Princess Moonbeam" from Mama's schoolfriend Ella.

Papa, always busy with new hobbies, was breeding canaries at the time and presented me with one of his birds. I called it "Johnny." Johnny occupied a pretty cage atop the kitchen cabinet. From this vantage point, he surveyed his little world. Up there, he was safe from eager little hands wanting to hold him and lavish affection on him that he was most unwilling and far too nervous to accept. Johnny remained very shy and never became tame. However, he hopped about quite happily in his little house, enjoyed the swing and, on cage cleaning occasions, flights around the kitchen with a rest on the curtain rod.

As time went by, we looked forward to hearing Johnny burst into the rolling and cascading trills that canaries are famous for but they never materialized. Johnny had a problem with his throat. Rapturous song eluded him. In time, he did manage a few modest melodies of his own, notably so when the sun brightened the kitchen and he heard other birds chirping in the trees outside. Johnny was part and parcel of the kitchen. I could not imagine it without him. He never seemed to grow older and I took his presence for granted. Johnny lived to be 14 years old and died of fright when Russian soldiers, who occupied the apartment in 1945, tried to take him out of his cage.

1931

February 2	Nazis demand that Germany quit League of Nations.
July 9	Hindenburg and Hitler meet in Berlin.
July 14	Banks close because of economic crisis.
August 5	Banks reopen after three week moratorium.
September 17	Feli Raubal, Hitler's niece, commits suicide by shooting herself.
October 11	Hitler gains commercial alliance with national leader and publisher, Hugenberg.
October 18	Confrontations between Fascists and Nazis. Hitler promises that he can maintain order.
November 7	Report indicates that Nazis would ensure "Nordic Dominance" by sterilizing certain races.
November 15	Nazis win elections in Hesse.
December	Unemployment reaches 5.6 million.
December 12	Hitler tells U.S. journalists, "I am a Democrat."
December 21	The author's sixth birthday.

In the early 1930s, masquerade balls enjoyed great popularity. Mama, Kurt and my aunts attended many masked balls. I pestered Mama for days to tell me what costume she was going to wear. Neither she nor anybody else gave me a clue and I became quite exasperated. I was nosy and felt hard done by for not being let into the secret. On one occasion, Mama relented and told me she would disguise herself as a bathing beauty and carry my large beach ball. After that, I left Mama in peace. I found out later that she told me a fib to stop me from badgering her. She really dressed in a very different costume, that of a Flamenco dancer. I resolved that I would attend many masked balls once I was old enough to do so. I spent lots of time imagining all the wonderful disguises I would wear. Most of all, I wanted to dress in a Rococo costume and white wig. Alas, by the time I was the right age, masked balls were a thing of the past.

Winter turned into spring and soon it was Easter. Easter goodies were usually hidden in the living room.

One year, a corner was transformed into a small landscape. It was a green Easter straw meadow with chicks and marzipan bunnies in chocolate boats cruising on a foil river. A chocolate car was parked near the "water."

I woke up on this Easter Sunday and eagerly ran into the living room, knowing that the Easter Bunny had come and left goodies for me. This time, most of the presents were not hidden but in full view on the couch. I found a yellow, embroidered pillow in the shape of a duck, a book called "Silver," which was a story about a cat and a large Easter bunny made of chocolate, carrying a basket on his back filled with little chocolate and other Easter eggs.

After Easter, I became ill. It started with a sore throat and an increasingly high temperature. My throat became so swollen that

I was unable to swallow. Mama sat by my bed all night. A shaded lamp provided subdued light while I, burning up with fever, laid my head on her lap. On my bedside table stood an array of glasses containing a variety of juices, water and milk to tempt me but I could swallow nothing. Our family physician, Dr. Schmitz, made several house calls. He was somewhat puzzled as to the nature of my illness. My throat was very swollen and covered with a thick white coating. He was afraid it might be diphtheria.

Dr. Schmitz was about to go on vacation. When he called on Friday, he wanted to take precautionary measures, just in case. Aunt Martha was sent to the pharmacy for an antidiphtheria serum. He injected this into my left thigh. A few hours later, I had a rather bad reaction. My left leg became completely stiff and I could not bend it at all. The paralysis lasted throughout the weekend. I remember vividly how difficult it was for me to get out of bed to go to the bathroom.

On Monday, Dr. Schmitz's partner, Dr. Baumann, called. He was not happy with the situation and arranged for me to be admitted to a hospital. We went by taxi to the Augusta Victoria Hospital in Schoeneberg.

Because I was only suspected of having diphtheria, I was admitted to the contagious disease pavilion but kept separate from the other patients who actually suffered from the disease. The hospital must have been short of private rooms because my bed was placed in a corridor with screens around it. I thought it was rather nice. There were windows all along one side and a lot of activity to be observed.

By Thursday morning, my throat had turned bright red. I was moved to the scarlet fever section and put in isolation. This time the isolation was complete. The room was designed for prisoners or mental patients. Located at the end of a corridor, that branched off the main corridor, it had a double door with an observation window, bars at the window and padded walls. There was no door handle and if, by chance, the door closed it was impossible to open it from inside the room. I was left there alone, except for the doctor who made the rounds in the morning accompanied by his entourage and the help bringing in my meals. I had no bathroom and I remember running down the corridor barefoot to call a nurse because I had to go potty. Nobody came near me all day. I had no toys and no books so I amused myself as best I could.

Now and then I got up and looked through the window at the hospital grounds where patients walked and sat on benches enjoying the spring sunshine. I felt very much alone and sad.

Visiting hours were restricted to one hour on Wednesday afternoons and evenings and one or one and a half hours on Sunday afternoons. I was moved into this room on Thursday. When Mama, Father and Mother came to visit on Sunday, Father blew his top. It was the only time I saw him really angry. He upbraided the matron and the resident for keeping a small child isolated without supervision in a room like that. He insisted on having me discharged the following day.

Father was working at that time, as was Mama, so Aunt Martha came on Monday morning to take me home. She brought one of my favorite dresses, dove grey with a white collar and a yoke embroidered with red and blue flowers. It was a wonderful day in May. The sun was shining, the birds were singing in the trees that had just turned a lovely shade of green. We walked along the gravel path to the hospital exit and took a cab home. I was still sick and had a temperature. I was put to bed as soon as I got into the apartment. A little later, the Riemanns brought me a large bowl of fresh strawberries and a toy, a small birdhouse with a bird sitting on top. When I pushed the bottom on the birdhouse, the bird made a chirping noise. I was very happy to be home. It turned out that I did not have diphtheria or scarlet fever, but rather an abscess in my throat.

During my hospital stay, I was very much impressed by the nurses. Many hospitals in Berlin were staffed by the Evangelical Nursing Order. They wore dark blue, ankle length dresses with very tiny white dots, black shoes and stockings, white starched caps tied under the chin with a small bow and a simple silver cross. For work, they dressed in blue and white striped cotton dresses, white aprons and white caps. I saw these nurses in the street mostly when we walked along the Hasenheide near a small hospital specializing in diseases of the chest. I had also seen a section in a cemetery reserved for the Sisters where they were laid to rest. All the graves were marked with identical simple crosses.

Father, Mother and I often walked along the Tempelhof Field to Tempelhof. The Tempelhof Field was a large open space. Until the end of WWI, it was used by the Imperial Army, stationed in adjacent barracks, as an exercise and parade ground where the Kaiser himself inspected his troops on many occasions. After WWI, the Tempelhof Field was converted into a modest airfield. Its entrance was on the Tempelhof side. The back bordered on garden allotments, tennis courts and the Sportpark on the Neukoelln side. We walked along the unpaved continuation of the Flughafenstrasse, which was closed to all but pedestrians and bicyclists.

Behind a brick wall on one side lay a cemetery, Invaliden Friedhof, with a military section. WWI casualties and Allied prisoners of war who had died of wounds or from other causes, were buried here. On the opposite side was the Turkish cemetery. I could peek in through a wrought iron gate in the brick wall and see tombstones and elaborately decorated obelisks surmounted by a crescent moon. It looked strange, exotic and mysterious.

After my hospital stay, when we walked this way, I ran to the opposite side of the path, instructing Father and Mother to pretend that I was a nurse. They were to say, loud enough for me to hear, "Look, isn't that Sister Elisabeth over there?" By now, I had decided to be a nurse when I grew up and to be known as "Sister Elisabeth."

The Hasenheide, beginning at the Hermannplatz, is a wide street with a median. At that time, it was lined with big old chestnut trees, garden restaurants and cafés. On weekends, families strolled here, met friends and sat under the trees, enjoying repasts, chatting and listening to the bands that played in almost all the restaurants. The Hasenheide was uncommonly attractive when the chestnut trees were in bloom.

Near the Hermannplatz was an entertainment center called The New World with a spacious garden. Adjoining The New World was an area called the Rifle Ranges, a sizeable wooded piece of land. The actual rifle ranges took up a small section along one side of it. Mama and I spent many summer afternoons there. She sat and read while I played.

The Rifle Ranges were a remnant of the original Hasenheide, which had been a large open area and had become Germany's first athletic field. It was used in the 19th century by the famous Friedrich Ludwig Jahn (1778-1852), the pioneer of physical education and gymnastics. His aim was to make German Youth physically fit to fight off Napoleon's forces. His followers' slogan was "Healthy, Devout, Joyful, Free." In 1935, the Rifle Ranges were transformed into a park, the Jahn Park. A statue of Jahn was erected overlooking a sweeping lawn.

I enjoyed the Rifle Ranges because they had been left in their natural, wild state. In comparison, the park was dull. All parks seemed boring and dull to me because visitors were forbidden to walk on the grass and had to stay on the gravel paths, which was altogether too orderly and artificial for my liking.

A new department store, Karstadt, had been built at the Hermannplatz. Karstadt took up the length of the square and was spectacular, with twin towers that rose majestically. They were topped by columns that lit up at night and turned into fluorescent purple beacons. In the lovely roof garden restaurant, well-known radio orchestras played every afternoon, led by the likes of Will Glahe (who went to school with Mama), Otto Kermbach and Barnabas von Gezy. Mama and Aunt Martha took me to the roof garden for lunch or afternoon coffee. I also had my photograph taken in the Karstadt studio wearing a cerise colored dress. The store's large display window became a main attraction, especially at holiday times, such as Easter, Pentecost and Christmas, and when the windows were used for live fashion shows.

If I remember rightly, it was this year that Father took Mother and me to Muencheberg, his hometown. It was a lovely, warm summer day. We stopped for lunch at the hotel on the market square where we sat on the veranda under a striped awning. It was furnished with wicker furniture. Tomato soup was the first course. I refused to eat it because I hated tomatoes. Later, we caught a train to Frankfurt/Oder. Something went wrong with our connections and it was well past midnight when we finally reached our destination and our relatives' house. We had to yell and keep knocking for a while to wake them up, much to Mother's discomfort.

The house had three apartments. The first floor was that of Aunt Adele's daughter, Emma, and son-in-law, Richard, the second floor was occupied by Aunt Adele's son, Alfred, his wife, Vera, and their daughters, Brigitte and Regina. The third floor was Aunt Adele's apartment.

Richard was badly wounded in WWI. He was almost completely blind and had a wonderful seeing eye dog, a German shepherd called Rex. He and Emma had two daughters, Irene and Edith. Edith was retarded in growth and in mind to the extent that she was unable to learn how to read and write. When Soviet troops occupied Frankfurt after WWII, two Soviet soldiers raped this poor little creature. I never learned any details as to how this incident happened. She, in her innocence, told everyone about it in great detail. Richard was beside himself. He stormed into the Soviet commandant's office and let loose a terrible tirade that was relayed to the officer by an interpreter. Consequently, the perpetrators were punished.

1932

January 7	Chancellor Heinrich Bruening: "Germany will not resume reparation payments." Bruening (1885-1970) led the presidential cabinet during the growing economic depression in 1930. Bruening asks Hitler to help extend von Hindenburg's term. The 84-year-old Hindenburg is reluctant to stay in office but is persuaded to run.
February 22	Hitler is nominated as the NSDAP candidate for the presidential elections.
March 2	Lindbergh baby is kidnaped.
March 13	Hindenburg receives 18 million votes, Hitler 11 million and the Communists 5 million. Hitler fails to gain majority.
April 10	Hindenburg gets a full majority in second ballot, defeating Hitler in two presidential elections.
April 13	Almost two-thirds of all German voters vote against Hitler in the presidential elections. Statutory Order on Safety and State Authority by Bruening bans Nazi military units (the SA and SS).
May 2	Prussian Diet Hall is wrecked in fight between Communists and Nazis.

May 30	Chancellor Bruening resigns over Hitler's refusal to allow small farmers use of bankrupt estates. Chancellor Bruening is replaced by Franz von Papen as chancellor. (Franz von Papen, 1879-1969, was the Reich Chancellor in 1932 and became the Vice Chancellor from 1933-1934. He was later ambassador to Vienna and Ankara and was acquitted in the Nuremberg war crime trials.)
May 31	A new cabinet excluding Nazis is formed by von Papen.
June 14	Hitler promises cooperation with von Papen's government.
June 16	The ban on the SA and SS is lifted by von Papen. Conference on war reparations begins in Lausanne.
June 24	German delegates tell France that reparations will not be paid.
July	Elections begin and end with fierce battle in Hamburg-Altona between Nazis and Communists. Nazis now have 229 seats in the Reichstag.
July 20	The Socialist Premier of Prussia is removed by von Papen, who also declares martial law.
July 31	Reichstag elections take place. As a result, Nazis now have 230 seats in new 608 seat Reichstag. NSDAP is largest party in Germany.
August 4	Communist and Nazi riots in Berlin. Reich threatens death penalty.

August 7	Foreign Minister Schleicher warns that Germany will not wait for reduction in reparations to create arms equality.
August 13	Hindenburg turns down Hitler as chancellor.
August 24	Nazi newspaper is banned for inciting riots.
August 30	Hermann Goering is elected president of the Reichstag.
September 1	Five Nazis, convicted of killing a Communist, get death sentence commuted to life imprisonment.
September 3	Three are killed in Berlin during a transit strike that paralyzes city.
September 12	After a vote of no confidence from the Communists, von Papen dissolves Reichstag.
October	"Reich can only pay debts with goods, not money," says von Papen.
October 18	Election terror increases, with more confrontations in Berlin.
November 3	Berlin Transit (BVG) strikes due to a proposed two pfennig reduction of hourly wages. The strike fails and ends on November 7.
November 6	Communists gain in elections. Nazis lose 35 seats.
November 21	Hitler refuses limited chancellorship offered to him by Hindenburg.
December 2	Kurt von Schleicher becomes chancellor.
December 21	The author's seventh birthday.

Unemployment in 1932/33 reached 6,013,612.

On January 3 it was reported in the papers that my idol, Gitta Alpar, together with many famous stars, including Richard Tauber, Bronislaw Huberman and Horst Wolfgang Korngold, appeared at the Kroll Opera House Charity Gala for the benefit of the Winter Relief Organization.

This interesting article appeared in a Berlin newspaper on January 10, 1932:

GENEALOGICAL RECORD BOOK

The leadership of the national socialist SS at this time intends to enforce a previously proposed racial Nazi law within their own ranks. Initially, it was their intention to force this law onto all German people. An order, issued by the Reich leadership of the SS, makes marriage approval by a racial authority compulsory for all SS members.

"The desired goal," so the order states, "is the continuity of the valuable hereditary health of German Nordic type people." Every member of the SS who wants to marry must announce this intention "at least three months before the event to the Reich leader of the SS. He must include a complete record of hereditary health certificates and certificates of good character for himself and his bride. His application is then examined by a racial authority. If approved, the applicant receives permission to marry. Together with his family he is entered in the Genealogical Record Book. Should an SS man marry in spite of being refused permission to do so, he will be discharged."

Perhaps it is permitted at this point to voice a few doubts about the feasibility of these exceptions. What is a "definitive Nordic man?" The racial problem is, in science and research, far too debatable and within the German people there exist so many types that the "pure Nordic race" must remain an illusion.

Secondly, the results of hereditary research are not yet in any way conclusive enough, as that one can predict the characteristics of descendants from the hereditary documents of their parents with any kind of certainty.

Thirdly, when a man is in love, even though he may be a definitive Nordic SS man, he will not care very much about racial authorities and a Genealogical Record Book. He will, like Goethe, deride a man who "full of youthful hormonal energy tries to fall in love according to a plan."

A speaking newsreel was shown for the first time in the Gloria Palast movie house and the papers reported, "The latest: A portable record player, not much bigger than a folding camera. It even has a tone arm on the inside. Finally, one can take one's beloved record player along on every outing."

Another interesting article entitled "Why Women Must Not Vote for Hitler!" appeared in March 1932. The article called the National Socialist Party "contrary and controversial because they want women to vote for them but they refuse to elect women. The Nazis are the sole faction in the Reichstag without a woman member." The article encouraged women to keep this in mind and to ask themselves on March 13, "why should I vote for Hitler?"

The article went on to point out that Hitler misinterpreted Darwin's theory and drew little known erroneous conclusions. At the National Socialist Party Rally in Nuernberg, Hitler declared: "If one million children a year were born in Germany and the state got rid of 700,000 to 800,000 of the weakest children then perhaps the end result might be increased strength." The danger is, that we ourselves cut off the natural selection process and by doing so slowly rob ourselves of the possibility to have "brains." It is not always the firstborn who are the talented ones or the strongest people. The purest racist city state in history, Sparta, executed these racial laws systematically.

The article outlined and exposed the Nazi philosophy that women are to be forced to bear as many children as possible, crimes against the fetus are to be punished with punishments that seem to come from the dark ages, and some authority is to be empowered with the right to make a selection among the children born and to destroy those they deem to be unsuitable. No details are known as to who will pronounce these death sentences and who will execute them.

In addition, the childless woman, whether married or not, "is not viewed as a worthwhile member of the Volk (Volk means the German people or nation) community."

Therefore, adultery by a man that results in a child is not legally to be interpreted as adultery. The article then questioned Hitler's ability to understand and apply Darwin's theory, blaming his misinterpretation on his lack of education.

The article concluded by encouraging women to consider these facts before voting on March 13, emphasizing the point that it did not only concern the political decision and material possessions, but German culture in general, which would not need to be bolshevized following a period of Hitler rule because by then that would already be a fact.

Now that I was six years old, I was no longer satisfied staying in the apartment. The time had come to venture out and I was allowed to play in the street and make friends with other children.

It was very early spring when I went out alone for the first time. I hung around the apartment house door, playing ball, not really knowing what to do with myself. Soon Arnold, a boy who was several years older than I, came by. His parents owned a cow shed and milk store. I don't recall what Arnold said to me but the next thing I knew he pointed a BB gun at my face and fired a load of plaster into my left eye. I screamed and ran upstairs where Mother washed my eye out. It looked angry and red and was quite sore. I was lucky it was not damaged. Father took me to see Arnold's mother and complained but she just shrugged it off. They always stuck up for their boy who was a bully and repeatedly got into trouble. We stopped patronizing their store.

When next I ventured out, I met two girls, Elke and her 3-year-old sister, Renate. Renate was sitting on the pavement, her back against the wall, while Elke was drawing a hopscotch pattern on the sidewalk. We played hopscotch. Soon I met other children: Hannelore, Dieter, Guenter, Loni, Martin, Peter and Rosie.

These children lived in apartment blocks owned by a building society. A building society builds houses for sale and apartments for rent for its members. In front of those buildings, which formed an L in relation to the street, a wire fence separated the landscaped walkway from an adjoining empty lot to the north, which also belonged to the same company. This lot had been partially excavated when WWI put an end to the building plans. The upheavals of the war and the postwar years prevented further development and it remained fenced in and empty.

The tenants' children were permitted to use the lot as a playground from late spring to early fall. Although I did not live in these apartments, I played there. At first, the janitor's daughter made it difficult for me and tried to stop me from getting in. However, I was determined and persisted because I wanted to be with my friends. Soon everybody took it for granted that I belonged there. This was a piece of good luck because it was so much nicer than playing in the street or going to a park.

There were public playgrounds nearby. For instance, a number of city squares had sandboxes and/or swings, and the Sportpark had swings, a roundabout, slides, seesaws, sandboxes, a sports stadium, tennis courts and a grassy playing field. Mama and Aunt Martha took me to this park at times but I did not enjoy it because I did not know any of the children and went there too infrequently to form friendships.

The apartment playground was perfect. The ground was uneven because the excavation had stopped midway. The part close to the apartments was level and grassy, then it sloped and was flat at the bottom with a sandy part at the lower end, good for digging and building sand castles. At the street side, the ground was flat and hard. Here we played ball, catch and other running games.

Our private play area was bordered and separated on its north side by the same type of wooden fence as on the street side from another large property that consisted of two parts: at street level, an open air market, with a concrete floor and permanently fixed light grey painted wooden tables. Market days were Tuesday and Thursday mornings until 1 p.m. The second level, lower and larger, was a fairground. The fairground hours were 6

57

p.m. to 10 p.m. on weeknights and 2 p.m. to 9 or 10 p.m. on weekends. It was closed during the winter months.

The fair had three roundabouts, or carousels, and tents for theatrical performances, such as sketches, contortionists, jugglers and other variety acts. The latter changed every week or every month. One could win food items, chocolates and knickknacks at raffles and two wheels of fortune. There were stands for throwing rings and dice, one or two shooting galleries, swings, a large ice cream parlor and vendors who sold candied apples, spun sugar, roasted peanuts and cookies.

I was not allowed to visit the fair alone when I was young. Once in a great while, Mama or Kurt took me to ride on the carousel. Father, Mother and my aunts never went. When I was older, I was allowed to go occasionally, either by myself or with friends.

The school year began in April. Already some time prior to this, stationery and department stores displayed and sold *Schultueten*. The *Schultueten* were colored cardboard cones trimmed with lacy gold foil and decorated with Victorian embossed paper cut-outs and came in various sizes. At its top, the *Schultueten* had a crepe paper insert extending beyond the cone tied with a narrow satin ribbon. Parents and relatives filled the cone with candy and chocolates. Children were presented with a *Schultuete* on their first day of school. The idea was the same as when Jewish grandparents put honey on a corner of a page in the Torah and make their grandchildren lick it off to signify that learning is sweet.

Some children carried their *Schultueten* to school on the first day, usually the kids who had the biggest ones and wanted to show off. However, looks could be deceiving. Times being what they were, big cones were often stuffed with paper and had only a few candies at the top, whereas smaller ones were usually filled all the way with goodies.

At 6 years of age, I was eligible to enter first grade. One fine April morning, wearing a new dress, a blue coat trimmed with white fur, and a blue and white angora beret, I marched off to school, without a *Schultuete*. On my back was my new leather satchel containing a slate and a pencil box with slate pencils. A small sponge and a cloth, attached by a string to the slate, dangled from the satchel. My school was an all girls school since schools were not coeducational.

My first day was exciting and fun. We were directed to our classroom where our teacher, Miss Roeder, was waiting for us. After roll call, she demonstrated on the blackboard how to draw a tulip. We copied this on our slates and colored it with chalks. When the bell rang to indicate the end of the class period, we were taken to the assembly room, called *Aula*. To mark this day as a special event for the first graders, the girls from higher grades put on a show, which included many songs, one of which was "Jumping Jack." We all knew it very well and needed no encouragement to join in singing it and acting it out. The eighth grade students put on a short play. Afterwards, we were dismissed.

When I returned home, I was presented with a lovely blue *Schultuete*. The little Riemann took my picture. My *Schultuete* was not the largest but it was big and filled to the very bottom with candy. It was so heavy that I could not hold still while a photo was being taken. The camera did not have a flashlight and, in order to take an indoor shot, the subject had to remain motionless for some time. As a result, the photo was blurred.

Our elementary school consisted of two L-shaped buildings bordering a school yard. The "Ls" were mirror images with the short part of the "Ls" facing the street. In the space between the ends of the buildings were gates and adjoining these was a building housing a small museum of local artifacts and our gym. One L building was the Boys School, the other the Girls School. The inside of our school was plain and utilitarian. The floors in the hallways and the stairs were terrazzo and the classroom floors were oiled wood. Classrooms had two large windows. The walls were painted with oil paint, usually in shades of light green. Along the walls opposite the windows and at the back of the room were hooks for our coats and hats.

We sat on benches and our satchels fit on a shelf under the attached table. On the top floor of the building was the *Aula*, an art instruction room and a chemistry lab. Teaching aids were at a minimum. Physical exercises took place in the gym and, weather permitting, in the yard.

At the beginning of each term, which was spring and fall, we received a lesson plan showing periods and subjects taught. All subjects were compulsory; there were no electives. Children stayed in their classrooms. After the bell had signaled the end of a class period, the teacher left. Five or ten minutes later, the teacher teaching the next period entered. We rose and the teacher said "Good morning." We answered and were given permission to sit down.

Classes began at 8 a.m. Monday through Saturday. In first grade, we went to school only from 8 a.m. to 10 a.m. during the first term. In the fall, the time was increased to three hours and in the following grades by at least one hour a day until finally we went from 8 a.m. until noon or 1 p.m. There were no extracurricular activities and no study periods. Our daily homework assignments were done at home and reviewed in class on the following day. Saturdays were homework free and we were dismissed at noon.

We went into the schoolyard for our half hour recess. Our school did not have a cafeteria, so most of the time I took sandwiches. Supervised by a teacher we either walked around in a circle, counterclockwise, eating our sandwiches or stood around in groups. We did not play. The boys kept to their half of the yard and the boys and girls ignored each other.

The economic situation in Germany was still deteriorating, as the number of unemployed people rose steadily. Many families were in dire straights. To help underprivileged children, schools through the Quaker Food Relief for Needy Europeans were able to provide a hot meal at the cost of a few pfennig. It was delivered from a central kitchen and served in a subterranean room on long tables covered with oil cloth. It was a very simple meal: a bowl of oatmeal with milk; lentil, pea or other thick vegetable soup; and once a week boiled potatoes, gravy and meat. Anybody could participate and I did for a short time. I still recall the gravy. It did not taste homemade but what I would now call "institutional." We were also able to buy plain, strawberry or chocolate milk that was ordered and paid for a week in advance, at the cost of ten pfennig a day.

On May 1, I remember that when I came home from school it was snowing. Father's brother, Wilhelm, wearing a green loden coat, stopped by for a visit after he had attended a May Day rally in center city.

Before Hitler came to power, May Day in Berlin was not a public holiday and was not celebrated in any way other than with a huge assembly in the Lustgarten with speeches by political and labor leaders. Attendance was entirely voluntary. After 1933, attendance became compulsory.

During the summer holidays, I went on vacation with Father and Mother to Koenigswusterhausen just outside Berlin. I remember taking long walks through the forest. Aunt Martha,

Uncle Gustav and the Schaefers came out for one weekend day. The Schaefers were lively, noisy and fun. While walking through the woods, the Schaefers started to sing but Aunt Martha suggested we should walk in silence and listen to the sounds of nature. She said we should enjoy hearing the wind rustling in the trees and the song of the birds. I preferred the singing. It was more fun for me because I went for quiet walks with Father and Mother every day with plenty of opportunities to hear the wind and the birds.

Mama had gone back to work after her divorce, first at the Ullstein Publishing House and later with the Scherl Publishing Company. After a while she began dating Kurt, a handsome young man, who also worked at Scherl. They had become engaged in 1931. Kurt was tall, with brown eyes, thick curly lashes and dark brown, straight hair. He spent a lot of time at our apartment and I liked him a lot. I went along to visit his parents, who lived in Charlottenburg, once in a while.

One day in August, Mother informed me that Mama and Kurt had been married on August 6, Kurt's birthday, and had gone to the Spreewald for their honeymoon. It had been a very quiet wedding at the Registrar's office. Nevertheless, I was very upset at being left out of it. No one had mentioned anything to me and I was crazy about weddings. It was quite a blow. Later on, I realized that at that time people like Mother still considered it embarrassing to have a divorce in the family and did nothing to attract attention to it or any remarriage. I was the only child in my elementary and high school classes whose parents were divorced. No one in our circle of friends and acquaintances was divorced.

When Mama and Kurt returned from their honeymoon, they took up residence in an apartment at the Hermannplatz. I loved visiting them because the Hermannplatz was busy. There was always something interesting going on. The beautiful new department store, Karstadt, held many attractions such as large decorated windows. But the most enticing place was a large ice cream parlor three doors from Mama's apartment house. It was my idea of heaven because I loved ice cream and this place offered many flavors. Apart from the usual vanilla, chocolate and strawberry, I remember hazelnut, coffee, lemon, banana, orange, sweet woodruff, cherry, pineapple and raspberry, all made with fresh fruit and only natural ingredients. Alas, most of the time I had to be content watching the big wheel of the ice cream maker in the window whirling round and round. Mother was against ice cream. She believed it was too cold for the stomach.

Around the corner from Mama's, in the Kaiser Friedrich Strasse, was a dairy store and cow shed. I often accompanied Mama to buy fresh milk there. The cow shed was located on the ground floor of the building behind the courtyard.

Occasionally, I went alone to fetch milk. On the way, I had to pass a showcase of some sort and noticed a reproduction of Goya's painting entitled, "3rd May, 1808, in Madrid, the shooting at Principe Pio Mountain." It fascinated me in a sort of horrible way. The painting depicted rebels facing the firing squad. Although I was repelled, I could not help stopping to look at it every time I passed.

Mama stopped working when she married Kurt. The Nazi regime encouraged women to stop working after they married. They actually said that a woman could not possibly be happy and fulfilled if she was working or had a career. Fulfillment came only by staying at home, keeping house, raising a family, all things that money cannot buy, that make life worthwhile and old age secure. In other words, unless a woman was forced to work out of economic necessity, her place was in the home. The government wanted to erase unemployment and the jobs relinquished by women became available to unemployed men.

So far the political and economic situation had only affected my life indirectly. Of course, no one discussed the situation or mentioned it to me. However, I often caught snatches of adult conversation about Hitler and politics. I was familiar with the names of leading politicians at the time since I heard them mentioned in conversations of adults and on the radio almost daily. I did not read the newspapers, naturally, but people talked and so I was aware of the fights between Communists, Nazis and Social Democrats. I also knew about elections.

In 1932, there were five elections. When we went out on election day, we passed the polling stations where I saw policemen, SA men and other party people wearing armbands standing outside. Placards and posters displayed everywhere could not be overlooked. I was able to read some slogans. Some said something about work and bread; others were against the Nazis. Apparently, the main difference between the Nazi Party slogans and those of the Communists and Social Democrats was that the latter promised better living conditions at some future time while the Nazis stressed work and bread NOW. This gave hope to the unemployed. Also, the Nazis constantly appealed to and played on people's emotions by condemning the Treaty of Versailles. This attracted many who were disillusioned because it promised to restore dignity and pride in Germany and being German.

Whenever I was out in our immediate neighborhood, I saw no demonstrations or fights between political factions nor did I see SA formations marching along the street. I think that their activities were concentrated in other parts of the city and, even in our district, kept to the main thoroughfares and squares where they would attract the most spectators and attention. I stayed for the most part close to home and I was not out at night. I noticed the flags that flew from apartment windows and balconies. Many were red. Red Communist flags continued to be flown in parts of Neukoelln for a long time, in fact, up to the day Hitler came to power.

We were not personally affected by the Depression and by the enormous unemployment. Father was working for the Government Printing Office as was Uncle Gustav. Mama was working at the Scherl Publishing House until she married Kurt. Aunt Marga worked at the G'sellius Booksellers and Rare Bookstore. Only Papa was out of work for a while.

In the fall, preparations and rehearsals began for a school play. It was quite a big production and all grades participated. I was excited, primarily because the night of the performance was December 21, my seventh birthday. The play was about two poor children who are alone in their cottage without food or presents on Christmas Eve. They fall asleep and in their dream they encounter many fairy-tale characters, among them Puss in Boots. Being one of the shortest girls in my class, I was chosen to play Puss. I memorized the long poem I was given but, when I realized that I would be all alone on stage while reciting it, I got cold feet and chickened out. I am sorry to this day that nobody encouraged me to go on. Instead of being Puss in Boots, I became one of a number of daisies who danced to the tune of "Softly the Snowflakes are Falling." Aunt Martha made a beautiful costume for me, with a bodice of green crepe paper and a pink tissue paper skirt shaped like the petals of a daisy. My hat had a green crown with a stem and a brim of pink petals.

The dress rehearsal took place in the afternoon of December 21 at the Saalbau in the Bergstrasse. The performance was scheduled to begin at 7 p.m. Before the show, we were served dinner in the restaurant part of the establishment and Miss

Bertram, one of the teachers, presented me with a box of chocolates because it was my birthday. The whole family came to see the play. I stayed up quite late. It was a memorable day.

1933

January 15	Nazis gain in the state of Lippe.
January 23	Schleicher resigns as chancellor.
January 30	Hindenburg appoints Hitler chancellor in a coalition government.
February 1	Hitler wins dissolution of Reichstag.
February 2	Hitler places curbs on leftist opposition.
February 6	Press censorship begins. Three days after Nazis come to power, homes of Communists are searched without warrants. 24 provincial governors and police chiefs are replaced with Nazis. People panic.
February 27-28	Reichstag burns down. Communists blamed.
February 28	Reichstag's Fire Decree (Protection of the People and State) is passed by presidential decree.
March 5	Last Reichstag election in a multiparty state. Hitler wins by a slim margin, 43.9 percent.
March 12	Hindenburg drops Flag of German Republic, which is replaced by the Swastika and the Empire Banner side by side.

March 21	Day of Potsdam.
March 23	Reichstag gives Hitler power to rule by decree.
March 28	Ban on Jews in business, professions and schools.
April 1	Einstein's funds seized by Nazis.
May 10	Burning of "un-German" books at Berlin University. Schools ordered to teach race science.
May 28	Communist Party property is confiscated.
June 18	Hitler threatens to take children from parents who fail to follow Nazi program. Social Democrats, the last opposition to Hitler, are outlawed.
July 3	Jews are evicted from Civil Service.
July 14	Hitler declares NSDAP the sole legal party.
July 15	Protestant churches are now the "German Evangelical Church."
July 31	26,789 people held as political prisoners.
September 29	Reichserbhofgesetz, the Hereditary Farm Law, is passed.
October 14	Dissolution of Reichstag - Hitler commits himself publicly to rearm Germany.
November 1	Germany's largest press, "Ullstein Press," is taken over by Nazis.
November 12	Hitler gets 92 percent of the vote at Reichstag election, 93 percent approve leaving League of Nations, three million cast invalid votes.
December	SS becomes official organ of the Reich.
December 21	The author's eighth birthday.

| December 22 | van der Lubbe sentenced to death for burning Reichstag. |

In 1933, the following public announcements were made in the newspapers:

May

SCHOOL AND NATION

At a conference of German cultural ministers, Reich Minister of the Interior Frick said: "The idea of liberal education has completely undermined the meaning of education and our educational institutions."

The national revolution issues a new law to German schools for their educational obligations: The German school must train the political person, whose reasoning and actions, service and sacrifice is rooted in his Volk as well as completely, indivisibly and deeply in the history and the fate of his Fatherland (Nation).

Volk and fatherland are the most important areas of education. The lure of exotic, foreign things from faraway places has at all times proved to be a great temptation for Germans, has enticed them into foreign countries and made it easy for them to be absorbed into foreign cultures.

One of our noblest, most valuable assets, the care of which must be close to our hearts, is our mother tongue, pleasant to the ear, powerful and flexible. We can be proud of it. Unfortunately, its purity is still not being nurtured the way it should be. Even official sources habitually use superfluous foreign words. We also want to think of German script, which should most definitely take precedence over Latinate script.

HISTORY AND RACE

History takes the first priority.

Next to a stronger emphasis on history and German culture values rank biology and race science.

Again and again, we realize that the character of a people and the fundamental strength of its historical development cannot be fathomed without sufficient knowledge of its utter uniqueness. Therefore, race science must be given sufficient time and attention in school so that the basic characteristics of the most important races become intimately known to the pupil and his/her continuous visual observation of racial differences will be honed.

The minister then addressed the importance of hereditary health education. These subjects must become second nature to the growing generation and influence their choice of a mate.

July 25

Land Year to begin as soon as 1934.

In accordance with the National Socialist principle of developing a close relationship between blood and soil, German youth will be sent to the country where work will create a strong bond with homeland and soil and will physically and mentally toughen them.

The Land Year constitutes a unique final education for elementary school pupils. At the same time, it prepares youth for pioneering Germany's new areas of development.

Author's note: (At the time, elementary school concluded with eighth grade and the Land Year was added as a compulsory ninth grade.)

Regulations for Good Friday.

For this year's Good Friday, April 14, the police regulations regarding the protection of Sundays and Holidays dated November 23, 1931 apply.

The following activities are forbidden:

Races, sport and physical exercise events of a commercial nature and similar performances, as well as sporting and physical training events of a noncommercial nature in as far as they are offered to a larger audience. Music featured in bars or pubs is prohibited, as is all other public entertainments, unless permitted according to the following ordinances.

Permitted are:

Theater and musical performances of a religious and solemn nature; that is, those which in content and presentation correspond to the special character of Good Friday as the day on which Jesus Christ died. Movies, which because of their religious or solemn character are considered suitable for Good Friday. These shows may be accompanied by serious music. Special interest lectures about art, science or Volk education. Radio programs must be solemn performances of a religious type or broadcasts of political daily and local news.

During the hours of main church services, from 9 a.m. to 11:30 a.m., all performances are forbidden. On Thursday, April 13 and Saturday evening, April 15, all public dances are forbidden.

School started again after the Christmas break and my life was back to normal. The same could not be said for the political situation. The worldwide depression, which began in 1929 deepened steadily until 1932. Poverty and mass unemployment were on the rise, which made more and more voters receptive to Nazis slogans such as:

"The needs of the people before the needs of the individual"

"Work and Bread for all"

"Down with the tyranny of investment capital"

Some people were deluded into believing that the NSDAP was a true national socialist party and supported it for that reason. Many trusted Hitler's promises. I heard concerns that Germany would become communist. I believe many felt the NSDAP was the only alternative to Communism and therefore the lesser of two evils. Even so, in April 1932 almost two-thirds of all German voters cast their ballots against Hitler in the presidential elections.

Reichstag elections were held in July 1932. Although the NSDAP made significant gains, their successes were short-lived and they fared much worse in the November elections. As a result, the NSDAP's financial backers were reluctant to continue their support and the survival of the party was at stake.

The Nazis, aware of their situation, decided on an all out effort to regain their strength, thinking it was life or death for the Nazi Party. They selected Lippe, a small state where regional elections were to be held on January 15, 1933, to make their stand. Lippe's capital is Detmold, which at that time had a population of approximately 18,000. Until 1932, the Nazis had no more than 3,000 followers in Lippe, less than the Communists, and no Nazi representative in the Lippe government.

In desperation, Hitler and Goebbels launched a gigantic propaganda campaign. There has been nothing like it before or since. Thousands of SA and SS men, speakers, newspaper reporters and agents from all over Germany converged on Lippe. Between January 4 and January 14, the Nazis organized 900 events, including 16 speeches by Hitler himself.

Even so, 60 percent of the voters did not vote for the Nazis. However, gaining 40 percent of the vote gave Hitler the edge he needed.

Nationwide headlines announced the Lippe election results, which helped make people believe that the NSDAP was strong, virile, and victorious. Two weeks later, on January 30, Hitler was named Chancellor by President Hindenburg.

I was too young to be aware of these events. What I do remember about this momentous, fateful day in the history of Germany is listening to the radio.

At the Hotel Kaiserhof, Hermann Goering read the announcement of Hitler's appointment as Chancellor just after noon on January 30. The Hotel Kaiserhof at the Potsdamer Platz, after the Hotel Adlon probably the most elegant and luxurious hotel in Berlin, had been Hitler's Berlin headquarters between February 1931 and January 30, 1933.

That night, thousands of SA men marched in a huge torchlight victory procession through the Brandenburg Gate, along Under den Linden to the Wilhelmstrasse and the Chancery. The events were relayed in live broadcasts and for a while I listened with Father and Mother. As thousands of SA men marched, I heard the music of bands accompanying rough men's voices singing the "Horst Wessel Song," the sound of boots hitting the pavement in unison and crowds cheering. The commentators were very excited. Their voices were louder and their speech was faster than normal as they described the scene, the light of the torches and the columns of SA.

The throng outside the Chancery was in high spirits, waiting for Hitler to make an appearance at the window. I could hear the crowd in the background. Shouts of individual *"Heils"* turned into a chorus of "We want to see our Fuehrer!" followed by *"Heil! Heil! Heil! Heil!"* as soon as Hitler showed himself. Back and forth the shouting alternated, as Hitler disappeared and reappeared again and again. I do not know how long people kept it up. It was long past my bedtime. I could not keep my eyes open any more and I went to bed. Father and Mother made no comments that evening nor the next morning, at least not in my presence.

I do not remember if the broadcast was mentioned in school the next day. My teachers were not in sympathy with Hitler. I know that for a fact borne out by their actions. I am sure they had to toe the line but did not do more than absolutely necessary and as little as they could, since regional school board representatives paid unannounced visits periodically to our school and observed class activities.

On my next visit to the cinema, I saw the events on a newsreel. It was spectacular and very dramatic, but I felt oppressed by the sight of so many uniforms. The light from the torches made crass contrasts on the stern, intense faces of the marchers, highlighting their features in the darkness of the night. It failed to give me a sense of exultation. I felt uncomfortable. The upturned faces of the crowd outside the Chancery were intense, excited, and almost fanatic, too. Something was missing. It was a celebration but it was not jolly. There was no laughter.

Not long thereafter, a shocking event occurred. In February, the Reichstag burned down. It was headline news and the topic of conversations. Reports claimed that the fire was started by a

Dutch communist, Van der Lubbe, who was arrested almost immediately. A short time later, I viewed the damage myself on one of my outings to the Tiergarten with Father. I stood and stared at the huge skeletal remains of the edifice of the Reichstag that had been dedicated "To the German People." Twisted, charred metal girders no longer crowned by the large patina green dome desolately bore witness to the ravages of flames.

The most far reaching and momentous consequence of the Reichstag fire was that on February 28 the "Protection of the People and State" decree was passed. It suspended civil liberties and police were now permitted to take suspects into protective custody. The decree was designed to pave the way for dealing with possible long-term state emergencies.

The elections continued. Large posters of Hitler and Hindenburg covered the advertising columns. Slogans once again defaced walls and fences.

On March 5, my family voted. I remember walking along the Hermannstrasse that afternoon with Mama and asking her for whom she had voted. At first she did not want to say, but I persisted. She said, "I voted SPD."

When the results were published, they revealed that the Nazi Party received 43.9 percent of the vote. The rest of the votes were split among the other political parties. Hitler had won, although by only a small margin. This was the last Reichstag election in a multiparty state until after WWII.

After this election, things began to change. The swastika was used by the Nazi party since its beginning. As of March 12, the red, black and gold flag of the German Republic no longer flew side by side with the Swastika flag. Instead, the red, white and black Empire Banner was used. A few areas in Berlin, like the Hermannplatz and the Wildenbruchplatz in Neukoelln, flew almost exclusively red Communist flags until January 30. Other streets displayed Swastika flags and Empire banners.

The new government announced that March 21 was designated "The Day of Potsdam," a day of special significance. Because of its historic connection with Prussian kings, primarily Frederick the Great, Potsdam was chosen as the setting. A religious service, held at the St. Nicholas Church, preceded the state ceremonies at the Garnisonkirche and Goering attended. Bishop Dibelius, the Protestant bishop, preached the sermon. Hitler and Goebbels, both raised Roman Catholic, did not attend. I don't think that this in itself would have prevented them from attending the service if it had suited their purpose. I do not know why they stayed away. In any case, I never heard or saw pictures of them attending regular church services.

Hitler and Hindenburg spoke at the state ceremony at the Garnisonkirche. A 21 gun salute was fired at the time a wreath was laid on the tomb of Frederick the Great. A parade followed, reviewed by Hitler and Hindenburg. Live radio broadcasts covered the events throughout the day and I listened to parts of the broadcasts. I heard the sound of the famous Garnisonkirche carillion playing its signature tune: "Be ever faithful ever true," the ringing of the bells, the description of what was happening outside the church, the sound of commands as the honor guard came to attention, the hushed voice of the reporter describing the arrival of important personages, and eventually the arrival of Hitler and Hindenburg. The only other thing I remember about the broadcast is the music inside the church and the rousing rendition of the chorale: "Now thank we all our God."

The newspapers not only described the events with many details and printed the speeches in their entirety but also told the story in pages of pictures.

A few days later, I saw the newsreel coverage of "The Day of Potsdam." Outside the church, the camera panned the church steeple, the crowds, the troops lining the street and the honor guard, as well as the arrival of diplomats, ministers and members of the aristocracy, among them the former Crown Prince Wilhelm and his wife, Cecilie. Most men were in uniform. Hitler, who normally dressed in uniform, chose on this occasion to appear in a cutaway and carry a top hat. Field Marshall von Hindenburg, although resplendent in his field marshal's uniform, looked very old. Then the cameras moved inside for the beginning of the celebration. The sound of the organ swelled, the choir and the congregation joined at some point in the magnificent chorale: "Now thank we all our God," which sent shivers up and down my spine.

I enjoyed the spectacle. The uniforms looked splendid in the sunshine, even though the film was black and white. That this event was of great importance communicated itself quite clearly, although the political significance and its ramifications escaped me entirely.

"The Day of Potsdam" had been a perfect day. The sun was shining and it was the first day of spring, synonymous with new beginnings. The new beginnings were not to be long in coming and would affect everyone.

Three days after Potsdam, the new parliament met at the famous Kroll Opera House, since the Reichstag building was gutted by fire. The papers reported that large numbers of SS and SA men provoked and harassed the SPD members as they entered the building. I saw the headlines and pictures in the paper but I could not read the articles because I was only 7 years old. It was at this particular Reichstag meeting that the intimidated non-Nazi Reichstag members, together with the Nazi members, voted 441 to 94 in favor of passing the so-called

"Enabling Act." The Social Democrats stood alone in opposing this bill.

The Enabling Act signified the end of the Constitution. It empowered the government to pass laws, to enter into treaties with foreign powers and to place the right of issuing laws into the hands of the Chancellor, Hitler himself. The Act rendered the president, at that time the aged Hindenburg, practically powerless. Hitler was now "master" of Germany.

The Enabling Act suspended basic civil rights such as:

- freedom of the person
- inviolability of the home
- secrecy in communication by letter, mail, telegraph and telephone
- freedom to express opinions
- freedom of the press
- freedom of assembly
- freedom of association
- right to private property

From 1933 until 1945, the German people had no basic civil rights. The guarantee of a person's rights to freedom, as we understand it, was not compatible with Nazi politics. Furthermore, key positions in the civil service were filled by Nazis who had joined the party before 1933 and were, therefore, considered politically trustworthy.

I did not understand what was going on nor could I fathom the consequences of what had happened but I did notice a number of changes. I saw no more posters and no graffiti of SPD and KPD on advertising pillars, fences and walls. All old slogans were painted over. Opposition posters were removed. Fighting between warring factions ceased. Beggars disappeared from the streets almost overnight.

Every day brought new ordinances, new laws and changes. Everything was, of course, reported in the papers but I was not aware of it at that time. For instance, on March 28, 1933, Jews were banned from professions, from teaching school and from owning businesses. We had no Jewish teachers in our school that I was aware. Our Jewish family doctor had retired some years ago and, at my age, I did not know any Jewish business people.

A boycott of Jewish shops, department stores, lawyers' and doctors' offices was organized and took place on Saturday, April 1. At 10 a.m., SA men took up positions at the doors of Jewish businesses, carried signs and discouraged people from entering.

Propaganda against the Jews was stepped up and culminated on May 10 with a large bonfire in front of the Humbold University where "un-German" books were burned, among them those of Heinrich Heine. We had, however, already memorized several poems by Heine at school and everyone knew and sang his song "The Lorelei" (*"Ich weiss nicht, was soll es bedeuten"* "I don't know what it means"). Now the song was no longer accredited to Heine but was labeled a German folk song.

On May 11, the newspapers were full of photographs and reports about the bonfire in front of the Humbold University. Later on, I saw newsreels of that night. SA men kept tossing books into the flames and sparks flew high into the night air. The men obviously enjoyed feeding the fire because they were laughing.

The changes continued. On June 18, the SPD, the last opposition to Hitler, was outlawed.

On July 3, Jews were evicted from their jobs in the Civil Service. On July 14, Hitler declared that "the NSDAP is now the only legal party in Germany." A new law prohibited the establishment of new parties.

A law against congenitally diseased descendants was enacted. Children of persons suffering from congenital mental illness, schizophrenia, manic depressive psychosis, epilepsy, Huntington's chorea, hereditary blindness, deafness, severe hereditary malformation or severe alcoholism, were forcibly sterilized. It is thought that by January 1, 1934, about 400,000 people had been sterilized.

On the following day, July 15, it was announced, "The Protestant Church will from this day on be known as The German Evangelical Church." "Art as of now on is to be strictly Nordic in character." "Schools must teach race science."

We learned about congenital diseases and how they were passed on. The main example given was that of the Wittelbachs, the Bavarian Royal Family. Cases of recurring madness showed up in the Wittelsbach family tree. The way hereditary characteristics were passed on was explained with the teachings of Mendel's Theory and his charts crossing different types of sweet peas.

Our school system was authoritarian even before 1933, a fact that apparently came in handy for the new regime. Although there were occasional parent/teacher conferences, parents had no influence on the system. Teachers were respected. Parents instructed their children to be obedient and upheld the authority of the teacher. We never had discussions in class. We listened to the teacher. We raised our hands if we knew the answer to questions. If we were picked to answer, we stood up and remained standing until the teacher said, "Sit down." We did not question the contents of our curriculum but we could ask questions in order to clarify something we did not understand. We voiced no opinions or criticisms about lesson contents.

Our new school year began in April and I entered second grade. I had a new teacher, a younger man. Our school day was longer than before and several new subjects, such as arithmetic, were added to our curriculum. We memorized the multiplication tables from one to 10. We learned a cursive writing, known as *Suetterlinschrift.* All our homework and our tests were now written in ink in our notebooks. We had one notebook for each subject and the notebooks had to be kept immaculately clean and neat. In addition, we wrote many pages very carefully in a special notebook labeled "Beautiful Writing."

In German class, we wrote essays and took dictation. Whenever we made a mistake in spelling, punctuation or grammar, we had to write the word or sentence three to five times and show it to the teacher.

The first class period, 8 a.m. to 9 a.m. on Mondays and Thursdays, was religion. Apart from the two Jewish girls, who were excused from this subject, we were all Protestants. The very first story in our first religion class was the Parable of Lazarus and the Rich Man. It impressed me deeply. I shuddered when I imagined the dogs licking the poor man's sores. I read and reread the story at home that afternoon sitting on the living room floor.

Needlework, another new subject, was taught by Miss Bertram. Our first project was to crochet a net to hold balls and the next was a dress for our favorite doll. We learned how to chain, slip stitch, single and double crochet, make loops and piquet. I purchased variegated wool in purples and oranges for the dress, which turned out very pretty. However, I had a very short attention span and was too fidgety to cope for long with the intricacies of crochet, so Aunt Schaefer, the wife of Uncle Schaefer and an expert needlewoman, finished the dress for me.

We did not have exams or finals. Teachers kept a record of the grades pupils received for their homework and in class tests. The final grade at the end of each term depended on these grades. Reports were issued twice a year. The report had to be signed by our father or guardian and shown to our teacher before we could take it home for keeps. We filed our reports in special hardcover folders marked "School Reports." Mine was the one Mama had used. It was dark blue with a fancy pattern and lettering in silver which said: *"Ohn' Fleiss kein Preis,"* which means:"No effort, no prize." Unfortunately, I lost it together with many other things during the war. It was customary to show reports to relatives, close friends and select neighbors. They usually rewarded good notes with a modest monetary gift and a reprimand for the poor ones. I always showed my card to my relatives but to others only at their request. I did not want it to look as if I were soliciting gifts.

There are two incidents I remember from second grade. One is that at some point we learned about water and waterworks. Our teacher asked us, "What do you think happens to water after it has been used?" Nobody knew. I raised my hand and said, "Perhaps it is cleaned and recycled." The teacher laughed, "If that were the case, I would never touch a drop of water again."

The second incident is one I cannot explain even now. One day, during a five minute break between classes when the teachers changed, I went to the back of the classroom. I lay down on the floor and began crawling on my stomach underneath the benches and tables until I came out at the front of the class. I was wearing a pale yellow dress with an embroidered bodice. When I got up, it was full of black greasy stains because our floors were wooden and oiled. The teacher asked me why on earth I had done this but I had no explanation whatsoever. I still don't.

At this time, the changes brought about by Hitler's power became more obvious. For instance, Neukoelln had several main thoroughfares. Beginning at the Hermannplatz, going east, was the Berliner Strasse extending into the Bergstrasse; the Kaiser

Friedrich Strasse also stretched east; the Hermannstrasse went south; the Hasenheide and the Urbanstrasse went west; and the Kottbusser Damm went west northwest. All but the Urbanstrasse and the Hasenheide were lined with shops of all kinds: butchers, bakers, clothing stores, leather good stores, gift shops, confectioners, branches of shoe store chains, jewelers, delicatessens, restaurants and more.

Some of these businesses were owned and operated by Jews. To me they were simply stores and we did not care who owned them. If they sold what we wanted to buy, we bought there.

The total population of Berlin in 1933 was 4,242,301, of whom 160,564 were Jewish. The total population of the Borough of Neukoelln was 315,632, of whom 2,941 were Jewish.

Suddenly, one day, signs appeared on Jewish shop windows:
"GERMANS BEWARE! DON'T BUY FROM JEWS!"
"THE TRUE GERMAN DOES NOT BUY IN JEWISH SHOPS!"

SA men stood outside preventing customers from entering. I don't know how long this lasted, maybe a day or longer. Mama was enraged and more determined than ever to buy where she wanted, regardless. Right away, she went out and bought something she did not even need. Many people were intimidated, at least for a time. Advertising columns were plastered with posters exclaiming:
"GERMANS, DEFEND YOURSELVES AGAINST JEWISH HORROR PROPAGANDA!
BUY ONLY FROM GERMANS!"

As the year progressed, the tentacles of the new regime started to reach ever more into our personal lives. At school, instead of saying "Good morning, Teacher" as we usually did, we were instructed to say "Heil Hitler!" However, it is hard to break the habits of a lifetime even though this lifetime spans only seven years. We still curtsied and said, "Good morning" to the teachers when we passed them on the stairs or in the corridors. None of them said "Heil Hitler!" in return.

The only time my family used "Heil Hitler!" was when we had to go to the police station, any government office, or, occasionally, to address party members. "Heil Hitler!" never took the place of the customary, everyday greetings. Mama and I discussed this. We agreed that it was really too ridiculous to start raising our arm and saying "Heil Hitler!" to our neighbors every time we met them in the staircase. I said that I would not do it in the street because I would be embarrassed to raise my arm. I knew that I would have to say "Heil Hitler!" to several party members whom I regularly passed in the street but I just said "Heil Hitler!" without raising my arm. Many people only bent their arm at the elbow instead of raising it all the way.

In school, we were told that German ethnic minorities in foreign countries were struggling to maintain their German cultural heritage and that we must help support their efforts by contributing 20 pfennig each month to the League of Germans in Foreign Countries (VDA - *Verein Deutscher im Ausland*). Many Germans had emigrated centuries ago, like those whose descendants still lived in Siebenbuergen, Romania. I particularly remember learning a lot about the Germans in Siebenbuergen and its capital, Kronstadt.

In addition, at least once a month a wooden board was passed from class to class. We were told in advance to bring money and for 10 pfennig we were allowed to hammer a fancy gold, silver, white, black or red nail into the design on the board, which had some Hitler Youth symbol on it. The money collected was for the benefit of the Hitler Youth. It was always a member of the Hitler Youth (HJ - Hitler *Jugend*), dressed in uniform, who came to the classroom with the board.

The economic situation had not improved as yet. There was still a lot of unemployment and people were scraping along. This was brought home to me one day when our teacher had to collect the 20 pfennig teaching aid contributions, which was mandatory for us to pay once a month. For a few children in my class, it was hard to come up with the money because their fathers were still unemployed or earned very little and they had sisters and brothers. One of the poorer girls did not have the contribution and our teacher was somewhat annoyed and upbraided her. I heard the girl, who was sitting in front of me, mutter under her breath, "I don't have the money. Twenty pfennig will buy four rolls."

In May, the People's Court was created specifically to try people for treason and offenses against the Reich and the People. Usually no detailed accounts of the trials, only short notices, appeared in the papers, such "John Doe was found guilty of (whatever offense) or of treason against the Reich and sentenced to imprisonment (or death) and the sentence has been carried out."

After Hitler came to power, May 1 became a paid official holiday. For me it was just another day off to be spent leisurely in the usual Sunday fashion. Kurt was ordered to attend the rally together with his colleagues and I suppose Papa was, too.

At my age, politics were of no interest and their meaning did not intrude into my personal little world nor into my conversations with other children. Later, when I was older, I gradually became aware of these things because Mama drew my attention to them and I began to read newspapers myself.

Other changes affecting every level of life were not publicized in either the papers or in radio newscasts. For example, the government interfered with the Protestant churches in many ways. Its Book of Psalms was rewritten in 1934 to eliminate references to the Jews. I did not know the Psalms so I could not tell the difference. The Fuehrer attempted to nazify the Protestant church by saying that he wanted to unify it and that Luther would have done the same. Protestant churches and many clergy stood strong and resisted the Nazification as long as they could but, ultimately, the Fuehrer won.

Radio, in its infancy when I was born, became a mass media soon after Hitler came to power. The *Volksempfaenger,* or Peoples' Receiver, an inexpensive set, was developed for the sole purpose of infiltrating as many homes as possible with Nazi propaganda. An even smaller and cheaper set, nicknamed "Goebbels Gob" also appeared on the market and millions of people who heretofore had been unable to afford a radio now bought one. Thus, Hitler, Goebbels and others had access to our homes. Of course, we still had a choice: we could turn the radio on or off. When Mama and Kurt were first married, they had a *Volksempfaenger* for a while until Mama bought a lovely large Grundig. Individual and independent local radio stations were soon united in a Reich Broadcast Company, the *Deutschlandsender* (Radio Germany) located in Koenigswusterhausen just outside Berlin. Local stations were Reichssender Cologne, Hamburg and Munich. I saw posters proclaiming, "All Germany hears the Fuehrer on the Peoples' Receiver."

Radio reception was not free. Telephone and radio came under the administration of the post office. A special delivery man called the *Geldbrieftraeger,* or money mailman, came knocking on the door once a month to collect the two marks for the radio. At the same time, he delivered Father's pension and was always offered a glass of sherry, which he accepted.

Mama liked music and listened to the radio a lot so I did most of my radio listening at her apartment. If I was at home, I listened to children's drama presentations on Sunday afternoons. I recall one about Albrecht Duerer. In my mind, I can still hear the voice of the child actor who played Duerer at an early age say, "There, it is accomplished," after he had drawn a perfect circle, one of the requirements to join the powerful Nuremberg artists' guild.

Father liked to listen to the news at midday and in the early evening. The rest of the day his radio remained silent. Aunt Martha, an opera buff, loved opera broadcasts as well as comedy programs, such as the "The Merry Fellows from Reichsender Koelle" with Jupp Hussels. She wanted to share her interest and her enthusiasm for opera with me and insisted on explaining the plots. Although I enjoyed the music, I did not like the plots because none of them had happy endings. Classical and chamber music was broadcast on Sunday mornings, while the afternoons featured popular and folk music. Of course, all speeches by leading Nazis and the Fuehrer were broadcast live.

In 1933, Hitler spoke fifty times on the radio, mostly at noon. Factories, schools and public squares installed loudspeakers. Everyone was expected to listen when the Fuehrer, as he was now referred to almost exclusively, spoke. Restaurants stopped serving during the more important speeches. Otherwise, business was conducted in whispers and conversation practically ceased while the Fuehrer was on the air.

At school, we had assembly in order to hear the Fuehrer's messages. I recall these occasions quite clearly. The Fuehrer inevitably commenced speaking in a normal tone of voice, beginning with "When I came to power on January 30, 1933" or "After the War in 1918" or "During the war 1914 to 1918." After that I tuned out and my mind wandered. I was aware that he droned on, getting louder, more passionate and progressively hoarse as he shouted rather than spoke. Applause followed nearly every one of his statements. Usually he stopped and waited for applause if it did not "spontaneously" interrupt him. Whatever he was talking about was way over my head; I was only in second grade. Over the years, I grew used to hearing the same type of speech over and over again, beginning with the same phrases, using the same tone of voice, building up to a shouted climax.

On occasion, we also had to listen to Baldur von Schirach, the youth leader, and Goebbels. Their speeches left no impression on my mind whatsoever, except that I can recall Goebbels' voice. They were spouting slogans and platitudes. I saw many of those on posters. The outstanding words that I heard and saw over and over again were "sacrifice," "duty," "honor," "blood and soil" and "the Fatherland." These words, and phrases containing them, were endlessly repeated. Speeches were very long, especially the Fuehrer's. We had to sit still, with no talking, no fidgeting, no getting up, no slouching, no putting our feet on chairs and no leaving the room.

In this and future speeches, the Fuehrer used the word "providence." He made it sound as though he was chosen by a deity for the special purpose of saving Germany and Western civilization from communism.

Father, Mother and I spent our summer vacation this year in Neuruppin, a city in the Mark Brandenburg northwest of Berlin, located at the Ruppiner Lake. Surrounded by pine forests, it was renowned for its healthy, balmy and fragrant air. The town was a popular vacation resort for Berliners. It was also the birthplace of the author and poet Theodor Fontane (1819-1898), who wrote ballads, novels and detailed descriptions of walking tours throughout the Mark Brandenburg. We lodged at a small hotel and spent our days sightseeing around the town, a delightful quaint place, and taking long walks through the lovely woods and along the lake. A café or restaurant was our destination on these walks, providing rest and refreshments before returning to our hotel.

During our time at Neuruppin, we made the acquaintance of a very nice couple, Mr. and Mrs. Bauer and their 13-year-old son, Jonathan. Mr. Bauer was a retired sea captain, Mrs. Bauer was Jewish and they lived in a suburb north of Berlin. We spent a lot of time together. Jonathan was a keen photographer. He darted ahead and pointed his camera, click, and we were caught walking toward him. Jonathan and I got on famously despite our age difference. He was handsome, with wavy hair, blue-grey eyes and thick lashes. He did not treat me like a child and was never condescending. I loved him. By the end of the vacation, Jonathan and I had decided that when we were grown up we would get married. It was my first proposal.

Over the next few years, our friendship with the Bauers grew. We visited them at their house, which had a pretty garden. In turn, they came to visit us in Berlin. Once the adults talked about some research that had been made on longevity. The results showed that women outlived men by several years. I was quite upset because this meant that Jonathan would die before I did and then what would I do without him? I lay in bed thinking about it for a long time before finally falling asleep. I did not mention this to Jonathan.

Mrs. Bauer played the piano well and sang. On one of our visits, she played and sang a song that I have not forgotten. The song lyrics began "Happiness passes, you'll see, in the time it takes to count from one to three." A somewhat sad sentiment but it must have been a popular song at the time.

The song proved prophetic for, unfortunately, Mrs. Bauer died about two years later of breast cancer. Father and I went to pay a visit of condolence. Poor Mr. Bauer was most distressed. It was winter and he stood with his back to the tile stove and cried. His face was red and his eyes were puffy. While the men conversed, Jonathan and I talked and he showed me his books. We kept in touch for a while until, two years later, Mr. Bauer remarried. I did not forget Jonathan.

Later, either in 1939 or 1940, when I was old enough to be allowed to go further afield by myself, I decided to visit the Emil Schaefers, Father's Skat club friends, who had moved to the same suburb as the Bauers. I walked over to the Bauer's house and I was quite nervous when I rang the bell. Jonathan's stepmother opened the door. I had never met her and introduced myself. She did not ask me in and she did not make me feel welcome. She simply said, "Jonathan is not home. He is still at school." Needless to say, I was very disappointed. I never saw Jonathan again but I often thought of him. I wonder how he got on during the war and if he had any trouble because his mother had been Jewish.

After the summer holidays, I was transferred to another second grade class taught by Mr. Lambert. Mr. Lambert was a bachelor in his mid to late 40s, I guess. He taught this particular group of students from first to eighth grade in all subjects except history. This was the only time he ever did a teaching marathon like this and, toward the end of it, he said that he would never do it again.

His birthday was on February 22. We usually prepared a surprise for him such as flowers, a small gift and a song on our mouth organs and recorders. As soon as we finished playing, he made us play it over and corrected our mistakes.

Mr. Lambert was much more than a teacher: he was an educator. He was very strict and demanding but, as a result, we learned a lot. He made us want to learn.

History began with local history. First, we learned about the Stone Age, then the Bronze Age and then the Iron Age. We visited the little museum next to our gym and looked at exhibits of Stone and Bronze Age origin, such as arrow tips, bronze buckles and clasps. Next we explored our own borough of Neukoelln, in particular a rather remarkable and interesting part, the Bohemian Village. It was during the reign of Friedrich Wilhelm, the Great Elector of Brandenburg (1640-1688) that a large number of people, persecuted for the sake of their religious beliefs, found sanctuary and refuge in Brandenburg. Among them were Bohemians and Huguenots. This policy was continued under the Elector's successor, King Friedrich Wilhelm I of Prussia, who was tolerant with regard to people's religious beliefs. When a large number of Bohemians arrived in Berlin in the spring of 1737, they were given land, which they developed into the Bohemian Village.

Upon entering the Bohemian Village for the first time, I felt myself transported into a bucolic idyll. There were farmhouses, barns, stables, a small schoolhouse, a smithy and a tiny church. I walked along the cobbled streets and alleys behind the barns. I heard cows lowing and cockerels crowing. I saw goats, ducks and geese. I was enchanted by the village. I loved to visit from that time on and was able to revisit in 1996 and 1997. Parts of it were destroyed by bombs during WWII. Unfortunately, modern buildings have also intruded and spoiled its character to some extent. The smithy, the church and the statue of the Elector still stand.

Another field trip took our class to the Invaliden Cemetery. We gathered around a large bronze sculpture in the war graves section. It showed a mortally wounded, or dead, soldier lying on the ground, covered by a blanket or a coat. One arm was raised and the hand, clenched into a fist, was sticking out from under the cover. Mr. Lambert asked us what it might mean. A gesture of defiance? Frustration at being killed? Hatred for the enemy? Our teacher left the interpretation to us to ponder.

We also took a trip to the Friedrichshain, a park with a well-known fountain surrounded by fairy tale figures. Then came visits to Britz, Buckow and Rudow. These had been villages until the growing city swallowed them up. Unlike Neukoelln, these boroughs had kept their original names. In their oldest parts, the boroughs still retained remnants of their past: old manor houses with ponds, village churches dating from the 13th century and the occasional windmill. The windmills, the churches, as well as some manor houses and other historical sites, remain even today. Right in the city, adjacent to the apartment house where Mama lived until she died in 1980, was a field on which a farmer still grew rye.

The Victoria Park was another popular park our class visited. I also went there many times with Father and Mama. It had an aviary with peacocks and golden pheasants. The Kreuzberg, a hill in the park, has a monument resembling a church tower on its summit. Centuries ago, the area was known as the Round Vineyard. Berlin was small in 1525 and the round vineyard was quite a way outside the city limits. Court astronomers predicted that on July 15, 1525, the heavens would open and a terrible flood would destroy Berlin. They convinced the Elector of Brandenburg that "the stars don't lie."

When the dreadful day dawned, it turned out to be sunny and cloudless. By midday dark clouds were spotted on the horizon but it grew larger as the day wore on. The Elector and his family were afraid. He ordered his coaches and he, his family and his court hastened to the summit of the round vineyard where they waited for the heavens to open and deluge the country. But the hours passed and nothing happened. Late in the evening, the

Elector and his entourage returned, rather shamefacedly, to his castle in Berlin.

We learned Berlin's history as well as numerous legends and sagas connected with it, such as the story of the Lions of the Parochial Church. An accomplished artisan designed and built a complex carillon for the Parochial church tower. The bells played a sacred hymn and the four lions on the corners of the tower roared once, twice, three, four times or more and Berliners knew what time it was. At noon and at midnight, the lions roared twelve times. The city councillors were very satisfied and paid a goodly sum to the master craftsman.

When the craftsman informed them that he wished to build an identical clock in another city, they shouted, "We forbid it!" They decided to make sure that theirs would remain the only clock of its kind and that the artist would never build another. They arrested the artist and ordered the hangman to blind him. The poor blind man ran out into the street and pitifully groped his way to the church where he pleaded with the verger, "Please, let me go up into the tower. I want to play my bells one last time." He felt his way up the many steps and played.

People in the street stopped and listened to the beautiful sound of the bells. Many sang along and the councillors rubbed their hands in glee. The big bells sang, the little bells exulted, the master played and the lions roared. Suddenly the playing stopped. The lions remained silent when the clock moved on the full hour. The craftsman vanished. The city councillors tried everything to find someone to restore the work, without success. Although the bells still played their songs, the lions remained silent.

The carillon of the Parochial Church, together with the upper part of the tower, were destroyed during WWII.

Each year took us a little further afield: to Unter den Linden, the Memorial to the Unknown Soldier, the Armory, the Dom and St. Hedwig's, the Roman Catholic cathedral. We visited the oldest parts of Berlin, including the St. Mary's and Nicolai churches built in the 1230s, the Museum Island and the Imperial Palace haunted by the White Lady. Apparently, when the White Lady appeared on the grand staircase it was an omen of an imminent death in the Royal Family. Many people claimed to have seen her. A popular story offers that an officer volunteered to keep watch one night after the White Lady had supposedly been sighted. When she did appear, he drew his sword. The following morning, he was discovered dead at the bottom of the staircase, slain with his own sword.

The story of St. Hedwig's cathedral is that during the time of Frederick II's reign, the Roman Catholics in Berlin desired to build a cathedral. They needed the monarch's permission and when it was granted, they inquired as to the style in which he wished the cathedral to be built. It is said that Frederick was having tea at the time the question was asked and he simply turned his teacup over and said: "Like this." Accordingly, the dome of St. Hedwig's resembled an upside down teacup.

History moved on from Berlin to the history of Mark Brandenburg and we learned how, at first, tribes living there fought, resisted and opposed Christianization and refused to acknowledge the Elector of Brandenburg. We visited many places connected with our history lessons. Some statues in the Tiergarten, namely those in the Siegesallee, represented the early rulers of the Mark Brandenburg, as well as statesmen and generals of later eras. Essentially, we were taught local, Brandenburg and Prussian history.

Then there was Potsdam. Every spring, when the magnolia trees bloomed, our class went to Potsdam, which means "under the oaks." It was my favorite field trip. We strolled around town and looked at the Nicolai Church and the Orphanage, where the sons of members of the Prussian armed forces and officer corps who had been killed in action were taken care of and educated. We visited the Dutch and Russian Quarters, Sanssouci, the New Palais, which was built as a guest house for Sanssouci, and the Orangerie, a former hot house for orange trees that had been transformed into a beautiful building used for concerts and social events. We walked through the beautiful park to the Friendship Temple, which housed a statue of Frederick's favorite sister, Wilhelmine. Other attractions were the Pagoda and the lovely Chinese Tea House. On each visit, we had our picture taken on the steps of the terraces at Sanssouci.

It was always great fun to go inside the castles. We slipped large felt slippers over our street shoes and slid rather than walked to prevent damage to the beautiful floors made of rosewood and other rare woods, inlaid with intricate patterns. I thought it was like skating, slithering from room to room. We went into the New Palais' fabulous ballroom, decorated with seashells and other sea related objects and then reached the small theater, which was decorated in white and gold and red. Sanssouci had a gorgeous library, paneled in a warm brown wood and embellished with gold arabesques. When the door was closed, it could barely be detected because it matched the walls and had bookshelves filled with books. The fabulous Voltaire room, with its reliefs of exotic birds, monkeys and fruits in many colors, and the library were my favorites.

The center room with its skylight was used by Frederick for intimate dinner parties and flute concerts. Naturally, I was familiar with Adolph von Menzel's paintings "Flute Concert at Sanssouci" and "The Dinner Party," both favorites of mine. Adolph von Menzel was a famous painter who lived from 1815

95

to 1905. He was very short and quite a character. He was affectionately known as "The Little Excellency."

Behind Sanssouci, across a valley and on a hill, lies a ruin, which was actually designed and built as a ruin around a reservoir in order to provide the water for the large fountain in front of the castle. The fountain never worked during Frederick's lifetime.

Adjacent to Sanssouci stood, and still stands, a windmill. The king complained that the mill made too much noise, so he wanted to put the miller out of business. The miller went to court, sued and won. Something quite extraordinary in the days of absolute rulers. But then, Frederick the Great was an extraordinary man and monarch.

Later, the story of the Mark Brandenburg became that of Prussia. Now history lessons were mostly about rulers and wars. We had to memorize the dates when the rulers ruled and of their wars. Personal data about kings and princes, other than what was connected with their official lives, was scarcely mentioned. This made the lessons rather dry. I hated figures anyway and hated memorizing dates but this was an important part of the lessons and we were required to answer numerous questions. Dates had to be correct in our essays as well.

The most fascinating historical personages to me and many other students were the Great Elector of Brandenburg, King Frederick I (the Soldier King) and Frederick II (Frederick the Great). The Fuehrer was thought to model himself in some respects on Frederick the Great.

Later on, my interest was captured by Queen Louise and Napoleon. After that, the outstanding personality we dwelt on in great length and detail was Bismarck, the Iron Chancellor.

Mr. Lambert also taught religion. The subjects he covered were The Ten Commandments, the Creed, the Lord's Prayer, grace, Easter, Ascension Day, Good Friday, Christmas, parables, many hymns and morning, noon and evening prayers.

This year Father celebrated his 65th birthday. At his party, I was eating soup and I had just taken a bite from my roll when Uncle Gustav clowned around while filling the wine glasses. I could not help laughing and the roll got stuck in my throat and choked me. I coughed and coughed but could not speak to tell anyone to hit me on the back. Tears were streaming down my face. Still, nobody took notice. I thought, "I am going to die if no one sees that I need help." Finally, someone hit me on the back and I recovered within minutes.

Before 1933, five Nazi Party Congresses had been held: January 27-29, 1923 in Munich; July 3-4, 1926 in Weimar; August 19-21, 1927 and August 4, 1929 in Nuremberg. From then on, a Reich Party Congress took place annually in Nuremberg. This year it was held from August 31 to September 3 under the motto "Victory of Faith." I do not remember seeing or hearing anything about it. I cannot recall newsreel or newspaper pictures.

Our national anthem, *"Deutschland, Deutschland ueber alles,"* was written in 1841 by Hoffmann von Fallersleben, a poet, using a 1797 Haydn hymn dedicated to the Austrian Emperor. Horst Wessel had written a poem, "Raise the Flag," which was first published in the Nazi newspaper *Der Angriff* on September 23, 1929. It was set to music and was known as the Horst Wessel Song. It became the custom to sing it following the national anthem, so it seemed to me that it was part of the anthem or that we had two anthems.

Richard Walther Darre joined the Nazi party in 1930 and became Reich Peasant Leader in 1933. He issued the Hereditary Farm Law in September. This law decreed that large farms must be preserved and protected from being split up among siblings into parcels too small to be worked profitably and support a family. The Hereditary Farm Law specified that only one son could be the heir, thus keeping the farm intact and in the same family for generations. The owner was not allowed to sell all or part of it.

Also, the hereditary peasant had to be debt free and prove his German ancestry back to the year 1800. A hereditary farm had to be 18.5 acres minimum, 212.5 acres maximum and cultivated exclusively by one peasant, which was now the new name for farmers who owned a hereditary farm. The name peasant was to confer standing and respect. As with manual labor, the peasant was to be honored and raised to a high level of respectability. All other people working farms smaller than hereditary farms were now called agriculturalists. We were reminded that through the ages, peasants, although vitally important, were inevitably looked down upon and ridiculed as country yokels by city folk and intellectuals. This was no longer so in the Third Reich.

On September 13, the Winter Assistance Program (WHW - *Winterhilfswerk*), began its collections. The new WHW slogan was "Nobody shall go hungry, nobody shall be cold." The WHW provided needy people with money, groceries, meals, clothing and fuel. "Winter Pfennig" collection tins were placed in stores and storekeepers encouraged people to put their change into the tins. The WHW was publicized in film, newspapers, by posters and on the radio.

The Red Cross and various religious organizations had been doing this type of welfare work in previous years. But the Fuehrer organized his own National Socialist Welfare (NSV - *Nationalsozialistische Volkswohlfahrt*) organization with its slogan "A nation takes care of itself."

During the months of September through March, weekend street collections took place for the benefit of the WHW. Film and stage stars, sports personalities like the boxer Max Schmeling and top Nazis like Goering and Goebbels were pressed into service for publicity purposes and to attract crowds, in addition to party functionaries and Hitler Youth. They were photographed and filmed standing on busy intersections shaking collection cans.

In recognition of one's contribution of 20 pfennig, one had a choice of various small emblems, which could be worn on the lapel or attached by a little loop to a button. The items were produced in economically depressed parts of Germany. They were beautifully handcrafted and so attractive that people could not resist buying whole sets, which I did as well.

Nazi representatives included block leaders, who were Party representatives responsible for one block or fifty households. They had authority to gain entrance to homes at any time for the purpose of enlightening people and spreading propaganda according to Goebbels, Berlin's regional party leader, collecting money, persuading people to subscribe to party newspapers, and persuading people to join welfare and other organizations. Cell leaders were in charge of four to eight block leaders and instructed block leaders according to Party directives. Ward Party Leaders were in charge of several thousand households in large cities. Party bigwigs were nicknamed "Golden Pheasants" because their brown uniforms were trimmed with much gold braid.

Another innovation reached into the family and into the kitchen. This was the One Pot Meal or Stew Sunday. Our usual Sunday dinner, eaten at noon, consisted of soup, a roast with two or three vegetables, salad, dessert and wine. Now, one Sunday a month from September through March was designated a One Pot Meal Sunday. On that day, the population was to sacrifice the typical Sunday repast for a simple, thick lentil, pea, green bean or cabbage stew. The difference in the cost of the meal was to be donated to the WHW. Party officials went door to door to collect the money. Again, people received a door sticker to show that they had complied with this requirement. Giving money was definitely not voluntary. Father contributed the minimum to avoid trouble. During the six months of One Pot Meal Sundays, newspapers published recipes and commented that the hausfrau was to be proud to fulfil her national obligation. Doing her national duty, so it said, would result in joy for the housewife and happiness in her home. However, just because we were made to contribute did not mean we changed our ways. I cannot remember a single Sunday when we had stew in place of the usual roast. On my twice monthly visits to Oma, she still had a chicken in the pot to make her excellent chicken noodle soup and a roast in the oven, as well as chocolate or vanilla pudding with vanilla or orange sauce and macaroons for dessert.

We did have to be careful because party officials were empowered to make spot-checks. We would have been in trouble had they found us with a roast on the table instead of stew. Of course, the Nazis found it hard to check everyone in a big city like Berlin. While we were not afraid, we were aware of the risks of noncompliance because the newspapers reported on offenders and their punishment.

On every One Pot Meal Sunday, leading Nazi personalities, including the Fuehrer, were photographed and filmed at various locations partaking in a One Pot Meal. Soon a little ditty made the rounds to the tune of a folk song. Part of it went like this, "and little Goebbels limps through the hall, calling pea soup or green beans, who is ready for another helping?"

Later in the year, restaurants were required to serve One Pot Meals on designated dates, which were published in the papers. The notices read: "The following Sundays are One Pot Sundays:

100

October 14, November 18, and December 16, 1934; January 13, February 17 and March 17, 1935. On October 14, only the following three one pot entrees may be offered in restaurants: pea soup, with the addition of either sausage, pigs ears or salted meat, beef noodle soup or vegetable stew with meat."

Later, monthly menus were published.

In conjunction with the WHW, the pound donation was instituted. Every household was expected to contribute one pound of prepackaged, nonperishable food to the monthly collection for distribution to poor people. Money could be substituted for food. I heard Mother and Mama grumble about it. Both of them would help out anyone in need but resented coercion. Mother usually gave flour, noodles or sugar. I don't know what Mama gave because I was never there when the food was collected.

On November 12, Germany had another voting session. In this connection, I want to mention that voters were often harassed at the polling stations by SA men before Hitler came to power. Mama told me later that after 1933 the ballot papers were printed on thin paper, transparent enough so it was possible to see how a person had voted. The Nazis simply destroyed an appropriate number of anti-Nazi ballots to ensure their victory. Mama was very bitter about it because she was SPD and hated Hitler.

The SS was declared an independent organization under Adolf Hitler on July 20, 1933 and in December the SS became an official organ of the Reich. SS men took an oath: "I swear to thee Adolf Hitler, as the Fuehrer and Chancellor, of the German Reich, loyalty and bravery. I vow to thee and to the superiors whom thou shalt appoint, obedience unto death, so help me God." SS men also had their blood type tattooed under their left armpit.

101

It was strange. To me, it seemed the whole atmosphere in Berlin changed as soon as Hitler came to power. I would not have been able to explain it at the time but I felt it. It was not the same as before. I felt that the rhythm of life changed. It accelerated and some of the famous *Gemuetlichkeit* was lost. *Gemuetlichkeit* is an atmosphere and mood of geniality, comfort, cosiness and kindliness. It appeared that our lives were manipulated. We were constantly reminded that the individual was nothing. The Volk as a whole was all important and came first at all times. Patriotism was fostered. It is hard to put into words how it felt.

Countless small things during a day could trigger an awareness of change, which I did not consciously acknowledge at that time but which nevertheless left lasting impressions. I certainly did not understand, question or think about why it was so. I just knew it was different. Public life became one of intensity, urgency, purpose, activity, changes, organization and control. The emphasis in Germany now was on "the community of German people" based on enhancing the values of honor, courage, strength, selflessness and a disdain of everything non-German.

It is only now, as an adult, that I can put into words what I felt then as a child. The time before 1933 can be compared to a warm, sunny, relaxing, late summer afternoon. After 1934, it compares to an early morning with brilliant but cold sunlight which increases in intensity as the day wears on to become a focused harsh spotlight.

The school year continued. For me, life was routine. The drama "Wilhelm Tell" by Friedrich von Schiller, the story of the Swiss national hero who embodies love of freedom, was banned from school reading. I don't know when this ban came into effect. No matter, for we read it in class. Mr. Lambert told us how remarkable it was that Schiller described the Swiss locations in great and accurate detail although he had never been there. December came and with it the holiday season. On December 11, Christmas trees appeared on the Berlin streets. A few days later, the father of a classmate, who owned a chocolate wholesale business, donated a Christmas tree and numerous boxes of chocolate ornaments to our class. The tree stood in the front left-hand corner of the room. We decorated it while Mr. Lambert stood by giving directions. On the day before our Christmas vacation, we were allowed to "plunder" the tree. Mr. Lambert saw to it that the children from poor families got most of the goodies.

It is still dark at 7:30 a.m. in Berlin during the month of December. When I woke up on December 21, my eighth birthday, I was delighted to find that Father and Mother had decorated the living room with strings of colored lanterns complete with burning candles. It was delightful. I had made the lanterns with Father's help. On winter evenings, Mother knitted, Father read aloud and I worked on a craft project, like the lanterns. Now, they made a lovely birthday surprise decoration.

Every year, usually just before the Christmas season, Aunt Marga brought home theater tickets to special children's productions. I loved it. This year we went to see "Peter's Trip to the Moon."

We spent Christmas and New Year's in much the same way as in other years. Christmas Eve with Mother and Father, First Christmas Day with Aunt Martha and the day after Christmas with Mama and Kurt. My Christmas presents included a new winter coat and a dark blue velvet dress with a cream-colored lace collar. There was also a new pair of patent leather shoes, a *Pummelchen* (a baby doll that was the latest and most popular on the market) and a new sled. On Christmas Day I visited Oma, Opa and Papa.

1934

January 2	Law for the regulation of national labor is passed.
March	Plans are made for 900 miles of autobahn.
April	Berlin Police Chief bans fortune-telling and horoscopes.
May 17	Trial of 1,000 alleged Communists.
June 30 to July 2	Roehm purge.
July 20	SS becomes an independent organization.
July 25	Dollfuss is murdered. Schuschnigg and Miklas are in control in Austria.
August 2	Hindenburg dies.
August 4	Hitler makes himself both president and chancellor. The Army swears an oath of unconditional obedience to Hitler personally.
September 4 to September 10	Party Congress in Nuremberg. The theme was "Triumph of the Will."
December 21	The author's ninth birthday.

Public announcements from the newspaper.
The 15th of January: A historic day.
Commemorative Celebration in Lippe.

Saturday, March 10.
400,000 less unemployed.

WHW emblem glass discs, as large as a one mark coin and featuring the German Eagle holding a swastika, were made in Thuringia and Lauscha.

The following are portions of a speech Goebbels made regarding women's place in politics:

"This area (politics) must be claimed absolutely and without reservation by men. Already, the differences between the sexes as viewed from nature points out that the woman is more suited to a life inside the walls of the house rather than a public life.

We do not consider that a woman's honor is elevated when she competes against the man in masculine areas but when the entire area of a woman's life becomes the ideal complement to that of man's life.

That does not mean to say that we want to push women out of professions. When today, old-fashioned people declare that women do not belong in offices, public office and social work establishments, this reasoning suffers from the ills of error. In days gone by, offices and social work establishments in this sense did not exist.

Nothing is more insufferable, more arrogant and insolent than when certain men try to impose their morals on women, while they vigorously object to women who try to impose their morals upon them. These moralizers claim the right to pronounce their

106

unauthorized judgment on all and sundry in the life of women.

They themselves smoke 20, 30, even 40 cigarettes a day but put up posters in restaurants that read: "The German woman does not smoke!" If a German woman smokes, it is her own business. I can imagine that among women the principle gains ground: "We won't smoke!" But the man does not have the right to dictate this to the woman. The woman, by the same right could go into a restaurant and put up moralizing posters saying: "The German man does not drink!" We know very well that smoking is more damaging to women's health than the health of men and, therefore, in the interest of offspring and Volk health should be refrained from. But it is stupid and mostly unsuccessful to communicate this to women in a way which dishonors them by posters in cafés. It would surely meet with more success if the man regarding non-smoking tries to influence the woman within the framework of the family.

We must most emphatically deny insinuations that we want to withhold something from women that is by rights theirs, that we actually confront women with enmity and that it is our intention to exclude or push out women all together from public life and from professions and thereby degrade women to second class creatures.

When we exclude women from the areas of public life, it is not because we want to dishonor them but because we would like to restore their true, intrinsic honor to them."

107

From now on, the Fuehrer's birthday was heralded long ahead of time. Many shops and department stores decorated their windows with flowers and a picture or a bust of Adolf Hitler. Flags were ordered to be flown. On the day itself, or on Friday if the day fell on a weekend, we had assembly in school. Each class contributed to a special program that was rehearsed at least once. There was group singing, solo singing, recitations of poems and a short address by our head mistress. Inevitably, the Fuehrer spoke on the radio. We listened. In my case, I was present in body though not in spirit. Details of the birthday programs were published long ahead of the event, followed by details of the festivities after the event. It was interesting to note the enormous number of gifts that arrived, apart from mountains of mail, so we were told, ranging from a cuckoo clock and a butterfly collection to 120 sandwiches, large cakes, flowers, as well as valuable antiques, paintings, sculptures and, believe it or not, the coat of arms of the Hitler family. Each year, every detail of this day was faithfully noted in all newspapers and magazines.

The government urged women to stay at home, as is illustrated by the following newspaper excerpts:

Girls Belong in the House.

Take cook pot, dustpan and broom
and you will land a husband soon.

The Goering Plan for combating unemployment considered household work and raising a family the natural occupation of women. The girl of today must take care of her loved ones.

And finally: should German girls rest their hands in their lap, waiting passively for a husband? Is that what women should do? In households and agriculture, workers are urgently needed. Germany has, indeed, a surplus of women but the actual possibilities for founding a family are, at the same time, not exhausted by a long shot. Besides, every man is pleased when a girl brings experience and expertise in housework to the marriage.

According to the Goering Plan, the city issues the decree: In the future, every young German man will only marry if his bride has spent at least one year working in a household or in agriculture prior to marriage.

Announcing the Reich Trade Occupational Competition - March 18 to March 23

"Our Ideal is Work!"

The willingness to attain the highest occupational achievement of the German Youth is tested in a great contest.

The following summons is issued on the occasion of the Reich Trade Occupational Competition Of German Youth:

"The ideal of the German People is Work. The German's desire is achievement and his desire is peace. We call the German Youth to participate in the Second Reich Trade Occupational Competition to take place from March 18 to March 23, 1935.

We are sure of the adherence of our young comrades. Heil Hitler!"

Signed: Goebbels, Frick, Darre and Seldte, Dr. Ley and Baldur von Schirach

Snow fell from before Christmas on through February. Mounds of it lined the sidewalks and it was very cold. After school, I often went sledding with the other children. There was practically no traffic in our street so it was quite safe to be on the road itself. At other times, I visited school friends.

One day, early in March, it was still cold enough to wear a winter coat and I went out after school to play with my tops. I was by myself. I whipped my top along the street. After one huge jump, the toy top hit the fence that separated the street from the market and disappeared through a space at the bottom. I walked to the door leading to the market and it was not locked. I went in and looked for my top. I saw it, picked it up and turned to leave but found myself confronted by a large German shepherd. I froze. The dog calmly walked up to me and bit my bottom. The owner of the dog immediately called the dog to him and grabbed his collar.

I screamed. Crying, I ran home and told Mother that I had been bitten by a dog. Mother undressed me and made me lie down on my stomach on the sofa. She washed the puncture wounds and put cold compresses on them until Dr. Baumann arrived. After a while, I calmed down. I was greatly surprised a little later when the doorbell rang and in marched a burly policeman, who had a handlebar moustache and was wearing his helmet. We called the policemen *Schupos*, short for *Schutzpolizei*. He was very cheerful and jolly. He removed his helmet, sat down on a chair next to me and asked me what had happened. He told Mother that he had to take a look at the injury, much to my embarrassment. The policeman informed us that the dog would be examined by a veterinarian to make sure it did not have rabies.

The owners of the dog were a married couple who lived in a caravan on the fairgrounds, a Mr. and Mrs. Hofer. Mr. Hofer had a job and Mrs. Hofer sold roasted nuts and cookies. The side of the caravan could be opened to form a marquis with a counter. After I recovered, I often visited Mrs. Hofer, bought peanuts and chatted with her. I thought it was very romantic to live in a caravan on the fairgrounds. We were friends for many years.

In December 1933, the Fuehrer broke ground for the first segment of the Autobahn in Frankfurt/Main. The plan was for 900 miles of road to be built. It was stated in the newspapers that the Autobahn, or German road, must be "a statement of its landscape and a statement of the German spirit. Bridges and curves are to blend with the landscape. They are works of art, symbols of eternity." "The mission of the Reich Autobahn is to become Adolf Hitler's road . . . to honor him not only today but for generations to come." The bridges were hewn in stone. People were very proud of the Autobahn. Of course, few people owned cars but this was to be remedied once the Volkswagen was available at a price everyone could afford.

The Fuehrer spoke on March 21 and said, "Today we worry about work and wages for millions of people. Tomorrow our concern will be how to increase their buying power and improve their standard of living." The latter concern was not translated into action. Consumer goods production was not increased. Living standards remained the same.

An avalanche of new institutions and organizations came into being every day. It was hard to keep up with them. My knowledge about them came from posters displayed on the advertising columns, snatches of grown-up conversations and current affairs as presented by teachers.

The new social services of the National Socialist Volk Welfare (NSV) were intended for young, congenitally healthy families in need. They included the Assistance Service for Mother and Child, a National Socialist Home Nurse's Service,

112

the Winter Assistance Program and more. Services included housing aid and settlement, employment assistance, kindergarten and nursery school placement, pediatric care, child rearing instruction and counseling, convalescent homes for mothers and children, and children's meals. Much of the work was done by volunteers. The NSV placed families with four or more children in better and larger apartments. When larger apartments became available, these families were given preference and landlords were required to accept them as tenants.

Motherhood was extolled as "the greatest mystery on earth" and was demanded and expected of every married woman. Intentional childlessness was said to be "against nature" and would lead to Volk death. Refusal to reproduce was grounds for divorce, as was infertility. The Germanic and Nordic peoples had always celebrated the mother as "the guardian of the sacred hearth fire, of life and honor." Mother love was praised as selfless and self-sacrificing. A woman had the responsibility to produce healthy offspring and married women were encouraged to stop working.

Marriage loans became available to help the unemployed. The loans were interest free and intended for needy, politically and eugenically reliable people. The loan came in the form of coupons that entitled the recipient to purchase furniture and household goods for up to 1,000 marks and were repayable at 1 percent interest a month. The loan was reduced by 250 marks with the birth of each child. By 1935, 523,000 people had applied for and received loans.

Married couples with children received a tax deduction. Large families were eligible for many benefits. Childless couples had to pay a tax penalty for not having children.

All pornographic literature was banned and sexual freedom was condemned, as was prostitution. The dangers of venereal diseases were stressed. At the time, none of this was mentioned in my presence or to me directly either at home or at school. Later, in high school, I learned about syphilis and that both Beethoven and Schubert died of it.

Also in March, the Berlin Police Chief issued a ban on fortune-telling and horoscopes. Aunt Marga was very interested in astrology, owned Tarot cards and continued to read books about astrology and horoscopes.

As far as fortune-telling is concerned, I knew nobody who practiced it as a business. There were gypsies and people with crystal balls who also read palms, tea leaves and coffee grounds and had Tarot cards at fairgrounds.

To impress us with the evils of fortune-telling, we were shown a movie at school about its dangers. The example given was that of a person who was feeling unwell but who was afraid to consult a physician. Instead, the person went to a fortune-teller who encouraged him to keep coming in order to be cured. Of course, it did not work and the person was finally admitted to a hospital. An examination revealed that it was too late. The delay in seeking medical help resulted in death. The moral was that fortune-tellers are dangerous and were, therefore, outlawed. They were criminals who endangered the life and health of the German people both physically and psychologically. I was impressed.

After Easter, I entered third grade. Having so far mastered, or at least become acquainted with, the rudiments of crochet, we now progressed to knitting. Our lessons were very practical. We always learned to produce something useful.

The first item was a bag for marbles. We started with two needles and learned how to cast on stitches and knit a square in stocking stitch. Then Miss Bertram showed us how to pick up stitches along the sides, which was no mean feat for small hands and fingers. Knitting with five needles, we proceeded to knit two inches. The next two inches were worked in "purl," much harder to do, followed by several rows in knit two, purl two. At the top of the bag, we worked in a row of holes (knit two together, yarn over, knit two together). The next rows were again in knit two, purl two. We were shown how to cast off and make a crochet chain to thread through the holes. Voila, the bag was finished and ready to use. I was very proud because I had done the whole thing by myself.

Our next project was more ambitious: socks. For a while I got on all right with it but when it came to the heels I was lost. Again, I was lucky. Mother was good at knitting socks. She "turned my heels." My teacher took one look and knew instantly that I had not knitted such a tidy heel. However, she still gave me a "2 = Good," probably for effort.

Oma and her daughters were very accomplished needlewomen. They knitted, crocheted, tatted and embroidered. Oma made beautiful, intricate crochet and knitted Viennese lace tablecloths. When they were finished, she stretched them on large frames. She could crochet a long sleeved man's sweater with knitted welts in two days. Oma produced layettes, sweaters, lace and embroidered tablecloths all the time, as did my aunts, but never made one item for me. This bothered me. I asked Aunt Marga to buy some wool. I took the wool to Oma and asked her to make something. She could not very well refuse and crocheted a pretty short sleeved sweater for me. I did not understand why she was like that and why she never hugged or kissed me.

Oma and my aunts were always busy when I visited them. On my weekday visits, Oma came home from work shortly before I arrived and the aunts and Papa arrived shortly thereafter. Once in a while when I visited on Sunday morning, I found Oma and Aunt Frieda in the laundry room doing their big wash. I have no idea what Oma, Opa and the aunts did when I was not there. They did not talk about it and they never took me anywhere except on visits to neighbors. They were friendly with many neighbors in their building. I met all of them and was particularly fond of Nora, who was in her late 20s. She had been engaged to be married when she was 22. Shortly before the wedding, she found out that she had an incurable, progressively debilitating disease. I have no idea what it was. All I know is that it started in her heel and she became increasingly crippled so the engagement was broken.

This year, Pentecost fell on a beautiful warm and sunny Sunday in May. Father, Mother and I paid one of our infrequent visits to Father's brother, Wilhelm. Uncle Wilhelm and his wife, Aunt Anna, lived in a cute little house in Heiligensee, a northwestern suburb of Berlin. Their older daughter, Else, was married. Their younger daughter, Anna, was single and lived with her parents. The house had a good sized garden that boasted numerous fruit trees, as well as berry bushes. Every year at the end of the summer, Uncle Wilhelm and Aunt Anna turned up at our apartment bearing large fruit filled baskets. I loved their visits and was sorry they did not come more often but it was a long way from Heiligensee to Neukoelln.

The SA had been the Nazi police force under the leadership of Roehm but Hitler eventually came to suspect that Roehm was turning the SA into a personal army and planning a coup. On June 30, so we were informed, an attempted coup by Roehm and several other SA members was foiled by the Fuehrer himself. Those involved in the coup were executed on what came to be called "the night of the long knives."

We were told in the newspapers and in radio news reports of Roehm's disloyalty and treason against the Fuehrer. I recall

116

seeing photographs of Roehm. Previous to this affair, I had not known who he was.

Beginning on June 30 and into July, SA purges took place. Later, the Fuehrer, speaking at the Reichstag, explained the circumstances of the purge. In order to keep the SA in line, the SA was relegated to conducting unimportant duties. I remember hearing all of this discussed at home and in school.

Meanwhile, Himmler and the SS waxed in importance and took over nearly all duties of policing the Reich. It was announced, "The SS will assume responsibilities once held by the SA." These changes confirmed the Fuehrer's increasing distrust of the SA.

The *"Voelkischer Beobachter,"* the official Nazi paper, stated: "Let everyone be aware that whoever dares to raise his hand against the State is sure to die."

Father's sister, Luise, and her family had lived in a village called Balz near Vietz on the Eastern Railroad, some 70 odd miles east of Berlin, halfway between the towns of Kuestrin and Landsberg in the Warthebruch, which is the fertile area along the river Warthe, a tributary of the Oder river. Aunt Luise Rothe was a midwife, beloved, respected and renowned for miles around.

Aunt Rothe had died a few years ago and Father went to the funeral. On his return, he recounted what had happened. His sister had slipped and fallen on the icy concrete walkway, in front of her house and injured her knee. She was taken to a hospital in Landsberg, where she died following surgery.

Surgery, even what we nowadays consider minor surgery and quite common routine proceedings, was in those days serious and risky. I heard of many people who died after appendectomies. Two of Mama and Kurt's close friends and a close friend of Aunt Martha and Uncle Gustav's died after surgery.

Aunt Rothe's funeral was a large affair attended by over 200 people. Most of the mourners were women whom she had assisted in childbirth over the years, as well as their daughters and daughters-in-law who had also called her when their delivery time came. She had retired several years before her death. However, the women in the area still wanted her to deliver their babies. "Children," she admonished them, "I am retired. You have a new midwife!"

Uncle Rothe and Aunt Rothe had three daughters: Ida, Charlotte and Christine. Christine died at age 21 of tuberculosis. At the time of her death, she had been engaged to be married and now her unused bridal myrtle wreath was mounted on pale blue satin under glass on the wall of her former bedroom. Ida lived in Berlin with her husband and family. I do not recall their last name. Charlotte was married to Otto. They had two sons, Hans and Gerhard, both a little older than I, and lived in Vietz.

After her mother's death, Charlotte, known as Aunt Lotte, and Otto went to live with Uncle Rothe, whose mother had been a member of an old Brandenburg family called von dem Borne (or von dem Busche). Uncle Rothe dressed meticulously in beige or olive green corduroy pants, a black waistcoat, a snow white shirt with a pleated front and a low stand-up collar and a navy blue or black cap. He looked stern, did not speak much, was serious and very strict. He expected children to be quiet and behave in his presence.

The property Uncle Rothe owned consisted of a few acres of land, not enough to support the family. Therefore, Uncle Otto had a full time job in Vietz with a feed company. On their land they grew rye, barley, potatoes and sugar beets.

This summer, Mama and I went to Balz for the first time for our summer vacation. We stayed with Aunt Lotte, Uncle Otto and Uncle Rothe. We boarded a train at the Schlesischer Bahnhof that took us via Kuestrin to Vietz. Hans was waiting for us at the station with a small cart to convey our luggage and we walked about a mile to their house.

The village of Balz was not a compact village clustered around a common or village green. It was what was called a "line" village, strung along a road, in this case the No. 1 highway that stretched clear across Germany from East Prussia to the Rhineland, and spread out each side of the road for several miles.

This was the first time I had been in the country proper for more than just a day trip and staying at Aunt Lotte's farm was a novel experience. An English walnut tree stood outside the front door. There were many lilac trees at the sides and the back of the one story house, which had a hall and kitchen with ceramic tile floors, a living room and three bedrooms. There was no indoor plumbing. The "little house," complete with a cut out heart in the door, was off to one side near a field and hidden by bushes. This, too, was a novelty. I was fascinated to discover that the toilet paper consisted of cut up newspapers and magazines.

At right angles to the house, flanking two sides of the yard, stood the barn and a stable. The immaculate stable accommodated one cow and three pigs. All edible leftovers were saved for the pigs. The potato peels were washed, cooked, mashed and mixed with skim milk, wheat germ and other leftovers. It smelled appetizing and the pigs loved it.

There was also a henhouse, home to a rooster and three hens. Daily before the crack of dawn, one of the hens laid her egg. As soon as she had accomplished this feat, she began strutting around the house cackling for hours.

First thing in the morning and again in the evening, Aunt Lotte milked the cow. The cow was given grass or hay and her tail was tied to her leg. Hans or Gerhard took up their position near the head of the cow and kept the flies away by fanning her with a long lilac tree branch with dried up leaves at the top. I was intrigued and wanted to try so Aunt Lotte showed me how. I don't think it was too much to the cow's liking, although, after a few practice sessions I did a pretty good job. The milk was put through a centrifuge and the cream was kept in cold storage.

Friday mornings were special because we made butter from the cream with a churn. The hard part was turning the handle until the cream turned into butter. I was curious and anxious to try my hand at it. I took turns cranking until my arms, unused to the task, hurt. As soon as the butter was made, we savored the fruits of our labor: "Second" breakfast, a most marvelous meal. We feasted on sourdough rye bread, baked in the brick oven that stood in one of their fields. These were big round loaves cut into such large slices as I had never known in the city. The bread was spread thickly with fresh butter and topped with slices of home cured smoked ham. Tall glasses of fresh, cool buttermilk proved to be the perfect drink to go with this repast.

I played with Hans and Gerhard when they had time after finishing their assigned chores. In the barn, we jumped from the crossbeams into the hay, played hide and seek, hopscotch, jump rope, ball games and catch. Other times, I occupied myself watching what Aunt Lotte did, explored the fields around the house, climbed fruit trees and played hopscotch by myself in the yard. I met a couple of the neighbors' children. They seemed quaint to me and I must have seemed strange to them. They showed me their garden and we climbed trees. The neighbors kept a few goats and one day the children tried to persuade me to eat goat droppings. They told me they were raisins, thinking they could fool the city slicker, but their attempts failed. I knew my raisins.

We ate our main meal at noon. I was astonished to see Uncle Rothe place his dessert onto the plate alongside meat and vegetables. He explained his strange habit saying, "It all ends up in the same stomach anyway."

Mama and I took walks to the village store and into Vietz where we looked at a mill and where I first encountered turkeys. I thought they were ugly and I was a little scared of them. We walked to the two lakes in the vicinity: the Dolgensee and the Raak See.

The Dolgensee, surrounded by tall pine trees, looked dark green and mysterious. It was said to be dangerous because of an eddy. Over the years, a number of swimmers had drowned in the lake. Water lilies floated on the surface in places, while proudly erect bull rushes bordered part of the shoreline. The Dolgensee lay an hour's walk from the main highway through the forest and the Raak See was an additional half hour's walk further along the same route.

The forest was lovely, mainly pine. Most tree trunks bore several diagonal narrow furrows bleeding sap into small containers, which were wired to the trees. The forester in charge of this territory took care of the trees and the animals within its boundaries.

The foresters, well trained professionals, wore green uniforms, hunting hats and guns. They were respected personages of importance and standing in any community. Foresters were usually accompanied by one or two dachshunds, the breed most associated with them.

I owned a series of four books about a boy whose uncle was a forester. The stories described the boy's experiences when he visits his uncle in the spring, summer, fall and winter. He learned about his uncle's work, the plants and the animals in the forest. I also read other books about foresters, their dogs and adventures related to their work.

Anyone wanting to gather berries and mushrooms had to buy a permit from the forester, although one did not need a permit if one only walked through the woods and ate berries on the way. Aunt Lotte had a permit, so occasionally we accompanied her and helped her fill her baskets with blueberries. She showed us where to find mushrooms. All but two species of mushrooms were edible but most of them were not eaten because they had no flavor. The ones we collected and savored were the delicious chanterelles and *Boletus edulis.*

In the evenings, after chores were completed, we sat in front of the house and enjoyed the cool of the evening. The adults talked and the children played. On weekends, we went to the movies in Vietz because Balz did not have a cinema.

Some Sundays an elderly couple, Uncle Otto's Aunt Anna and Uncle Wilhelm, walked over from Vietz to share afternoon coffee and cake with us, as well as supper and a bottle of homemade beer. Uncle Wilhelm loved to eat, most of all roast pork. Unfortunately, he had great difficulty chewing because he had no teeth and was too poor to buy dentures.

A fortnight later, Mama went back to Berlin and Father and Mother came to stay for the next two weeks.

On August 2, while we were still in Balz, President Paul von Hindenburg died. I had often heard people talk about him with respect and as the hero of Tannenberg. Tannenberg, a small place in East Prussia, was the scene of his greatest victory over the Russians in WWI. Hindenburg was buried with great pomp in the Tannenberg Battle Memorial. Reports stated that torches lit the 65 mile route to Hindenburg's tomb. The State funeral was broadcast and shown in the cinemas. Magazines and newspapers amply illustrated the story and covered the event in detail.

On the day after Hindenburg died, August 3, the Fuehrer declared himself to be both President and Chancellor of Germany. Members of the Armed Forces were required to swear an oath of unconditional obedience to Hitler personally:

"I swear before God this sacred oath:

I will render unconditional obedience to Adolf Hitler,

the Fuehrer of the German Nation and People,

Supreme Commander of the Armed Forces,

and as a brave soldier I am ready to risk my life

at any time in obedience to this oath."

Hitler was now the absolute dictator of Germany. There were no checks to challenge his power. I was at the time oblivious to the significance and consequences of this decree.

The farmers in the village of Balz worked hard all week but on Sundays some of them dressed in their SA uniforms, held meetings and shooting target practices. They met either in Vietz or in a Balz village pub. Uncle Otto did not belong to the SA, and Hans and Gerhard did not belong to the Hitler Youth.

Upon returning from vacation I found that Mama and Kurt, assisted by Aunt Martha and Uncle Gustav, had accomplished a move to a different apartment for themselves, as well as Father, Mother and me.

During WWI, the building of private residences and apartment houses practically came to a standstill and it was never resumed full-scale, owing to the political and economic situation following WWI. The result was a great housing shortage. In order to get an apartment, one had to find a party who was giving up an apartment or a party who would swap. Mama gave up her apartment. She and Kurt moved into one vacated by the people who moved into Father and Mother's. Father and Mother rented

123

one of two apartments that became available when the local police precinct relocated to larger quarters. Now we lived on the first floor and Mama was only a couple of blocks away from us on the same street.

I was very excited about the move. People did not move often. Father and Mother had lived in their last apartment for over 30 years. Aunt Martha lived in the same apartment building for over 50 years. This was not unusual. Even today, a school friend of mine has been living in the same apartment in Berlin for 47 years.

The other first floor apartment at our new location was occupied by newlyweds, Mr. and Mrs. Schlosser. I became quite friendly with Mrs. Schlosser. Mr. Schlosser was a party member and, I think, a Block Warden. I did not pay too much attention to these things. He was a quiet man and I did not know him well because I visited with Mrs. Schlosser during the day when he was at work.

Our former neighbors, the Riemann sisters, had visitors this summer. Not just ordinary visitors, but their American cousins. I did not find out much about them, like where they came from. Prior to the arrival of their visitors, the sisters spent a lot of time and care sewing a fabulous wardrobe for a beautiful doll that the cousins took back to America. The Americans created quite a sensation because they arrived in a large recreational vehicle, something we had not seen before. I doubt if there had been many like it in Berlin. I was sorry I did not meet the cousins but they only stayed a couple of days.

When school started in late August, Hindenburg was discussed. We learned about his life, his military career and the great victory at Tannenberg. We were shown pictures of the huge monument that was erected at the scene of the battle and where he was now laid to rest. I had seen most of this already in the papers.

We also learned about Hitler's life, that is, the official version of it and I had a pictorial history of Hitler's life. Adolf Hitler was born in Braunau at the Inn in Austria. His father was a civil servant. Adolf was very fond of his mother, Klara. Adolf wanted to be an artist and did not want to follow in his father's footsteps and become a civil servant, as was his father's wish. His refusal to comply led to a break in their relationship. Adolf left home and went to Vienna where he tried to join the Academy of Fine Arts but he was not accepted. He then tried to earn his living by painting but he painted more houses than pictures in order to survive.

When WWI broke out, Adolf joined the army. He served in France and was wounded. In addition, he was exposed to mustard gas, illegally used by the enemy. As a result, he lost his sight temporarily. After the war, Adolf lived in Munich where, by chance, he attended a meeting of the very small German Labor Party. He was enthused about their party platform and joined. He went on public speaking tours and soon reformed the German Labor Party into the National Socialist German Labor Party, became its leader and continued the struggle for power. His struggle eventually led to his victory in 1933.

In those turbulent years of many parties and many factions, unrest, strife, fighting between parties and hecklers interrupted his meetings and public appearances. Therefore, the more brawny of his followers formed the *Sturm Abteilung* (SA), or Storm Troopers. It was their job to throw out hecklers and troublemakers. The SA distributed posters, marched in demonstrations, infiltrated communist and socialist neighborhoods and so forth. Frequently, fights erupted between opposing political factions and a number of SA men were injured. Some were killed and became martyrs of the party. One of them was Horst Wessel.

Horst Wessel, so our school text stated, was a hero of the Nazi movement, a martyr who died in the line of duty. Horst Wessel became an SA leader of Storm Unit 5 in the Communist stronghold of Berlin-Friedrichshain. He worked and fought for the National Socialists until Red Front militarists went to his apartment one day. Horst Wessel opened the door and was shot point blank in the mouth. He was taken to a hospital where he died a few days later. He was given a big funeral, which turned into a demonstration. I heard about it on the radio.

At some point, it became necessary to form another organization, the *Schutz Staffel* (SS), the Fuehrer's personal bodyguard. The SS motto was: "Our Honor is Loyalty." SS men wore belt buckles bearing this motto and carried knives engraved with their motto. SS men swore the following oath:

"I swear to thee Adolf Hitler
as the Fuehrer and Chancellor
of the German Reich
Loyalty and bravery.
I vow to thee and to the superiors
whom thou shalt appoint
obedience unto death
so help me God."

The next spectacular public event was the annual Nazi Party Rally in Nuremberg. This year it promised to be, and was, the biggest and showiest since the Fuehrer had come to power. The rally began on September 4 and lasted two weeks.

Each day, every event was covered in minute detail and lavishly illustrated in the press, which always published the Fuehrer's speeches verbatim. Live radio broadcasts allowed people to hear all the speeches, the singing and the descriptions

126

by enthusiastic commentators of the marching, the setting and the actions taking place. "The Horst Wessel Song" was heard over and over again. Our radio remained mostly silent. Father and Mother rarely listened to anything except the midday and evening news and the weather forecast.

Other activities at the rally were sports demonstrations, ceremonies to honor those who died for the Nazi movement and vows of fidelity by the various factions. Most interesting were the very apologetic and nervously fervent protestations of fidelity voiced by the SA spokesman, triggered, no doubt, by the Rhoem affair and purges.

All the events were shown at length in the cinemas. We went frequently to the movies and I saw practically the entire footage. It was most spectacular. Thousands of SA and SS men, Labor Service men with shouldered spades and Hitler Youths marched in impeccably straight columns through the city for hours. Ten thousands of cheering, flag-waving and flower throwing people lined the streets. Houses were bedecked with flags and garlands. People leaned out of every window. From the reviewing stand, the Fuehrer and other leading Nazis acknowledged and returned the marchers' salutes.

At night, thousands of people stood shoulder to shoulder outside the Fuehrer's hotel shouting in unison: "We want to see our Fuehrer" (*"Acht, neun, zehn, wir wollen unsern Fuehrer seh'n."*). I tried to imagine what it was like standing in a crowd like that but I knew that I would never want to be part of it neither did I feel any enthusiasm for, nor could I identify with, their excitement.

The organization and the logistics of this rally, and all other rallies, were stupendous. Films of the gigantic assemblies in the specially built stadium showed a sea of fluttering flags and thousands of standards being carried and marched around the

127

stadium by the SA and others to the sound of rousing march music. The thousands of SA men marching in perfect columns were reminiscent of Roman legions. Each delegation's standard bore the name of their part of Germany.

One night, a seemingly endless torchlight parade wound its way through the ancient streets of Nuremberg, past the floodlit 15th and 16th century buildings of this beautiful old city, to the Zeppelin Meadow, a huge assembly place. A sea of 21,000 flags and torches were carried by as many people and were then posted around the entire grounds. Just before the Fuehrer made his appearance, the music stopped. An expectant hush fell over the huge stadium. It was as if the crowd held its breath. Then the bands struck up the "Badenweiler March."

The Fuehrer finally made his dramatic entrance. He walked alone, followed at a distance by Goering, Goebbels, Hess, Himmler and others. The "Badenweiler March" became associated with the Fuehrer, the same as "Hail to the Chief" is with the U.S. President. This march, the Fueher's favorite, was composed by Georg Fuerst to commemorate the capture of Badon-viller in the Vosges mountains. On May 17, 1939, a police ordinance was issued that stated that the "Badenweiler March" was to be performed publicly only in the presence of Adolf Hitler. Heroes' Memorial Day was marked by Beethoven's "Eroica."

At this and all other rallies, the "Blood Flag," the one carried during the unsuccessful Munich *putsch* (the attempt to overthrow Bavarian government) in 1923 and stained with the blood of the slain Nazis, was accorded the place of honor. The Fuehrer held a corner of it and touched all new flags and standards as they were presented to him, in order to dedicate them.

Speeches, parades and assemblies filled the days. Thousands of Labor Service men, spades shouldered, spoke as one voice, reciting something about where they came from, what they were about, how they were serving the Reich and the Fuehrer. I recall one particular chant: "WE WANT ONLY ONE LEADER! NOTHING FOR US! ALL FOR GERMANY! HEIL HITLER!"

Hitler Youth also had their day. Baldur von Schirach, the Youth Leader, and the Fuehrer himself addressed them.

The rally ended with a huge torchlight parade through the city. At the Stadium where the torchlight procession ended, antiaircraft search lights, placed close together around the upper outside rim of the stadium, aimed to meet spectacularly at a central point above it. "A cathedral of light" was the way the press described it. To me, it was overwhelming, intimidating and awesome when I saw the newsreel of the event.

The fanatical fervor of the participants and Hitler's frequent references to the part providence had played and was playing almost suggested a kind of religious belief that the Fuehrer was the chosen redeemer of the German Volk and, indeed, of the world. This impression was deliberately created and sustained.

Leni Riefenstahl, an actress turned producer was commissioned by Hitler and Goebbels to capture the entire event on film, thus preserving it for posterity. Her "Triumph of the Will" is a most revealing documentary.

One of the things that communicated itself very clearly to me was the earnestness and determination accompanying every action. There was no laughter, there was no fun. Everything was duty, honor, blood and sacrifice. These heavy concepts left me feeling weighed down rather than uplifted. Obviously, this was not the way the participants felt. They were elated.

Anti-Nazi sentiment was still alive in 1934, born out by an incident reported in the paper from Munich. Lutherans marched in Munich on October 11 singing anti-Nazi songs. The Munich police, using sabers, attacked the marchers.

129

After the Fuehrer came to power, the Nazis announced that every German worker should be in a position to take his family on a 10 day vacation every year. This was to be accomplished through the offices of an organization called Strength through Joy (KdF - *Nationalsozialistische Gemeinschaft Kraft durch Freude*), a branch of the German Labor Front (DAF - *Deutsche Arbeitsfront*), which took the place of the outlawed unions.

On November 27, Rudolf Hess (the Fuehrer's deputy), Dr. Goebbels (the propaganda minister) and Dr. Ley (the Reich Organization Leader), spoke in the huge machine hall of the Berlin AEG (Power and Light Co.) to mark the first anniversary of the KdF. Dr. Ley said in his speech, "Only sleep is a private affair. We no longer have private people. The time when everyone could do as he pleased is over."

Every worker had a small contribution automatically deducted from his wages that constituted the membership dues for KdF. Members were encouraged to take advantage of the various programs offered: travel, theater, concerts, opera, exhibitions, sport and hiking groups, folk dancing, movies and continuing education courses. Certain restrictions did apply. People had to take the tickets given to them without a choice of seats. They were expected to use them because their employers had to subsidize these events. The tickets were available at half price but if the tickets were not used the ticket holder was required to reimburse the firm for the full admission amount.

Once KdF was implemented, thousands of people took advantage of the trips and cruises. Some of Kurt's colleagues, one couple we knew, plus several friends and neighbors took vacations or cruises. Although workers were entitled to 6 to 12 days vacation, many could not go away because they could not afford it. Most blue collar workers did not make enough money (which was an average of 28 marks per week) to even take the vacation time to which they were entitled. They worked instead.

For instance, Kurt only made 35 to 40 marks a week. An all-inclusive KdF trip from Berlin to the Bavarian Forest for one week was 39 marks per person. Two weeks at Lake Constance cost 65 marks, the Harz Mountains cost 28 marks and the Mosel River cost 43 marks.

As an example of how tight budgets were for an average family, I usually ate with Father and Mother but I did notice that once in a while Mama prepared a very simple meal of home fried potatoes with bacon for supper. Mama told me years later that she could not make ends meet and had to borrow a mark from Mother in order to be able to put a simple meal such as this on the table a day or so before payday.

I recall that KdF cruise ships, called the Peace Fleet, went to Norway, Madeira and Italy, plus other destinations. KdF ships were one class ships. There was no first class. This was, according to Dr. Ley, to emphasize that "we do not send the educated intellectual as a representative of the new Germany. Instead, we send the German laborer as our representative to the world." I remember being told at school that these large KdF passenger liners were designed in such a way that in case of war they could speedily be converted into hospital ships.

KdF vacation trips were not always available during the summer months, the height of the travel season, but were mostly offered in the spring and in the fall. They did not include the most expensive and exclusive vacation spots but small places in economically less affluent areas in order to bolster the local economy.

KdF was not created simply for enjoyment but was intended to make people better workers and increase productivity. Leisure activities were organized to prevent boredom, which could lead to inflammatory and even criminal ideas.

Another KdF program was called Beauty at Work. I heard our friends talk about improvements that were made at their work places, such as redecoration, better lighting, plants in offices and so on. Luncheon facilities were improved. Many offices and factories now had nurseries for the children of working mothers. I noticed external improvements when I traveled by bus: fresh paint, renovations and landscaping.

Everyone in my family took a summer vacation. Uncle Gustav and Aunt Martha usually went to the Baltic Sea. Aunt Marga traveled extensively to Austria, Switzerland, France, Denmark and many places in Germany. Mama, Kurt, Father, Mother and I stayed closer to home. We went to the country. Mama did not want to go on any KdF trips, partly because they were government organized and partly because she did not like group travel. Many of my friends, schoolmates and their parents never had a vacation outside of Berlin and spent every summer in the city and/or on their little garden plots on the outskirts of Berlin.

By now, new construction had begun on various government projects, such as the new chancery and the new Tempelhof airport. Goering wanted a Reich Air Ministry building in the Wilhelmstrasse and got it. The Reich Sport Field was enlarged. At the trade fairgrounds near the Funkturm, a central Hall of Honor was taking shape. These changes were not decided upon by the City of Berlin. The city actually had no say in these matters. Rather, the Fuehrer decreed all changes.

I saw an entire issue of the "Illustrated," a magazine, devoted to the remodeling of Berlin by Albert Speer. These changes were overwhelming. Pictures showed models of wide avenues and gigantic edifices. Grandiose but to me they looked intimidating, strange and somewhat scary. I particularly remember the picture of the Great Hall, a building of gigantic proportions. It was to be 315 meters long, crowned by a dome that was 100 meters in diameter, rising 320 meters above ground and bearing a globe of the world.

Two major center city thoroughfares were planned: the East-West Axis and North-South Axis. The East-West Axis was a continuation of Unter den Linden through the Brandenburg Gate and the Tiergarten to the Big Star Circle. The projected completion date was 1950 but it was already completed in 1939. The North-South Axis was never started as far as I remember.

As the Christmas season began, theaters once again offered special matinee performances of dramatized fairy tales: "Max and Moritz," a popular story of two very naughty boys, and "Peter's Flight to the Moon," adapted for the stage from a children's book by Thea von Harbou, "Hansel and Gretel," "Rosina's Dangerous Journey," "Little Red Riding Hood" and more. Every year, Father and Mother took me to see one or two shows and I loved it. The atmosphere was so festive and exciting. This year, we saw "Hansel and Gretel" by Engelbert Humperdinck.

Once I went with Mama to the State Opera, located on Unter den Linden, to see "Puss in Boots." We had front row center seats. The production was fabulous, with costumes made of splendid pastel colored satins, velvets and lace. The prince, wearing a pale green satin coat embroidered with gold and white satin breeches, arrived on stage in a golden coach drawn by white horses. To me, his entrance was stunning.

I also vividly remember the scene of the Old Crone's Mill. Members of the Corps de Ballet, wearing drab dark cloaks and rags, barely able to walk with the help of crutches and canes, slowly and painfully dragged themselves up a ramp leading into

133

the big mill. After a magic spell, the mill began to turn its wings to magical music and one by one dancers came sliding down a shoot, dressed in crisp white tu tus. The mill had miraculously transformed the old crones into beautiful young girls.

The splendor was not confined to the stage. Many children in the audience were elegantly attired. The boys wore suits, some of velvet, or sailor suits. The girls wore pastel colored floor length dresses, white ankle socks, black patent leather shoes and silk flower wreaths in their hair. My best winter dresses were invariably of dark blue or burgundy velvet with a lace collar. This time I wore a dark blue one.

The Opera house was beautiful. As in most of our theaters, the decor was white and gold with deep red plush seats, even up to the last row on the fourth and highest tier. All corridors encircling the theater were similarly decorated and, in addition, mirrors and statues gave them a stately, elegant appearance. During the intermission, we walked through these corridors sipping beverages we had purchased in the vestibule on the first floor.

During Advent, our class presented a Christmas Program. Mr. Lambert chose a rendition of the "Christmas Story." Several girls, including myself, were chosen to recite parts of St. Luke's gospel. Between readings and recitations, the audience, made up of parents and relatives, were to sing Christmas carols while the children danced.

On the appointed evening, I wore a peasant costume. The skirt was green, with two rows of black velvet ribbon near the hem. The white short sleeved peasant blouse had a black velvet bodice embroidered with flowers. White ankle socks and patent leather shoes completed my costume. When it was my turn, I got up, walked to the front of the audience, turned to face them and began, "In the same night, there were shepherds in the fields."

As I continued, I began to talk faster and faster. Mr. Lambert was furious and extremely disappointed in me. I don't know why I did it. I suppose it was nerves. After this, I do not remember any more Christmas celebrations at school.

Every year, the Nazi party organized Christmas Eve parties for needy children. The events took place out-of-doors in city squares of working class boroughs. I saw the preparations several times. A large Christmas tree was put up in the square with long trestle tables, covered with white tablecloths, placed around it. Entertainment was provided by SA, SS bands and either HJ, BDM, or school choirs. SA, SS and usually the Nazi Women's Organization handled the refreshments and the distribution of gifts. The gifts were purchased with monies collected for the Winter Relief Program. The "Morgenpost" reported that "The National Socialist Movement is making every effort to turn the Christmas holidays into a festival for every Volk member." In addition, the Nazi party encouraged people to invite single persons who were alone at Christmas into their homes. The Nazi slogans were: "Well-to-do families should invite a poor family or single poor people" or "well-to-do single people should visit a poor family."

On December 21, I celebrated my ninth birthday.

Christmas and New Year's Eve were spent in the usual way. I always enjoyed going out on the balcony just after midnight on New Year's, lighting some Bengal lights (long tapers, similar to sparklers, which burned red or green for at least two minutes), shouting "Happy New Year" and listening to the church bells ringing in the New Year.

1935

January 13	In the Saar Plebescite, 90 percent of the Saar population wants to return to Germany.
January 17	League of Nations votes to award Germany the Saar Basin on March 1.
February 18	Two women were beheaded by Nazi government for revealing military secrets.
March 1	German troops march into Saar.
March 15	Goebbels bans four Berlin newspapers.
March 16	Military conscription reintroduced. Goebbels announces that Hitler has removed the military sections of the Versailles Treaty and has restored military service. Hitler proclaims the formation of a conscript army of 12 army corps comprised of 36 divisions.
March 17	Heldengedenktag. War Heroes Remembrance Day. Nazis arrest 700 Protestant pastors.
March 25	Hitler says that Soviets imperil peace in Europe.
April 9	Goering marries Emmy Sonnemann.
April 17	League of Nations condemns German rearmament.
April 19	Army pays Hitler a birthday tribute.
April 20	Reich rejects League verdict on rearmament.

April 30	Berlin court upholds Hitler's plea for nonbelief in Nazism as ground for divorce.
June 26	Compulsory labor service for men from age 18 to 25 is implemented.
July 8	Hitler announces building of two battleships and 28 U-boats.
September 17	7th NSDAP Congress in Nuremberg. Proclamation of the Nuremberg Laws. The Swastika is proclaimed to be the only German flag.
October 12	Jazz banned from radio broadcasts.
November 6	Hitler promises to remove anti-Jewish signs during the Olympic Games.
November 28	All men 18 to 45 are declared army reservists.
December 21	The author's 10th birthday.

Announcements from the newspaper in 1935:

January 16

Berlin celebrates the Saar victory. Celebrations in front of the Reichtag. Dr. Goebbels thanks the Saar. Torchlight procession of thousands.

March 1

THE SAAR IS GERMAN AGAIN!

One minute silence, flags fly in the Reich, church bells ring for one hour.

March 15

Large mosaic commemorative plaques have been placed at the Berlin City Hall, as well as in all borough city halls, for the benefit of the WHW. For 20 pfennig you can buy a mosaic stone and place it according to the large design on display. Slowly, a complete artistic mosaic picture emerges that, in time to come, will bear testimony to the heroic work of the German WHW 1934/35.

March 19

Blackout Test in Greater Berlin.

From 10 p.m. to midnight. Blackout measures in effect for public transportation, theaters and cinemas.

Insulting the Fuehrer can constitute a reason for divorce.

Church celebrations on April 20 and May 1.

The following directions were issued by the Reich Bishop for church participation in national celebrations of April 20 and May 1.

The Fuehrer's birthday is essentially to be recognized during church services on Easter Sunday, April 21, in sermons and prayers. Wherever local National Socialist organizations or part of the congregation express the desire to hold a church service in celebration of the Fuehrer's birthday on April 20 itself, it is to be acceded to within the framework suitable to the solemn character of the period between Good Friday and Easter.

Flags must be flown from church buildings on April 20.

May 1 is to be celebrated as follows:

Wherever local national socialist formations express the wish to attend a church service on May 1, within the framework of the day's events, or if they accept the invitation of a church congregation, a church service must be scheduled at a time best suited to fit in with planned activities. Otherwise, the eve of both days is the most suitable time for a church service and invitations to official, nonchurch and National Socialist organizations must be issued.

Naturally, the church service must begin and end with church bells ringing. If church services are to be the main event of their activities on May 1 itself, and this is desired by or suggested by the Reich government in press or on radio, this request has to be met.

For church services on the eve and on May 1 itself, flags must be flown.

A street collection took place on May 10 and 11 for the benefit of the Reich Mothers' Service.

May 12

The highest priority of our population policies is the protection and nurturing of the German Family.

A worthy beginning to Mother's day: The exhibit "Woman and Volk" opens. Opening speech by the

Minister of the Interior Dr. Frick who said: "This event will show that all people and all organizations in the fatherland, every man and woman, state and movement, should work together in the interest of the German future. For all of us, the German Mother's Day should not simply be something external but a day of contemplation of the things we have to thank German mothers for, what they mean to us and how, accordingly, their position and their tasks in private life and in public should be molded. The dangers of degeneration of the German people, as we saw it in Germany during the years following WWI, can only be eliminated when the German woman (wife) and mother recognizes them, and if she, with fervor and tenaciousness, is determined to lead the German people and the German youth in a new direction.

The task of women is not only the continuation of the species and the physical care of children but, first and foremost, the inner calling to be the educator of the entire Volk. In this respect, she is more important than all organizations of the state and the movement. In contrast to women leaders of times past, the National Socialist women's leadership considers it to be its noblest task to change German women psychologically and to prepare them for life."

"State and movement," the minister continued, "will do everything to support and strengthen women and mothers and family life. Our population and race policies must be aimed at the protection and promotion of German families. A race hygienically oriented state will always strive to avoid war because, even in case of victory, it robs the Volk particularly of its most worthy

141

young men who are essential for its survival. Furthermore, innocent women and children would become victims of any future war. Therefore, it is foolish to believe that a government like Adolf Hitler's, who himself views the Volk as the most precious commodity on this earth, would wantonly expose this Volk to annihilation."

He ended the speech: "We German men rely on and trust our German women (wives) and mothers. Together with our children, we owe thanks to them for everything they did for us and our Volk in order to celebrate in joyful confidence this year's Mother's Day with them."

May 18

On May 17, 1,550 Berlin children go to the country through the offices of the National Socialist Volk Welfare Service (NSV).

From several Berlin boroughs, 700 children left for a 6 week vacation in Thuringia where they will stay in private foster homes.

Another 700 children left two days ago for East Prussia and 150 left yesterday morning to stay at the NSV home in Mueritz.

Oct. 14

Three Eintopf entrees for restaurants: beef noodle soup, savoy cabbage with beef or lamb, mushrooms with egg or bread dumplings.

These directives are for restaurants only. Housewives may prepare meals of their own choice.

Our winter was, as always, cold and snow had been on the ground since before Christmas. Additional snow fell after New Year's Day. My friends and I played with our sleds, taking advantage of the slight incline of the street to gather momentum, which carried us at a reasonable speed downhill. There were hardly any cars at that time to interfere with us.

On January 30, I was out sledding. It was bitter cold and none of my friends were around. I went to Elke and Renate's apartment to ask if they would come out to play. Her mother said, "No, I am sorry. The Fuehrer is speaking. They must stay and listen to him. Why don't you come in and join us?" I did but I soon got bored, made an excuse, saying I was expected home, and left. Elke and Renate were always made to listen to the Fuehrer's speeches. If they happened to be out playing, they either knew they must be home at a certain time or their mother came to fetch them.

The Fuehrer was determined to reclaim the territories Germany had lost as a result of the Versailles peace treaty. The area he targeted next was the Saar, which was rich in coal and important to the economy. For some time we read references and articles and heard radio programs about the "German Saar," with emphasis on how the ethnic Germans were chafing under French rule. The ethnic Germans, so we were told, desired nothing more fervently than to "come home into the Reich." The Saar Song was played over and over on the radio, day after day, week after week. The lyrics, "The Saar is German, German forever," were sung to the tune of a traditional, well-known miners' song that we had learned at school.

In January, a plebiscite in the Saar showed that 90 percent of the population was in favor of returning "home." On January 17,

144

the League of Nations voted that the Saar be restored to Germany on March 1.

Many people, including Father, were apprehensive about French reaction, knowing the Saar issue would, in all probability, intensify the animosity between our countries. The French had not forgotten the war of 1870/71 or WWI.

The Fuehrer naturally made the most of the return of the Saar. Newsreels showed the Fuehrer and German troops entering the Saar. He was given a tumultuous welcome despite the fact that it rained all day. People were crying, singing, waving flags, throwing flowers and shouting. Flowers and flags were everywhere. It was very emotional.

The Saar, being the topical subject of the day, was studied in our geography lessons. As always, our teachers refrained from making political comments or voicing opinions. I think this class was taught by our headmistress, Miss Dahme, who was not a party member. She was a fine woman and teacher. I was very fond of her and after I went to high school, she invited me to visit her in her home, which was quite an honor.

On February 1, the Fuehrer opened the biggest car show ever held in Berlin. It was at this show that the Volkswagen (People's Car) was first introduced to the public. It was to be affordable, costing 900 marks, and available to everyone. "Every member of the Volk can have a Volkswagen," was the slogan on posters displayed on the advertising columns. Although none of the automobiles were as yet on the market it was possible to order a car and pay for it in advance by installments. Five marks were deducted from each paycheck. Once someone had paid 75 percent of the purchase price, he or she received a voucher with an order number. The slogan circulating at the time said: "You must save five marks a week if you want to drive your own car." More than 300,000 orders were placed by 1940 but not one car was ever delivered because the factory was switched over to war production.

Goebbels spoke on March 16 and announced that the Fuehrer had wiped out the military sections of the Versailles Peace Treaty. He informed his listeners that the Fuehrer had restored military service. Military conscription was again a fact.

This year, Memorial Day fell on March 17 and was celebrated at noon with an assembly of all Nazi leaders at the State Opera. The program, broadcast live, included funeral music by Beethoven and appropriate speeches. The radio continued broadcasting serious music for the rest of the day, which was customary. In the afternoon, the Fuehrer reviewed a large military parade to underline the fact that Germany was officially rearming.

I also recall that we had a blackout practice that year on March 19. I did not notice that we did anything in particular about it because the heavy outside storm blinds we lowered every night were a natural blackout at Father and Mother's apartment.

Among Mama's acquaintances was a couple, Magda and Leo, who had emigrated to Australia in the early 1920s. In those days when people left their native country to live in Australia or other far off places, they knew that they would not be able to come back for a very long time, more than likely never. It takes time to get used to living in a strange country, using a language other than your own. Homesickness is a given. It hits sooner or later at shorter or longer intervals and in varying degrees of severity. People had to grin and bear it and get over it as best they could. Magda and Leo did not have it easy at first but were about to reap the benefits of their hard work. They, too, suffered from homesickness.

After Hitler came to power, their relatives began writing in glowing terms of how wonderful things were in Germany under the Fuehrer. Everyone had work. Everything was great. The future looked rosy. These letters were no cure for homesickness. Hearing nothing but good news for years, Magda and Leo decided to return to Germany. They sold everything and took a ship home.

Soon after their arrival, they found out that things were not quite as rosy as they had been led to believe. For one thing, Leo was hard put to find work. Although he was good at many things, he had no formal training in anything particular and ended up working in a warehouse at low pay. The family had to live with Magda's parents and it took more than a year before they were able to move into their own apartment.

I loved to hear Magda talk about Australia. Once when I was sick, she visited and told me how hot it was in the summer and that sometimes they only ate homemade ice cream. This sounded like heaven to me because I was very seldom allowed to have ice cream and was always yearning for it.

The social event of the year was the wedding of Hermann Goering to actress Emmy Sonnemann on April 9. Goering was popular. Of course, ordinary folk did not get to know any of the top Nazis personally. They remained remote. People's opinions were based on what they read and impressions from newsreels. Goering always appeared to be jovial and was frequently smiling.

As an ex-fighter pilot ace, he still retained the aura of a hero even though he was no longer young and dashing but becoming quite rotund, to put it politely. He was also flamboyant. Goering owned an estate in the Schorfheide north of Berlin where, among other things, he kept buffalo. His estate was named Karinhall after his late wife, Karin Goering. Karin had divorced her first husband in order to marry Goering in Munich on February 3, 1923. She died of heart disease in 1931 and was buried in Sweden. Her body was brought back from Sweden on April 19, 1934 and placed in a mausoleum at Karinhall. The Fuehrer attended the reburial.

Now Goering was to be married with much pomp. On the wedding eve, the bridal pair attended a gala performance at the State Opera. The bride-to-be wore a pale gray evening gown, a diamond tiara and carried a large bouquet of white carnations. The musical performance was followed by a reception and a torchlight parade. The wedding ceremony was performed in two parts. First, the civil ceremony took place at the Berlin City Hall followed in the afternoon by a religious ceremony in the Berlin Dom. The Fuehrer acted as best man and Hitler Youths carried the bride's train. The population, starved of extraordinarily glamorous events, lapped up every detail of the festivities, a welcome change from blood, soil, duty and sacrifice. Thousands of Berliners stood outside the Dom and along the route the couple traveled to the reception in an open conveyance.

My friends and I talked about the wedding and commented on the Fuehrer. He was single. We speculated if and when he might get married. We wondered why we never heard or saw any sign of a woman in his life. Later, I repeatedly heard him called a "castrated tomcat."

Employment books were reintroduced in 1935 and were issued by employment offices. The books had previously been in use during the reign of Kaiser Wilhelm. Without an employment book, one could not obtain work. Control was the objective in the Third Reich and the book gave employers control over their employees.

Employment books were handed over and kept by the employer when the employee began work. If the employer did not want an employee to leave, he could refuse to return the book to the employee, preventing the individual from changing jobs. Should an employee be foolish enough to protest, the employer was required to report him to the Gestapo who had their own methods of keeping people in line.

The employment office regularly channeled people into jobs that were not of their choosing. School graduates who went to the *Arbeitsamt*, or employment office, to seek jobs or apprenticeships were pushed into industries that needed workers. Pressure was used to make young people accept the jobs they were offered. The daughter of an acquaintance was pushed into an apprenticeship to become a salesgirl in a shoe store. She told us that she did not want to do it but was pressured into it because at the time the employment office had to fill positions in this category. When construction began on the Autobahn, unemployed men were offered jobs on it. Some of them did not want to accept because it meant being sent away from home for long periods and for many of them it was not in their own line of work. Nevertheless, the choice they were given was to accept and work or refuse and lose unemployment benefits immediately.

Gleichschaltung was a word I heard many times. It meant a complete coordination with Nazism and at the same time the elimination of class distinctions. *Gleichschaltung* also meant the synchronization of German lands and provinces.

Great emphasis was placed on the "nobility" of work and of the working man. The working man, the laborer, the blue collar worker was equal, nay, maybe even superior to other workers. Nobility and equality were stressed again and again. People were to feel equal to each other. Any remaining class distinctions were to disappear and did seem to disappear, on the surface anyway.

I saw a film in which an "upper class intellectual" falls in love with the daughter of a blue collar, uneducated working man and proposes marriage. It was played in such a way that the blue collar father tried to pull the intellectual boyfriend more or less to his level. The father did not exactly look down on the intellectual boyfriend but he did not look up to him either. The boyfriend on his part was ill at ease trying to fit into the laborer's environment.

I cannot say that I experienced class distinction in a personal way. The Fuehrer, so I remember being told at school, erased them. He himself was above classes and above material interest. I never heard that he went shopping or that he bought something and I had no idea if he got paid.

Life close to the soil was upheld as the ideal way of life. The importance of farmers, farm work, closeness to the soil and roots in German soil was extolled. Great pains were taken to ennoble these occupations by bolstering self-respect, as well as instilling a feeling of importance and pride, in those engaged in them. Many posters pictured peasant families and peasants at work in the fields.

Harvest Thanksgiving, the Harvest Home celebration, took place on the Bueckeberg, a hill that was part of the Wester mountain range. It was an elaborate festival that received much publicity. Peasants came from all parts of Germany, dressed in their regional costumes. The Fuehrer, of course, attended, made speeches and was photographed with them. One farm couple was chosen to be crowned with the harvest crown by the Fuehrer for special achievement.

Unemployment had decreased but wages were extremely low, hours were long and deductions, including taxes, social programs, health insurance, Labor Front dues and obligatory contributions to the Nazi welfare agencies (such as the Winter

Aid Program and Strength through Joy), were high. Kurt was not working in his field. He was a skilled mechanic but worked at the Scherl Publishing house operating an off-set press. His pay was low. After compulsory deductions, a budget had to accommodate utilities, food and clothing.

At this time, however, I think most people were glad they had a job. Things seemed to have stabilized and were looking up, now that there was no longer a threat of unemployment or inflation. It was possible to relax a little and enjoy whatever one was able to enjoy, even though it might be modest in character. Wages were still low and people could not afford much but there was enough to eat on the table and perhaps a little money left over for a few extras.

People were very careful with their money. Older people had lost their life's savings following the WWI collapse, when savings accounts were wiped out, and were forced to start from scratch. Father and Mother were among them.

Although all our friends and acquaintances were working, I did not notice significant changes in their lifestyles. It was an event when someone acquired a new piece or a set of furniture because it did not happen often. People took extremely good care of their possessions and their clothes to make them last a long time. One of Mama's friends kept her living room furniture covered with sheets. I thought this was going a little too far. How could she enjoy it if she never saw it? I felt extremely uncomfortable when we visited.

I think most people spent more money on food. I heard people criticize some of their acquaintances, saying, "Can you imagine, they put margarine, cottage cheese and tomatoes on the table, even when they have company." Therefore, it was deduced, these people were very stingy, for they could not possibly be too poor to afford cold cuts. It was almost construed

151

as an insult not to offer your guests a good spread and guests expected it.

Our living standard remained constant. Father had retired in 1933. He and Mother lived on his retirement pay, a pension. I have no idea how much that was and I do not know if they had any other savings or source of income. Money was not discussed with me because I was a child. I had no idea what anybody's income was and I was not concerned. It did not interest me.

We lived comfortably and simply. I did not receive an allowance. When I needed anything, such as school supplies, I said so and was given enough money to buy them. On Sundays, I was given 30 pfennig for the movies plus another 20 pfennig for candy. At other times, I would ask for 10 pfennig to buy lollipops. They cost five pfennigs and were available in the shape of roosters, ducks and other animals, in lovely rich colors of red, pale yellow and emerald green each, transparent as glass. Another kind, at 10 pfennig a piece, was tri-colored, orange changing into green then yellow. It was opaque and tart. I preferred the latter.

I hardly ever went grocery shopping. This, like all other housework, was taken care of while I was at school. Occasionally, Mother sent me to the store to pick up an item for her. I did not like grocery shopping but on Saturdays I liked to walk through the markets and look at the stalls of fishmongers, green grocers, novelty items, cloth and clothing. I did not pay attention to prices. I had no idea about money.

The actual reduction in unemployment was not as great as it appeared on the surface. Nevertheless, the progress made so far greatly impressed many people and justified the trust placed in the Fuehrer in 1933: namely to deliver what he had promised, Work and Bread. I think for a while many people were satisfied with what the Fuehrer did, although in Berlin the majority of those I knew remained skeptical and cautious. They simply took things in their stride and adopted an attitude of "Let's wait and see."

Berliners are survivors. They are realistic. They accept the inevitable and make the best of any given situation. They have a very strongly developed sense of biting humor. They come up instantly with nicknames for anything new in the city. For example, the Congress Hall (Pregnant Oyster), Berlin Air Lift Memorial (Hunger Fork), the Berlin Symphony Hall (Karajan's Circus). Berliners are down-to-earth and very outspoken. They love nature, animals and love to be out-of-doors. But above all, they love Berlin and are proud to be Berliners.

A few people in our neighborhood were party members. They were easily recognizable by their party button, nicknamed "Bon-bon," which they wore on their lapel. Required to wear their party button, they were proud to do so. Nazi sympathizers, that is nonparty members, were harder to pinpoint and they were known by their reputation. One was careful when talking and dealing with both kinds. A couple of Mama's acquaintances and a few neighbors fell into the latter category. Therefore, politics was a subject to be strictly avoided. Friends and neighbors warned each other about suspect persons.

When our summer vacation started, Mama and I went again to Balz. This time we did not stay with Aunt Lotte because her sister was visiting her. We stayed at the Forest Guest House located at the very edge of the forest. The house, surrounded by a spacious garden, had a big veranda and a lounge, which contained a piano and a selection of books and games. Breakfast was available from 7 a.m. until 8:30 a.m., lunch was at noon and dinner was at 6 p.m. Meals were served family style with everybody sitting at a long table. Afternoon coffee was offered to those who were around at 3:30 p.m. Between meals and after supper, guests were free to do as they pleased. However, there was not much to do in Balz except to walk in the woods, to one of the three village pubs or about two miles to Vietz for movies on weekends.

The host family, after completing their evening chores, entertained their guests. The son and two daughters played guitars and sang, while the mother sang and played the piano. We joined in the singing and listened to folk songs and ballads. Sometimes, one of the guests recited poems, read a short story or told a tale. We played charades, musical chairs and such. I enjoyed it a lot because a number of guests were families with one or more children. I always had somebody to play with instead of being alone most of the time.

When Kurt came to spend his vacation with us, we walked to the Dolgensee almost every day because he liked to swim. Mama, dressed in her bathing suit, made a great show of running down to the water as though ready to throw herself into the lake only to stop an inch short of the water's edge, turn and retreat to sit in the shade of the pine trees. The Raak See, blue and smiling amid meadows, presented a much friendlier scene than the dark Dolgensee but nobody went swimming there. I don't know why. The local forester and his family lived at the Raak See. We usually stopped in to drink milk, which was deliciously cool, sweet and very creamy.

Our holidays came to an end, school started and life reverted to routine: homework, playing with friends, visits to relatives and to the cinema. Mother's birthday, on September 21, was celebrated with a large platter of fancy pastries in addition to the traditional plum cake. This large sheet cake had a yeast pastry foundation covered with blue plums and was served with whipped cream. It was everybody's favorite.

The Annual Reich Party Congress took place in Nuremberg from September 10 to September 16. It was, of course, covered live on radio, extensively in the newspapers and shown on film. The motto for the 1935 Congress was "Reich's Party Congress of Freedom." A number of congress facilities, designed and planned by Albert Speer, were still under construction. They promised to be gigantic. One congress hall would hold 60,000 people. However, the Luitpold Arena in Nuremberg was already completed and available this year so the Congress was held there.

As in 1934, immense assemblies of 150,000 men and youths, standing in "blocks" on the field, took place daily. At night, antiaircraft searchlights, positioned around the huge assembly area and aimed to meet high above it, created the now famous dome of light. This extraordinary display was planned for the utmost emotional and psychological effect on the assembled multitude. Even in black and white movies, it came across as more than just spectacular. What struck me when I saw the newsreels was that each participant was a minute, anonymous part of the whole show. Uniformity eliminated personality and individuality.

SA, SS, Labor Service, Army units and Hitler Youth marched through Nuremberg's streets to the cheers of the population. Houses, particularly those along the route, flew only Swastika flags and were decorated with garlands of evergreens and flowers. Cheering people by the thousands lined the streets, waving and throwing flowers. Women with small children or babies in their arms broke through the police cordon when the Fuehrer's cavalcade passed and rushed to the car holding the infants up for him to see and touch.

At night, a torchlight parade wound through the old city. People cheered the Fuehrer and stood for hours outside his hotel shouting themselves hoarse asking him to appear so that they could catch a glimpse of him.

Two very important proclamations were made at this Congress. First, the Swastika became the only national flag of Germany. Until now it had flown alongside the red, white and black Empire Banner. I noticed that, all at once, "old" German flags disappeared from the scene. The second announcement proclaimed the Nuremberg Racial Laws.

The racial laws deprived Jews of their German citizenship. As a result, they were not allowed to vote or participate in politics. Further, German citizenship laws prohibited marriages between races, such as Germans and Jews. Marriages were now subject to scrutiny. The racial laws dealt with Jews, gypsies and others, including homosexuals. We numbered a homosexual couple among our friends. They lived quietly and continued to do so for decades. Nobody ever bothered them. Mama once mentioned that the husband of a school friend was homosexual. She said, "He and other homosexuals got married to avoid suspicion and to be safe." People had to submit to medical exams prior to marriage in order to prevent congenitally diseased offspring.

The Nazi regime pronounced it socially acceptable for single women to have children, provided the father was an SS man. Girls, through the various youth organizations, were given the chance to volunteer to have a child "for the Fuehrer." The Fount of Life provided SS men as prospective fathers. Marriage was not required. I heard a statement made in a speech that not every girl could expect to get a husband but that she could have a child.

The Fount of Life established homes in various parts of Germany for women and girls who were expecting babies from SS men. In a statute dated September 13, 1936, it was decreed that every SS man must have at least four children, in or out of wedlock. SS men came under the Betrothal Order, the obligatory duty to report their engagement. Their brides were carefully checked to ensure they had met racial and health qualifications. The children were to be born in a Fount of Life Home where wed and unwed mothers were protected from the outside world. Children of unwed mothers were provided with child support and birth certificates by the home, which also recruited adoptive parents for the children. The homes were supported and financed by compulsory contributions from the SS leadership. By 1944, thirteen Fount of Life Homes were in existence and 11,000 children had been born there.

While at the home, the women were taught how to be good housewives and mothers. At the same time, they were systematically indoctrinated in Nazi ideology. Only Nazi newspapers and books were available in the homes and the girls had to listen to all the Nazi broadcasts on the radio.

I did not read the newspapers that reported every word of every speech and announcement but I became aware of their consequences. Current events, so a directive instructed, had a place of priority in schools. Practically all our dictation and essay themes dealt with current events. I am sure the text for dictation was handed to teachers, that it certainly was neither spontaneous nor of their own choosing.

Our teachers treated all children in class alike. Two girls in our class were Jewish, Sara and Eva. I spent a lot of time with Sara, mostly during our long recess. We also teamed up on class outings and day trips. Eva told me that she was taking private English lessons. She and her family were emigrating to Palestine. I do not remember when she left school.

Not too long afterwards, Sara and her family emigrated to Montevideo, Uruguay. I was sad to see her go. I suppose the writing was on the wall and these two families heeded it. I thought it was romantic, exotic and exciting to move to South America. I have often thought of Sara over the years and wondered what her life was like. She was a pretty girl with dark brown hair, worn in pigtails, large blue eyes with black lashes and a complexion as delicate as that of a Dresden porcelain figurine.

After the spring of 1935, signs reading "Jews not Welcome" appeared in hotels and restaurants in Southern Bavaria. As early as the fall of 1934, they had appeared in Franconia.

Mama and I discovered the sign "Jews not Welcome," above the ticket window at a local cinema. I wondered if the Jews heeded the warning. I could not tell a Jew from a non-Jew and never looked at people trying to figure out if they were Jewish. To me, they were just people, that's all. Mama did not say anything while we were at the cinema but when we came home she vented her anger.

On October 18, 1935, another law for the protection of German congenital health came into effect. From then on, couples who wanted to marry had to submit to counseling and medical examinations. If these examinations revealed incurable, hereditary diseases in the family or any deformities, the couple could not marry unless they agreed to be sterilized prior to marriage to make it impossible to pass diseases to future generations.

In Balz, I knew a family who had five children, all of whom had physical deformities. At least one was born subsequent to the passing of this law. One boy had a hand adjoining his shoulder. A couple of the girls had deformed forearms and club feet. Villagers talked about the family and said it was a shame to have more children like that and pitied the children. This family was somewhat ostracized. They lived in a house along Route 1 at the east end of the village in a house that looked neglected. They were obviously poor and the children were poorly dressed. I do not know, if in compliance with the law, both or either of the parents were at some point sterilized.

The Nazis adopted the "Theory of Descent." This theory purports that all our present day species were arrived at as a result of natural selection. Inevitably, in the struggle for existence only the best adapted specimens survive and reproduce. Naturally, this theory was to be the Nazi model of human society, peoples and races.

In high school, we learned that only the fittest do and should survive. This is the case in nature, where the deformed are killed and the sickly are left to die. With people, wars achieve the opposite. The sick stay at home and the healthiest specimens have to go to war, to be killed and maimed. This leaves the unhealthy to reproduce. This was the way our biology teacher told us about the theory of descent. Mama said, "What about Goebbels? He has a club foot and here he goes having one child after another."

An increase in daily reports drew our attention anew to the conflict between Italy and Abyssinia. Abyssinia was a country with approximately 12 million inhabitants. Italy had tried, and failed, to establish itself as a colonial power in Abyssinia as early as 1896 and made several attempts thereafter. Italy's claims were recognized by Great Britain and France in 1906.

For some time, there had been rumblings in Abyssinia (now Ethiopia). The conflict brewing between Italy and Abyssinia, came to a head on October 2, when 360,000 Italian troops marched against Addis Ababa, the capital of Abyssinia. Hereafter, reports appeared regularly in the press about this war, which despite Italy's military superiority, dragged on for a long time.

However, the events in Africa were overshadowed by the exciting fact that the XI Olympic Summer Games were scheduled to take place in Berlin. Construction started on the Olympic Village, which would house the athletes, and on the Olympic Stadium complex. The old linden trees on Unter den Linden were chopped down and replaced with young ones. Apartment houses, hotels and guest houses were spruced up, renovated and painted. The Tempelhof airport, too small to handle the influx of flights, was enlarged and completely changed. Part of the enlargement took in the area of the Sportpark as well as the Turkish and the Invaliden Cemeteries. To facilitate this, graves were opened, remains unearthed, deposited in new coffins and reburied somewhere else. The Flughafenstrasse was extended and our old walkway became the Columbia Damm. The old airport building was replaced by a semicircle in the "new" neoclassical style on the Tempelhofer Damm side. The Tempelhof Airport was unique because it was the only airport located almost in the center of a capital city. Although used to accommodate the Olympic traffic, it was not entirely completed and did not officially open until 1939.

Other changes included the completion of the East-West Axis. This necessitated the rearrangement of the Tiergarten, to the Brandenburg Gate which, as a result, was practically torn apart to allow the Axis to run as a continuation of Unter den Linden through the Brandenburg Gate to the Big Star Circle. The Victory Boulevard in the Tiergarten and all its statues were relocated. The Triumphal Column, commemorating the Franco-Prussian war of 1870-71, was moved from the Koenigsplatz to the Great Star Circle.

I did not feel good about the changes. I had liked the Tiergarten the way it was. It seemed to be just right for things to stay the way they were. It gave me a feeling of security, continuity and safety. I suppose that as a child, I registered many events only at the periphery of my small world. Nevertheless, they influenced me and produced subconscious feelings. One of these was the effect of the new buildings that were going up in Berlin. I found them intimidating, plain and uninteresting. They made me feel uneasy. I did not like what they represented (the Nazi regime) and I instinctively rejected them. I did not like the idea that all of Berlin would one day be dominated by similar structures.

To me, the "new" Berlin of the Third Reich was impersonal, cold and sterile in comparison to the old familiar Berlin. I liked my Berlin the way it was: multifaceted, comfortable and familiar. Each part of town had its own distinct atmosphere. Now the Tiergarten was torn apart and Unter den Linden denuded. Years later, during the war, we nostalgically sang the song "As long as the OLD linden trees line Unter den Linden nothing can defeat the spirit of Berlin, Berlin remains Berlin. "Yes," we would say sadly, "HE cut down the old linden trees and look what happened, the trouble we're in." But that lay as yet in the future.

Father was always interested in what was going on in Berlin. He went and looked at the new buildings, the Tiergarten, the Tempelhof Airport, the East-West Axis. He compared what was being done to what had been there before. He remembered how it had been and commented on the changes. Father was flexible and no stick-in-the-mud. He was in favor of progress but he was not in favor of the new styles and he called the buildings "propagandistic and pretentious."

1936

February 4	Nazi Wilhelm Gustloff killed.
February 6	Hitler opens Winter Olympic Games in Garmish-Partenkirchen.
February 11	First Volkswagen (VW) factory opened by Hitler in Fallersleben, Saxony.
March 7	Hitler orders troops into demilitarized Rhineland and reclaims it for Germany.
March 29	A plebiscite on Hitler's policies results in 99 percent approval.
April 5	Germans who failed to vote begin to lose jobs.
April 20	Hitler's birthday celebrated with military parade to demonstrate his power.
May 2	Addis Ababa falls, Negus flees and Italians use mustard gas.
June 17	Himmler is now the Reichsfuehrer of the SS and chief of German police.
June 19	Max Schmeling knocks out Joe Louis in 12th round.
July 18	Spanish Civil War begins.
August 1	Hitler opens Olympic Games in Berlin.
August 25	German planes sent to Spain to aid Franco.

September 9 to 14	Party Congress in Nuremberg. Four Year Plan announced. Hitler denies plans for war and insists Germany has right to colonies. Largest German military maneuvers since 1914.
October 25	Berlin-Rome Axis created through treaty between Italy and Germany.
November 8	Thousands of foreign words banned from vocabulary.
December 6	Germany-Japan-Italy form Axis, fulfilling Hitler's dream of worldwide anticommunist bloc.
December 21	The author's 11th birthday.
December 23	Germany sends Condor unit to fight in Spain.

Announcements and articles from the Berlin newspapers in 1936:

October 13

Appeal to housewives to quell complaints about the shortages of certain food items, including pork.

Rudolf Hess made an appeal to housewives: "You, my German housewives, influence not only, and we do not want to kid ourselves about this, influence not only the moods of your own husbands but on you, on the mood you emanate depends the mood of the German Volk in large measure.

Every good housewife knows how to keep her family happy, especially those of you who have, apart from the greater picture, experienced personal economic difficulties. You know how one can prepare a good meal with very simple ingredients even if once in a while it contains neither meat nor butter nor eggs.

Competent German housewives know what to do to be active in the service of our great German Family: the German Volk, when it must overcome temporary minor emergencies. Knowing what is in the interest of the greater German Family, housewives adjust their buying habits accordingly! Housewives avoid trying to find and buy items that are not in season but comply by buying what is available in quantity. No good housewife regrets the absence of a quarter pound of pork, which she is unable to obtain. Every good German housewife is part mother to the whole German People. In many cases, she has the same and higher duties to fulfil as the men of our Volk, who respect and honor her. German women, show what you can do!"

December

Hitler Youth collect beechnuts in German forests, as part of the Four Year Plan, to be made into cooking oil.

Their pay has been increased from 18 marks to 25 marks for 100 kilograms (200 pounds) of beechnuts.

Reports about Madrid included the following: Tuesday, July 21, 1936-Bloody Street Fighting in Madrid and Heavy Fighting in the Whole of Spain; Sunday, July 26, 1936-The Ring Around Madrid Closes, Terror Days for Germans in San Sebastian; Tuesday, July 28, 1936- Captured Nationalists locked into church and burned.

Saturday, August 1
Olympia's Sacred Flame Lights Germany.
Opening of the Olympic Games:

The Fuehrer and Reich Chancellor said: "Sporting and chivalrous competitions awaken the best of human ideals. They do not divide but unite the combatants in mutual understanding and respect. They help to create bonds of peace between nations. For this reason, may the Olympic Flame never be extinguished."

The headlines at the time were:

THE REICH CAPITAL WELCOMES
THE OLYMPIC FIRE
THE ROUTE OF THE TORCH
THROUGH BERLIN
FLAGS OF 53 NATIONS FLUTTER OVER THE
REICH SPORT STADIUM

Sunday, August 9
March of the Hitler Youth to Nuremberg.

Chief Regional Leader Axmann bids good-bye at the Berlin city limits in Lichtenrade to 50 Hitler Youths who will march to Nuremberg (615 kilometers in 34 days) to attend the Reich Party Congress.

Excitement and anticipation of the Olympics had grown steadily throughout 1935. However, the murder of Wilhelm Gustloff on February 4, 1936, made headlines and interrupted the Olympic fever. Wilhelm Gustloff, a devoted Hitler follower, was shot in his home by a Jewish student, David Frankfurter, who wanted to strike a blow at the Nazi persecutors. The world Jewry was blamed for the murder and Gustloff was given a state funeral. Later on, one of the KdF cruise ships was named for him.

Now only a few days remained until the start of the Winter Olympics in Garmisch-Partenkirchen, a renowned, expensive winter sports resort in the Bavarian Alps, which was fashionable, elegant and beautiful.

The Fuehrer opened the Games on February 6. All events were fervently followed as they were reported on the radio, in the press and in the movies. The papers consisted of pages and pages listing every single event. It was very exciting for me and for everyone.

Mama's interest in sports was limited to figure skating competitions. She went to see many championship events when they were held in Berlin's Sportpalast but her sense of fair play was on occasion offended by what she considered prejudiced judging. She did not attend the Winter Olympics.

Two significant political events took place in March.

On March 7, German troops marched into the demilitarized Rhineland, which the Fuehrer, by taking this action, reclaimed for Germany. Occupied zones after WWI were the left bank of the Rhine with bridgeheads on the right side of the Rhine, i.e., Cologne, Koblenz, Mainz and Kehl. These areas were occupied on January 10, 1920 by French and British troops according to the Versailles Treaty and were to be gradually evacuated. Failure

167

to make reparation payments would result in continued occupation or reoccupation of these territories. Evacuation had been delayed but ended now as a result of this bold move on the part of the Fuehrer. Many people, including Father, held their breath while awaiting foreign, primarily French and British, reaction.

The second event was the Plebiscite on the Fuehrer's policies, taken on March 29. The result was that 99 percent of the voters approved. It was compulsory for Germans to vote and early in April many who had failed to do so lost their jobs. Mama voted. She said to me that she felt good about being able to vote "No," to feel that she could express her disagreement with Hitler.

While the preparation for the Olympic Summer Games continued, the Fuehrer's birthday was celebrated on April 20 with the usual pomp and a huge military parade. Nobody in our family was interested in going to see it. I certainly was not. The thought of standing for three or four hours watching a military parade go by failed to inspire me with enthusiasm. I thought it extremely boring to watch earnest looking soldiers marching with tanks, motorcycles and armored cars rolling by. No fun at all except for the bands and the horses. In any case, I saw excerpts from the parade in the cinema because newsreels were part of every program.

The Olympic complex, and Reichssportfeld or Olympic Stadium, covered an area of 50 square miles. In the spring, our class went on a field trip to look at the Olympic Stadium, the Swim Stadium and the Dietrich Eckhard open air theater. The Stadium could hold an audience of 100,000. When we saw it, we were the only people there. With only 30 10-year-old girls standing in one of the top rows, the huge place felt eerie. I tried to imagine what it would be like when filled to capacity but could not quite do it because I had never been in a crowd anywhere near that size.

The Berlin Transport Company (BVG - *Berliner Verkehrsgesellschaft*) advertised and ran bus tours to the Olympic Village in Doeberitz, a suburb of Berlin, which was an Army maneuver base. Father, Mother and I took the bus to Doeberitz one Sunday.

The village boasted a spacious reception area, shops, a post office, a bank, rooms for visitors and a great number of telephones. The guide told us that there were 134 houses to accommodate 3,000 athletes and 40 kitchens. I noticed that each house bore the name of a German town or city. The actual layout of the village was attractive and it was nicely landscaped. However, I was a little disappointed that the village, as well as the furnishings, were so plain, utilitarian and not luxurious or beautiful. It was, of course, built in the neoclassic style like other recently completed edifices in Berlin, which I disliked intensely. The Olympic village reminded me of barracks. It was, I knew, to house athletes but I suppose I had expected a little more color and decor.

The war that had been raging in Abyssinia since October 1935 continued. Reports from the theater of war were strongly colored in favor of Italy, ridiculing the Negus, a title by which the emperor of Abyssinia was known, and his feeble attempts at defending his country. I remember seeing the discrepancies of the fighting forces on film. Italy attacked with a modern army and modern weapons. The Abyssinians fought with bows and arrows, clubs, a few antiquated rifles and not much more. They did not even have uniforms for the soldiers and many wore tribal clothes.

It was no match. It was pathetic. It was sad. Not so in the words of the reporters and commentators who held the defenders and the Negus up for constant ridicule. It was sickening. Mama bristled at the unfair contest. It was slaughter. It was inhuman. It was only a question of time when the fighting would end and the outcome was obvious. The Italian Army, superior in training and equipment, whipped the natives who put up a desperate fight. On May 2, the Abyssinian capital, Addis Ababa, fell and the Negus, Haile Selassie, fled. It was discovered later that the Italians had used mustard gas, which was illegal.

The Italian army finally conquered Abyssinia on May 5. It was amazing that the fighting lasted so long considering the inequality of the combatants. Although Great Britain and France had recognized Italy's claim to colonial rights in Abyssinia, they now reacted unfavorably to the war and pushed for economic sanctions against Italy. Italy acquired Abyssinia on May 9, 1936, but lost it in 1941.

Meanwhile, political events in Spain came to a head and the Spanish Civil War broke out on July 18. It was a very brutal and bloody war between the nationalists, fascists and conservatives against Republicans, socialists, communists and anarchist forces. It ended in March 1939 with the victory of the fascists. Generalissimo Franco, the Caudillo, became head of state.

An event of great interest to sports fans took place on July 19. It was the much publicized heavyweight fight between Germany's champion Max Schmeling and the American Joe Louis. The fight was broadcast live on radio. People were glued to their seats, listening to the radio. Even Father tuned in and so I heard it all. The commentators' enthusiasm in describing the event clearly communicated itself to all listeners. With each round, the pitch of excitement and tension rose as we heard the raised voices of the commentators give a blow-by-blow description. Its culmination came with the shouting and tumultuous cheering of both commentators and spectators when Schmeling knocked out Joe Louis in the 12th round. The jubilation seemed not to end. Schmeling was the hero of more than just the hour.

Max Schmeling was popular in Germany long before he fought Joe Louis. He married a well-known and well loved film star, Annie Ondra. The attractive couple was the object of great affection and admiration by their fans, who craved news and details of their lives. Any item about them was eagerly gobbled up by the adoring public. During the war, Max Schmeling served in the paratroopers and his picture often appeared in newspapers and magazines.

In Berlin, the imminent Summer Olympics dominated coverage by the press and conversations among people in the city. Everybody was intensely interested. The events were listed in the papers and anticipation ran high. Papers stated that price increases and price inflations because of the Olympic Games were strictly prohibited. The Games were scheduled to open on August 1. Along main streets, squares and in center city, flagpoles soon flew Olympic flags side by side with the Swastika. The Triumphal Column was draped with flags. Banners and flags fluttered in the summer winds all around the Big Star Circle. House facades received face-lifts, were renovated and refinished; parks and city squares were groomed and planted with flowers.

Souvenirs decorated with the Olympic symbols appeared in shops and department stores all over Berlin. Interestingly, when Hitler came to power he had forbidden the use of the Swastika and all National Socialist emblems on souvenirs and gift articles of any kind. He had considered it undignified and in poor taste.

Thousands of foreign visitors were expected. Newspapers published appeals asking people to open their homes to house the overflow of guests who could not be accommodated in hotels and guest houses. I would have loved to meet some since I had never met foreigners before. So I was all ears and my heart beat faster when, during a conversation, Aunt Martha · remarked casually, "I am going to have foreign visitors in my apartment." I was agog and wanted to know who was coming and when. I kept plying her with questions. She was hedging, evasive and mysterious. She would not give me a straight answer until she realized I was getting exasperated to the point of giving up.

She finally announced, "Yes, I am going to have foreigners, Americans and Cameroons." That statement had the effect of a pinprick to a high-flying balloon. What a joke and the joke was on me. I was upset because once again, she had succeeded in getting the better of me. Why was I upset? Because "Americans" and "Cameroons" were types of pastry! I should have known. Uncle Gustav and Aunt Martha liked to tease me and they could always count on getting a rise out of me.

When school let out, Father, Mother and I spent our vacation in a part of the Mark Brandenburg called the Spreewald. The river Spree flows through Berlin. Some distance before it reaches the city, the Spree divides into numerous shallow rivulets and creates a unique landscape of many small, mostly wooded islands. It was a popular vacation spot for Berliners. Remnants of ancient Slavic people, the Wenden/Sorben, retreated into this region and settled there centuries ago. The fascinating part was that the farmland and a number of villages were actually situated on islands. The farmhouse, the stables and the barns were in some cases located on separate islands. The common method of transportation was by flat bottomed boats, propelled by punting like the gondolas in Venice. Only the waterways and an occasional tall, slender wooden bridge connected the islands. Farmers brought home the hay, the cows and the harvest by boat. Children went to school by boat. The mailman used a boat, as did wedding parties and funerals. In short, everything moved by boat. In the winter, all rivulets froze and the method of transportation changed from boats to skates and sleds.

The Spreewald is famous for producing sauerkraut and pickled cucumbers. When trains stopped in the towns, especially Luebbenau, vendors walked along the platforms pushing carts, selling jars of sauerkraut and pickles.

We stayed in a village called Burg. Burg attracted many tourists who came primarily to watch local people arrive for church on Sunday dressed in their regional costumes. We joined the sightseers and admired the lovely outfits and their wearers. I believe the men were dressed in dark jackets, dark hats and waistcoats, with sturdy shoes sporting a large buckle. I cannot be more specific. I did not pay much attention to the men because their clothes were not as eye catching as those of the women.

The women wore voluminous ankle length skirts with many starched petticoats to make them stand out. Skirts were of shot silks and moire taffeta in colors of dark blue or brown. The aprons worn over the skirts were made of lace. Beautifully embroidered, fringed scarves covered the women's shoulders. However, the most distinctive item of the costume by far was the headdress. There were two groups. One exclusively wore black, navy blue or brown headdresses. The other wore only white or pastel colored ones (pale pink, pale blue, white, pale green or pale yellow.) Apparently, as it was explained to me later by a native, the difference in colors signified that the wearers belonged to different tribes.

The headdresses were elaborately embroidered on the front as well as on the back. This regional dress was well known all over Germany, particularly so in Berlin. For many years before WWI, the Spreewald girls and women were sought after nannies. They were seen pushing prams along Unter den Linden and in the Tiergarten and were part of the Berlin scene.

Tourists could hire boats for sightseeing trips through the Spreewald. Father, Mother and I did this. It was lovely to glide silently along, accompanied by the sounds of the water being churned up by the punting pole, the birds singing and the wind rustling the leaves of the tall alder trees.

We stayed at a local inn, which was also a farm with livestock and a pond with geese and ducks. I explored the neighborhood and one day came to a field near our lodgings where a young farmer's wife was turning hay. I started a conversation with her and after a few minutes I asked to be given a rake so I could help. This was, of course, a novelty for me, the city child. The woman wore her weekday working clothes: an ankle length bright red fine corduroy skirt, banded near the hem with two rows of narrow black satin or velvet ribbon. She wore a white blouse and a black vest. She told me that she and her husband were of old Wendish stock. I was fascinated when, another time, I heard her converse in a strange tongue with a neighbor. I became quite friendly with her and saw her almost every day, visiting her house and helping with the hay. She was an attractive woman and her husband was good looking but she was sad because they had no children.

I loved this vacation because it was different with many unusual things for me to do and to see. The Spreewald was idyllic, rustic and far removed from the hubbub of the big city, newspapers and radios. Father picked up a paper now and then but I paid little attention to it.

Olympic preparations in Berlin continued and thousands of visitors began to arrive. We read in the papers on July 8: "5,000 members of the National Socialist Motor Bike Corps ready for the Olympics. They will welcome guests at the city limit lead-in roads and serve as pilots to guide them through the traffic. More than one thousand telephones installed at the Olympic Stadium complex."

Prior to the Olympic Games, the Berlin Zoo announced: "Sensational! Berlin's lions in their new natural habitat!" As soon as possible upon our return home, I paid a visit to the zoo to see this unique lion exhibit. Of course, many Berliners had the same idea and it was very crowded.

As early as the end of June and in July, newspapers began publishing the history of the Olympic Games and how the Olympic Flame would be lit on Mount Olympus. From there it was to be carried by runners to Berlin. This was exceptionally exciting because it was the first time in Olympic history that the flame was carried from Mount Olympus to the site of the Games. We talked about it in school and saw a documentary.

The day after the flame was lit, I saw photos of the scene. And again, as always, a few days later the newsreel showed the ceremonies. I saw the ritual performed by young people dressed in simple, classic Greek garments. The flame was ignited by sun rays passing through glass.

Soon newspapers published maps of the runners' route, as well as daily progress reports. At school, we followed the flame's progress by marking a map. It was thrilling to think of how many runners carried the torch through many countries all the way to our capital city. As the flame neared Berlin, another map showed the route the runners would take on the last laps through Berlin itself to the Olympic Stadium. I was very excited. I saw that the flame would be carried along the Tempelhofer

Damm, within walking distance of my home, at approximately noon on August 1.

I wanted to see the runner and Father agreed to take me. On the morning of August 1, Father and I walked to Tempelhof. Hundreds of people lined the route. We joined them and waited quite some time. The crowd was animated; everyone was talking about the games and about the torch carrier. I had fun peeping out to see if I could catch a first glimpse of the runner. It was suspenseful. Traffic had been stopped and only the convoy accompanying the runner would be coming down the street. Shouts went up and necks craned when the first police motorcycle escort came into view. We cheered and clapped enthusiastically as the runner approached and passed by, all too quickly. I was proud and elated to have witnessed this event.

Later in the day, the opening ceremonies were broadcast live on the radio and we made a point of listening to the commentator, the fanfare, the music and the clapping. I was particularly interested to hear the cheering and the commentaries when the runner carrying the flame arrived at the stadium, circled it and made his way up the steps to light the fire that would burn for the duration of the Games. Of course, the Fuehrer made a speech and declared the Games open. I do not remember one word he said except the sentence: "I declare the Olympic Games of Berlin 1936 open!"

The weather was beautiful and everything went according to plan, very smoothly and orderly. I was impressed and excited when on the newsreels I saw the athletes from the participating nations in their special outfits march proudly into the stadium. The U.S.A. had, what looked to me, the largest contingent of participants. It was mentioned that the Stars and Stripes were not dipped in salute to the Fuehrer. Of course, the cheers were especially loud and enthusiastic for the German team that entered last. The Fuehrer smiled benevolently and continuously, as did all the other Nazi leaders who shared the box with him. The Games and everything connected with them were well organized and lavishly run to make the most favorable impression possible on every visitor and participant.

Newspaper pages were filled almost exclusively with reports of the Games. Every day they published detailed lists of the events that were to take place on that particular day and the results of the previous day's competitions. Very little room was left for other news. We made sure we went to the movies to see as many of the Olympic events as possible. It never occurred to me that we should have bought tickets to go and see them in person. The subject was never mentioned at home. Kurt was the only sports fan in the family. I had no idea what the tickets cost and how one would get them. Nobody I knew went to any of the events. The Fuehrer visited the games almost every day. I read in the papers that 3,000 people watched the events in public television rooms in Berlin.

It was around this time that, by pure coincidence, I had an interesting experience. It came about like this. Coffee is an important beverage in Germany, far more popular than tea. We had shops that specialized in coffee and a small selection of teas. Late one afternoon in August, Father and I walked to the particular coffee shop we patronized located on the Kottbusser Damm. Big sacks of raw beans stood on the floor along one wall and shelves behind the counter held cans and prepackaged coffee. The establishment sold a great variety of raw beans and roasted beans from different coffee growing countries. By far, the most interesting object in the place was the big roasting machine in the window. The enticing smell of freshly roasted coffee beans pervaded not only the interior of the store but wafted outside.

Father made his purchase and we started for home. As we approached the junction where the Kottbusser Damm begins, at the northwest corner of the Hermannplatz, we saw that the police stopped the traffic and pedestrians from crossing the street. We had no choice but to wait. We stood in the front row at the curb. Father inquired of the policeman what was going on and was told that the Fuehrer was on his way back to town from the Regatta at Gruenau. I don't know how long we stood there. It must have been almost an hour. Eventually, the motorcade came into view and there he was, the Fuehrer, in his convertible. He was wearing his usual uniform and cap. He was smiling and saluting. He looked exactly like his photos. I don't know who sat next to him in the car. Of course, traffic had been stopped long before he came and a sizeable crowd had accumulated. Many people were caught on their way home from work. Thus, Hitler was not driving along empty streets.

Every crowd included people who shouted "Heil!" if not from conviction then because they did not want to be noticed by the police or plainclothes Gestapo for not joining in the salute. Even if one did not feel like shouting "Heil Hitler!" it was safer to raise one's arm at least. On this particular occasion, many raised their arms but a few others, including Father, did not and I only raised mine for a moment when I saw a policeman look my way. Also, I did not raise my arm for the whole time because then my view would have been obstructed. The "Heil!" shouts were comparatively sparse. A few minutes after the cavalcade passed, we were free to leave.

During the Olympic Games, hundreds of Hitler Youth boys acted as guides and messengers. Many of them participated in Olympic ceremonies, especially the closing ceremony, which was impressive. The Olympics closed with the singing of the chorus from Beethoven's *A* Ninth Symphony, Ode to Joy."

While this was being sung, huge bonfires were lit and burned outside the stadium. Searchlights formed the famous dome of light just as at the Nuremberg Party Congress. The rousing music, the flames combined with the silvery beams of the searchlights and the flags being displayed by flag bearers around the upper rim of the stadium created a sensational atmosphere that sent shivers up and down my spine.

Germany won 33 gold medals, 36 silver medals, 30 bronze medals and was ahead of the U.S.A., Hungary and Italy. Newspaper reports, heralded by our leadership, came from London, Paris and Rome. They wrote: "Berlin Surpasses Everything" and "Berlin Breathes the Spirit of Youth."

The Olympic Games were a most memorable event for Berliners who were caught up in the enthusiasm and excitement. We Berliners were proud to have the Games take place in our city. After they were over, conversations still centered around them for a while before everyday life reclaimed our undivided attention.

September came and, with it, the Reich Party Congress held from September 8 to September 14 in Nuremberg. This year's motto was: "Reich Party Congress of Honor," to celebrate the Olympic Games and the successful occupation of the Rhineland.

Formations of the various Nazi organizations marched onto the Zeppelin Field. It was enormous and held well over 100,000 people. Banners flew from stone ramparts with stone turrets bordering the field, which boasted a main platform with an elaborate portico. The logistics of these gatherings were staggering, but everything was organized to the last detail and went like clockwork.

Earlier in the year, Leni Riefenstahl's documentary of the 1934 Congress, "Triumph of the Will," premiered following much advance publicity, fanfare and heralding. School children were taken during school hours to see it. It was stupendous. What impressed me most was the choral speaking of the Labor Service men. They seemed to speak in one voice. I thought they looked and sounded almost like robots. I was also overwhelmed by the number of uniformed, unsmiling men and their intensity, by the procession of thousands of flags onto the field and the searchlights forming the dome of light. I still cannot quite express the feelings these pictures created in me. I was awed by the spectacle and at the same time, deep down, I felt a faint stirring of uneasiness.

During the Congress, the Four Year Plan was announced. Goering was named the plan's executive director. I was to hear a lot about it in the coming months and years. Speaking at the Congress, the Fuehrer denied that he planned war but, at the same time, he held the largest maneuvers since 1914. Another subject the Fuehrer belabored at length was Germany's right to colonies. Every other nation had colonies–Belgium, Holland, England, France–and Germany needed them badly.

I am certain a directive was issued to schools regarding this subject because in geography, now called Earth Science, emphasis was placed on learning about all the former German colonies in Africa. We wrote essays about them and went over the points of the Four Year Plan. The need for German economic self sufficiency was emphasized. We were told repeatedly that independence from foreign sources of raw materials was the primary goal. Germany must be self-sufficient.

I noticed that the British were a particular target for propaganda because they, and to a lesser extent the French, had, according to Hitler, at all times conspired to obtain colonies at the most strategic positions, such as Gibraltar, Malta, Egypt, the Suez Canal and more. Not only had they acquired these valuable properties but, at the same time, they had successfully put obstacles in Germany's way that prevented her from acquiring colonies. Much to their chagrin, Germany did manage to establish colonies in Africa. However, in 1918, the Versailles Peace Treaty deprived Germany of them. The Fuehrer wanted our former colonies back. I didn't know how he was going to achieve this goal.

Since we did not have colonies, so we were told at school, we were short of vital raw materials. But German ingenuity was hard at work to find solutions and synthetic materials that could be produced in Germany. Foreign spies were eager to get their hands on certain formulas, hence we had to be on the alert for foreign espionage and sabotage action. Our class was taken to the cinema together with many other schoolchildren, for a special showing of a film, "Traitor." It was about industrial espionage, a tense drama full of propaganda about how foreign powers were intent on hindering German progress.

A few years later, in high school, we were asked, "Do you know why German goods are marked 'Made in Germany'?" Of course, we had no idea. The answer was that the British tried to squeeze Germany out of foreign markets. Britain was jealous, envious and afraid of German efficiency, industry, know-how and competition. They reasoned that if German goods were marked "Made in Germany" and were found wanting, Germany would lose out. However, the British miscalculated and the imprint "Made in Germany" soon became a hallmark of excellence owing to the unequaled, superior quality of German workmanship. Not only did existing markets expand but new ones opened up because people preferred to buy German products. I thought this was neat because something that I believed was planned with bad intent did not have the desired success.

The Hitler Youth was established as early as 1933. I was oblivious to any announcements about it and remained so for several years to come. As time went on, I saw children in HJ uniforms in the street going to or coming from their HJ meetings. I occasionally saw HJ or BDM units march or walk along one of Neukoelln's main streets but I never saw any formations in our street probably because they preferred the busier thoroughfares for maximum effect on the public. At the time, I was not familiar with all of the following details, which I include for the reader's edification

The Hitler Youth was very strictly organized right from the very beginning. The National Youth Leader was Baldur von Schirach. The Hitler Youth Slogan was, "Fuehrer, command, we follow!"

Baldur von Schirach composed "The Hitler Youth Song":
Forward! Forward! Blare the bright trumpets!
Forward! Forward! Youth fears no danger!
Germany, you must stand radiant even though we may perish
Our flag flutters ahead of us,
man by man we advance into the future.
For Hitler we march through night and peril,
with (following) the flag of youth for freedom and bread.
Our flag flutters ahead of us.
Our flag represents the new era.
Our flag leads us into eternity.
Yes, the flag means more than death.

The Junior division of the HJ was called Wolf Cubs for boys age 10 to 14. HJ was comprised of boys age 14 to 18 (at 18 boys were called up into the armed forces). Transfer from Wolf Cubs to HJ was automatic. The HJ was organized and sub-divided into:

- Comradeships

- Troops
- Followings
- Clans
- Regiments or Banne (Bann is an Old German word for area of command and authority.)

The League of German Girls (BDM - *Bund Deutscher Maedchen*): Girls age 10 to 14 were organized into Young Girlships of 10 girls, 10 Girlships equaled a Troop, 4 troops equaled a Group, 3-5 Groups equaled a Ring, 4-6 Rings equaled a Sub-*Gau* (*Gau* is Germanic for subdivision of a clan area) and 20 Sub-Gaus equaled an Upper *Gau.*

The youth leaders were ardent Nazis. Adolf Hitler, the boys and girls were taught, was the infallible leader. The boys dressed in black shorts and brown shirts, white knee socks and black shoes in the summer, with leather webbing. In the winter, they wore black ski suits similar to sweat suits and a peaked cap with a swastika emblem. The boys wore patches and various other insignia, earned for various achievements, on the sleeves.

The Hitler Youth had many different branches boys could choose to join: flying, communications, naval, drum corps, fanfare, music and motor. The HJ was for the most part intended to provide preliminary military training and make the boys combat ready, although, at the time, the other kids and I did not realize this was the aim.

The HJ took part in parades, rallies, mass meetings, song fests, gym tournaments, shooting matches and represented Germany at international sports events, street collections, harvest and more.

BDM members aged 14 to 21 were also members of the suborganization Faith and Beauty. At age 21, young women became members of the League of German Women.

The BDM's purpose was to mold girls as closely as possible to conform with the Nazi ideal of womanhood. They were to learn to be obedient, dutiful, disciplined and self-sacrificing. These virtues were to be emphasized and continually reinforced so the girls would become willing and faithful followers of Nazi doctrine. Great emphasis was placed on physical fitness and discipline. Most activities were devoted to sports and the rest to ideological instruction. Girls were constantly reminded that women are born to be mothers and caretakers, while always keeping in mind that "Germans are the superior race."

Germany was divided, for HJ purposes, into 40 regions. Boys and girls were strictly segregated. On the whole, the Third Reich was quite puritanical and stressed high morals. Everything was to be wholesome, Nazi goal oriented and regimented.

The ceremony of dedication for the League of German Girls took place, like all the other HJ dedications, on April 19, the eve of the Fuehrer's birthday. The leader spoke the text of the dedication and the girls repeated it after her. The script was as follows:

Leader: *"Jungmaedel* (young girls), you are to be integrated into the BDM today."

Girls: "I swear to serve the Fuehrer, Adolf Hitler, faithfully and selflessly in the Hitler Youth.

I vow that I will at all times work for the unity and comradeship of the German Youth.

I pledge obedience to the Reich Youth Leader and all leaders of the BDM.

I vow by our sacred flag that I will always strive to be worthy of it, so help me God."

Leader: "In my capacity as a responsible BDM leader, I admit you into the ranks of the League of German Girls."

A song about loyalty was then sung.

First Speaker: "We are the followers of these exalted flags that people more significant than us created from nothing. Now we see flags flying victoriously. All that remains of past struggle and dying is to us but a distant memory."

Second speaker: "But we are young! It would be treason if all we did was walk along the smooth paths without remembering those who prepared it. Already the symbol glows above new horizons and our own deeds reach forward like a steely pointer."

BDM girls wore long, straight black skirts, white short sleeved blouses, black kerchiefs held in a leather knot at the front and black flat heeled shoes. Berchtesgaden cardigans, part of the Berchtesgaden regional costume, became very popular because Hitler's famous estate was near Berchtesgaden. Soon most girls owned and wore one, including myself. Practically all BDM girls had one but it never was and never became part of their uniform. The cardigan was black and knitted in a fine rib. It had a yoke with a green, a red and then another green stripe, equal in size at the top and silver buttons down the front.

The Hitler Youth maintained hostels and youth homes throughout Germany. The Hitler Youth went to separate vacation camps for boys and girls. Days at camp followed a routine of roll calls, marches, tasks and chores. Sometimes the children were quartered in barracks. Camps and camping served to further indoctrinate the youth. The Hitler Youth also organized vocational training camps.

Members of the Hitler Youth took part in the Adolf Hitler March. From all over Germany, 2,000 youths marched to Nuremberg to attend the Party Congress, some of them from as far away as 490 miles. Baldur von Schirach, the Reich Youth Leader, said about this march: "We are marching TO the Fuehrer. If he so desires, we will also march FOR him."

Physical exercises and athletic competitions became an integral part of achieving the important goal of attaining physical fitness and toughness.

The BDM and HJ attended May Day celebrations and solstice festivals, and collected money for the WHW and other causes. They also made and repaired toys at Christmas time, more so during WWII. These toys were distributed at Nazi organization Christmas parties to needy children and, later, to children of soldiers.

The HJ, including BDM, held regular weekly meetings called Home Evenings apart from and in addition to other mandatory activities and services. Attendance was compulsory and considered an honorable service to the Volk. I heard from my playmates that Home Evenings were spent listening to lectures on history, race and folklore, reading politically oriented books, learning songs and crafts. Periodically, my friends had to take exams on what they learned, for which the boys and girls received certificates of accomplishment. The HJ was big on awards. The boys were rewarded with arm patches and other insignia for excelling in various areas, like shooting, making models of planes, physical training and more.

HJ and BDM members were encouraged to talk about their parents and their parents' views and reactions to political events. They were also to report any person making politically incorrect statements, including family members. Mama told me once that some HJ members had ratted on their parents who, consequently, were arrested by the Gestapo. It was a reminder for me to watch what I said and to whom I said it.

No gathering was complete without music. The leaders or members played recorders, guitars and accordions. Songs were an integral part of all get-togethers. Numerous songs were especially written and associated with the Hitler Youth, such as

"Flame, Rise Up," "Emerging from Grey City Walls" and "Wild Geese Rustle through the Night."

The song "Sublime Night of Clear Stars" was meant to be a hymn but was used mainly during the winter solstice on December 21. Solstice celebrations were intended to eventually replace Christmas. This never happened. People were not inclined to change. We learned this particular song in school but it was in no way implied, neither did it occur to me, that it would ever take the place of "Silent Night, Holy Night."

The radio stations, too, scheduled regular programs for the Hitler Youth, boys and girls. These included broadcasts of music played by the various HJ music corps.

It was general knowledge that boys and girls on reaching the age of 10 should join the Hitler Youth. Posters on advertising columns served as reminders to do so. So far, membership in the Hitler Youth was voluntary and no pressure to join was brought to bear on us at school or, at least, not at my school. In my class of 30 girls, only six were members of the BDM. No effort was made by party organizations to recruit us.

The reasons why children voluntarily joined varied. In the days before television, portable radios, cassette players and individually owned cars, many children found the HJ was a place to meet with peers. It was a place where they felt important, away from parental control, where they felt that they were an integral part of something significantly larger and very much removed from their rather ordinary everyday life. I knew what life in Balz was like, for instance, and I suppose life in other villages in Germany was much the same. It did not offer much of anything in the way of entertainment or excitement to young people. Movie houses were more than a mile's walk away and were open only on weekends. And now, suddenly, there were opportunities to do something and to be involved with peers. I am sure that a number of boys and girls realized that in the HJ they would be able to satisfy their craving for power and exercise their authority once they became leaders. One of my playmates became a leader later on.

Some children probably felt attracted to the organization while others thought it was the thing to do, to belong. Some parents probably felt it was to their children's advantage to join the HJ. Some children were probably brainwashed at home by their Nazi parents.

Young people, in particular, think they are immune to brainwashing and propaganda. I was subjected to both during the 12 years of the Third Reich, mainly during my high school years. To what extent this constant exposure would have been successful I cannot say because I was fortunate in having an antidote, which came into play as soon as I arrived home from school: Mama. Without her, I might have believed many things I was told as gospel truth. Another factor that helped to prevent me from being brainwashed is that I am not the type by nature to go for the Nazi kind of ideology. Anything smacking of fanaticism turned me off and made me feel very uncomfortable.

Guenter, Martin and Elke were my age and they joined the HJ when they were 10 years old. In the case of Elke (and later Renate), joining the BDM was a given since her family strongly supported the Fuehrer and the Nazis. For Martin, it was different. He was crazy about airplanes and flying. Therefore, the Flying HJ provided an irresistible incentive to join. National Socialism had nothing to do with his decision. Boys in this branch learned about aeronautics, aerodynamics, how to build glider models and gliders, learned to fly gliders and so on. It was actually preliminary training for joining the air force when they were old enough to do so and, alternatively, it was preparation for 14-

year-olds who left school to enter aircraft production plants as apprentices.

I have mentioned that in 1935 joining the HJ was voluntary and no pressure was used. However, this changed after 1936. I heard that from now on officials of the party and the HJ visited schools at the beginning of the school year and enrolled all 10-year-old boys and girls. Theoretically, membership was still voluntary. No one came to my classroom this or the following years.

When my other friends reached the age of 10, they were automatically enlisted in the Hitler Youth. I know that they were neither enthusiastic nor fanatic about the HJ or National Socialism. They had to join and it was part of life. My friends were required to attend meetings at least once a week, mostly after school or in the early evening hours as well as Saturday and/or on Sunday mornings. We rarely talked about the subject among ourselves. When we were together, we played and concentrated on our games. However, I learned a number of things from their remarks.

Everything within the HJ was organized with a view to the Nazi spirit. There was no play apart from ball games. It was marching, drilling, singing ideological songs, memorizing Nazi poems, reading Nazi literature, learning about race, and Germanic and Nordic customs and festivals. At the meetings, much time was spent on indoctrination in Nazi ideology. The girls had a special song book called "We Girls Sing." In addition to Nazi songs, it contained numerous folk songs from all parts of Germany. I owned a copy because I liked music and knew practically all the folk songs in it, having learned them at school. HJ and BDM marched for local sports events, attended local and national rallies and other special events.

Saturday and Sunday mornings were given over to sports and physical training irrespective of the weather. In the summer, the children were made to do strenuous exercises in the full midday sun. I remember that Elke, of all people, complained about it. Apparently, several girls passed out. I was appalled. I thought it was unreasonable. I felt there was a difference between physical fitness training and endangering one's health and voiced my disapproval. Elke gave me some of her brainwashed ideas about having to be tough for the Fuehrer, so I did not pursue the subject. However, I talked about it at home. I said how happy I was not to have to participate in the things Elke and the other girls had to do.

Elke once took me to their meeting place. It was not a very big room in a ground floor apartment facing the courtyard. Furnished with a large table, a Nazi flag and chairs, its bookshelves were filled with Nazi literature. It did not look particularly tidy, cheerful or bright.

One evening a week was reserved for basic physical training and schooling, one evening for voluntary achievement sport and two obligatory evenings or afternoons per week for other purposes. Service on two Sundays per month in the summer and one Sunday in the winter were required. It was stated that time for church was to be left free but that did not work out most of the time since Nazi activities were scheduled regardless.

Attendance at all HJ and BDM meetings, as well as all other events, as I said before, was compulsory. Only sickness, with a proper written excuse, was a reason for being absent. I believe a death in the immediate family was also an acceptable excuse.

About two years later, when Mama and I were in Balz on vacation, we met a Berlin couple from the borough of Reinickendorf, Mr. and Mrs. Lange. They had a son, Eberhard, who was my age. After we returned to Berlin, Mama and I visited them several times. Once our visit happened to fall on a day when Eberhard had an HJ meeting. Because we were visiting, Mrs. Lange told Eberhard that he could stay home. Eberhard and I went outside to play ball, ride bikes and run around. Unfortunately, one of the other HJ boys must have seen us because later on he arrived at the apartment with a note from Eberhard's leader demanding to know why Eberhard had been absent. His mother told the boy the reason: "We have company." He replied emphatically that this was an unacceptable excuse.

Mrs. Lange was quite upset. It spoiled the pleasant time we had spent together. Mama telephoned Mrs. Lange a few days later and found out that she had been summoned to appear before the leader with Eberhard and Eberhard was to be punished. Mama and I were upset. I had heard some children mention that their leaders were bullies and I hoped that Eberhard would not get into too much trouble. I did not find out what his punishment was.

Leaders had the authority to punish wayward members, who had no appeals available. Depending upon the nature and commitment of the leader, punishments could be nasty. Girls, I heard, had to clean the meeting place and scrub the floor left deliberately dirty and untidy by order of the leader. Boys were made to do excessive physical exercises and drills. All were berated in front of their peers partly as a punishment, partly as a deterrent to others. Sometimes their comrades were made to take part in the punishment by taunting them or they made the culprit run the gauntlet.

I went my own way. I was 10 years old but I had neither the intention nor the inclination to join the BDM. I was never one to run with the crowd. I disliked, instinctively, all regimented activities as well as the organization's uniforms. The thought of being subject to the whims of a fanatic leadership, in fact, being at their mercy and having to obey blindly, was abhorrent to me. Once or twice, I was asked by various people why I had not joined or when was I going to join. I replied that I did not feel I wanted to do so.

The Nazis published a number of illustrated magazines for children. One of them was "Join In to Help." I don't remember if we had to subscribe to it at school or how it was distributed. I remember reading some issues but I cannot recall anything I read in them.

Several Nazi newspapers were published, for instance the *Stuermer*, the *Angriff* and the *Voelkischer Beobachter*. The only time I saw these papers was in showcases displaying them at various points in the streets.

Hateful propaganda against the Jews increased. The HJ sang rude songs about the Jews, such as: "Throw out the whole Jewish baggage, throw them out of our fatherland. Send all of them to Jerusalem, but cut off their legs or they will come back again." I heard it several times, that is why I remember it. When I told Father about it, he and Mother were horrified, as was the rest of my family. They were horrified that children were taught and encouraged to sing such a song and told me never to repeat it. I did not need to be told not to sing it. I thought it was gruesome to chop off anyone's legs. Besides, I had no quarrel with the Jewish people I knew.

Father said, "These people are Germans. Many of them fought in WWI. They deserve the respect due to veterans." Father listened to the Sabbath services broadcast from synagogues and temples before the Nazis came to power and for as long as these broadcasts were permitted thereafter. He loved the singing and the chanting and repeatedly remarked to me that the cantors had excellent voices.

After the summer holidays, school began again and I settled into my usual routine. However, the outstanding and exciting feature of school this fall was a wonderful three day field trip to the Werbellinsee, located in the Schorfheide north of Berlin. We stayed at a school hostel. The buildings stood among pine trees and the grounds extended to the edge of the lake. The accommodations were spartan. We slept in bunk beds in dormitories. Our teacher, Mr. Lambert, had to sleep in the dormitory with us. He had the bed next to mine.

One of the highlights was a visit to the large game preserve where we saw otters, sheep, wild pig, cranes and some other wild animals such as pine martens and bustards. I was very interested to learn that hunters must shoot bustards from the back. Buckshot would not penetrate if coming from the front of the bird because their plumage is so smooth. I really did not like to hear about them being shot at all.

We took long walks, explored the fields and forest, and learned about plant and animal life. The animals probably went into hiding when they heard us approach. This explains that we saw more flora than fauna, apart from insects and beautiful butterflies. I was so excited to find so many plants I had not seen before that I ran here and there and back to Mr. Lambert to ask him the name of each plant I found. He finally said, "Gisela, you must have walked three times the distance we did by running back and forth like this." Insects were very much in evidence at night, primarily thousands of mosquitos. For many of my classmates, field trips, like the annual excursion to Potsdam and the steamer trip to the Mueggelsee, constituted their only vacation.

Throughout the year, housewives were reminded to buy and use whatever produce was in season. Shopping was done daily because few people owned refrigerators. Now, a bumper crop of cabbage caused our daily newspapers to urge its readers to eat more cabbage, stressing the health benefits of cabbage and sauerkraut. Variations of the usual cabbage with lamb dish were suggested to enable the hausfrau to keep her family happy eating cabbage three or more times a week. Here are a few examples:

Fish/Cabbage Rolls

3 pounds of cabbage, 2 pounds of fish, 1/4 pound of smoked bacon, 1 large onion, 1 handful dried mushrooms, salt and pepper.

Soak the mushrooms over night. Before using, squeeze as much water as possible from the mushrooms but reserve the soaking water. Chop raw fish, bacon, onion and mushrooms, salt and pepper. Mix all ingredients.

Blanch cabbage to make it easy to remove the leaves. Take two large leaves and top with two small leaves. Fill leaves with the fish mixture, roll up tightly, secure with toothpicks or yarn to hold cabbage roll together.

In a heavy skillet, melt butter and place cabbage rolls closely together so they cover the bottom of the pan and brown slightly. Pour the soaking water and enough boiling water over the cabbage rolls to cover them. Simmer until done.

Cabbage Dumplings

1 small head of cabbage, butter, 1 large onion, a few tablespoons of breadcrumbs. Two eggs, small cup of sour milk, 100 grams of flour.

Cut cabbage into wedges and cook until half done. Drain, squeeze out excess water, chop finely. Saute chopped onions in butter until glassy in appearance, add breadcrumbs. Let cool. When cold, add egg yolks, sour milk and flour, blend. Fold in stiffly beaten egg whites and as many breadcrumbs as needed to make it possible to form dumplings. Simmer dumplings in salt water until done.

Fish and Cabbage Casserole
Fish filets, marinate filets in vinegar and water.

Potatoes boiled in their skin, small head of cabbage, caraway seeds, thinly sliced pickled cucumbers, tomato or horseradish sauce or leftover gravy.

Peel and slice cold potatoes. Shred cabbage very fine and steam in very little water with caraway seeds.

Cut fish into half inch slices.

Grease a casserole dish and layer: potatoes, cabbage, fish, very thin slices of pickled cucumber, repeat layers. Pour either tomato or horseradish sauce or leftover gravy over the casserole and bake for half an hour at 350 degrees.

Cabbage Strudel
Make a noodle dough from 1 egg, 1 cup of lukewarm water, 1 tablespoon of butter, salt and flour. Kneed vigorously. Let dough rest under a warm dish. Stretch dough out on a floured cloth with the flat of your hands until very thin.

Filling: Cabbage or Savoy cabbage is steamed for a few minutes with salt and pepper. Add leftover chopped meat.

195

Place filling on strudel dough. Roll into a strudel and bake on a greased baking sheet or cut into thick slices and fry in butter.

Cabbage Pie

Fill a pie crust with chopped cabbage that has been steamed for a few minutes with salt, pepper and caraway seeds if desired. Add any leftover chopped meat. Mix one cup of buttermilk or milk with 1 egg yolk, 1 tablespoon of flour and salt. Pour over filling. Top with pie crust, cut slits in top of crust to allow steam to escape. Bake.

Cabbage Rolls with Mushroom/Nut Filling

2 stale rolls (soaked and squeezed out), 1 pound of mushrooms, 1 onion, 2 eggs, 3 tablespoons of ground hazelnuts, nutmeg, marjoram, paprika and chopped parsley.

Saute chopped mushrooms and chopped onions in butter. Mix with rolls, hazelnuts, paprika, parsley, salt, pepper and marjoram. Add beaten eggs.

Fill cabbage leaves, roll up tightly. If necessary, use yarn to keep them together. Brown cabbage rolls lightly in butter. Place in a baking dish. Dribble with oil and bake for 1 1/2 hours.

Another law passed in October made it compulsory for schools to include PT in their curriculum. Our school already had PT twice a week for an hour prior to this law.

Sports were designed to improve and develop physical fitness but our sessions were not competitive in character. No one was singled out for special training or attention. We did floor exercises most of the time. I liked them a lot. In addition, we worked on rings, parallel bars, the horse, climbing ropes and poles. Later, in high school, we had a large sandbox and practiced jumping, vaulting, shot-put, discus and javelin throwing. Weather permitting, we also played ball games and ran in the school yard. We did not engage in competitions or contests with other schools. Competitive games and sports took place within the HJ.

At the end of October, the important news item was that Italy and Germany signed a treaty making them allies, thereby creating the so-called Axis Berlin-Rome. Later on, in December, a treaty with Japan added the name of Tokyo to the Axis.

Over the years, I made many friends and was invited to their homes to play. One of my friends was Anneliese, the daughter of grocery storekeepers just around the corner from where I lived. For a while, we spent a lot of time together and Anneliese asked me to her birthday party. The girls wore Sunday dresses and the birthday girl was presented with books, games, candy and flowers. It was fun. We played pin the tail on the donkey, word games, threw dice to win chocolates and wore paper hats.

Anneliese later invited me to go with her to the Baptist church Sunday school. The church was located on the ground floor of an apartment house in our neighborhood. Anneliese said that she would get a prize for bringing a new person to Sunday school. It was okay but I soon stopped going. I really cannot say why.

Mama was reading the paper one day. She said to me, "It says here that a fortune-teller has been sentenced to six months in jail. Fancy that."

My birthday, so close to Christmas, was a problem because everyone was busy and had no time for a party. Nevertheless, my family made it a special day for me. I received many flowers, such as white paper narcissus, yellow mimosas, several poinsettias and red flowers of the anemone family. I always received birthday gifts as well as Christmas gifts.

In December, we celebrated Advent by lighting the candles on our Advent wreath on Sunday afternoons. I loved this quiet time. At school, we lit our Advent candles during the first hour on Monday mornings and sang a Christmas carol. As usual, Christmas trees and Christmas markets made their appearance on our streets on December 11.

Aunt Marga brought home tickets for the theater. I went to see "Peter's Trip to the Moon" with Father and Mother for the second or third time, as well as "Max and Moritz."

On December 21, I celebrated my 11th birthday.

My family celebrated Christmas Eve at Father and Mother's apartment. I visited Oma, Opa and Papa on Christmas Day. We had no school until after New Year's and I spent a lot of time sledding, as well as skating.

The year 1936 drew to a close. On New Year's Eve, my family gathered at Aunt Martha's. I was happy to help prepare the party food. We played games. The Schaefers, who were lively, helped to make the evening jolly. Aunt Marga placed a small table in a corner and provided some new puzzles for my amusement. She promised to pay me 50 pfennig for every time I solved a puzzle. This was an exciting incentive because I did not receive pocket money. I solved the puzzles several times. Sad to say, Aunt Marga failed to pay up.

1937

January 30	Four year extension of Enabling Law.
April 20	Hitler's birthday, now a public holiday.
May 6	The dirigible "Hindenburg" burns in Lakehurst.
May 11	Hitler bans hydrogen zeppelin flights.
June	Five more Protestant pastors arrested in Berlin, including Pastor Jacobi of the Memorial Church. Strict restrictions regarding foreign currency come into effect.
July	Hitler orders the arrest of Pastor Niemoeller.
July 19	Hitler opens House of German Art in Munich.
August 8	Protests in Berlin about the arrest of Niemoeller result in 111 arrested.
September 25-29	State visit of Mussolini. Biggest Nazi party rally in Nuremberg to date.
December 21	The author's 12th birthday.

January 30, the anniversary of the Fuehrer's coming to power was usually hyped-up and celebrated with a mass meeting at the Berlin Sportpalast. There were speeches, nationwide assemblies, declarations and demonstrations of loyalty. The Fuehrer was, of course, the focal point and his speech was the main event of the day.

But this year was different. Our school was directly involved in the anniversary celebrations. On January 30, the Reichsminister for Propaganda and Public Enlightenment, Dr. Joseph Goebbels, was scheduled to visit our school and deliver an address that would be broadcast live.

Our teacher broke the news to us some time before the event and acquainted us with the itinerary: All children were to take up positions in the school yard some time before Goebbels' arrival. He would be welcomed at the entrance to the gym by the headmaster of the boy's school. A girl, not from our class, and a boy were chosen to present Goebbels with a bouquet. As soon as the minister entered the gym, the children in the yard would make their way to the art room to listen to the broadcast. After the speech, we were to return to the school yard for Goebbels' departure. A rehearsal took place a few days prior to January 30.

The big day dawned. Everyone was nervous. Dutifully, we trooped into the yard and into position. It was cloudy and cold. Apart from getting cold feet, it was bearable. We were dressed warmly, wore hats and gloves and stood close together. A few minutes later, Hitler Youth units arrived and arranged themselves shoulder to shoulder in front of us. Soon after they were in place, a detachment of 6 feet tall SS men marched in and took their places in front of the Hitler Youth. Now we could not see anything except the backs of the HJ and the towering backs of the SS men.

We chatted and stamped our feet to keep warm. We were somewhat chagrined that our view was blocked so completely. "What was the point of standing there for ages if we could not see anything?" we grumbled. We stood for over an hour and were quite chilled and bored. Finally, I heard a band strike up in the street. This signaled the VIP's arrival. I could not see what was going on but I guessed that Goebbels had been welcomed and escorted into the gym. We continued to stand there until we were told to go to the art room. Perhaps children who were very close to the gym entrance and people who had, no doubt, gathered in the street, joined in some "Heil!" shouts. All I remember is hearing the band followed by indistinguishable sounds.

We settled down to listen to the Reichsminister's speech of which I recall nothing. No talking, fidgeting or leaving the room was allowed. When it ended, we took our places in the school yard, once more behind the SS and HJ. We remained until Goebbels and his entourage had left to the strains of the band and the HJ and SS detachments had marched off. Before being dismissed, we were allowed to peek inside our gym. It had been transformed by masses of flags and garlands of evergreens to be quite unrecognizable. It looked very festive in the Nazi decorations. Our teacher did not refer to the visit nor did he make any personal observations about it the next day but in February we had to write an essay about it.

Newspapers reported that Reichminister Goebbels was given a "tumultuous welcome" by 350 school children, was greeted by the headmaster, and presented with bouquets by a boy and a pretty girl.

During the preceding year, additional directives had been issued to schools, one of them a ban on using "alien" and "foreign" words. For instance, all Latin designations in grammar were replaced by German words. We no longer learned genitive, dative and so on. Now we simply called it 1st Case, 2nd Case, 3rd Case and 4th Case. No longer did we have nouns but "chief or major words." The adjective became an characterizing word, the preposition was a relation word, the verb was a do-word and an adjective was a connecting word.

An attempt was made to replace the names of the months. For example, January was *Hartung*, February was *Hornung*, March was *Lenzing*, May was *Wonnemond*, August or September was *Erntemond*, November was *Neblung* and December was *Julmond*. Like so many other attempts to change the old established customs, it did not work.

Some words of foreign origin or root were retained and called borrowed words, or inherited words. It is really quite amusing that when I visit Germany now I notice how these words have changed not only back into what was then considered an "alien" vocabulary but how many other foreign words, mainly English ones, have found their way into the everyday language.

There must have been numerous directives to the schools that the pupils did not know about. Not knowing what these directives were I could not tell what changes, if any, in the contents of school books were made because I did not see the previous editions. Reading books for our German lessons were not exchanged at this point for new ones; we continued using them for the remainder of the school year.

Teachers were not obligated to join the party. In fact, the party was very particular as to who was admitted. However, all teachers were forced to become members of the National

Socialist Teachers League (NSLB - *Nationalsocialister Lehrer Bund*). As members of the NSLB, they were required to attend compulsory training seminars, which were always held during vacations. Our teachers were never absent from class to attend a seminar and our school was never closed for that reason. None of my elementary school teachers, including the headmistress, were party members. No matter what subject they taught, they refrained at all times from making political comments or voicing personal opinions on political and current events.

On most Sunday afternoons, especially in the winter, I went to a children's matinee at a local cinema. Sometimes the entire program consisted of American Mickey Mouse and other cartoons. I saw all the Shirley Temple films. She was extremely popular, not only with children but also with adults. Her films were always dubbed by a German girl, a couple of years older than Shirley, who made perfect voice-overs for Shirley. Then there were movies with Pat and Patachon, Tom Mix, Charlie Chapman, and Laurel and Hardy. I saw "Babes in Toyland" more than just once. Programs included a documentary and a newsreel. I remember documentaries about African tribes, foreign countries, animals and the building of the Autobahn.

Movies were strictly rated for general audiences over 18 years of age, for audiences over 14 years of age, and for audiences over six years of age. Most of the time, one did not have to show identification but the ushers asked for ID if a patron looked too young and would not admit him/her without it. Of course, younger kids would try to get into a movie rated for older ages. I always looked much younger than my age and did not even try.

I recall Mama taking me to the cinema when I was very small. The movies were still silent movies at that time. Hard to imagine now. She told me later that she loved to go to the children's shows because she enjoyed the children's reactions more than the movies. I remember Mama taking me to see "Snow White." It was black and white and silent. Pandemonium broke out when the stepmother turned up with the poisoned apple. Hundreds of excited children jumped off their seats yelling, "Don't take it! Don't take it! It is poisoned! She is evil," and so on. It was very exciting and, to Mama, hilarious.

In spite of not feeling quite my usual self, I had gone to a matinee on the last Sunday in February. When I returned home, I felt very sick. I had a temperature and a very sore throat that developed quite suddenly. Then I threw up bright yellow vomit. I went to bed. Dr. Baumann visited on Monday morning. He came again on Tuesday, March 2, Aunt Marga's birthday. By then I had broken out in a rash. Dr. Baumann's diagnosis was scarlet fever. This meant a hospital admission because scarlet fever is very contagious. Remembering my past and only hospital experience, I was adamant that I did not want to be hospitalized.

We had only one option: quarantine at Aunt Martha's apartment. One of the bedrooms would have to be converted into a sickroom. The person attending me must change outer clothes each time upon entering and leaving the sickroom, wear a mask and observe strict sterile techniques. It was far too complicated but I refused to see reason and insisted on staying home.

I was overruled and shortly after noon the ambulance arrived. I got onto the stretcher myself. Mother kissed me and I was carried out. Aunt Marga had just arrived for lunch. I saw her standing on the sidewalk as I peeked out from under the sheet that covered my face.

This time I was taken to the Urban Hospital, a large complex consisting of separate buildings for different diseases, situated in a garden surrounded by a brick wall. One of the buildings was the isolation pavilion for scarlet fever, another one was for diphtheria. Both were feared and dangerous children's diseases. Diphtheria was exceptionally deadly.

I spent the first day and night in a ward with many children. It was awful. I was burning up with fever, aching, miserable and could not sleep although I was very tired. Whatever chance of sleep I had was ruined by the boy in the bed next to mine. He snored loudly all night.

Visiting hours were on Wednesdays from 2 p.m. to 3 p.m. and from 6 p.m. to 7 p.m. and on Sundays from 2 p.m. to 3 p.m. The day after I was admitted was Wednesday, hence it was visiting day.

Because we were in a contagious disease pavilion and in the most contagious stage of the illness, no visitors were allowed inside our ward. The ward was on the ground floor. Outside, wooden steps were placed beneath each window, enabling visitors to peek in. Verbal communication was virtually impossible because the windows remained closed. Patients and visitors could smile and wave to each other. I was still upset at being in the hospital and, after a sleepless night, very grouchy. I am ashamed to say that I very ungraciously turned my back on my visitors.

The following day, I was moved into a room with three beds, also on the ground floor and out of earshot of the snorer. That made me very happy.

About two and a half weeks after admission, I was moved to the large ward on the second floor. At the time I contracted the disease there must have been a scarlet fever epidemic. Apparently, one child in an orphanage came down with it and the disease spread throughout the orphanage. At least a dozen children from the institution occupied beds in my ward.

At visiting time, visitors were still not allowed into the ward. The large double door leading to the ward was opened but roped off. Visitors had to stay behind the rope. I was lucky, my bed was the first inside the door to the right therefore I could easily converse with my visitors. While on the first floor, I remember that Papa came once or twice with his wife, Aunt Elsbeth. Mama, Father and Mother came every time. Everyone in the family visited several times during my six weeks stay.

Strict bed rest was observed while I still ran a temperature but I had fun. I colored, read and talked to the girls in the beds next to mine. Once my temperature was down to normal, I was allowed to get up in the afternoons but during visiting hours we had to remain in bed. I could now talk and play with the bedridden children in the ward and help feed the very small ones. After our main meal at noon, we napped while the nurses went for their lunch. A maid served us our afternoon corn coffee, made from roasted barley, and a snack at 2 or 2:30 p.m.

One day, I noticed that a little 3-year-old girl, sitting in her bed, amused herself by happily pouring her coffee into her empty potty and back into her cup, not very successfully. I went and stopped her. I began to enjoy being in the company of children all day and I also became quite friendly with the nurses.

Mornings were busy. At wake up time, very early, nurses brought wash basins, towels and soap. Our teeth had to be brushed and temperatures were taken before breakfast was served at 7 or 7:30 a.m. After the beds were made, we were ready for the chief physician who made his rounds accompanied by a retinue of residents, interns, the matron and nurses.

I do not recall taking medication. These were the days before antibiotics. Scarlet fever was a treacherous disease and always had some side effect. Most children developed middle ear infections and a few developed kidney trouble. I was one of the few with heart trouble. This was probably due to the throat abscess I had at age 5. At least, it was attributed to the strength of the serum I was given at that time.

For the first two weeks or so, while on the ground floor, I was on a strict diet. Breakfast consisted of porridge and corn coffee with milk. For second breakfast, I had open rye bread sandwiches, cut into four sections, with farmer's cheese or a boiled, sliced egg. The main meal at noon was also meatless; thick vegetable soup or boiled potatoes and spinach.

Visitors were allowed to bring three pieces of fruit. I invariably received a huge Jaffa orange, a large banana and a large Golden Delicious apple. The diet did not allow cake, candy or chocolates. For supper, I had a choice of sandwiches and mint tea without sugar. It was a low fat, meatless and sugarless diet. Once I was on the second floor and fever free, I was on a regular, but still sugar free, diet. The food was good.

The hospital was staffed by the Evangelical Lutheran Nursing order I mentioned before. The nurses were very efficient. My favorite was Sister Babette, who was cheerful, always smiling and a lot of fun.

Finally, on April 12, I was released. After spending six weeks indoors I looked as white as a sheet and felt weak. As Mama and I walked through the hospital garden to the exit, we met a woman patient who was looking up at the diphtheria pavilion. When she saw us, she said something to Mama. We stopped to talk with her for a minute. She told us that every day she walked over to look at this building because years ago her little girl had died there of the disease. I was sad and never forgot the incident.

At home, I found that neighbors and friends had left bouquets of spring flowers. The living room looked like a veritable flower shop. It was delightful. I had to rest a lot and did not go back to school for another two or three weeks. When I did, I had a great amount of work to catch up on but I managed to do so before the summer holidays. Easter was especially nice this year because I was once again allowed to eat candy and chocolate.

At the time, under the health system in Germany, one had a family physician but when a patient was admitted to the hospital, he or she passed into the care of the hospital's medical staff. After discharge, the patient went back to his or her own physician. I visited my family doctor for a checkup and was told that I was not allowed to participate in any sports or swimming for a year because I had a heart murmur.

During the 1936 Nuremberg Rally, Hitler had spoken at length about Germany's right to colonies. I am sure a directive was issued to schools regarding this subject because in geography, now called earth science, the emphasis was on learning about the former German colonies. We were again told how Germany's colonies were acquired in the face of and despite foreign opposition and intrigue, specifically that of Great Britain. German colonies had been run in an exemplary manner and had greatly improved the natives' standard of living and education. At the same time, the importance of raw materials and Germany's independence from foreign suppliers was stressed. The Fuehrer did not want to depend on the goodwill of other nations for important and vital supplies of raw materials. We were told that German scientists were busy experimenting and discovering new formulas for synthetic rubber and fuel.

Race science was added to our curriculum this term. Although we were shown pictures of various races, we were not shown pictures of Jews in my classroom. Jews, not really a race, were probably in a category by themselves. I do not recall reading anti-Semitic material in my reading books. The different races in Germany–Nordic, Eastern, (West)phalian and Dinaric– were illustrated on a chart, with photos showing typical representatives of each race. Mr. Lambert did not go beyond this. Later, in high school, instruction on this subject was more detailed.

We learned about Teutonic and Germanic tribes. Among other things, we heard about *Thing* (pronounced "ting") plays. Strictly speaking, they were not really plays but a type of choral speaking and choral poetry. Dressed in plain robes, the performers stood around on an open air stage or strode around in a solemn and ritualistic manner. Apparently, a number of open air theaters in various parts of Germany performed *Thing* plays. For example, 10 such plays were performed in Heidelberg. Some were performed at the Dietrich Eckard Buehne on the Olympic stadium compound in Berlin. Aunt Marga was very interested in the theater but I don't think she went to see it. I gathered that the *Thing* was not popular. After a short time, *Thing* plays disappeared from the scene.

We learned a lot about Valhalla and Nordic gods, such as Odin, Thor, Loki and the Valkyries and about the Irish monks who came to Germany as missionaries, chiefly Bonifacius. We learned about Charlemagne, the slaughter of the Saxons, about runes and how the old Germans (Teutons) met under oak trees and held all their ceremonies out-of-doors.

My usual routine of school and homework was overshadowed completely by an event that was much more important and exciting: my father's younger sister, Aunt Gertrud, was getting married on May 15, the day before Pentecost. I, the only niece of the bride, and Ruth, who was my age and the niece of the bridegroom, were to be in the wedding party. I was very excited and filled with eager anticipation.

209

So far, I had never been invited to a wedding. Mama and Kurt were married very quietly in a Registrar's Office and I was only told about it after the fact. Likewise, I heard about Papa's second marriage after it had taken place. I was also very disappointed when I found out after the fact that Papa's older sister, Frieda, had been married.

I loved weddings. On my way to visit Aunt Martha on a Saturday, I often saw a bridal coach waiting at the Genezareth church in the Herrfurth Square. I inevitably stopped, waited to hear the bells ring, and watched the guests and bridal couple enter or leave the church. The men wore tuxedos and top hats. The ladies wore long dresses and carried long stemmed flowers in the crook of their arm. There were no bridesmaids. Occasionally, children attended the bridal couple as flower girls or carried the bride's train.

I always stopped when I came upon a wedding carriage waiting outside an apartment building to see the bride and groom emerge from the building. It was customary for the bridegroom to pick up the bride at her house. The janitor put out a red carpet runner from the door to the carriage.

Now, finally, my dream to be part of a wedding was coming true. Aunt Gertrud's fiancé, Herbert, lived in Goerlitz, an old city in Silesia. He owned and operated an upholstery business.

The majority of weddings took place on a Saturday and it was customary to celebrate *Polterabend*, a party on the eve of the wedding to which all wedding guests were invited. The party took place at Oma and Opa's home. Guests in festive attire gathered for a sit-down dinner. During the course of the evening, neighbors and friends came to smash crockery on the doorstep for good luck. Each time this happened, the bride and groom had to open the door and sweep up the pieces. It was great fun. Aunt Gertrud and Uncle Herbert were kept busy until quite late.

This party was also a kind of shower. Guests brought small gifts and the giver could chose to recite a verse or poem appropriate to the gift. One could buy books with verses fitting all sorts of household articles. More often than not, guests dressed up to match the gift. For example, if the presents were baking or cooking utensils the giver could come as a chef or baker. The bridal wreath and the veil were usually presented by the bride's sister, if she had one.

My family decided that I should recite a poem. I abhorred doing so because I was self-conscious and not accustomed to performing in public but the pressure was on. Didn't the bridegroom have a niece? Surely she would recite and it would be a disgrace if I did not. A little book of poems was purchased, I picked a gift of serving utensils and memorized my little verses.

A few weeks before the exciting event, decisions were made as to what I was to wear for the two occasions. I was to have a new dress for the wedding and was to wear my Easter dress for the *Polterabend*. The Easter dress was a pink silk dress, striped with satin, one inch matte, one inch shiny and it had tiny black dots all over. There were finely pleated ruffles around the hem and neck. It had puffed sleeves and I loved it.

I was thrilled to be at such a big party although most of the people were strangers. I met Uncle Herbert's parents and his niece, Ruth. She was about my height, with dark hair and was pretty. I was nervous about reciting my piece. I got all hot and bothered before I started but I got through it all right. Ruth did not recite anything. I was allowed to stay until 10 p.m. when Father came to pick me up.

A religious wedding ceremony was not legal. Couples were legally married at the Registrar's office and Aunt Gertrud and Uncle Herbert were married there at 11 a.m. The bride wore a

211

suit and a hat and carried red roses. Afterwards, the couple and their witnesses went to a restaurant for a toast.

The church wedding was scheduled to take place at 3 p.m. After lunch, Mama walked me to Oma's apartment. I wore my new dress made of pale pink silk with a pattern of tiny sprays of red and blue rosebuds. Ruth wore a white dress with a floral pattern. Both of us wore wreaths of silk flowers in our hair.

The bride, Oma, Opa and Ruth were in the living room waiting for the bridegroom. When he arrived, Opa gave the bride away and he and Oma left for church. A few minutes later, the bride, groom, Ruth and I followed. A red runner covered the sidewalk and the bridal coach stood at the curb. Neighbors and passersby lined each side of the carpet and clapped as we emerged from the house.

The wedding coach, the traditional conveyance for bridal couples, was upholstered in white satin. The windows were decorated with garlands and a small wreath of myrtle. It was drawn by two white horses. Two coachmen, dressed in long off-white corduroy coats, black boots and top hats with cockades, sat on the coach box. One held the reins and the other jumped off to open and close the doors.

Off we drove to the Martin Luther Church just a few blocks away. The bells were ringing, the sun was shining and the service was long. The bridal couple sat in front of the altar, with wedding guests on either side. Ruth and I had to stand on each side of the couple, facing each other. Friends and neighbors who were not invited guests sat in the pews.

Aunt Marga had guessed my size and bought me a very pretty pair of black suede shoes. They were a size too small and pinched something awful. I shifted from one foot to the other foot. Later, I was severely criticized for not standing still during the hour-long ceremony. Ruth was held up as an example but then her feet were not hurting.

After the ceremony, we returned to the apartment where a banquet table had been set up. We were served dinner, which was interrupted by many toasts to the bride and groom. Papa had prepared and read the traditional "wedding newspaper." A wedding newspaper featured episodes and anecdotes about the bride and groom's lives, humorous references to their meeting, their love and predictions for their future.

Later in the evening after a cold supper, the help removed the tables and cleared the floor for dancing. The music was provided by an accordion player and violinist. Much to my chagrin, I had to leave at 11 p.m. I wanted so much to stay longer because at midnight the bridal veil was "danced away." For this tradition, the bridal couple danced while guests tried to tear off little pieces of the veil to keep as good luck tokens. To me, this was to be the most exciting part of the evening. Alas, Mama was waiting downstairs and Papa took me to meet her. This was the only time I saw Mama and Papa together after the divorce. They did not speak to each other.

With Pentecost past, the long summer holidays seemed to be just around the corner. One company benefit of the Scherl Publishing House where Kurt worked was that children of employees could apply to be sent to one of three children's holiday homes maintained jointly by Scherl, the Post Office and the UFA Film Studios. The homes were located on Norderney, in the Harz Mountains and at the Brenner Pass in the Alps. Applicants were given a medical examination and the examining physician determined where the child was to go. This year, I applied for the first time and the doctor decided that it would be most beneficial for me to spend four weeks on the North Sea island of Norderney. Norderney, one of the Frisian islands, was at that time a very fashionable, expensive seaside resort and spa.

Early on the given day, Father and Mama accompanied me to the Lehrter railroad station. Like all the other children, I was given an identification card to be worn around my neck. Together with my fellow vacationers, I boarded the special coach reserved for us and our escorts. We traveled via Bremen and Emden to Norden where we disembarked and continued by steamer to Norderney.

Norderney is small, only 2 kilometers wide and 13 kilometers long. It is slightly kidney shaped and curls toward the mainland, creating a bay and natural harbor on its western end where the only town is situated. To prevent erosion, a seawall with a promenade along its top extended for several kilometers from the town along the north shore. The rest of the island consisted of dunes and grassy areas that supported a few cows and sheep. All food, as well as consumer goods, were ferried over from the mainland.

During low tide, the water between the mainland and the island practically disappears. One can walk around, collect shrimp, look at what all is creeping and crawling around and enjoy digging bare feet and toes into the wet sand. However, it can be dangerous to walk too far from shore as the incoming tide rushes in suddenly. Many a careless person has drowned there.

The Home was a three building complex, consisting of the two story home, a storage unit and a single three story house. Girls and boys were separated into age groups. We all shared a dining room where we ate at long tables. Each group sat with their own young supervisor, who was in charge at all times and also planned activities. The table for the administrative staff and the director of the home was placed across the top end of the dining room.

I loved this vacation. It was my first visit to the seaside. We rose at 7 a.m., put on our black shorts and white athletic shirts and went outdoors for physical exercise followed by showers and a flag raising ceremony. Next, we trooped into the dining room for breakfast. Most mornings, weather permitting, we went swimming at a designated beach close to town that had lifeguards. People were not allowed to swim anywhere else. Because of my heart condition, I was not permitted to swim. It was hard for me to watch the others. Most afternoons, following our siesta, which lasted until 3 p.m., we played on our private beach. Now and then, we walked into town and bought postcards, stamps, ice cream cones and listened to the band that played in the formal park. On overcast or rainy days, we played games, sang, read or wrote letters indoors.

The warm sunlit days passed quickly. Before leaving for Berlin, we ordered smoked shrimp and smoked flounder and picked them up on the morning of departure. They were still warm and smelled mouth wateringly delicious. Suntanned and refreshed, we were ready to go home.

In July, Pastor Niemoeller, a Lutheran minister, was arrested and jailed on charges of sedition. Father explained to me that Pastor Niemoeller had been critical of the government. This was not the first time I heard Pastor Niemoeller's name mentioned and it was not the last time. Shortly after Pastor Niemoeller's arrest, I read in the paper that more than a hundred people were arrested in Berlin for protesting this action. I believe it was the only time I heard of an antigovernment public demonstration apart from the Munich incident some years before.

Berlin was 700 years old in 1937. Not old by European standards; nevertheless, it was an occasion to be celebrated. A varied and impressive program was to take place from August 14 to August 22. The festivities began with a reception at the Berlin

City Hall, followed on August 15 by a huge parade depicting the historic development of the oldest part of Berlin, as well as the historic development of those Berlin boroughs, which had once been independent communities. The last section of the parade emphasized Berlin's importance as the capital of the Third Reich.

"Berlin through Seven Centuries" was the title of a festival held at the Olympic stadium, which included many musical numbers performed by orchestras and choirs, as well as contributions by school children, the armed forces and party organizations. An exhibition, "700 Years Berlin," at the Kaiserdamm and many additional activities were scheduled to take place at the Funkturn exhibition grounds. Formal, elegant concerts were arranged at different castles in Berlin, like "Music at Castle Lietzenburg 1702." Boroughs arranged their own celebrations. Souvenirs and commemorative items included a specially minted coin and a historic book about the city. I was delighted when Aunt Marga brought the book home for me. Unfortunately, it got lost during the war.

Our school, together with all other Neukoelln schools, attended the program arranged at the Neukoelln Stadium. An SS band played and Hitler Youth marched in bearing flags. A boy's choir sang and high school boys showed their expertise in sports by doing exercises on various equipment, followed by relay races. Girls in dirndl dresses performed folk dances. A soccer game was followed by a men's chorus singing and a speech by Neukoelln Mayor Samson, who also presided over the winner's recognition ceremony. I enjoyed the program but wished that our class could have taken part in the dancing.

This year, the G'sellius Book Sellers, where Aunt Marga worked, celebrated their 200th business anniversary. The firm had remained in the same family since 1737. A week of special events, climaxing in a Gala Dinner for management, staff and guests marked the occasion. G'sellius was the "in" bookseller. The diplomatic corps and the old aristocracy were its regular patrons. After 1933, leading Nazis frequently visited and became regular customers. Aunt Marga usually mentioned when Goebbels, Goering, von Schirach and others had shopped at G'sellius.

The 1937 Nuremberg Party Congress took place from September 6 to September 13. Its theme was "Reich Party Congress of Labor." The attendance of 100,000 participants, with 32,000 flags and banners, and the dome of light made this rally as impressive as the previous ones.

Benito Mussolini, the Duce, was scheduled to pay a state visit to Germany from September 25 to September 29. The Fuehrer was showing off his Reich and numerous special events throughout Germany and Berlin were scheduled for Mussolini's benefit. Berliners were ordered to hang out their flags so thousands of German and Italian flags decorated the city. One particularly large one, measuring 30 yards in length, flew from a 126-foot flagpole in the Adolph Hitler Platz.

After Hitler had come to power, many street and square names were changed to bear his name. In Berlin, the square known as *Reichskanzlerplatz* was renamed Adolf Hitler Platz but today it is called Theodor Heuss Platz. I think it's the only place renamed for Hitler in Berlin. Bremen renamed seven streets and squares, Hamburg five, Munich seven and Stuttgart eight.

After what had turned out to be a triumphal tour, the Duce and the Fuehrer arrived in Berlin by train. They actually traveled in separate trains that traveled side by side until, shortly before reaching Berlin, the Fuehrer's train pulled ahead so the Fuehrer could be on the platform to welcome the Duce when he alighted from his own train.

September 28 was declared a holiday in Berlin. On the following day, September 29, the two leaders first laid wreaths at the War Memorial Unter den Linden before they continued on to Charlottenburg. Here, with their respective entourage, they took their places on the reviewing stand outside the Technical High School to watch a 600,000 strong military parade.

For once, I saw a parade in person. Kurt decided to go and I went along. It was a beautiful warm, sunny day. We found a good spot at the curb diagonally across from the reviewing stand. The march lasted at least four hours. Seemingly never ending ranks of soldiers, bands, tanks, motorcycles, armored cars, motorized units and some cavalry units passed. I liked the horses, the bands and the kettle drums best. The rest was not at all interesting to me. After a while, I was tired of watching unit after unit of serious looking soldiers in their grey-green uniforms marching or sitting stock still in their armored cars and tanks. They all looked alike.

When the parade was over, I stepped into the street to get a clear view of the reviewing stand. Just then, the Fuehrer and Mussolini began to descend the steps from the platform to the street where a convertible waited. They were talking to each other and after they got into the car they were smiling, looking around and acknowledging the cheers with salutes. I was astonished to see how short Mussolini was. Both of them looked exactly like they did in photos and on film except that this was living color. Hitler's hat hid his forehead and overshadowed his eyes, but Mussolini's face was easy to see because his cap left it free. They drove off and the crowd began to disperse. I was pretty tired after standing for hours in the same spot and welcomed the walk to the U-Bahn station.

The whole city was lavishly decorated for this State visit. Many decorations remained in place for some time after the Duce's departure. Berliners flocked by the thousands to see them. The evening of October 6, Papa's birthday, he took me to see Unter den Linden, the Pariser Platz and the Brandenburg Gate. I remember well walking down the median of Unter den Linden, stopping every now and then to turn and take in the view. There were four rows of 33 feet high pylons, each crowned by a golden eagle and flooded in a golden yellow light on one side with red on the other. The new Linden trees, which had replaced the old ones the year before, were still small and completely hidden by the columns. We walked almost the whole length of Unter den Linden looking this way and that to catch the effect. It was very crowded. The fountains at the Pariser Platz just inside the Brandenburg Gate, and the gate itself was floodlit in different colors, as were all other government and historic buildings. Huge banners and flags flew from the Brandenburg Gate. What a sight! I remember it for another reason, too: it was the only time Papa took me somewhere.

The Olympic Stadium was the setting this year and in years to come (until the outbreak of war) for elaborate Summer Solstice celebrations with huge bonfires, flags, singing and choral speaking. It was attended mostly by members of the Nazi youth organizations.

Something was always going on somewhere in Berlin and in Germany that kept the Fuehrer in the public eye. The past July, for instance, the Fuehrer opened the House of German Art in Munich. In the fall, a documentary covering the event and the exhibits was ready to be shown. Our class and many other school children from local schools were taken to see it. It was a color

219

film, something new and unusual as most movies at that time were black and white. I liked this film and I really enjoyed it. I was not entirely ignorant about art. Aunt Marga made sure that I had many books with reproductions of works by famous artists. I was familiar with Botticelli, Titian, Rembrandt, Duerer, Holbein, Frans Hals, Michelangelo, Rafael and other old masters. I knew nothing of modern art or abstract paintings because they had been banned long ago. Although I had often looked at my art books, I was hardly an expert or a judge of art. I liked realistic paintings and loved many that were shown in this film. Some were landscapes and some were portraits. The camera zoomed in on the picture so one could no longer see the frame and to me it seemed that we were looking at a real live landscape. One portrait in particular impressed me. It was the full length figure of a lady wearing a pale blue gown, sitting in a chair. A close-up showed her hand, which rested on the arm of the chair, with its pale skin and the delicate network of veins. It looked absolutely lifelike.

Art for art's sake was not important in Nazi Germany. Art was to be strictly Nordic or modeled after classic Greek and used to portray the people of the "new" Germany. Heroes and a heroic past were idolized. The famous sculptors at this time–Georg Kolbe, Arno Brecker and Joseph Thorak–produced reliefs, busts, colossal sculptures of horses, naked muscular men, groups of men, men and women, and families. These statues, reminiscent of Greek statues, were overwhelming in size, some 50 feet high. Sculptures of women supposedly represented grace and devotion.

We were shown a documentary about Thorak, an Austrian who worked in bronze and marble. Architects Albert Speer and Professor Troost planned to place these statues in public squares outside various new buildings and the Olympic stadium. I found art in the Third Reich somewhat strange, especially the sculptures and murals. They were gigantic, nude and uniform in body and face. I saw them as stern, purposeful, dull, uninspiring and sterile. They had no identity. They seemed overpowering simply by size. Smiles were conspicuous by their absence. Although nude, the figures were not at all sexy. They symbolized the essence of Nazi ideology: duty, heroism, the State, the ideal race, the ideal family and sacrifice. Many paintings and murals were along the same lines but also extolled the virtues of farming, closeness to the soil and the nobility of mostly manual labor.

Another exhibition opened a few blocks from the House of German Art in Munich. It was entitled "Degenerate Art by Artists of the Era of Decay." Articles appeared in the press condemning this style of painting and sculpture along with the artists who had created it. This propaganda backfired because the show attracted more visitors than the new German art exhibit. I saw only a few examples of the degenerate art, which were published in the papers. I did not understand all of them. The Fuehrer, after visiting the exhibit, commented that "patience was henceforth at an end as far as all those who had not fallen into line in the area of fine art were concerned."

The Spanish Civil War had broken out in July 1936. At that time, much of the news about it was overshadowed by the Olympic Games. Once the games were over, the papers reported more fully on the war, particularly that the Fuehrer had sent the Condor Legion to support Generalissimo Franco. A total of 6,000 Germans went to Spain, including air force, communication, transport and tank units.

Our local paper, which always published a novel in installments, now printed one set in Spain. The story was about a young couple who wanted to marry. Political events and the

221

outbreak of the civil war separated them before the wedding. To me, it was so romantic and fascinating and I lapped it up. I could hardly wait to read the next installment when I got home from school. I felt for the unfortunate lovers.

The news about the fighting was anything but romantic. The press stressed and publicized chiefly the atrocities committed by the Communists. I tried not to look at the pictures. It all sounded frightful and made me shudder.

The annual harvest festival took place on the Bueckeberg early in October, as in previous years. It was an impressive production. On the slopes of the Bueckeberg, 1.2 million German peasants wearing their regional costumes assembled. Alone, ahead of his entourage, the Fuehrer strode slowly up a wide aisle to the cheers of the multitude, who also waved and threw flowers. Upon arriving on the top of the mountain, the Fuehrer was presented with and accepted the harvest crown. He was photographed and filmed with many groups of peasants. He especially liked to have his picture taken with mothers and children. After 1937, the government encouraged local harvest celebrations to take the place of the Bueckeberg spectacular.

Girls, ages 17 to 21, who were not already members by virtue of belonging to the BDM, were encouraged to join the Faith and Beauty organization. Among other things, members were taught how to perform rhythmic exercises akin to dancing, sometimes using huge balls and large hoops. They dressed in flowing dresses, shorts and athletic shirts or ancient Greek type garments for their public appearances. Large firms encouraged girls in their employ to join.

At about this time, our school went to the Neukoelln stadium and watched several hundred girls from one of the big shoe manufacturers, Stiller, perform various aerobic type exercises and dances using hoops and large balls. For one number they wore blue dresses, for another they wore multicolored flowing robes. I enjoyed the pretty sight.

I was very happy to find out that our class was scheduled to go on another three day field trip. This time we went to the Spreewald. We stayed at a school hostel again but I cannot remember the first thing about it. I loved the trip because we spent most of our time sightseeing on boats.

The next public event on the Nazi calendar took place on November 9. Led by the Fuehrer, survivors of the attack on Nazis in 1923 marched in a silent, solemn procession to the Feldherrnhalle.

Occasionally, when leafing through the newspaper, a headline would catch my attention and I would read the article. One day, I read that a law had been passed some time ago that affected parents who refused to teach their children Nazi ideology. In November, a Court in Waldenberg ruled in a case to take children from their parents. The parents were members of a Christian Sect, International Bible Researchers. They were pacifists and were accused of creating an environment where children would grow up as enemies of the State. The children were taken into State custody because the parents had refused to teach them Nazi ideology. The Judge said: "The law as a racial and national instrument entrusts German parents with the education of their children only under the condition that they educate them in the fashion acceptable to the nation and the Nazi State."

During the winter months, the tennis courts at Neukoelln's border of the Tempelhof Field, and others in the city, were covered with water creating skating rinks open to the public every afternoon and evening. The entrance fee was 10 pfennig. Recorded music was relayed over a loudspeaker and overhead electric lights provided illumination after dusk. There was a little wooden hut that was divided into two parts. One part was a bare room with benches around the walls and a big potbelly stove. It served as a place where everyone went periodically to get warm. The other room offered refreshments such as hot chocolate, hot cider, hot dogs, candy and doughnuts.

I had learned to skate using Mama's old skates. I wore my lace up winter boots, carried the skates and, when I got to the rink, I sat on a bench and attached the skates to my boots, tightening them with a key. The first time was terrible. I thought I would never be able to keep my balance and clung to Mama until she gave me some good tips on how to stay on my feet and glide.

As Christmas approached, I visited Aunt Martha for fittings. As usual, she was working on a new Sunday dress and a new coat for me as Christmas gifts. This year, she made an additional present for me, a beautiful black wool skating outfit trimmed with grey fake Persian lamb and lined with multicolor patterned heavy silk. Aunt Martha completed the outfit by creating a cute matching hat and a muff.

On December 21, I celebrated my 12th birthday. I did not have a party but I was allowed to invite a friend. We had cake and cocoa, and, when Kurt came home, we played board games. The little Riemann's present was a small wooden sewing stand with a pin cushion, needles, yarn, a thimble and a small pair of scissors. The cute stand was painted pale green and decorated with little flowers. She had attached a note that said, "Now that you are 12, you are old enough to take some of the little chores off Mother's shoulders, like sewing on buttons, for instance." I was not thrilled. I hated sewing on buttons and dusting, the only things I was allowed to do around the house. I would much rather have cleaned windows and mirrors and ironed.

Besides my beautiful skating costume, I was delighted to find a pair of real skating boots under the Christmas tree. I was thrilled and went skating as often as possible. I became more ambitious with my new skates. I tried figure skating. I practiced left and right turns, skating forward and backward, spinning and skating with one leg extended back and up. I could do great figure eights. I loved it and was happy when one of the adult skaters took the trouble to help me and correct my efforts.

Unfortunately, my skating career ended too soon. We had a very early spring and the ice melted. The rinks closed and I never went skating again. I remember hurrying to the tennis court one afternoon in late February hoping against hope that it would still be open but it was closed. I stood for a while gazing woefully through the wire fence at the pools of water that had formed on the melting ice. At the time, I knew of only one artificial ice rink in Berlin. It was quite a distance from where I lived, in the Friedrichshain. I did not have anyone to go with and, although Mama encouraged me, I was too shy to venture there alone.

1938

February	Schuschnigg meets Hitler and agrees to amnesty for Austrian Nazis. Goering is made a field marshal. Hitler seizes control of the army and is now Supreme Commander of the Armed Forces.
February 20	Hitler demands self-determination for Germans in Austria and Czechoslovakia.
March	Hitler masses troops at Austrian border. Schuschnigg resigns and Nazi Seyss Inquart takes over.
March 11-12	Austria is annexed and German troops march in.
April 2	London recognizes German seizure of Austria.
April 6	U.S.A. recognizes German seizure of Austria.
April 24	Sudeten Chief Heinlein demands concessions for Germans in Czechoslovakia.
May	Hitler visits Italy. Crisis in Czechoslovakia results in Czech troops on German/Czech border.
September	Sudeten Germans hold mass demonstrations for union with Reich.

September 15	Chamberlain and Daladier in Munich to meet with Hitler.
September 16	It is reported that 23,000 Sudeten Germans have fled to Germany.
September 26	France and Britain give in to Hitler and ask Czechoslovakia to surrender German areas to Hitler.
September 29-30	Chamberlain comes again to Munich and agrees not to stop Germans from occupying the Sudetenland if Hitler promises to stop aggression in Europe. France and Britain sign agreement in Munich, allowing Hitler to take the Sudetenland.
October 1	German troops move into the Sudetenland. Hitler demands return of all lost German colonies.
November	German Embassy Aide in Paris, Ernst vom Rath, is shot by Grynspan. American Ambassador recalled from Berlin. German Ambassador recalled from Washington.
November 9	Kristallnacht. A night of organized Nazi rioting resulting in the breaking of Jewish store windows and the burning of synagogues.
December 21	The author's 13th birthday.

In his annual January speech, the Fuehrer again expounded at length on the importance of the Four Year Plan and its execution. In school and in the press, it was constantly emphasized that Germany must stand on her own feet and must not depend on imports of raw material and other goods from foreign nations.

We were urged to collect scrap metal, paper, bones, rags and leftover food. Every household received a cute pink cardboard pig imprinted with a list of what pigs eat, as well as a list of what they cannot and do not eat. We affixed it to our pantry door and I remember it well.

At the same time, a container was placed in each yard to receive every tenant's kitchen refuse, which was collected daily and used to feed pigs in order to increase Germany's meat production. Posters appeared on advertising columns and in food stores in the form of a piglet saying: "Combat spoilage." Bones, collected by Hitler Youth and at school, were ground into bonemeal and used to manufacture glue. I made sure to save the bones from our roasts, cutlets and chickens so I could take them to school for the collections. It was advisable to contribute regularly and avoid attracting the wrong kind of attention.

Housewives were encouraged to use their own shopping bags and nets to cut down on the use of paper bags and wrapping paper.

Newspapers provided instructions for saving empty tubes and cans in accordance with the Four Year Plan's demands for economy. Mustard, mayonnaise, tomato paste, anchovy paste, toothpaste and many ointments came in tubes. "Attention! Please do not throw away empty tubes. They are made of materials we urgently need and, in part, must import from abroad. Save empty tubes. You will help save foreign currency!" This also applied to keys for opening cans. Since iron and steel were rationed, our cans of sardines and other fish no longer came with keys. Instead, the shopkeeper supplied one key for every two tins. "Every key can be used several times and the savings will be even greater if everyone uses their own can opener instead of a key," we were admonished.

During the course of 1937 and continuing on into 1938, we were bombarded with speeches, newspaper articles and all sorts of propaganda about Austria which claimed and emphasized how much the Austrians longed to return "home" to become part of the German Reich. It was stressed again and again that the Germans in Austria and in Czechoslovakia must be allowed to determine their destinies but were prevented from doing so by their governments. We heard that Nazis in Austria and Czechoslovakia suffered persecution, were arrested and languished in prisons. The Fuehrer and leading Nazis ranted and raved on this subject. The Fuehrer demanded self-determination for the Germans in Austria and Czechoslovakia in his many speeches.

Every day in every newscast and in every paper the names of Schuschnigg, the Austrian Chancellor from 1934 to 1938, and Seyss-Inquart, the Austrian Nazi leader, surfaced. These names became household words. Schuschnigg and his actions were portrayed as evil in the news. Every day brought additional reports and horror stories about him. In February, Schuschnigg met the Fuehrer in Germany. Under pressure, Schuschnigg agreed to grant amnesty to Austrian Nazis.

The Fuehrer spoke on February 20. In his speech he again demanded self-determination for the Germans in Austria and Czechoslovakia. Once more Europe faced a crisis and, as a result, tensions grew.

A new slogan surfaced: "One Volk! One Reich! One Fuehrer!" Posters depicting the Fuehrer and the slogan were used in extensive propaganda campaigns for a "Greater Germany," a Germany that would include all German speaking peoples in one state.

I was very much aware of the tension but I was not worried. Although there was talk of war it seemed to me to be a complete improbability. Why should we have a war and with whom? The Austrians? Ridiculous. Or the Czechs? Impossible. I read and heard about British and French concern over the situation. I saw photos and newsreels documenting Chamberlain's visits to the Fuehrer. People were tense and worried. There were reports about riots in Vienna, fighting and shooting with communists, looting, chaos and unrest. The Fuehrer had provoked the crisis. People feared the reaction of England and France. I heard Father, friends and acquaintances discuss and speculate on it. Father expressed his concern but I was not bothered by the situation. I felt quite carefree.

At school, I learned a poem by Ernst Moritz Arndt, "What is the German's Fatherland? The entire Germany." The poem was actually written in the middle of the 19th century when Germany, as a nation, did not exist. It consisted of numerous individually ruled principalities and kingdoms. A patriotic movement was trying to unite these fractions into a united nation: Germany. I do recall that we did not cover that particular period in history in detail, at least not this particular struggle. We learned more about the struggle against Napoleon. As a result, I thought of the poem simply as a patriotic poem. As in many other instances, the subtle or maybe not so subtle propaganda intent escaped me. I was inclined to take things at face value.

We discussed Austria in our geography lessons, which included the physical geography as well as the economy. I gathered that post-WWI Austria had not been a prosperous nation and never recovered from the loss of her Imperial territories. Its economic situation at the moment was far from rosy. I heard about this not only in school but overheard friends and neighbors mentioning the fact that Austria was in poor shape. People said that the Austrians believed their lot would improve greatly once they were part of Germany and its strong economy. The general opinion was that, of course, the Austrians were not as disciplined, precise and industrious as the Germans. There was what was called the "Austrian *Schlendrian,*" the more relaxed, laid-back attitude to life. But everyone agreed that the Austrians, especially the Viennese, had undeniable charm and their accent was delightful. I could testify to the latter because Aunt Martha's neighbor was Viennese.

On March 12, the Fuehrer and German troops marched into Austria to the jubilant cheers of the Austrian population who turned out en masse to welcome their Fuehrer. The caption under a newspaper photo read: "Austria, Heldenplatz in Vienna. Amid thunderous jubilation, Adolf Hitler's homeland comes home."

Newsreels showed the Austrians dressed in their best regional costumes, shouting, "Heil! Heil." They threw flowers and wildly waved Swastika flags in a completely spontaneous welcome for their Fuehrer. There was nothing forced about it. All the church bells were ringing. Austrians were deliriously happy and proud to be part of what was now to be known as Greater Germany, except for a few anti-Nazis and Jews who feared the Nazis. Their premonitions were soon confirmed when thousands were arrested and Goering cautioned the Jews to leave Austria. Austria was henceforth known at the "Ostmark."

Any remaining fears of a war subsided completely when the British government recognized the German seizure of Austria on April 2. This was followed by the U.S. government's recognition on April 6. Internal and international tensions regarding the annexation of Austria dissolved. Everyone breathed a sigh of relief and relaxed.

Early in May, attention focused on the zeppelin "Hindenburg" when it departed once again on its transatlantic crossing. I had seen this dirigible on any number of occasions cruising majestically over Berlin. The long, slim, cigar shaped, silver zeppelin, gleaming in the sunshine, was such an unusual sight that people in the street excitedly pointed it out to each other and kids yelled, "The zeppelin! Look at the zeppelin."

Therefore, news of the tragedy at Lakehurst when the airship burst into flames and burned shocked not only Germany but the world. Everyone who could do so, including myself, was glued to the radio listening to news from New Jersey. Commentators, one of them in tears, explained what had happened in detail and brought us up-to-date on what was taking place. I shuddered when they described the dreadful, excruciatingly painful burns suffered by the crew and the passengers. Of the 97 people aboard, 33 perished. At first, radio reports stated that there was hope for the badly injured Captain Lehman. Unfortunately, he died on Friday night, May 7. I was quite upset and very sad. The zeppelin had been an object of pride and the world's first transatlantic passenger airliner.

The tragedy remained a topic of conversation for a long time as reports continued to come in about investigations into the causes of the crash. Newspapers were snatched up fast as they hit the street. Pictures were far more eloquent than words. Our nation mourned.

Nevertheless, life and politics went on. The cheers in Austria had hardly died down when propaganda about the ethnic Germans, primarily the Sudeten Germans, in Czechoslovakia began dominating the headlines. The Sudeten Germans voiced their demands for concessions through their spokesman and

233

leader, Heinlein. Daily papers were filled with reports about fights, persecution, anti-German demonstrations, suppression and atrocities committed. When the Fuehrer paid a state visit to Italy in May, the reports and newsreels covering his visit provided a welcome relief from the constant hammering away about the Sudetenland. It was reported that Czech troops were massed at the German border and that Czech men aged 16 to 60 were required to report for defense work.

Hermann and Emmy Goering's daughter was born on June 2. She was named Edda after Mussolini's daughter and in time was christened in Karinhall with proper pomp and circumstance. The Fuehrer attended and many pictures appeared in the papers and illustrated magazines.

Goebbels and his wife, Magda, had five children. They were occasionally seen in photos with their mother. I don't recall seeing any with their father. They often visited the Fuehrer at the Obersalzberg where they posed with him or where the photographers took snapshots. One little girl, Helga, was the Fuehrer's favorite. Magda Goebbels was an attractive woman. Personally, I could never understand any woman actually marrying somebody like Goebbels because he was short, skinny and ugly.

The Fuehrer loved to be seen and photographed with children and German shepherd dogs. Many of the photos were taken at his house and estate in Berchtesgaden on the occasion of his birthday. Never ever was there a hint of a woman in the Fuehrer's life. He was always alone. I did not hear about Eva Braun until late in 1945 after it was all over. I was flabbergasted and I was not the only one. This goes to show how well secrets could be kept in the Third Reich.

I don't recall what type of personal identification cards, if any, people carried in Germany before 1938 but it was decreed on July 22, that every person over the age of 14 was to carry photo identification at all times.

Some time during the school year, I do not remember whether it was before our long summer vacation or after, Mr. Lambert announced that each of us must ask our parents for a written declaration, called a Certificate of Descent, stating that we and our parents were of Aryan descent. Father wrote a note for me and Papa wrote the other. That took care of it for me. One girl in my class ran into a little problem. Her name could have been Jewish and she had dark brown hair and dark brown eyes. She was asked to bring additional proof that nobody in her family was Jewish.

The Certificate of Descent had to be accompanied by supporting evidence, such as birth, baptismal and marriage certificates. A person was considered an Aryan if he or she had four non-Jewish grandparents. A person was "mixed" if he or she had one or two Jewish grandparents or a person was non-Aryan if he or she had three or four Jewish grandparents.

Since the Nuremberg racial laws had been passed, we were encouraged to research and keep a record of our ancestors in an booklet called "Forebear's passport," sold at stationery stores for 60 pfennig. I did not buy one.

When school let out for our summer vacation, I went for five weeks to the Harz Mountains, again through the auspices of the Scherl Publishing House. It was quite exciting because the children's home was an authentic old castle, Schloss Stiege. It was great. The boys even had a Knights' Hall. Schloss Stiege stood on a hill surrounded by beautiful trees and meadows where we played and picked flowers. We hiked through the mountains and walked in the lovely forests where murmuring brooks tumbled over mossy rocks. We collected pebbles in shades of turquoise, green and pink.

We took a day trip to the Witches' Dance Plateau. Legend has it that once a year on *Walpurgisnacht*, the night before May 1, witches and warlocks gather here for a great ball. Once even the devil came but for some reason he had to flee. He was cornered and spurred his horse to make such a mighty leap from one cliff across a deep cleft to the other side that the imprint of its hooves can still be seen in the rock today. Local souvenirs offered were small witches riding on brooms.

The Harz Mountains were also famous for their beautiful singing canaries (bred, not wild) called "Harzer Rollers" for the way they trilled.

The food at Schloss Stiege was much better than in Norderney. One first for me and others was that for supper we repeatedly had fresh red currants or blueberries with goat's milk. It tasted much stronger and seemed richer than cow's milk. I did not acquire a taste for it.

One night, a severe thunderstorm became almost stationary over our castle. It was the longest thunderstorm I had ever experienced, lasting from 7 p.m. through the night until 7 a.m. The castle had a lightning rod and lightning hit it many times during the course of the storm. I saw sparks coming from our light switch and in the morning we were amazed to see a black zigzag on the enamel behind a water spout.

We spent a lot of time playing in the meadows, which were fragrant with flowers. A huge old oak tree provided shade and was a favorite gathering place in the evenings when boys and girls sat under its branches and sang to the accompaniment of guitars played by our supervisors.

At Schloss Stiege, we followed more or less the same routine as in Norderney: physical exercise, flag raising, breakfast, writing letters, marching into town singing, shopping for postcards, stamps and souvenirs, hiking, playing and the evening flag lowering.

When rain kept us indoors, we played games and charades in a large lounge. Our group's supervisor also read short stories to us on these occasions. I recall one of the stories clearly. It was called "The Coffin Procession." I had to stay and listen when all the while I wanted to leave. This story described the annual pilgrimage of villagers to a shrine in a distant town. Apparently, every year a person had died during the pilgrimage so people began to carry an empty coffin along.

One time they walked to their destination and fulfilled their religious obligations. Nothing untoward happened. Nobody died. A spirit of rejoicing spread through the throng. While they walked home, they happily burst into a song of thanksgiving. Much to their distress, a messenger caught up with them to say that one member of the group was no longer with them. At a local hostelry, he had made a bet that he could eat a dozen or more hard-boiled eggs, proceeded to do so and died a short time later as a result. Instantly, the mood changed to one of sorrow. I cannot remember additional details but I did not like the story. Anything to do with death and coffins made me feel very uncomfortable and I hated stories or movies that did not have a happy ending.

All too soon, the five vacation weeks were over and we boarded the tiny local railroad train which connected with the main line. I stood by the open window gazing sadly at the lovely landscape I had to leave behind. Berlin seemed dusty, noisy, hot, uncomfortable, crowded and oppressive in comparison. It took me a week to adjust to city life.

Once again, I became aware of the Sudetenland situation which I had happily forgotten while I was in the Harz Mountains. Now, however, things heated up considerably and developed into a serious crisis. Ethnic Germans held demonstrations, shouting their desire to return home into the Reich.

The Fuehrer demanded that the Sudetenland become part of Greater Germany. Czech and German troops massed at the German/Czech border, while Sudeten Germans fled from persecution. Every day, radio broadcasts and newspapers were filled with detailed reports of the sufferings of the Germans in Czechoslovakia. Tensions increased. Chamberlain and Daladier flew to Munich to meet with Hitler in Berchtesgaden.

In contrast to the Austrian crisis, this one made me nervous. The general mood was somber. Being naive, I kept thinking, "Why, after generations of living under Czech law, are these Sudeten Germans suddenly demonstrating? How is it that, suddenly, they are being persecuted and want to be part of Germany?" Later, of course, I found out that a lot this agitation and many of the incidents were actually staged by the Nazis.

It went on and on. We learned how Germans, who lived there, hated being under Czech rule, how industrious they were, how the Czechs envied them their achievements, how "slovenly" the Czechs and Slovaks were. After all, they were of the Slavic race and everybody knew about the "slovenly" Slavic and so it went on, day after day.

While the media reported on the situation, many reports were brought up in current affairs at school. For instance, there were reports that ethnic German women and children in the Sudetenland were mowed down by machine guns. It was reported that the Fuehrer was massing German troops on the border and that the Czechs were mobilized. It was all very disturbing and I felt quite nervous as to the immediate future.

While this crisis built, the Reich Party Congress took place in Nuremberg from September 5 to September 12 under the motto "Greater Germany."

On September 22, the Fuehrer met with Mr. Chamberlain, the British Prime Minister. Apparently, the talks lasted for hours. More talks were scheduled for the following day and it sounded quite hopeful. However, on September 24, the Fuehrer issued an ultimatum to Czechoslovakia. The Czechs were to hand over the Sudetenland by or before October 1. The ultimatum was to be formally transmitted to the Czech government by Mr. Chamberlain. This was the outcome of the talks that had taken place. Official German government statements stressed that the Fuehrer and Mr. Chamberlain were working day and night for peace. Then the Fuehrer spoke at the Sportpalast on September 26, demanding that the Sudetenland become part of Greater Germany. He shouted and shrieked in his usual way that he would have the Sudetenland on October 1. If Benes, the Czech President, did not hand it over, he would go to war on Saturday! The crowd applauded less than usual. I did not notice any "war fever," only apprehension coupled with the fervent hope that war could be avoided. The crisis was very real and very serious. I became more concerned and nervous. This was not like the Austrian crisis. Of course, I did not spend all my time worrying. I went out to play after school and forgot all about it. But every day I heard conversations, at school as well as at home, which reminded me of the explosive situation.

Hitler said that the Sudetenland was absolutely his last territorial demand in Europe. Absolutely. I don't know if anybody believed him because there were still other areas he might claim. There was the Memel district in East Prussia, Danzig, the Corridor and Upper Silesia with its rich coal mines, which were areas ceded to Poland after WWI by the Versailles Treaty.

With regards to Czechoslovakia, the Fuehrer assured Chamberlain that "the Czechs have reconciled themselves with their other minorities. The Czech State no longer interests me. If you so desire, I will give you another guarantee: We do not want any Czechs." The Fuehrer placed the blame for this crisis squarely on Benes and held him responsible for war or peace.

Czech and German troops continued to mass at the border. The Fuehrer invited Mussolini, Chamberlain and Daladier to meet again in Munich on September 28.

On September 30, it was all over. At 12:30 a.m. Hitler, Mussolini, Chamberlain and Daladier signed a pact turning the Sudetenland over to Germany. Czechoslovakia was not consulted. Czechoslovakia was simply told it had to accept. The Czech prime minister also signed a pact ceding the Sudetenland to Germany.

We watched the newsreels showing Hitler, Chamberlain and Daladier on the terrace of Hitler's house in Berchtesgaden. We also saw the departure of Chamberlain and his famous arrival in London, waving the paper, saying "Peace in our time. Peace with honor."

Everyone breathed a sigh of relief. The crisis was over, so it seemed. War had once again been averted.

I felt a great sense of relief, as did my family and, for that matter, the majority of people. Although the Fuehrer had once again succeeded in getting his way, I saw no sign of public celebration or jubilation. The newspapers lauded the Fuehrer's actions but, for my family and myself, life continued in its usual way. The Fuehrer ordered his troops to march into the Sudetenland on October 1. The occupation was completed by October 10. The Fuehrer followed his troops almost immediately and was greeted with much flag waving, flower throwing and crowds cheering. It was a victory procession.

Hitler had declared that this was to be his last territorial claim in Europe. But now the Fuehrer demanded the return of all former German colonies. In geography, we dwelt at length on our ex-colonies in Africa. We learned how badly the British had treated their colonial subjects, especially the Boers in South Africa. Some considerable time was spent on the Boer War and how the British had starved Boer women and children who were interned under inhuman conditions in camps.

At this time, for some reason, Berlin experienced a butter shortage. Shops were instructed to sell only an eighth or a quarter pound of butter per family at a time.

Naturally, just because there was a shortage, people came out in force to buy butter. Long lines formed at the groceries. Everyone went to their regular store first and then to other stores where no one knew them in order to get more than the allotted amount of butter.

Now this happened at the time when my mind was set on getting a recorder. I had been pestering to get this instrument. When I came home with my eighth of a pound of butter, Mother told me that Father had bought the recorder for me. I was ecstatic. "Where is it?" I wanted to know. She told me that Father was still standing in line for butter. Mother had sent him to her regular store with the thought that the grocer would not know Father since he seldom accompanied her. I was far too impatient to wait until he got home.

Mother remonstrated with me that if I went to the store I "would blow his cover" because the store owners knew me and knew that Mother and I had been there a short while before to purchase butter. I remember vividly how excited and impatient I was. I remember well how I rushed up to him, snatched the bag

241

containing the flute almost in passing and ran home. Later I worried but he was able to purchase the butter without any problems.

Conscription Rules came into effect late in June. Conscription Rules were a type of draft whereby both blue and white collar workers could be drafted away from their regular jobs and made to work at particularly important jobs, that is, particularly important to the state. When first instituted, the draft was for a limited period only; later on, it became permanent in nature. In January 1943, this draft was extended to women between the ages of 17 and 45 for national defense reasons. I repeatedly heard it mentioned in conversations that so and so had been conscripted to such and such a firm or job.

Work on the Westwall, the large fortification along the French-German border, began in May. The Westwall was 400 miles long and had 14,000 bunkers. Later the Allies called it the "Siegfried Line." This enormous enterprise required a large work force of approximately 100,000 men. In order to meet this demand, the Employment Offices were empowered, as of June 22, to draft workers from their regular jobs. In all, close to half a million workers were drafted for a period of several months to build the Westwall. The draft began almost immediately. Mama heard about it when Kurt came home from work saying that people from Scherl would also be affected. Many men quickly signed up for their vacation to avoid it. Mama kept telling Kurt, "Put your name down for vacation right away, don't wait. Take your vacation. Don't you see that everyone else is doing it? The wise guys are trying to beat going to the Westwall. If you don't take your vacation, you will be caught."

Kurt, however, hesitated and was drafted. He had to report with many others and was shipped to the Palatine to work on the

Westwall. I cannot remember the place he was sent but he was away from August 18 to December 3.

Kurt was unhappy and hated being away from home. Workers were billeted in private homes and most of the local host families were not too happy at having to accept guest workers. The population in that part of Germany is predominantly Roman Catholic. Berliners and people from northern Germany are predominately Protestant. Kurt wrote that his host family was very devout. Every night the family congregated in the living room and recited the rosary and many Hail Mary's. Kurt took refuge in the kitchen behind his newspaper. He felt like an intruder.

The Westwall was finished in 1939 shortly before the outbreak of war.

In November, large headlines reported the murder of a German Embassy official in Paris. Ernst vom Rath was shot by a Jew. Dramatic news reports and newsreels covered the affair and the propaganda machine was running at full speed. The murder, an international incident, was a serious matter. The American Ambassador was recalled from Berlin and the German Ambassador was recalled from Washington.

Ernst vom Rath's murderer was Hershel Grynszpan, a student, who was born in Hannover on March 28, 1921. His family had fled from persecution in Poland in 1911. Hershel was visiting relatives in Paris when he received the news that his parents, together with other former Polish Jews, were deported from Germany to Poland. He was outraged and in retaliation he planned to murder the German Ambassador to France. However, on November 7, he shot Ernst vom Rath instead. Furor against the Jews was fanned more than ever. At the time, I had no idea that Jews were being deported to Poland.

The Nazis used the assassination to pass a decree on November 12 prohibiting Jews from attending theaters, cinemas, concerts and public exhibitions. Jewish children were forbidden to attend public schools. I did not know there were schools for Jewish children in Berlin and I didn't hear about the decree.

A few days after the murder and the decree, we awoke to hear that during the night Jewish businesses throughout the city, and all of Germany, had their windows smashed. Synagogues in Berlin were burning. Jewish people were attacked and beaten by members of the SA dressed in civilian clothes. The papers and newscasts proclaimed that it was the "spontaneous reaction of the population to the murder of Ernst vom Rath." This night became known as *Kristallnacht.*

Father said right away that these incidents were not spontaneous but organized and deliberate. Not at that time nor at any other time did I myself encounter ordinary people in a state of excitement or rage. Thousands of people would have had to be very passionate and angry enough to take to the streets and vent these feelings in order for such attacks to occur spontaneously.

Like everyone in my circle, I was sad that this young diplomat lost his life. However, it would never have occurred to me to go out in the middle of the night and throw bricks, if I knew where to find one, at shop windows and go on a rampage. First of all, I was brought up to be very law abiding. The aforementioned actions would for this reason be unthinkable. Secondly, I did not fly into an uncontrollable rage over this crime, in spite of sympathy for the victim, that would make me forget my upbringing and the consequences of criminal actions for an ordinary person like me.

Father, a very circumspect person, although at all times interested in what happened in Berlin, never went anywhere near demonstrations and such. We, therefore, did not join the sightseers who walked around to look at the damage.

However, on my way to Oma's on my regular visiting day, I saw a broken and boarded up shop window in the Berliner Strasse obviously damaged during the anti-Jewish demonstrations. Apart from this, I only remember seeing newspaper photos of burning synagogues and other shops that had been damaged. Many of the photos showed SA men at the scenes of the attacks. I saw no photos of people being beaten. These incidents were reported only by word of mouth. I did not like what I saw and heard. It was frightening and I felt shudders, like "somebody walking over my grave." Mama was quite outspoken as usual and condemned the Nazi action in no uncertain terms.

As I grew older, I gradually became more aware of how the state intruded and interfered in everyone's life. Everything seemed dead earnest. It was all duty, sacrifice and courage. Where was the fun, laughter, spontaneity, individuality and romance? It all seemed to have disappeared like the sun behind dark clouds.

Even women's clothing was supposed to become drab. The Nazi fashion favored a uniformly cut, calf length dress, with a well-defined waistline. Shoes were thick soled with wedge heels. These clothes were to undercut class distinctions. Frivolous and exclusive clothes were frowned upon. Women did not wear pants in those days. The only time pants and shorts were worn was on vacation, at the beach or while engaged in sports or physical exercise activity.

The Nazis also discouraged makeup. Makeup and lipstick were labeled "unnatural" and "decadent war paint." The ideal German woman in the Third Reich, whose purpose in life was to be the mother of many healthy children and a comrade, would

245

have no use for makeup since it was not in line with party policy. "The German woman does not paint her face." There was so much propaganda about it, that if a woman went out obviously wearing lipstick, rouge and mascara, children taunted her by shouting, "Paint box, paint box." It happened to me a few years later. Girls were supposed to let their hair grow, wear it in pigtails or plaited into a crown, later on in a bun or short and straight. Deodorants and other products which helped to eliminate unpleasant body odors continued to be used.

Only a few hard core Nazi women followed the regime's formula. The majority of women in Berlin, young girls in particular, were fashion conscious. Trends and colors continued to change each season as before. One year the "in" fashion was summer dresses with multi colored skirts and navy or black tops trimmed with the skirt material, and light beige colored summer coats. Hats continued to be worn, too. Still, women generally wore no or very little make up and those who did, used it discreetly.

I loved to study fashion magazines and was looking forward impatiently to the time when I would be allowed to wear high heels. Mama, my aunts and I liked to express our individuality by choosing different fashions and colors.

The Nazi movement and regime were strictly masculine and male dominated. It was, in one word, chauvinistic. Women definitely took a back seat. Men did not cook, clean, go shopping, push prams or diaper babies.

In order to further solve the problem of an acute female labor shortage in rural areas and households, and to attain the goals set for the Four Year Plan, the government instituted the Duty Year. Serving the Duty Year was compulsory for girls under the age of 25. Females working on farms or as domestics were exempt. The Duty Year was another device to control and regulate the labor market. Completion of the Duty Year was noted in the employment book and was a prerequisite for obtaining a job. Mama's reaction to the Duty Year was that it forcibly reduced young girls to unpaid servants. She and I agreed there and then that we would do everything we could to see that I could avoid it, although we had no idea how we were going to accomplish this feat.

The Labor Service was another matter. The motto of the women's Labor Service was: "The girl must be capable of being a rank and file soldier."

Camps, so it was stated in a directive, were to be rather primitive with straw mattresses and simple bathroom facilities. Girls must get used to do without beauty and personal hygiene aids in order to toughen them up. The camps served to educate girls in self discipline, sobriety, obedience, endurance and stringency against self.

All this I gathered from what I heard and read. It did not appeal to me. I hated the thought of having to live in such a society, of having no privacy, of having everything planned, prescribed and supervised.

Each time I heard an announcement of yet another compulsory duty being added to the ones already in existence, I felt as though another link was added to a chain, a chain that choked personal freedom.

On my visits to Balz, I saw Labor Service maidens, as they were called, who worked on farms. I saw their camp and their leaders. It was enough to make me feel uptight. The camp was very simple, although not primitive. I simply could not imagine myself as part of this service. Everything in me rebelled against it. I am sure a lot of girls probably enjoyed it. The novelty, the comradery, appealed to some but not to me. I am also sure that not all leaders were fanatic Nazis but were decent and treated the girls under their "command" fairly. Unfortunately, I do not have more first hand knowledge about the Labor Service. I did not get a chance to talk to any of the maidens.

I have mentioned Faith and Beauty was an offshoot of the League of German Girls. Its main purpose was to prepare girls for their future role of housewife and mother. They also were taught personal hygiene, housekeeping and home decorating. I was not aware of this aspect of the organization. Most of what I saw and heard about Faith and Beauty girls was that they did aerobic dancing and gymnastics with large balls and hoops or skipping ropes. Following membership in the BDM and Faith and Beauty, young women automatically passed into the National Socialist Women's League.

Women were to break with tradition and customs and get married in a Nazi ceremony rather than in church. It was their duty to produce children and the more the better, that is, if they were intelligent and healthy. A woman who was "blessed" with many children was entitled to have a Duty Year girl to do the chores.

Throughout the years, posters extolled the family, primarily one blessed with many children, showing stereotypes of blond, Nordic looking couples and their offspring.

In all the talk about marriage, children and family, personal relationships, apart from being comrades, were not mentioned. I noticed the word "love" was not mentioned. It was all the State, the German People, the Volk community. There was no room for individualism, originality, creativity or for development of individual traits and personality. People were to be small impersonal cogs in the impersonal political state machinery. Achievement for personal reasons and gain was out and subjectivity to the whole was in.

To me this "recipe" for life was most depressing. The people, even on the posters, were not smiling but looked stern. Time was organized to suppress individuality. The more I thought about it, I felt as if a big stone lay on my chest making it hard to breathe. Of course, I did not go around thinking about it all the time but when I did, I did not like it, not at all. Each person's whole life was to be centered around the State with no room left for oneself. Everything one did and thought was for the State or the State's and the people's welfare. The man one married was to be chosen for his racial qualities, his involvement with the Nazi system and his outstanding health. Preferably he was to be a party member, in the military, the SA or SS. It all seemed so predetermined by the State.

I was vividly reminded of Dr. Ley's statement: "Only sleep is a private affair. We no longer have private people. The time when everyone could do as he pleased is over!" No wonder I retreated into the world of fiction and fantasy and gobbled up romance novels, stories about travel, faraway exotic places, anything that was the opposite of reality. Anything to escape. I read my mother's old books, novels about aristocrats and romance, of poor girls and poor young men making good, of good being rewarded, of evil being punished. I loved movies with happy endings, musicals and operettas with lilting tunes. Secretly, I longed for something really exciting to happen in my life.

As I grew older, I became increasingly apprehensive. I became more aware of the dangers around me. I was warned all the time over the years to keep quiet, not to express an opinion on anything other than harmless things. I was warned to watch what I talked about in public places and to watch what I said and to whom. I was warned never to talk to strangers. In public, the

249

weather, clothes or personal gossip were safe topics. I learned to stick to them.

Winter came. Christmas carols and plays were banned from schools but we continued to bring our candles and pine branches for Advent and sang a carol as before. Yuletide celebrations were advocated. Perhaps people in rural areas were more inclined to stage them but in Berlin people did not give them a second thought. Christmas remained Christmas as of old.

On December 21, I celebrated my 13th birthday.

Germany before 1945

Berlin

Mama, Gisela, Papa
1926

Skat Club
1930

Karstadt

Gisela saw Adolf Hitler while standing at lower left
streetcorner, near the Karstadt department store.

Gita Alpa

Gisela in 1931.

Gisela at the park in 1932.

Jonathan would race ahead and take photos
as we took our afternoon walk.

Snapshot taken by Jonathan while
on vacation in Neuruppin.

Gisela's class photo from 1934.
She is second from left in front row.

Class photo taken at Sansoucci.
Gisla is second from the right in the second row.

Spreewald.

Gisela with Father and Mother on a
sightseeing trip in the Spreewald.

Pumpkin farm in the Spreewald.

Spreewald costume.

Unter den Linden with Berlin City Hall and
Dom in the distance.

Unter den Linden at night.

Partial view of Kempinski
Haus Vaterland.

Goering's Air Ministry building.

Employment Book, 1935.

Drawing of Mother's Cross, 1938.

Example of Schultuette and satchel.

Aunt Trudchen's wedding, May 15, 1938.

The bridal carriage arrives.

Confirmation, March 17, 1940.

Gisela and Mama with Tante Lotte
and Uncle Otto in Balz.

Gisela and Hans, Balz 1941.

Bakery next to Ziegler's Inn, Balz.

Woman on Russian front.

A farmer and her children in Russia.

Russia. Photo taken by Kurt.

Kurt's photos of the Russian front included these boys,
1941-42.

Russian boy, 1941-42.

Kurt, on leave, with Mama, 1942.

Gisela with Mama's friend and son who were
later killed by bombs, 1942.

Gisela and Dieter leaving the Genezareth
Church after Dieter's confirmation,
March 1943.

Dieter on his confirmation day.

Gisela and Gertraud with Gisela's yellow duck
in the background.

Teens with Commissionaire at Scherl clean up,
June 1944. Gisela is first from left.

Goerlitz, November 1944.

Charlottenburg Castle at war's end.

Karstadt at the end of the war.

1939

February 3	Goebbels ends career of five actors for misrepresenting Nazism.
February 14	Battleship Bismarck is launched.
March 14	Slovaks declare independence.
March 15	March into Bohemia and Moravia. Hitler arrives in Prague only eight hours after troops march in.
March 16	Slovakia joins Moravia and Bohemia and becomes part of the German Protectorate.
March 17	Chamberlain recalls envoy from Berlin.
March 22	Hitler annexes Memel from Lithuania.
April 7	Italians move into Albania.
April 23	British envoy returns to Berlin.
June	In Czechoslovakia, a German policeman is killed and 1,000 are arrested.
July 13	Germany leases Trieste from Italy.
July 18	2,000 Nazi guards arrive in Danzig.
July 30	More troops move to Libya through Trieste. France and Britain warn Hitler about Danzig but Hitler ignores the warnings.
August 8	Hitler orders men aged 15 to 70 to register in preparation for wartime assignments.
August 16	Hitler demands Danzig.

August 20	Polish troops ordered to German border.
August 21	Russian/German Nonaggression Pact announced.
August 22	France and Britain reaffirm pledge to aid Poland.
August 23	Belgium declares neutrality while France mobilizes.
August 26	Hitler demands Danzig, the corridor and all other German territories lost in 1918. Reich demands an end to the Great Britain-Polish alliance.
August 29	USSR masses troops on its western border.
September 1	German troops move into Poland and Danzig is ceded to Reich.
September 3	War with France and England.
September 4	Royal Air Force (RAF) bombs Cuxhaven and Wilhelmshaven for the first time.
September 5	Graudenz falls. Krakow is surrounded.
September 6	Krakow and Kielce fall. A new decree provides for the death penalty for anyone endangering the defensive power of the German people.
September 9	German high command announces that German troops have reached Warsaw.
September 14	U-boat sinks two British ships in Atlantic, for a total of 19 so far.
September 16	British aircraft carrier Courageous sunk, with 500 men lost. Ultimatum to Warsaw: surrender.
September 17	Soviets cross into Poland on its eastern border.

September 23	General von Fritsch killed in action.
September 27	Warsaw surrenders. The establishment of Reich main security office combines security police with security service resulting in the most powerful instrument of police terror (Gestapo, Kripo (Kriminalpolizei) and Security Service).
October	Hitler signs note authorizing mercy killing of "Lives Not Worth Living," or the Euthanasia Program.
November 9	A bomb explodes 12 minutes after Hitler left Buergerbraeu in Munich, killing seven and wounding 63.
November 11	State funeral for Buergerbraeu victims.
November 18	Nine students in Prague shot for staging anti-German demonstration and 10 hour work days are introduced.
November 21	Two 19-year-old youths in Augsburg sentenced to death for stealing from home of a soldier.
December 12	German offensive along the Rhine.
December 20	The ship Graf Spee is down near Montevideo. After long battle with the British, the captain scuttles ship on Hitler's orders, then shoots himself.
December 21	The author's 14th birthday.

From the media 1939:

German Airplanes Attacked Again!
Secretary of State Stuckart in great danger!

On their flight back from Danzig to Berlin Polish anti-aircraft attacked. Plane saved only by pilot's presence of mind/ East Prussia too threatened/ Dreadful mass murder in Lodz and Bielitz: Thirty-two dead.

August 18, 1939
76,000 Germans flee Poland!

August 22, 1939
Dogs set on German refugees!

Saturday, December 16, 1939
Four Years Penitentiary for listening to foreign radio stations.

The accused was also stripped of his civil rights for two years and his radio was confiscated.

Two Ethnic Germans Buried Alive.

German Special Court sentenced six Polish bandits to death who had buried two ethnic Germans, aged 19 and 20 respectively, alive after torturing them in a bestial fashion. Two additional perpetrators could not be sentenced because they are still at large.

The Fuehrer held the official New Year's reception in the new Chancery. The glittering occasion was attended by all the leading Nazis and their wives, as well as the diplomatic corps and other special guests. Naturally, it was well publicized and the public had the opportunity to see scenes on film of the reception and the grandiose setting. The walls of the high ceilinged, spacious rooms were decorated with large paintings and tapestries. I remember marble floors, pillars and many mirrors.

It was one of the rare occasions when wives of leading Nazis were seen at a public function, although gala performances at the State Opera were attended by wives. At times, Madga Goebbels was used as an example of perfect German motherhood and photographed with her children. Emmy Goering was photographed at her wedding, at the christening of her daughter Edda and in some publicity shots with Edda during the war but photos of Emmy Goering were rare.

Otherwise, the wives led private lives. Women had no place among the Nazi leadership. The only woman who held a position in the government, and at best it was a subordinate one, was Gertrud Scholtz-Klink. She was tall, blond and had 11 children from two marriages. She was a dyed-in-the-wool Nazi and had joined the Nazi party in 1928. She was the leader of the National Socialist Women's League. Eventually, she was promoted to the top post of Reich Women's Leader. However, she was not the leader of the BDM girls, who came under the leadership of a man, Baldur von Schirach.

I encountered the expression *arbeitsscheu*, "work shy," on a number of occasions but don't recall precisely where. I think it must have been mentioned in some speeches that we were made to listen to at school or when I overheard adult conversations. The way it sounded to me was that it referred to a person who was averse to the idea of work as a whole and regular employment in particular, like a drifter who did not want to do anything but be lazy.

What I did not know at the time was that the Nazi definition of "work shy" in the year 1938 was that of a person capable of work who rejected offers of employment twice or who left two jobs shortly after starting. Whether the work offered or the job the person left was suitable work for that individual or matched the person's qualifications was immaterial. The employment booklet and the employment office were the sources of detection of "work shy" people. The Gestapo was instructed to send work shy people to a concentration camp. There was no legal recourse. Not only did I not know the definition of *arbeitsscheu*, I did not know the consequences of being labeled "work shy." I do not recall hearing of anyone in our circle of acquaintances or in our neighborhood being picked up by the Gestapo.

Higher education was not taken for granted. Based on the child's performance over the years, teachers recommended either the middle school or the high school. The schools were not free. Middle school tuition was 10 marks per month and high school tuition was 20 marks per month, plus the cost of books. This does not sound like much by today's standards but many people at that time could not spare that amount. Most children left school at age 14.

If parents could afford to send their child to either the middle school or the high school and if his or her grades were high enough, the child was required to sit for a qualifying examination at age 10. The examinations were not easy but designed to weed out those who were not higher education material. I missed this exam because I was sick. That was that. No provisions existed for make up exams at a later date. All places were filled.

However, I did have another opportunity. There was an institution called the intermediate school. Entrance exams were tougher because the institution taught the curriculum in three instead of six years. At the end of 1938, or early in 1939, I sat for the entrance examination. It took all morning and covered every subject. In German, I was given a choice of three subjects for an essay. They were all National Socialist oriented, so really it was not much of a choice at all. I wrote the life story of Horst Wessel. The following day, Mr. Lambert questioned me in detail about the test. He was upset because I had obviously made some mistakes in math. Nevertheless, I passed and left my elementary school at the end of the school year.

In the spring, before our school year ended, the deaconess from the Martin Luther Church visited our classroom and enrolled us in confirmation classes. These began after Easter in preparation for our confirmation the following spring. When the new school year began, I went every Monday and every Thursday morning from 8 a.m. to 9 a.m. to the congregational building for instruction. Here I was reunited with my former elementary school classmates.

Confirmation was a milestone, a very important event in young people's lives. We had known for years that we would be confirmed one day and, as the time grew nearer, we spent some time thinking and talking about it. Even though most of us never set foot in a church, we all wanted to be confirmed.

Classes were taught by the deaconess and the pastor, Pastor Saran. Pastor Saran was an elderly, distinguished looking, white haired gentleman whom we loved and respected. As he kindly instructed us, his own faith and love of God communicated itself to us. Part of the time was spent learning hymns. Occasionally, we sang anthems during the service, accompanied by the organist. We learned about the life of Luther, the history of the Reformation, the social institutions of the church, such as the Bethel Institute and, of course, scripture. Politics did not enter into our confirmation instruction.

An integral part of the confirmation preparation involved church attendance. I was required to attend church every Sunday, if possible. I was given a pink card bearing my name. Upon entering the church for the Sunday service, I handed the card to the verger, who signed and marked it as proof of my presence and handed it back to me as I left the church.

The church arranged two field trips for us, one to Luther's town of Wittenberg and one to an institution near Potsdam for deaf, mute and blind people. I was unable to go to Wittenberg but I did go on the second trip. The institution was immaculately clean and the floors shone like mirrors. The rooms were spartanly furnished, containing a minimum of furniture: a bed, a bedside table, a chest, a wardrobe and a chair. There were no rugs on the floors and no mirrors. Everything was practical and simple so the occupants could easily familiarize themselves with their surroundings and memorize each item in each room in the whole building.

We did not meet any of the residents because they were at work, engaged in broom and brush making and a few other occupations that required skilled hands. I tried to imagine what it was like to be blind and deaf, to live in such silent, dark isolation. It was a very sobering experience and made me appreciate my good health and all my faculties. Our guide, the matron, demonstrated their method of communication, which was by tapping on a person's hand using various combinations of finger tips.

The new school year started after the Easter vacation. It was with some trepidation, but with more anticipation and excitement, that I went to my first class at the new school. There were 36 girls in my class. Our home room teacher, Miss Kunz, was also new to this school. She was 32, blond, slim, tanned and she had a bit of an overbite. She had just returned from a holiday in Sweden.

Some girls were quite smitten with her but I was cautious. I realized during the ensuing weeks and months that Miss Kunz was definitely "brown." She enthusiastically supported the Fuehrer and repeated Goebbels' propaganda, which made me increasingly dislike and distrust her. Consequently, I kept very quiet and only answered when spoken to. In any case, we were never on friendly or intimate terms with our teachers, who remained aloof and were approached with respect and, at times, anxiety. Miss Kunz told us she had applied for party membership and was waiting to hear that she had been approved. It was not that easy to join the party. One requirement was that a person had to supply proof of German or related descent back to the year 1800.

Our headmistress was a party member. She and my homeroom teacher did most or all of the constant indoctrination to which we were subjected. We had several other teachers, one each for religion, for music and needlework, for English, and one for science and math. None of the teachers, apart from the music teacher, were married. As teachers, none of them measured up to Mr. Lambert. We speculated as to whether Miss Kunz had a boyfriend and whether she would get married because she was the youngest and best looking of all.

School became something of a drudge: Work, work and more work because we had to get through the curriculum twice as fast as other schools. This alone did not bother me but it bothered me that I did not have a fair teacher. Miss Kunz soon showed favoritism and antipathies. A few girls in class were her pets so they could do no wrong. She picked on a few others whom she seemed to dislike for some reason. The majority, including me, were treated with indifference. This showed itself in my marks. No matter how well I did my work, my marks always stayed the same: satisfactory. However, when we were taught the same subject by another teacher, my marks went up to "very good" and "good." After a while I did not try as hard as I had before because it seemed pointless. The only "very good" Miss Kunz gave me was for behavior. When she handed out report cards, she remarked, "Gisela gets 'very good' for behavior but then what else would you expect? She is so quiet, one hardly knows she is here."

We had no discussion periods. When called upon to answer questions, we stood up and remained standing while we answered. We raised our hands if we knew the answer or if we wanted to ask a question. Mostly we only asked for explanations if we had not understood something. It was very formal and we were well behaved and polite.

Meanwhile, in the world outside our classroom, the tensions between Slovakia, Bohemia and Moravia came to a head in March when the Slovaks declared their independence. Their independence was short-lived. The Fuehrer moved German troops across the border, occupying not only Slovakia but also Bohemia and Moravia, declaring all of them a German Protectorate. The Fuehrer himself followed hot on the heels of his soldiers. He was in Prague eight hours after his army had marched in.

This action created yet another international crisis. The Fuehrer had broken his promises to the international community. In April, speaking at the Reichstag, he declared that he would give President Roosevelt his word that he would not attack other independent nations in Europe. At the same time, he conscripted all German youths. Adults around me were uneasy, fearing the outcome and the reaction of the European community.

The Fuehrer's birthday in April was one of those special birthdays, his 50th, and was celebrated accordingly. The official celebration climaxed in a four hour military parade and the opening of the East-West Axis, which I saw on the newsreels.

As stated before, the BDM's purpose was to mold girls as closely as possible to conform with the Nazi ideal of womanhood. A girl was to learn to be obedient and dutiful, disciplined and self-sacrificing. Great emphasis was placed on physical fitness. More than half of the BDM's activities were devoted to sports, the rest to ideological instruction. Girls, like boys, met weekly and attendance was obligatory.

Some girls in my class enjoyed being members of the BDM. I had the impression they derived a feeling of belonging and importance from their membership. It introduced an element of excitement into their lives. In Berlin, the Hitler Youth was constantly drawn into action and received publicity, which added to their sense of importance.

Of the 36 girls in my class, only six were *not* BDM members, just the reverse of my grade school class, where out of 30 only six were *in* the BDM. It did not take long for our headmistress to become aware of this fact. One day, she visited our classroom for the specific purpose of giving us a pep talk. She told us, the six of us that is, about the disadvantages we would encounter if we did not join the BDM forthwith. She informed us that we would find it very difficult, if not impossible, to obtain apprenticeships in our chosen professions. Some professions would be entirely closed to us. We would, in all probability, not be admitted to a university and we would not find it easy to get jobs, especially in the civil service. She earnestly recommended and expected us to join the BDM as soon as possible.

Now I did not seem to have a choice. I was trapped and was forced into something I had so far happily and successfully avoided. I talked to Father and I was nervous. I had butterflies in my stomach but there was nothing for it. I knew I must go to the regional office and join the BDM. A few days later, after school, Father and I walked to the regional office. The office was empty except for two BDM leaders who were listening to swing or jazz records, a definite no-no and banned on radio. They were dancing with each other. Neither of them bothered to come to the counter. From across the room they asked us what we wanted. When I told them, they said, "You don't have to do anything now. We will come to the schools and admit all girls who are not yet members." Then they resumed their dancing and we left. Quickly.

I was much relieved and did not give the matter another thought. I had been given a reprieve and felt wonderful. Nothing further was said at school and no one ever came to check up on us or make us join.

In addition to the subjects I was taught in grade school, I now had English, algebra and higher math. All subjects were requirements. The curriculum also required us to be taught Latin and French. However, shortly before school started the Latin/French teacher died. He was not replaced so Father offered to teach me Latin. We did have a few sessions but then I quit.

Our English teacher was an English lady. I do not remember her name but she was middle-aged, slim, dark haired and serious. I clearly recall the first lesson. I was excited and expectant. The teacher entered our classroom, walked to the window and opened it, saying: "I walk to the window and I open the window. I close the window."

Miss Fischer, who was a short woman in her middle or late 40s of undistinguished looks, appearance and grooming, taught arithmetic, mathematics, physics, algebra, chemistry and biology.

Those of us who were as yet naive and ignorant of the facts of life as well as those who knew a lot, wondered when and how she would broach the subject of sex and reproduction of the human race. Time went on and nothing happened. We had already learned about Mendel's law of heredity in grade school. It was reviewed, expanded upon and expounded in order to stress once again the hereditary nature of diseases such as insanity, deformities, hemophilia and criminal insanity and how these could, in fact must, show up at some time or another, even after skipping several generations.

Miss Fischer also talked about the notion that while the half moons on our fingernails were white, Negroes and mulattos tried to hide their nails because their half moons were not white and they were ashamed of it. I tried to imagine how hard it must be to hide one's hands and fingers at all times. I could not see why they should be ashamed; after all, they had not done anything wrong. We were told that Negroes, mulattos and people of mixed blood were mentally, and often physically, inferior to the white race. The only Negro I ever saw as a child was an old man walking in the street.

Mr. Lambert had talked about the different races without any elaboration. Miss Kunz went a little further in race science class, than just naming them. She enumerated various characteristics and proceeded to pick out girls who best represented each of these races. They had to get up and stand in front of the class while she pointed out features. The girls were embarrassed. The Eastern were usually White Russians: round heads, round faces, light colored eyes and blond hair, with white skin. We were all familiar with Nordic people, the superior race, tall, blond, blue-eyed, long faces, elongated skulls and white skin.

(West)phalians had square heads, Dinarics had distinctive noses and dark hair. There were Latins, such as Italians, Spaniards and French people. Slavs (Poles, Czechs, Hungarians, Slovaks, Yugoslavs and Albanians) who had darker, swarthy complexions, were short in stature, and had dark hair and brown eyes. Jews were of two kinds: the Eastern type, known as Ashkenazim, were from Poland, Russia and other Eastern European areas, and were described as dirty, ugly, unkempt and altogether repulsive. The Sephardim were from Spain and Portugal and were described as more civilized and palatable. Then there were gypsies, who were described as good-for-nothing nomads, lazy, dirty, thieves and thugs.

It was impressed upon us repeatedly that our duty to the Fuehrer and Germany was to have children. Four children was to be the norm in order to ensure that our superior genes were multiplying more than those of people of lesser intellect, who usually produced too many offspring. It was expected of us to offset this trend. In fact, because we had high IQs, we were obligated to exceed the minimum of four children.

Religion was taught by a lady in her 50s. There were no lessons dealing with faith or with the Old or the New Testaments. Instead, we reviewed the lives of the Reformers, church architecture and some religious art.

Only one girl in our class was Roman Catholic and two were what was called God-believing, followers of a modern German cult of non-Christian theism. I understood this to mean that they believed in God but had no other religious beliefs or church affiliations. These three girls were excused from attending the religion class. Once, one of the God-believing girls hid in a wall closet before the religion class started. She thought it was funny that we knew she was there and the teacher did not. During this

288

hour, we were a little on edge and inattentive in case she would do something to reveal her presence.

Our homeroom teacher, Miss Kunz, also taught gym several times a week. In addition to floor exercises, rings and bars, we spent time outside, when the weather permitted, practicing long jump, high jump, shot put, throwing javelins and running. We often played dodge ball. I liked this game. I deliberately stayed out of the crowd and waited until almost everybody was "out." Then came my chance to get into action, play more or less by myself, until I was finally alone. That was fun and I loved it.

In music instruction we were introduced to the classical composers, listened to records of symphonies and concerts, and learned songs by Schubert, Schumann, Mozart and others.

We had no school library. Also, we did not receive art instruction. We did not learn how to play an instrument and we did not have a school band.

School still started at 8 a.m. and lasted until 2 p.m. on weekdays and on Saturdays went until noon or 1 p.m. Since we were taught an accelerated curriculum, we were given much homework. It usually kept me busy for three hours or more. We had no extracurricular activities. All of us lived in different parts of Berlin or in the suburbs and so many were a considerable distance from school. Most of us did not arrive home until three or four in the afternoon or later. This was not conducive to forming close and lasting friendships or meetings after school hours.

I did make friends with the girl who sat next to me, Lydia. Her mother was deceased and she had a stepmother. She and her parents lived in a neat single house with a garden in Gruenau, a suburb of Berlin. She invited me to her home but I only went once. It was too far to visit on a regular basis. However, we were good friends during school hours. A number of other girls and I also struck up friendly relationships and walked to our respective train and bus stops together. We talked mostly about movies and movie stars. Some talked about boys but none of us had boyfriends.

On special holidays connected with the regime, we had assembly. Beforehand, we practiced songs and memorized poems suitable for the particular occasion. Several girls loved to recite and were always picked because they could be relied upon to do a good job. Otherwise, in class we were all called upon to recite poetry. We memorized a lot by Geibel, Moericke, Uhland, Goethe, ballads by Schiller, Eichendorff, Adalbert von Chamisso and others. Many of the poems were set to music. We learned to sing these in music classes both in elementary and high school. I made a list which shows that I memorized more than 170 songs and 130 poems.

Our neighbors, the Schlossers, were expecting a baby. I was thrilled and felt inspired to knit a pair of baby booties. I had learned the basics of knitting and crocheting but I never had the patience to finish a project myself, though I did crochet lace edging around many a handkerchief as gifts for my aunts, Mama and Mother. In the past, I had always been lucky in enlisting the help of others. Now I enlisted a former needlework teacher, Miss Kemp, who lived nearby and graciously consented to assist me. On my consequent visits, we became quite friendly. Aunt Marga managed to procure hard to obtain illustrated travel books of Spain, Italy and Greece for her as a thank you, much to her delight.

The baby, a girl, arrived in April and was named Erna. I was very disappointed because I had more unusual names in mind. I learned later from Mama that the Nazis had issued a list of names unacceptable to the regime. Mama knew a couple who had a baby girl and wanted to name her Jutta but were not allowed to do so. Once I read in a magazine that a couple had named their new daughter, Hitlerine. I wonder what became of Hitlerine after 1945.

Even before Hitler came to power, the Nazis blamed the Jews for everything that was wrong in Germany. After the Jews were excluded from public life and most of them had emigrated, Mama remarked, "The Nazis blamed everything on the Jews. Now the Jews have been thrown out of Germany but the conditions they were blamed for still exist. Who is to be blamed now? The Nazis no longer have the Jews to serve as scapegoats. Only Christians are left. Obviously, they are now responsible for whatever is wrong. Just look how badly many treat their fellow man. And the Nazis wanted to make us believe that only Jews behave like that."

Neukoelln had relatively few Jews and Jewish businesses. I remember several Jews in our neighborhood. In the next street was a potato shop owned by an old Jewish couple. They retired from the business when I was quite small, which accounts for my not remembering them clearly. Across the street from the apartment house where I was born was a storefront where a young Jewish couple operated a rag collecting business. Instead of throwing away old clothes, blankets and other textiles no longer needed, we took them to the rag store. Mr. Salomon weighed the rags and gave us a few pennies for them. I occasionally went there and watched the couple sorting and taking the rags apart, bundling them for collection. It was dusty in the place and the young woman always wore a kerchief over her dark hair. They were nice looking, petite and very quiet and did not engage in any unnecessary conversation. They emigrated before the war.

Soon after the war began, I heard Mama talking to some women in the street who said that a very old Jewish woman lived in a small ground floor apartment a couple of streets from us. Her neighbors took her food and looked after her. It must have been the woman who had run a potato shop at that address. Mama found out a short time later that the old lady had died.

Mr. and Mrs. Silbermann lived on the second floor of our apartment house and they owned a shoe store. The Silbermanns had no children. They were tall, slim, dark haired, good-looking and elegant. I remember going to their store for shoes with Mama and Mother on numerous occasions. Apart from this, my contact with them was limited to chance meetings in the apartment house hall when I curtsied and said, "Good morning," "Good day" or "Good evening." I was mostly by myself when I met them. The Silbermanns, like all other tenants in the house and people in general, kept to themselves but talked briefly with other tenants when they met in the house or on the street.

In March, Father spoke with Mr. Silbermann, who told him that they were going to emigrate. However, Mrs. Silbermann had been ill for some time (with terminal cancer as it turned out.) Her sister moved in with them and nursed her. Mr. Silbermann said they could not meet the deadline set for their departure because Mrs. Silbermann was too sick to travel. He had received permission to stay until after her death and funeral. When I came home from school one day in April, Mother informed me that Mrs. Silbermann had died.

When I went to the bakery that afternoon, I noticed a hearse outside a house across from the bakery. People stood watching. Inside the bakery, I heard some customers say that a woman had killed herself and her 11-year-old son by "turning on the gas." The women wondered if mother and son could be buried in the same coffin or had to have separate ones. I left the store and ran along the street as though chased by furies. I could not get into our apartment quickly enough. A short time later, I heard noises in the hall. I looked through the spy hole and I saw the undertakers carrying out a coffin with Mrs. Silbermann's body.

That evening, Uncle Gustav and Aunt Martha came to visit. When they heard about Mrs. Silbermann, Uncle Gustav began talking about Jewish burial customs. There was no way I could excuse myself. I had to stay and listen. Both these events haunted me terribly from then on. I could not bring myself to talk about it to anybody. It took a long time before I got over the shock. Death upset and scared me. Every time I had to walk past an undertaker's establishment, where coffins, blankets and pillows were visible through the windows, I held my breath and walked by really fast, looking in another direction.

When Mr. Silbermann emigrated, his large apartment was rented to an underprivileged family "rich in children." The NSV Mother and Child organization subsidized the rent.

Easter was over and Mother's Day was approaching. Heretofore, it had been celebrated on the second Sunday in May. This year it was permanently changed to the third Sunday in May. I have no idea why. On Mother's Day, mothers were not only remembered and honored by their families but, in the new Germany, by the state. It was the day chosen for the presentation of the Mother's Cross of Honor award, instituted in 1938. It was actually an extension of a Military Cross of Honor. Women who had given birth to numerous offspring had shown the same "dedication of body and life" as "frontline soldiers in the thunder of battle" said the *"Voelkischer Beobachter"* newspaper. Women who had four or five children were entitled to a bronze cross. Women who had six or seven children were given a silver cross and those with eight and more children were presented with a gold cross.

The cross was accompanied by a certificate which stated:
"The most beautiful name on earth is
Mother!"
Honor Card of
German Mothers
rich in children
(A swastika was printed here)
Protecting the German Mother
is the honorific duty of every German."

We learned new poems written for Mother's Day and a few lines from one of them have remained with me. It went like this: "Of men and heroes, people will talk for as long as the earth exists. But traces of the mothers who carried them soon blow away in the wind." At school, we had assembly on the Friday before Mother's Day. Every class contributed to the program.

The Mother's Cross, it was stated, was created to emphasize the mothers' importance as keepers of the sacred home fires, life and its honor, since it was important to exalt motherhood. These ideas were taken from the values and traditions of Nordic and Germanic peoples. Mother love was exalted in literature and films, such as "Mother Love," which was the story of a mother who donates one of her eyes to restore her son's sight.

Mother had five children but two died when they were babies. Four children entitled a woman to the Bronze Mother's Cross and Aunt Marga decided that her mother deserved this recognition. She must have filled in the papers or whatever was required and, in due course, Mother received her cross. The presentation was usually made during a special ceremony at some official party place. Mother didn't want it and was embarrassed so she refused to attend the ceremony. I think somebody came to the apartment to make the presentation because I am sure Mother's back trouble was used as an excuse not to attend the official ceremonies. The cross, in its box, was deposited in a drawer and later was lost.

Mama's friend Vicki was a character. She was one of those women who could put a flower pot on her head and look like a million dollars. She had a smoky, husky voice and managed to look elegant in everything she wore. She married Wolfgang when I was five. Wolfgang, a very young war veteran, found himself unemployed after WWI and the economic crisis which followed so he joined the SA before Hitler came to power. Mama told me that he fearlessly went into the streets to paste posters for the Nazi Party on walls and advertising pillars amid hails of bullets.

After Hitler came to power, Wolfgang held some kind of rank in the SA. I think he may have been a Sturmbannfuehrer. At first, he worked out of his apartment and later he had an office. Mama said he would do anything for people who came to him for help. He went to great lengths to secure jobs and assist in any way he could.

Mama said Wolfgang had been quite a boy. On one occasion, Wolfgang was told to stay in a bedroom while his mother visited with a friend. When his mother was ready to leave several hours later, she and her friend discovered that Wolfgang, left on his own with no toys and no books, had amused himself by neatly cutting out all the roses from the curtain material.

Wolfgang was a fun person and I liked him a lot. I never heard him talk about politics; at least, he did not say anything within my hearing and I never saw him in uniform.

Vicki and Wolfgang lived in a lovely apartment. I loved their living room because it had a big bay window one step higher than the rest of the room. One evening in the fall of 1938, Mama and I visited them. We enjoyed a pleasant evening and savored the luscious Turkish gateau we were served. As usual, I entertained myself while the adults talked.

It was a warm evening and when Mama and I walked home, the sky still light with the afterglow of the recent sunset. Mama said they had talked about Nostradamus so I asked, "Who is Nostradamus?" Mama explained that Nostradamus was a 16th century French astrologer who had written a book predicting the future. The book was banned in Germany, as were all forms of fortune-telling. But Vicki somehow managed to obtain a copy and showed it to Mama. Mama said one of Nostradamus' predictions was that the entire city of Berlin would one day be a sea of flames. A chill ran down my spine and my knees felt weak. I was profoundly shocked and frightened. I could not imagine what that would be like. The prospect was unimaginably horrible but it did come true.

By April 1939, Wolfgang was ill. He was admitted to the hospital in the Hasenheide. We visited once but he was in bed and could not speak. Mama said he had something wrong with his throat and his tongue. In May, I heard that he had cancer and had undergone surgery. Mama visited again and shortly thereafter he died.

Mama went to the funeral, which took place on a lovely warm and sunny day in May. I stayed home and played with my friends but kept thinking of Wolfgang. The funeral was a huge affair and police had to direct traffic outside the cemetery. Hundreds of people attended, mostly members of the SA who also provided the honor guard and a band, as well as high ranking government officials. I think Mama said there was a wreath from Hitler. Vicki was dressed in black and widow's weeds. Mama said Vicki did not cry but, when they had to raise their hand in the Hitler salute while the anthems were played, Vicki's arm shook visibly.

Soon afterwards, we visited Vicki. She and Mama talked about Wolfgang, his death and his funeral. Vicki said some people had been critical. They made snide remarks about her being dry-eyed at the grave side and, therefore, unfeeling and unemotional. "What are they talking about?" Mama exclaimed. "That just goes to show how people will distort things. Anybody with eyes could see how hard it was for you to control yourself, not to cry in front of all those people. Surely everybody must have seen how your arm was shaking during the salute." Vicki and Wolfgang had had a happy marriage and Vicki was devastated but she was not a person to sit and feel sorry for herself. I don't know what Vicki did after Wolfgang died because I did not see her again for a long time.

Time seemed to be passing more swiftly for me. I still played with my friends, although I had less free time now. Occasionally, I read them a story from my English book because they were curious about the language and wanted to hear how it sounded.

Summer arrived and, with it, our seven week vacation. I had once again applied to be sent to a Scherl children's home. The doctor again recommended Norderney and this time I went for six weeks.

Things in Norderney were much the same as on my previous visit except that the food seemed worse. Our day began at 7 a.m. when, dressed in our black shorts, white athletic shirts, socks and gym shoes, we went outside for physical exercises and running, followed by showers, dressing and the morning flag raising ceremony. The older boys took turns raising the flag and the older girls were responsible for reciting an appropriate verse while it was hoisted. I took my turn as well. We raised our arms in salute and sang the national anthems, "Deutschland, Deutschland Ueber Alles" and the "Horst Wessel Song." While we sang, we fidgeted with our arms in the air because the anthems were long and it was somewhat of a strain to keep our arms up. This ceremony was repeated after supper when the flag was lowered.

Flag raising was followed by breakfast. Most mornings, it consisted of thick hot vanilla, chocolate, or farina soup. The cooks were apprentices and inexperienced so, more often than not, the soup was burned, not just a little but a lot. It tasted awful. Nevertheless, we had to eat two deep bowls full of the stuff. We overcame the taste by holding our noses while spooning the soup into our mouths and swallowing as quickly as possible. In addition to the soup, we had black bread with some sour tasting farmer's cheese. This was not the most delicious start for the day.

Upon entering the dining room, all the children went to their tables and remained standing behind their chairs until the director and her staff came in and took their places at the head table facing us. At every mealtime, except second breakfast, a verse was recited by one of us. Only then did the director say, "You may be seated." The only verse I remember is "Well-rounded potatoes, white as alabaster, make a satisfying meal for any man, woman and child." It was a popular verse due to its brevity, since verses had to be memorized.

After breakfast, we returned to our rooms and made our beds, took care of our clothing, wrote postcards and talked until it was time for second breakfast at 10 a.m. Second breakfasts consisted of corn coffee, thick slices of gray or black bread spread with margarine, sour farmers' cheese and, on occasion, cold cuts. There was also a piece of fruit to go along with the sandwiches. Nobody liked the sandwiches. The boys usually

298

started flipping pieces of bread across the room at the other tables. They got away with it only because we were not supervised during this meal.

Then we were ready to go out. We usually went into town, walking in twos and threes, when the sky was overcast and it was not warm enough to go swimming. As soon as we reached the main street we stopped, lined up properly and, on the given command, marched in step and sang to make a good impression on the general public. During inclement weather, we spent our time in the recreation room, where we sang, played games, read and wrote letters.

Of the songs I learned in the homes, many were HJ and BDM songs. I sang them along with the other girls, sometimes with the boys, but I never stopped to analyze the lyrics. They were just songs and I liked some melodies better than others. I did not identify with the lyrics, for instance in the song "Forward! Forward! Blare the Bright Trumpets" where it says "even though we may perish, the flag is more important than death." I never thought of myself perishing or dying, most certainly not a sacrificial death for the Fuehrer.

Most mornings, we went swimming. The beach closest to town was the public bathing beach, the only place people were allowed to swim. It had changing facilities and lifeguards. The rest of the beach was divided into sections for individual hotels. The various children's homes had their own beaches farthest along the promenade. The water in the North Sea is cold and that July and August it was only about 55 degrees Fahrenheit. Bathing time was strictly monitored and the first time we were only allowed to be in the water for two minutes. After a few days, a minute was added each time, up to a maximum of 15 minutes. Occasionally, we went to the indoor pool. This was great fun because periodically machine made waves convulsed the water to make it resemble the sea. After swimming, we returned to the home to rest until our main meal at noon.

We followed the same ritual at our main meal at noon as we did at breakfast. We stood until a verse had been recited and the director told us to sit down. The meals were not very filling. Many times we had boiled potatoes, scrambled eggs and lettuce. I cannot remember if we had dessert. If we did, it was some kind of pudding or stewed fruit. I do remember that often I was still hungry when I got up from the table.

Our rest period after lunch lasted until 3 p.m. During this time, we had to lie down on our beds and keep quiet. Following the siesta, we usually walked to our own beach where we stayed until supper time. Occasionally, our supervisors organized ball games but for the most part we were left to our own devices. We amused ourselves by building sand castles, jumping from the promenade down into the sand, walking along the edge of the water, looking for shells, sitting around talking and playing catch.

Our supervisors, girls between the ages of 18 and 21, were training to be kindergarten teachers. Outwardly, they were very much the type of the "Ideal Young German Woman" with straight hair worn in a bun, no make-up, and wearing sporty, simple clothing. In every other way, they displayed traits like those of other young women their age. Their minds were on boyfriends and what to do in their spare time. When we were at the beach, they usually took off for a long break at an open-air café. Some times, when we got bored being left on our own for hours, a few of us climbed to the top of a dune overlooking the café to spy on them, not that there was anything to see or hear but it gave us something to do.

The summer was exceptionally lovely and warm. The sky was a deep, deep blue. It looked so close I thought I could touch it.

A few days after we arrived, another group of children came in from Cologne. They were children of post office employees from the Rhineland. Several girls joined our group at supper time. One of them sat opposite me and I am afraid I completely lost my appetite because she had deformed feet. I suppose they were club feet. She wore black lace up orthopedic boots. This alone would not have bothered me but she also had deformed hands and forearms. The hands had no fingers, only little round knobs with a nail in the middle. She had no thumb, just the division between the hand and the place where the thumb normally branches off from the hand. I was mesmerized and could not stop looking at her. At the same time, I was repelled and could not eat.

I could hardly sleep that night because I felt wretched for the girl. The following day when we walked to the beach, she was limping along all by herself. It seemed no one wanted to walk with her. I retraced my steps, joined her and began talking to her. Her name was Katrin and she was 14, blond and blue-eyed, with a very pleasant personality.

From then on, I spent most of my time with her. I gathered that she did not have much of a life back home. Her mother had passed away and she had a stepmother, stepbrothers and stepsisters. She was not complaining but it sounded as if she was barely tolerated, lonely and unhappy. I felt terribly sorry for her. She mentioned that her deformity was blamed on her father's heavy drinking. Whether or not that was true is hard to say. We had learned at school that children of alcoholics could suffer deformities. For this reason, we were told, the new Germany did not allow people with such family histories to marry in order to prevent perpetuating congenital diseases and defects. Seeing this poor girl, I thought it was a good law because people would not have to have unhappy deformed, sick or mentally ill children. I thought it was sad because these children were unable to have a normal childhood and life. They were often treated cruelly, abused, neglected and ridiculed by their peers.

Katrin and I exchanged addresses. I also exchanged addresses with a couple of other girls, one from Kassel and another one from the island of Usedom in the Baltic Sea. Sad to say, these holiday friendships rarely survived for long. We exchanged a few letters but time terminated the fragile link. I wrote to Katrin but she never replied. I have wondered what happened to her, especially when Cologne suffered heavy bombing raids during the war.

As I mentioned before, our meals were not the best or the most satisfying. Since we were out almost all day, the sun, wind, water and plenty of exercise stimulated our appetites and sometimes we were still hungry after our midday meal. We would have liked to buy snacks to supplement our meals but we had no money. It was customary for us to hand our spending money over to our supervisor on arrival. She kept book and paid for our purchases when we went shopping. The girl from Kassel, who was in my room, secretly held part of her money back. One day during our rest period, we were so hungry, we decided that one of us should sneak out and buy something to eat. I was a very fast runner and was elected to do so. I tiptoed downstairs, out of the house and streaked into town to the nearest grocery store, where I bought a loaf of bread and cold cuts. I raced back at top speed. If someone had clocked me, I might have been the first person to run a mile in four minutes. People stopped and stared, wondering where the fire was.

We quickly made sandwiches. I was just about to place another piece of bread on top of the cold cut when I heard the caretaker's wife coming on her rounds. I slapped down my open sandwich under my pillow and pretended to be asleep. As soon as she had gone, I retrieved it and I found it had left a big round grease mark on my pillow case. We laughed and enjoyed our treat. When I returned to Berlin, Dr. Baumann was shocked to discover that I had lost three pounds.

After lunch, the mail was distributed. The director called out the names and we went to the head table to pick it up. I received a great deal of mail and Aunt Marga frequently sent me small parcels with candy and novelty items. One day the director, holding a parcel, called my name. One of the girls in my group commented, loud enough for her to hear, "What, another parcel?" Whereupon the director said, "Well, Gisela, you are getting more than your share. I think this time we will give the parcel to your supervisor to distribute the contents among the girls in your group." The director of the home was definitely "brown" and I believe she was a party member.

I was furious. Not because I had to share, I always shared with my roommates, but because someone ratted on me. Most of all, I was upset because it was from Oma, who never gave me anything. Now Oma had actually sent me a parcel and I would never know what was in it. Besides, I thought it grossly improper, if not illegal, that someone could confiscate my personal mail, my personal property, just like that. I cried. The girls in my room were very sympathetic. My share of the parcel's contents was two candies.

During our stay, we went for walks in the Wattenmeer, when the sands were exposed during ebb tide between the mainland and the island. It felt strange but pleasant to sink my toes into the soft, wet, mushy sand and watch crabs and shrimp dig themselves in. It was not so much fun stepping on jellyfish. They felt much more solid than they looked in the water.

We walked on the promenade and/or around the park on some afternoons or evenings while the band played in the bandstand. It was the thing to do, after all, because Norderney was a spa. Once we paid a visit to the Norderney airfield. An air force corporal was our guide. He told us that it was easy to learn how to fly a plane. "It's easier than learning to ride a bike," he commented.

My six weeks passed quickly. I was deeply tanned and my hair was bleached almost white by the sun and the sea. On the morning of our departure, we went to the smokehouse and picked up our orders of smoked shrimp and smoked flounder, still warm, with a mouth-watering aroma. After lunch, we boarded the boat to Norden where the express to Berlin stood in the station, ready to depart.

When we pulled into Bremen, the whole station and what else I could see of the city from the train was one sea of flags and swastika decorations. I surmised that the Fuehrer had just paid a visit or was about to do so.

Our train made a one minute stop in a Berlin suburb and I was astonished to see Aunt Marga on the platform looking for me. She was not allowed to enter our carriage but could hand me a posy of chocolate flowers through the open window. The chocolates were wrapped in purple, pink and gold foil, the leaves in green foil and the whole posy was surrounded by a lace doily. It looked very cute and I was delighted with it. Aunt Marga rode in a different carriage for the last leg of our journey. We arrived at the Lehrter Bahnhof at about 9:30 p.m. on this lovely warm summer evening. The rest of the family was waiting for me, as were all the other children's relatives.

It always took me a few days to get used to the city again after returning from the country or the seaside. On my return this time, I found the atmosphere in Berlin to be restless and tense.

School started in late August. Miss Kunz had spent the long vacation in Sweden. I could not understand why she came back because I would have stayed in Sweden. Mama had told me of her dream to emigrate to Sweden as a young girl. She had seen job ads in the papers. Unfortunately for her, her parents did not permit their young daughter to travel alone, not to mention emigrate to a foreign country. Mama always dreamed of visiting Sweden and Norway but she never realized her dream.

For six weeks, I had been blissfully oblivious to what was going on in the real world. I had not heard any news or seen newspapers. I came down to earth with a bang. Current events were anything but reassuring. They were awful and getting worse with every passing day. Miss Kunz spent some time reviewing the plight of the ethnic Germans living in Poland. The Poles persecuted, murdered and tortured ethnic Germans. One day, she told us that a German farmer was found nailed to his barn door; he had been emasculated. Gruesome. Others were beaten, killed, terrorized and farms were burned. Thousands of ethnic Germans fled into Germany and every day brought additional horror stories. The government spewed venom against the Poles, saying that Poles were slovenly, lazy and dirty and that their farms were a disgrace, mismanaged and neglected. The expression "Polish mess" was used to mean slovenliness, neglect and confusion. How dare they ill-treat the ethnic Germans, who lived mainly in West Prussia, known as the Corridor, which by right belonged to Germany but had been handed to the Poles by the Versailles Treaty.

The Corridor was approximately 6,125 square miles of fertile farmland with a population of 330,600, of which 50

305

percent were German speaking. It was situated between the Vistula, a river near the city of Danzig, and Pomerania. The Corridor separated East Prussia from the rest of Germany. Travel through the Corridor was guaranteed but trains were sealed at the border. There were no customs inspections.

In early 1939, the Poles began to expel Germans from West Prussia. On March 21, Hitler issued an ultimatum demanding additional access routes through the Corridor, a plebescite and a 25 year nonaggression pact. Poland rejected all demands on March 26.

Earlier in the month, the Fuehrer voiced his demand for the return of Danzig. In response, Polish troops were reported to be massing on the German border. France and Britain reaffirmed their intention to aid Poland in case of German aggression. Belgium declared itself neutral. France and Holland mobilized while the Soviet Union massed troops on Poland's eastern border. Every day, almost every hour, brought new distressing developments. We were told that there was chaos in Poland. German families fled and German passenger planes were attacked while flying over the Corridor. German farms were looted and torched. It was frightening to me.

On August 26, Hitler demanded that Danzig, the Corridor and all other territories Germany had lost to Poland as a result of the Versailles Treaty, including Upper Silesia, be returned.

As the political crisis escalated, talk turned to memories of WWI and of the hardships and shortages suffered. Mother, Mama and my aunts looked stricken and unhappy. They vividly remembered the hardships. In the end, there was nothing to eat but rutabagas for a long time. Bread was made from sawdust and rutabagas. Roast rutabagas were used to make ersatz coffee. Everyone was sick and hungry. Children suffered from malnutrition. Shops were devoid of consumer goods, such as soap, personal hygiene articles and so on. I was quite shaken by their accounts. We were all sick with the thought of war. Mother's brother, Ernst, had been killed in Flanders. After WWI, Mother and Father, along with millions of others, had lost all their savings. No wonder we dreaded the future.

On August 23, the German Foreign Minister von Ribbentrop, was in Russia to sign a Nonaggression Pact. This allowed the Soviets to acquire the Baltic States (Lithuania, Latvia and Estonia) and divide Poland. Our teacher said that the whole world admired the Fuehrer's brilliant move, except for Mr. Chamberlain and Lord Halifax of England, who were shocked.

In current affairs, communist Russia and Communism were invariably portrayed as the archenemy and the Fuehrer as the chosen one, the redeemer who would save, or was already saving, the world from Communism. Our classroom wall was graced, if one can call it that, by a framed anticommunist quotation. On the day after von Ribbentrop signed the German/Russian Nonaggression Pact, Miss Kunz turned it to the wall. "For as long as we have a Nonaggression Pact," she announced.

Tensions increased further. People I knew were visibly worried. Talk centered on the situation and on the future. Was there a chance for peace? Was there any chance that war could be and would be avoided? But, everything pointed to the inevitability of armed conflict. I avidly listened to the news. Rumors circulated about rationing of food and other commodities. I hated the idea.

On Sunday, August 28, ration cards were hand delivered to every household. It was a blow to everyone. Rationing began on August 29. A normal consumer was allotted 1 pound 3.5 ounces of meat, 9 ounces of sugar, 14 ounces of coffee substitute, 5.25

pounds of bread, 10 ounces of fat (not butter, but butter fat), 3.5 ounces of jam, 5.3 ounces of pasta or cereal and 1.75 ounces of cheese per week. Every month, 4.3 ounces of soap and 0.7 ounces of tea were allowed. Whole milk was reserved for children under 14, invalids and expectant mothers only. Eggs were distributed occasionally, one per person.

The bread we ate was not white bread but rye bread which was much heavier than white bread. Therefore, it might look as though we received an enormous bread ration but, because of its weight. This really was not the case. We ate white bread only once in a while, either for breakfast or in the afternoon, with butter and preserves instead of cake.

I found out after the war that our ration cards had been printed as early as 1937. At first, one card was valid for all foods. Later, individual cards for meat, fat, cereal and pasta, and bread were issued. The cards were valid for various lengths of time and color keyed to different goods and to the age of the person entitled to buy them. Separate ration cards were issued to soldiers home on leave and for travel. A 20 percent tax was imposed upon beer, hard liquor and cigarettes. There was a separate coupon for dog food.

I was shocked when I heard that clothing and shoes could no longer be bought without a permit. Permits had to be applied for and the chance of one being issued was small. I had been eyeing a lovely pair of blue and white shoes for weeks. I realized that I would not be able to have them. I was very upset and cried. I could not understand why, when the writing was on the wall, no one had bought them before the restrictions came into effect. To me, that would have been the logical thing to do.

The crisis was beginning to get to me. I was haunted by fears and had trouble sleeping. I lay in bed for a long time trying to fall asleep. How would war come? What would war be like?

How did one react to such an overwhelming event? War seemed imminent and rumors were rife. The ones concerning rationing of food and clothing had already become a reality with the issuing of ration cards. What next?

I did not want war and I was apprehensive. The situation was grim, the atmosphere tense and growing more stressful by the hour. Mama said, "Who cares about the Polish Corridor? We were without it all these years and everything was peaceful. Why stir up trouble? Why go to war over it? I want peace. I do not want war." Many of our friends and "safe" acquaintances asked the same questions.

I listened to the news for details. The Fuehrer made demands, one of which called for a plebiscite to determine what would happen to the Corridor. It was grim. I felt dejected, unhappy, tense and apprehensive.

At 9 p.m. on August 31, the radio station interrupted its regular broadcast. A special report acquainted us with the terms and proposals the Fuehrer made to Poland. The Poles refused to come to Berlin to discuss them. They would not return Danzig even in the event that the Corridor voted in favor of return to Germany.

The annual Party Congress scheduled to be held in Nuremberg, under the motto "Reich Party Congress of Peace," was called off because of the impending war. Poland was reported to be in a war fever, mobilizing and moving troops to the German border. Silesia was reported to be in an uproar. I tried to imagine how war would be announced. In my imagination, I saw our newspaper's front page and under the heading one word in huge red letters filling the entire page: WAR! That would sum it up. What else could be said? What else was there to say? What difference would any other additional words make? They were of no import. The fact was: WAR! That is how I, a 13-year-old girl in Berlin, imagined the start of WWII.

Of course, it did not happen that way in the real world. Friday, September 1, dawned. It was a lovely summer day in Berlin, with an almost cloudless blue sky and temperatures around 72 degrees. When I got up at 7 a.m., as I always did, we were already at war, although I did not know it yet. I had imagined the beginning of a war to be a terrifying experience. In actuality, it was almost an ordinary day. Nothing seemed to have changed, on the surface.

It was announced in the morning news broadcast that the Fuehrer would address the Reichstag at 10 a.m. And so he did. "This night for the first time, Polish regulars fired on our own territory. Since 5:45 a.m. we have been returning the fire and from now on bombs will be met with bombs." The Fuehrer had spoken. He had announced that "in self-defense" German troops returned enemy fire. The Poles provoked the attack. He did not make a formal declaration of war; there was never to be one.

At school, we had assembly and after the Fuehrer's speech we were dismissed. I remember it clearly. I was dressed in one of my dirndl dresses, black with fine white lines dividing it into squares patterned with posies of poppies, cornflowers and daisies. The dress had puffed sleeves, a tight bodice and a gathered skirt. When I came home, I went to our private playground. All my friends were there. We played ball games. It seemed like any other day, except for the nervous feeling in my stomach.

German troops had crossed into Poland. The fighting had begun. This was war? After lunch with Mama, I walked over to Father and Mother's. I did not notice anything different in the streets. No one was jubilant. Everything looked quite normal and people were going about their business. People did not congregate in the street and I did not speak to anyone. Mother was sitting by the kitchen window reading the paper. There were no red headlines.

So this was war. I was frightened and, at the same time, relieved. It was a relief from the tension of the past months, the rumors, the uncertainty of not knowing what would happen yet knowing all the time that we were teetering on the brink. Now the die was cast. War was a fact. My fear of the unknown remained, however.

Almost immediately, special news bulletins informed us of the troops' progress. Panzers rolled, infantry marched and Stukas (short for *Sturzkampf* bombers) attacked. Gone were the horror stories of persecution, murder and torture suffered by ethnic Germans living in Poland. There was no longer a need for propaganda. The flames had been fanned and the fire started. People I knew were subdued and resigned to the situation. What could they do? The war machine was clicking into gear and nothing could stop it. But there was no enthusiasm for war.

Mother recalled how at the outbreak of WWI people had flocked into the streets, presented flowers to the troops marching to the station, cheered, clapped and laughed. People were caught up in a frenzy of enthusiasm that was almost a celebration. I saw nothing like that and nothing like it happened in Berlin this time.

The eventful day was drawing to a close but not without an unpleasant surprise. At 7 p.m., the air raid sirens sounded. It was an eerie wailing sound. I was amazed and hoped it was a mistake. I was at Mama's and we went into the basement. It was a very strange feeling sitting with so many people in this comparatively small, dimly lit room. I don't know how long it was before the all clear sounded, I think within less than half an hour. Everybody smiled and laughed, much relieved that nothing

311

had happened. Mama wondered if it was a deliberate reminder to drive home the fact that the war was for real.

A decree, issued on the first day of war, said we were forbidden to listen to foreign radio stations. Blackout regulations came into effect immediately. From then on, newspapers published a boxed notice giving the times of sunrise and sunset and the correct hours during which complete blackout must be observed and maintained. Air raid shelters for all buildings had become compulsory in August and in several parts of town bunkers were erected to serve as shelters. Air raid wardens had already been appointed and volunteers trained to cope with emergencies. Quite some time ago, we were ordered to empty our storage units in the attic of all unnecessary items to reduce the fire hazard. Soon thereafter, all attics were emptied completely and the wooden partitions were taken down.

We had been issued with gas masks. Of course, we had to try them on. Mother said she would not. Father tried his and I tried mine. I hated it. We looked like strange insects with huge glassy eyes and a weird snout. The rubber fitted very snugly and the elastic entangled my hair. All I wanted to do was tear the mask off as quickly as possible. I have no recollection of what happened to the masks. We took them to the shelter, but we never, thank God, needed to wear them in earnest.

Air raid wardens held training sessions in the street. They stressed the importance of going to the shelter as soon as the alarm sounded, of keeping buckets filled with water and sand on staircase landings, and filling kettles and other containers with water for drinking. They emphasized the importance of a complete blackout. Wardens made their rounds at night to check on people's blackouts. Tenants were severely reprimanded if it was not perfect. Repeat offenders were subject to severe punishment.

312

Saturday, September 2, brought renewed tension. Would Great Britain and France stand by their agreement and support Poland?

Sunday dawned and was another gorgeous day. More people than usual went to church. I know because I had been attending church regularly this year, in preparation for my confirmation. When I came home after church, I heard that England and France had declared war on Germany. This was another blow. Father was sitting by the window reading the Sunday paper. I was anxious to read it myself. There were long articles about England and France, their warmongering and their failure to recognize German claims to former territories and so on. It still seemed unreal; I felt dazed. Again, I had envisioned that such an absolutely world-shaking event would warrant a most dramatic announcement and that people's reactions would be public and noticeable. It was nothing like that. Sunday morning and the rest of the day remained quiet and normal, with no people gathering in the streets. I didn't detect anything unusual at all when I went out in the afternoon. However, Father was anxious and Mama was upset. I was shaken. What effect would this latest development have on us?

Radio newscasts included the first reports from the front in Poland. It was a depressing Sunday. In spite of the sunshine, it seemed gray to me. Mama was worried about Kurt being called up. Kurt was depressed at the thought of having to go into the army. All around the mood was sober, somber and serious. People remembered the casualties of WWI. Now troops were in the field. Already there must be dead and wounded. The first casualty obituaries appeared in the papers in September. The politically correct phrase to use was "died for Fuehrer." Most of the ones I saw read, "died for their Fatherland" or simply "died in action."

313

Monday morning school started at 8 a.m., as usual. Before class began, one of the more vocal girls, Rosemarie, voiced the opinion that we should no longer take English. It was unpatriotic to learn the enemy's language. I listened. No one asked my opinion. Had someone done so, I would not have given it. Privately, I thought it was silly to make a fuss. English was part of our education and I wanted to continue. At the beginning of term, we were informed by Miss Kunz that our English teacher was no longer with us. Henceforth, the subject would be taught by herself and by our headmistress.

Rosemarie raised her hand and said, "We really do not want to continue our English lessons. We feel it is unpatriotic." Miss Kunz received this statement earnestly and commended us for our patriotism. She was going to pass the message on to our headmistress.

A couple of days later, our headmistress visited our classroom. On this occasion, she was dressed in a dark blue or dark gray pin-striped suit. She wore a hat and a mink around her neck. She smiled in her patronizing way and launched into a spiel about how important it was for us to continue with our English studies. Just how important? "Because of my knowledge of English, I have been drafted to serve our Fuehrer and our Fatherland as an interpreter and translator. A significant task, you will agree. I will be gone from time to time to fulfill my obligations and do my duty," our headmistress explained. "Meanwhile, girls, continue your studies, study diligently." Suitably impressed by our headmistress's speech, our class graciously agreed to continue learning the English language.

New rumors circulated, this time about the British. The British were planning to drop poison gas on Berlin. In spite of Goering's boasts that no enemy plane would ever darken the airspace over Berlin, these rumors persisted.

❖   ❖   ❖

Mama was worried. She loved coffee. Brewing coffee was a ritual she repeated in the morning, afternoon and evening. First, the already spotless coffee pot was rinsed once more with hot water, carefully dried and placed on a warm spot on the back of the stove. The tap was turned on until the water ran really cold, to ensure its freshness. The kettle was filled and put on to boil. At just the right moment before the water reached the boiling point, Mama took out the coffee grinder, unscrewed a jar holding freshly roasted coffee beans and measured beans into the coffee grinder. She carefully closed the jar and then ground the coffee beans. By the time the kettle began to whistle, the ground coffee had been transferred to the pot, with a tiny pinch of salt. Mama poured water, a little at a time, into the coffee pot, replacing the kettle after each pouring to bring it again to a boil before pouring more. This procedure was very important, Mama explained, to ensure that the coffee was properly brewed. Nothing but freshly boiling water would do. To give an idea of how serious she was about brewing coffee, many years later, when she was on vacation in Austria, Mama almost suffered her first apoplexy. The landlady of the guest house had asked her, "Do you mind if I boil your breakfast eggs in your coffee water?"

When the coffee pot was full, Mama replaced the lid, covered the pot with a thick, quilted cozy and let it stand for a few minutes to allow the grounds to settle. A heavenly aroma filled the kitchen while Mama, in preparation for the delight to come, took out her favorite bone china cup and saucer.

At the outbreak of war, Mama had six pounds of coffee beans in airtight glass jars. When she heard the rumors, she was frantic. "My coffee," she wailed. "The British will drop poison gas and spoil my coffee! I can't stand it! We cannot get any more and what I have will be ruined!" She did not seem at all

315

concerned about what would happen to our food and to us as a result of the gas. She could only think of her coffee. To me, that was funny. To forestall the disaster, Mama proceeded to brew coffee, twice a day, strong enough to shrivel a coffee spoon should it have the misfortune of ending up in a cup. In less than two weeks, Mama's jars were empty. Satisfied that nothing and no one could now deprive her of her coffee, Mama relaxed as much as her palpitating heart would let her. She was wide awake at night and jittery from all the caffeine, but nevertheless happy.

Weeks went by. Nothing happened. No air raid. No poison gas. No more coffee. Poor Mama had time to repent at leisure and bemoan the fact that she could have enjoyed afternoon coffee for many a week if she had not panicked but had rationed her coffee beans.

When rationing had come into effect, Mama and Mother were required to register at the grocery, the greengrocer's, the fishmonger's, the game store and the butcher's. Greengrocers, fishmongers and game sellers issued a number to each customer. When produce was available, it was distributed in numerical order. Those customers whose numbers were displayed on the blackboard outside the store were entitled to a piece of fish or game. During the first year or so of the war, we had fish once or twice. I don't remember ever getting a piece of game. Even at the greengrocer's everything was rationed: potatoes, fruit and vegetables. Mama and Mother had to stand in line for hours to obtain whatever was available. The meat ration was used for meat or cold cuts. Coffee, tea and cocoa were rationed out in extremely small quantities at unpredictable times. Adults received only skim milk. This is not to be compared with the skim milk we buy today. Wartime skim milk was nothing more than slightly opaque blue water. Cheese rations were minute.

In restaurants, the menu listed how many ration coupons must be given over for a meal. For instance, a meat entree might require 1.5 or 3.5 ounces worth of meat coupons. This applied to fat, bread and cake, as well.

To comply with air defense regulations, several storage units had been eliminated in the basement to make room for an air raid shelter large enough to accommodate all tenants. The windows were covered and the caretaker kept the place clean.

In Berlin, a number of large aboveground bunkers had been built to shelter several thousand people each. We did not have one in our immediate vicinity. Even if there had been one, I would not have gone. I did not feel comfortable being shut up in a place like that with so many people.

The first victories in Poland were announced with great fanfare. Much to everyone's dismay, the RAF attacked Wilhelshaven on September 4 and 5, as well as the North Sea Canal and Cuxhaven. War had come to Germany itself.

We followed war events in class. On September 5, the city of Graudenz fell. Krakow was surrounded and fell on September 6. Rumors began circulating that as soon as Poland was defeated there would be peace. I hoped so. Even though the news from the front was one continuous high, I wanted the war to be over.

It seems strange to look back to a time without television coverage of all these earthshaking events. Television was around and before the war television sets were available for 650 marks. I don't know of anyone who bought one and never saw a set in a shop. I do recall that there was a public television viewing room in Neukoelln. I passed it on my way to my swimming lessons some years before the war. I remember looking in the door and seeing that the TV was turned on. During the Olympic Games, events were televised. However, I heard nothing about television programs during the war.

Kurt was called up and I moved in with Mama. We relied on the radio for the latest news. Mama listened almost all day. After school, I did my homework in the kitchen. Fanfare and music by Wagner repeatedly interrupted scheduled programs with reports of victories.

A new decree was instituted: the death penalty for anyone who endangered the defensive power of the German people. Three youths in Hannover were caught snatching a lady's purse during blackout. They were sentenced to death and executed. The crime rate in the Third Reich was extremely low, as a result.

The German High Command (OKW) announced at 7:15 p.m. on September 8 that German troops had reached Warsaw. The announcement was followed by the national anthem and the "Horst Wessel Song."

In addition to bulletins from Poland, special news bulletins reminded us of U-boat actions. Fanfare heralded every announcement and the new "England Song," which became the signature tune for all special news regarding the maritime war, was played following reports about the sinking of British vessels in the North Sea and the Atlantic. For instance, on September 14, the sinking of two British ships was announced. The total number of ships sunk so far was given as 19. The announcement was followed by the "England Song":

"Today we'll sing a song and drink cool wine.

We'll clink our glasses for we must part.

Give me your hand, your white hand, farewell my love, farewell, my love, farewell,

For we are sailing, we are sailing, we are sailing against England."

I was doing my homework and Mama was preparing supper on September 16 when a special bulletin announced that the British aircraft carrier, *Courageous*, had been sunk, with the loss of many lives. On the down side, the government had to admit that the British had bombed Kiel, a major German naval base. But, so the report stated, antiaircraft fire downed five enemy planes. Rumor had it that a large number of our ships were destroyed or damaged.

On September 17, Soviet troops invaded Poland from the east.

We celebrated Mother's 70th birthday on September 21 with flowers, small gifts, pastries and plum cake. We were able to buy cake by giving up food stamps. Alas, this time we had no whipped cream.

A somber voice informed radio listeners on September 23 or 24 that General von Fritsch had been killed in action outside Warsaw. The general was buried in Berlin on September 26, a cold, rainy and overcast day. The newspapers stated that General von Fritsch "died for the Fatherland." The official, politically correct phrase "died for the Fuehrer" was conspicuously absent. The Fuehrer did not attend the funeral. This was strange, considering that von Fritsch was the first General killed in action. The Fuehrer's absence was explained by pressing war related duties. Rumor had it that the general was shot by Himmler on orders from the Fuehrer or that he had committed suicide.

On September 25, we received new ration cards. The meat ration was cut from 1 pound 3.5 ounces to 1 pound a week.

Our history lessons emphasized England's policy of encirclement and keeping the European balance of power. We were told that the "crafty" British signed agreements with other states which would result in the complete encirclement of Germany. Germany would be isolated and left without allies. In addition, we were told, that England had for decades, maybe even centuries, a policy of setting European powers against each other thus controlling the political balance in Europe. Although I admired the diplomatic skills of the British, the idea of being encircled and friendless was scary.

The British were portrayed as plutocrats, ruled by greed and money, with Jews pulling the strings in the background. I had no clear conception of what a plutocrat was. I had no idea what life in England was like. My knowledge of England was limited to what I learned from the stories in my English lesson books. The characters in my book were ordinary people who went shopping at the neighborhood grocery stores and ate plum pudding at Christmas, which was full of great ingredients and had to be steamed for eight hours.

Current events receded into the background after school while I played with my friends and during the evening. But when I went to bed and before I fell asleep, they preyed upon my mind, keeping me awake for a long time as I worried about what would happen next.

On September 27, barely three weeks after the German troops crossed the Polish border, Warsaw surrendered. The war in Poland was over. Would there be peace? That was the question. The Fuehrer had emphasized repeatedly that he only wanted to reclaim the territories lost in 1918. But there was no peace. Hitler spoke to the Reichstag on October 3. He made peace overtures to England and France but they were rejected. The Fuehrer was furious and placed the blame for the continuation of the war squarely on those two countries. He reasoned that Poland was defeated and, therefore, their pact with Poland was now null and void. So why did France and England want to continue the war? Because they were warmongers, he stated.

A radio request program for the armed forces began on October 1. The concert was broadcast every Sunday from 4 p.m. to 8 p.m. from the main studio in Berlin. Requests were made by people at home for soldiers at the front and the other way around. They included greetings, news of loved ones, congratulations on the occasions of wedding anniversaries, particularly silver and golden anniversaries, wedding announcements and special birthdays. Birth announcements were introduced by the sound of a baby's cry.

Among the most requested songs were "Lili Marlene," "Erika," "You Cannot Shock a Sailor" and "Come Back" or "J'attendrai." The program was very popular. A few requests were for short excerpts of classical or light classical music. The concert program invited donations for the German Red Cross.

The Reichstag met on October 6 in the Kroll Opera House in Berlin and the Fuehrer addressed it. He stated that the Soviets had annexed the Baltic States. He talked about peace proposals and warned Britain and France to stay out of "German Living Space" in Eastern Europe. Miss Kunz read to us from the *"Voelkischer Beobachter"* newspaper, "Germany wants peace. Germany has no war aims against France and England. Germany will make no more claims except for the former German colonies. Germany wants cooperation with all nations of Europe. Germany proposes a conference."

Extra editions appeared on the streets on October 15: "German submarine sinks British battleship *Royal Oak* at Scapa Flow, the British Naval base." The captain of the German sub that had successfully penetrated into Scapa Flow was Captain Prien. He was awarded the Knight's Cross and his picture appeared everywhere. He was the object of widespread hero worship and was killed later on in the war.

November brought more air raids on Wilhelmshaven and the RAF was reported to have lost fifteen planes. Newspapers called for bombing raids on Britain. Editorials jubilantly announced every loss the Royal Navy and British Merchant Navy suffered. Goebbels spouted hatred and blasted Churchill, calling him a liar. The anti-British hate campaign intensified.

On the home front, the 10 hour work day was introduced.

Hope for peace died. I resigned myself to this fact.

Publicity about the Fount of Life homes was renewed to break down prejudice regarding illegitimate children. In October, Himmler decreed that despite bourgeois prejudices it was now the duty of German girls and women of "good blood" to have children by soldiers going off to war, even outside marriage. It was no longer to be viewed as a disgrace to have a child, or children, out of wedlock; it was now to be considered acceptable with no shame attached to it. Himmler promised that the SS would take over the guardianship of all legitimate and illegitimate children of Aryan blood whose fathers met death at the front. The men and women who stayed at home had the "sacred obligation" to have additional children.

On November 9, the Fuehrer undertook his annual pilgrimage to Munich for special ceremonies to honor the victims of the 1923 Putsch. Later, the Fuehrer addressed his old combatants in a beer hall but, pleading urgent government business, he left earlier than anticipated. Shortly after his departure, a bomb exploded in the hall. It was obviously intended for him. The government blamed foreign agents for the attack and the newspapers held Britain responsible. Six people were killed and many injured. The victims were given a much publicized state funeral on November 11, which I saw on newsreel.

On November 12, ration cards for clothing were distributed. Men, women, children and babies were issued separate cards. Everyone, except babies, received 100 points. Socks and stockings cost 5 points but were limited to five pairs a year. Pajamas cost 30 points, a nightdress 25 points, an overcoat or a suit 60 points. Items were also limited by season.

Himmler reported on November 21 that the man who planted the bomb in the Munich beer hall had been found and arrested. His name was Georg Else, age 36. Himmler claimed that British Intelligence and Otto Strasse, a former Nazi leader, were responsible for planning the incident. To my knowledge, no further reports on the matter appeared in the paper. There was no mention of a trial or execution.

The Advent season arrived and I celebrated it in the usual way. At this school, too, we brought candles and fir tree branches into the classroom on Monday mornings and put them in front of us on our desk. For the first class period, the candles provided the only light and we sang a Christmas carol just as in my elementary school. I was delighted when a bell sounded outside the classroom door. The door opened and in came an angel carrying a lighted candle. The angel was followed by a girl, dressed as a shepherd boy, who played a recorder. The angel walked to the front of the classroom, sang a carol and departed. On the successive Advent Mondays, two, three and four angels visited us and sang. It was a charming custom.

The leading news item on December 20 was that the German battleship *Graf Spee* had gone down near Montevideo, Uruguay. Reports stated that the Fuehrer had ordered the captain to scuttle the ship rather than surrender and the captain had gone down with his ship. However, this was not the case. In reality, he committed suicide. He shot himself in his hotel room in Buenos Aires on the Fuehrer's orders. The *Graf Spee* had been engaged in a long battle with the British and tried to escape into a neutral harbor. She had not been lucky like the passenger liner, the *Bremen*, which had made it back to Germany earlier in December.

Life, apart from all these events, went on much the same. I went to school and did my homework. I still went out to play and spent some evenings at my friend Dieter's apartment helping him with his homework and playing games. I attended my confirmation classes. I went to church every Sunday and on Reformation Day, October 31, a public holiday. I went to see Goethe's "Iphigenie at Tauris" performed at the State Theater.

Women were needed to fill the gaps in the work force left by men drafted into the forces. Soon we saw streetcar conductresses and drivers, as well as women delivering mail just as in WW1. It was now acceptable for working women to wear pants because they were more practical and warmer in the winter. However, pants were not worn at other times. Instead of hats, working women and housewives alike wore turbans and decorative hair nets. New hats were hard to get. The turbans were for the most part fashioned by tying scarves that way, but more attractive preshaped turbans were available at the stores. Hair nets were made of coarse yarns, usually crocheted, and tied at the top with velvet ribbons. They came in various colors but were mostly black, navy blue, beige or white. These nets covered the hair which was worn behind the ears. For dressy occasions, we wore hats.

Uncle Herbert, Uncle Otto and Uncle Willi were called up. Uwe Schaefer, son of the Emil Schaefers, had joined the Navy before the war. Occasionally, when he was on leave, he paid us a short visit. I was very proud to walk down the street with him.

He looked extremely smart and handsome in his Navy uniform and was something of a sensation because we hardly ever saw a sailor in our part of town. I wrote letters to Kurt and Uncle Herbert. Before Christmas, Dieter's mother helped me bake cookies for them. It was hard not to eat them myself. Dieter snatched one and I upbraided him for it, poor guy.

Rye Flour Cookies
2 pounds of rye flour, 1 egg, 40 grams of margarine, 250 grams of sugar, 65 grams of honey, 2 or 3 tablespoons milk, 1 package of baking powder (two teaspoons), lemon zest. Mix ingredients, add baking powder, knead and roll out on table sprinkled with ordinary flour. Cut out cookies. Bake.

Cinnamon Stars
80 grams of flour, half a teaspoon cinnamon, 200 grams of sugar, 50 grams of fat, 200 grams of chopped oats, 6 tablespoons of milk, mix in order of ingredients listed, let rest for an hour, roll out, cut out stars, bake at 350 degrees.

Semolina (or farina) cookies
1 pound of semolina, half a pound of sugar, 1 egg, 20 gram fat, 1 teaspoon baking powder, lemon zest.

Beat fat until creamy, add other ingredients, place dough by the teaspoonful on baking sheet, bake at 350.

On December 21, I celebrated my 14th birthday. As usual, I did not have a party because everyone was too busy so close to Christmas. However, I received flowers and presents.

Christmas shopping presented something of a challenge. Shop windows displayed goods but most of them were rationed and we did not have enough coupons to buy them. Heretofore, popular presents had been clothing, fine toilet soaps, perfumes, jewelry and candy. Now these were no longer easily available. Books, radios, gramophone records and jewelry became sought after gift items. However, if one wanted a new record, one had to give up an old record in order to buy it.

No goose spluttered in our oven. Our Christmas fare was meager. But whatever Mother cooked was tasty and we did not go hungry. Extra rations for Christmas were a quarter of a pound of butter, 3.5 ounces of meat and four eggs instead of one. The traditional Christmas plates were missing. Fruit, if available, was strictly rationed. Infrequently, there would be a few fresh lemons from Italy or Spain. I did not see bananas, coconuts, grapes, mandarins, dates or figs again until well after the war. After my 14th birthday, I counted as an adult and was consequently on smaller, adult rations and no longer entitled to milk.

Christmas was subdued with Kurt away. But we still had Christmas trees and Christmas Eve was spent at Father and Mother's. On the morning of the First Christmas Day, I visited Oma and Opa. The afternoon and evening were spent at Aunt Martha's. On the second Christmas Day, I visited Papa in Weissensee and he actually gave me presents: a set of matching lingerie and a fan. I found out years later that Papa always received a children's allowance but he never spent it on me as he should have. This was the only gift I ever got from him except for Johnnie, the canary.

The official Nazi Christmas message was delivered by Dr. Robert Ley, the Reich Organization Leader. I did not hear or read his message myself but the subject came up in school after the Christmas holidays. Dr. Ley had said: "The Fuehrer is always right. Obey the Fuehrer. A mother is the highest expression of womanhood. A soldier is the highest expression of manhood. God is not punishing us with this war. He is giving us the opportunity to prove whether or not we are worthy of our freedom."

Mama and I were invited to spend New Year's Eve with one of her school friends, whose husband was also in the army, along with a few other friends. Her daughter Sonja, who was my age, and I were excluded from the adult party and spent a seemingly endless, extremely boring evening sitting in the kitchen. We did not even have a radio. We grew tired and all we wanted to do was sleep. This year, there were no fireworks at midnight and no church bells rang. The city was dark and quiet.

Shortly after 1 a.m., Mama and I walked home. The streetcars had stopped running and it was very cold. We were practically the only people on the street because Berlin night life had been curtailed. By Himmler's orders, all bars and restaurants were required to close at 1 a.m. and the public was officially warned against excessive drinking on New Year's night. In contrast with the New Year's Eve celebrations of 1938, this evening was dismal. I wondered whether it was an indication of what the new year would be like.

1940

January 30	Hitler warns there may be total war.
February 14	Great Britain: merchant ships will be armed.
February 15	Hitler: British merchant ships will be considered warships.
February 19	Germany sinks sixth British destroyer.
April 9	Invasion of Denmark and Norway by Germany.
April 15	French and British land at Narvik, Norway.
April 22	German bombers smash Norwegian towns in air blitz.
May 10	Invasion of Holland, Belgium, Luxembourg and France. Churchill becomes Prime Minister.
May 12	Allies bomb Krupp plants and Rhine area.
May 13	Germans take Sedan.
May 15	Holland surrenders after severe bombing of Rotterdam.
May 17	Germany cuts through French lines on 62 mile front.
May 21	Allies trapped at Dunkirk. German troops are 60 miles from Paris.

May 26	Allies begin to evacuate Dunkirk, Calais falls.
May 28	Belgium capitulates unconditionally. King stays in Belgium until further notice.
May 29	Prince William of Prussia killed in action.
June 10	Norway capitulates.
June 14	Paris occupied by German troops.
June 15	German flag flies over Versailles.
June 22	France surrenders.
July 24	Hitler annexes Alsace-Lorraine.
July 29	Hitler annexes Eupen, Malmedy and Moresnet in Belgium.
August 8	Of 800 German planes flying over London, 53 are shot down.
August 12/13	Big air attacks on Britain.
August 14	Air raid on Berlin at 2 a.m.
August 18	German blockade of England.
August 20	Air raid on Berlin.
August 26	First big air raid on Berlin 12:20 a.m. and all clear at 3:23 a.m. British bombers over Berlin drop more leaflets than bombs so there is minimal damage.
August 28	Heavy air raid on Berlin by British.
September 1-2	Air raid on Berlin at 11:45 p.m.
September 8	Massive reprisal air attack on London.
September 9	London burns.
September 10	Air raid on Berlin.
September 11	Heaviest air raid on Berlin yet, with more fire bombs than before.
September 11	Buckingham palace hit.
September 19	In Rome, Ribbentrop warns Mussolini against attack on Greece and Yugoslavia.

September 23-24	Four hour air raid on Berlin, with damage to northern industrial districts and Stettiner and Lehrter railroad stations.
September 25-26	Longest air raid on Berlin so far: 11 p.m. to 4 a.m.
September 29-30	Air raid on Berlin lasts two hours.
September 30	Children under 14 to be evacuated from Berlin. Air raid on Berlin.
October 23	In Berlin, Franco meets Hitler. St. Paul's Cathedral in London hit.
October 28	Mussolini attacks Greece.
November 12	Molotov visits Berlin.
November 14	Coventry destroyed by 500 bombers in raid, resulting in 1,000 dead.
November 17	Documentary "Victory in the West."
November 23	Air raid on Berlin.
November 24	Slovakia joins Axis.
December 13	Marita plan approval results in invasion of Greece.
December 21	The author's 15th birthday.

The New Year began with the coldest January I could remember. In fact, it was the coldest January Europe had experienced in 14 years and one of the snowiest. Piles of snow 5 and 6 feet high lined our sidewalks.

Coal, used as heating fuel, was rationed and had to be conserved. The icy blasts of an east wind did not let up. Mama's apartment, on the top floor of the building and exposed to the east, was frigid. We placed newspapers between the double windows and hung blankets halfway across but it was all to little avail. We huddled around the stove, dressed in our warmest clothes, and went to bed early to keep warm. Temperatures dropped to 5 degrees Fahrenheit.

Kohlenklau, an imaginary antisocial parasite who wastes energy, was introduced at the onset of winter. Posters appeared in public places, U-Bahn stations, on advertising columns, in stores and on matchboxes. *Kohlenklau* literally translated means coal thief. It was the subject of radio sketches and used in an intensive campaign exhorting us to use as little fuel as possible and preserve energy by not leaving lights on when no one was in the room. We were told not to leave windows open for long periods and heat only one room instead of the whole house or apartment.

A number of schools closed in order to preserve fuel. Those that remained open, such as mine, doubled up. I went to the morning session and children from another school came in for an afternoon session.

A novelty item appeared on the market in the fall of 1939: fluorescent pins to be worn on outer garments during blackout. Fairly plain at first, they soon became more elaborate and cute. One could not purchase much so it was fun to select and buy new and larger pins. During the day, the pins had to be exposed to strong light in order to glow for any length of time in the dark.

Their luminescence was really too weak to be of any significant help. One had to come pretty close to a person before one could see the pin. But we did not mind and enjoyed them anyway.

Broadcasts were interrupted by special bulletins announcing mostly the sinking of British ships, followed by the "England Song." They always mentioned the gross tonnage involved, which did not mean anything to me since I had no idea what gross tonnage was.

The Fuehrer spoke as usual on January 30. In his speech, he voiced a warning that the war could well turn into a Total War. I did not know the difference.

In February, the Fuehrer declared that "as of now," British merchant vessels were to be considered warships because the British had decided to arm them. Announcements about the sinking of British vessels increased; several in one day were no exception.

U-boat captains and crews were heroes and were decorated with the Iron Cross and the Knight's Cross, with or without oak leaves. The latter was awarded by the Fuehrer personally and photos of the recipients were published. The other extensively publicized heros were fighter pilots. One of them was the dashing Captain Moelders, a good looking daring fighter pilot, and another was Major Galland. Major Galland headed the Richthofen Squadron. He had served in the Condor Legion during the Spanish Civil War and shot down 104 enemy planes.

I went to school, did my homework and went to the movies much as usual. Movies were our number one entertainment and, over the years, became more and more important as an escape from reality. This was especially so in the winter when the days were short and the weather depressing. Going to the movies helped a lot to lift flagging spirits. Here, after seeing the latest reports from the front in the "New German Newsreel" (which

333

avoided showing German casualties except on rare occasions, like a slightly wounded soldier), we were able to transport ourselves into the world of make-believe, into a no-man's-land, entirely apolitical that seemed to exist in another time and place where everything was, above all, peaceful.

The worst of the winter passed, temperatures rose and another scrap metal collection began on March 3. Hitler youths went knocking on apartment doors. We were urged to bring scrap metal to school. I visited Aunt Martha, Mama, Oma, Aunt Frieda and asked for scrap items but they had nothing left.

All through the winter, I was conscious of the fact that a few weeks hence I would be confirmed. Sundays in Lent, including Passion and Palm Sunday, were days when the Rite of Confirmation took place in Protestant churches. Boys and girls were confirmed at the age of 14. On the Sunday before confirmation, the confirmands submitted to a public oral examination by their pastor at a special service. For both occasions, boys wore navy blue or dark grey suits, long pants for the first time, gloves, hats and a myrtle boutonniere. Girls wore a Sunday dress for examination and for their confirmation, they wore black dresses, black shoes and carried a bouquet of fresh lilies of the valley or yellow roses tied with an embroidered tulle veil. Boys and girls carried hymn books.

The Nazi party instituted Youth Dedication ceremonies scheduled at the same time as confirmations, with the intent of replacing confirmations.

My confirmation was to take place on March 17 at 9 a.m. The preceding Sunday, March 10, was set for our examination.

I frequently visited Aunt Martha and spent hours perusing fashion magazines to find the right patterns for my confirmation dress and the dress I would wear on Examination Sunday. In addition to the two dresses, I was to have a dark blue coat.

Because I was still growing, I was entitled to a new pair of shoes so we applied for and received a permit to purchase them. I made a point of looking at the window displays of every shoe store in our neighborhood until I spotted "my" shoes. To me, they were the height of elegance: black suede and patent leather. I decided that the shoes should be Papa's contribution to my confirmation. I was thrilled to receive my very first pair of silk stockings to complete my outfit.

After New Year's, florist shops stretched wires across their windows and hung up the veils that were used to tie the confirmation bouquets. Every time I passed the florist nearest home, I stopped. I had my eye on a simple veil, edged with a delicate pattern. Mama pointed out another that she liked better, one with an applique of white silk flowers, but I insisted on my choice. Mama tried to talk me out of it. I gave in, then I was sorry and changed back to mine. This tug of war went on for some time. Even Father entered into it and said I should be left alone to chose what I wanted because, after all, it was my day. But the pressure continued. In the end, I gave up and ordered the one Mama liked. It sounds trivial now but it was important to me at the time.

I visited Aunt Martha numerous times for fittings and one day I returned from school to find my dresses and my new coat hanging in the bedroom. The examination dress was of heavy medium blue satin with the matte surface on the outside. The three-quarter length sleeves had inset pleats, the bodice had tiny buttons down the front and the skirt was circular. My confirmation dress was of heavy black taffeta with a flared skirt, fitted waist and bodice. It had elbow length sleeves puffed at the shoulder and a high neckline with a narrow lace collar. The skirt, sleeves and front were trimmed with 1/2" pleated frills. I thought it was elegant.

I was lucky that I had no problems with clothes. Aunt Martha still had a stock of yard goods and notions which lasted throughout the war. She was also very adept at making a new garment out of two older or unfashionable ones. My dresses were always one of a kind and simply lovely.

On Saturday, March 9, I was given my very first permanent at a small beauty parlor which specialized in oil permanents. We considered these to be particularly suitable for my short baby fine hair. The permanent cost the "horrendous" sum of 2.50 marks including cut, perm, shampoo and set. This was the best permanent I have ever had. It lasted for 9 months and was never frizzy.

Sunday afternoon, March 10, at 3 p.m., members of the congregation, confirmands and their families attended the special examination service. Confirmands sat in the front pews, with girls on the right and boys on the left. At one point during the service, Pastor Saran asked questions and I was picked to answer two of them. I was quite excited and remember how my heart pounded when I rose to answer. I answered correctly, I might add.

My examination day also happened to be Memorial Day. Newspaper articles concurred that we should remember the dead but, they continued, this was no time to be sentimental. Men were dying for Germany. A person's personal fate was unimportant. The *"Voelkischer Beobachter"* wrote, "Certainly we think earnestly of the dead but we do not mourn." The front page carried a red headline across the whole page that read: "OVER THE GRAVE FORWARD." I saw this in school when Miss Kunz showed us a copy. The Fuehrer made a speech at the Armory located on Unter den Linden but I did not hear it. We were in church and otherwise occupied. Apparently, he was full of venom and promised that at the end of the war Germany would have achieved the most glorious victory and military triumph in history.

The following week was one of preparation. On Thursday, I attended our last confirmation class and we rehearsed Sunday's ceremony. On Saturday afternoon, I had my hair done. It was waved softly and set in small curls at the nape of the neck. Late in the afternoon I picked up my flowers, a bouquet of fresh lilies of the valley. We placed it in a vase and put it on the balcony to keep fresh. I was very tense and it took me a long time to fall asleep that night.

We rose early because I had to be at the church by 8 a.m. Of course, I could hardly eat any breakfast. I also was thrilled to dress in all new clothes. I wore a ruby and diamond pendant necklace, as well as a ring with an emerald cut hyacinth, which were presents from Aunt Marga. The morning was bright and sunny but very cold. Snow still lay in small piles at the edge of the sidewalks. I felt the cold more keenly because I was nervous.

I joined my fellow confirmands in the congregational building. Pastor Saran came and said a prayer. Then we lined up in pairs on the stairway waiting for our cue to process into the church. Mr. Lambert came walking up the stairs and talked to his pupils whom he had taught and guided for these past eight years. He stopped and talked to me and asked what we were having for dinner. I told him we were having meatloaf and he moved on.

At the sound of the organ intoning the entrance hymn, we processed into the church, which was crowded. Rows of chairs had been placed on each side of the altar. Boys went to sit on the left, the girls on the right. I recall very little of the service and nothing of the sermon Pastor Saran preached. I do remember parts of the sermon he gave at the previous year's rite, which we had been required to attend. Now, at my own confirmation, I was far too nervous. His words went right over my head. I could not concentrate.

When the time came, we went forward in groups of four, knelt at the altar and Pastor Saran confirmed us. Calling each of us by name, he took each one of us by the hand and recited the Bible verse he had chosen for each confirmand as a guide through life and a remembrance of this special day. Many girls and boys received the first verse of Psalm 23, "The Lord is My Shepherd, I Shall not Want." I had a different, longer one: Isaiah 54:10. I loved it and was very proud of it. I always thought of it as something very special. "For the mountains may depart and the hills be removed, but my steadfast love shall not depart from you, and my covenant of peace shall not be removed, says the Lord, who has compassion on you."

The service ended. The sound of the organ swelled. We processed out, went upstairs to get our coats and then met our families. As we emerged from the church, trumpets sounded from the church balcony, church bells pealed and the sun was shining.

Papa had come with Aunt Elsbeth, Aunt Frieda and Oma. We walked around the block to Oma's apartment. Papa made a color movie which I remember well. He started with a view of the church tower, then panned down to the musicians on the balcony and to the crowd streaming out of the church. He filmed me, my aunts and Oma as we stood around and walked along the street. He never gave me a copy of the film and I only had a chance to watch it once. I inquired about it after the war but was told that it was lost. Papa also took a couple of black and white photos. Usually, confirmands had a studio picture taken but I did not. Somehow, the subject of having it done never came up.

March 17 was also Opa's birthday. I stayed with Papa, Oma and Opa until noon and then Papa walked me home. Aunt Marga opened the door and I entered to the sound of a record playing, "May God Bless You." I felt self-conscious and was blushing while I stood there, hoping the song would end soon. Mama, Aunt Martha, Uncle Gustav and the four Schaefers were there. I missed Kurt and Uwe. I had been allowed to invite two friends so I asked Loni and Dieter. We had just taken our places for dinner when the doorbell rang. It was Guenter, carrying a potted myrtle tree and he was invited to stay. The adults sat at the big table, while my friends and I sat at a small table. This might seem strange but it was quite the accepted thing to seat young adults separately.

Karl and Minna Schaefer were very nice but not my favorites. There was something about them that put me off, though I could never put my finger on it. Karl was gregarious and enthusiastic while Minna was quiet, like a little lamb, and completely dominated by her husband. I never liked to visit them. They had a nice sunny apartment in Britz but the atmosphere was strange to me. It seemed to communicate sadness, which I cannot explain. Karl was quite enamored of the Fuehrer and I am not sure if he joined the party but he held some small office. Minna, as a dutiful wife, was a member of the National Socialist Women's Organization. Karl was always full of what the Fuehrer did and how great he was. I can still see him on this occasion sitting at the table and hear his voice as he held forth about the great qualities of the Fuehrer, his accomplishments, all he had done and all he would do for Germany, for us. Karl's trust in his Fuehrer was implicit.

At some point during the meal, Father made a speech and proposed a toast. I was embarrassed because I had not been singled out for such attention before. My friends thought it was great. At 3 p.m., my friends and I took a long walk to an ice cream parlor at the Kottbusser Damm to buy ice cream. Luckily, the afternoon was cold so the ice cream did not melt before we got it home.

We enjoyed coffee, ice cream, cake and a scrumptious walnut mocca gateau. Our really fabulous pastry shop made it especially for this occasion. Afterwards, we played games until my friends went home. The adults stayed until late and my special day came to an end.

I received a number of small gifts. Father and Mother gave me money and the hymn book, Mama gave the bouquet and veil, stockings and lingerie. Aunt Martha made the dresses and the coat. Aunt Marga gave me the necklace and the ring. Aunt Schaefer knitted a lovely sweater made of burgundy yarn with a white silk thread running through it. Karl and Minna Schaefer gave me a bone china place setting and a myrtle, as did Dieter and Loni. I received money from the Riemanns and flowers from Mama's friends and neighbors. All in all, quite modest gifts by later standards but not during wartime.

Myrtle trees were a traditional gift. Girls tended the plants carefully, to make them grow and bloom. In time, the branches were to be braided into traditional bridal wreaths when the girls married. My plants did not make it.

Papa finally agreed to pay for my shoes but not before Oma lectured me on how Papa had to pay support for me for years. The shoes cost 12.50 marks. I do not remember receiving a gift from Oma or Papa's sisters.

After school on Monday, I changed into my confirmation finery, took my bouquet and called on friends, neighbors and good acquaintances to be congratulated and admired. This was customary and people, who had not already done so, presented the confirmand with a small gift, usually money. I only called on the Riemanns, Dieter's and Loni's parents, and a few neighbors. I walked to Aunt Martha's to thank her for making my clothes. I

340

felt self-conscious walking along the streets carrying my bouquet and was glad when it was over.

Not all the girls in my class were confirmed on the same Sunday. When all of us had been confirmed, we wore our confirmation dresses to class on a specified day.

On the Sunday after Easter, we took Holy Communion for the first time. Now we were officially adult members of the congregation and the community. Most of us stopped attending church services after that.

A little footnote about my confirmation dinner. I mentioned earlier that Mr. Lambert asked me on the church stairs what we were having as a main dish. I replied truthfully that we were having meatloaf, gravy, red cabbage, roast potatoes and apple sauce, whereupon he moved on. I found out much later, that he went to another girl's home for dinner and to my school friend Kirsten's home for coffee. In times like these, a chance of a good meal, like a roast with all the trimmings and home baked pastry was not to be missed.

The type of meatloaf we had was called "Mock Hare." It was a mixture of ground pork, beef and veal with one egg, a few breadcrumbs, onions, salt and pepper. Pieces of smoked bacon, 1 to 2 inches long and 1/4 inch wide, were inserted all over. It was baked and basted until crisp and brown on top. Of course, this was a very ordinary, everyday meal. Certainly, it was not a dish one would serve on a special occasion. I did not think anything of it at the time. I was not involved in household affairs and meal planning.

Much later, Mama told me the reason we were forced to have such a simple entree. For several months before my confirmation, Mother saved up meat rations. People were not allowed to save the coupons. The coupons were only valid during the current ration period, usually a calendar month.

Mother, who had been a customer at the same neighborhood butcher for 30 years, explained to the proprietress that she would like to have a nice roast for my special day. Mother asked if she could surrender meat coupons every week on account. The woman agreed and clipped mother's coupons every week. A few days before March 17, Mother went to order the roast. The butcher's wife looked Mother straight in the eye and said, "What roast? What meat coupons?" Imagine Mother's horror. Poor Mother was devastated and humiliated beyond belief. Mother had given up her entire meat rations and deprived herself of much needed food for a long time. It was a disaster. But she never said a word to me about it.

I am sorry she did not tell me because I would not have continued to curtsy and greet the butcher's wife had I known about her treachery. But that was typical of the way I was treated. Everything unpleasant or worrisome was kept from me. Nothing was discussed. I was to have a carefree childhood. Thus I was oblivious, innocent and naive to a great extent as to what went on the real world. I lived in my little cocoon, protected and shielded, not learning much about people.

While I was preoccupied with my confirmation, Laws for the Protection of Youth were passed. Persons under the age of 18 were required to be off the streets after dark, out of cinemas, restaurants and places of entertainment by 9 p.m., unless accompanied by an adult.

I don't recall what we did this year at Easter. There were, of course, few of the usual Easter confections but I think we received one extra egg per person.

After the Easter vacation, the new school year began. I advanced to the next grade and once more life was routine except for whatever new regulations our leaders ordained.

Papers published mysterious messages hinting at imminent momentous events and actions planned personally, so it was implied, by our Fuehrer. From the *Voelkischer Beobachter* on April 7, 1940: "Germany is ready. All eyes are upon the Fuehrer." We were wondering what it might be and what was going to happen. Our curiosity was satisfied and our questions answered when we awoke on April 9 to the news that German troops had invaded Denmark and Norway. The newscasts and lead articles in the papers proclaimed how Denmark had offered no resistance at all, being completely stunned by the sudden and unexpected invasion. We were told that "these countries have to be protected from the Allies. We have to defend their neutrality." The Norwegians, however, were not quite so easily persuaded to accept the Fuehrer's protection. But, willing or not, they were now safe from the Allies under the umbrella of the Fuehrer's army. Blitz air attacks would take care of any and all remaining resistance.

On May 6, we had assembly in order to listen to Rust, Minister of Education, make a special broadcast addressed to schoolchildren. The following is a quote from his speech: "God created the world as a place for work and struggle. Whoever doesn't understand the laws of life's struggles will be counted out, as in the boxing ring. All good things on this earth are like trophies. The strong win them. The weak lose them. The German people under Hitler did not take up arms in order to invade foreign countries and subdue people to serve them. The German people were forced into action by foreign nations who blocked our access to bread and solidarity."

Somewhere in his speech Rust appealed to girls to bring their combed out hair to school. The combings would be collected and used in felt production. A collection container was placed in the school entrance hall. I had short, fine hair and did not bring any combings to school.

Four days later, on May 10, Germany invaded Holland, Belgium, Luxembourg and France. On the same day, Churchill became Prime Minister. He was immediately ridiculed and vilified in our press and on radio.

A headline and report, dated May 11, read:
"CHIEF WARMONGER CHURCHILL BECOMES PRIME MINISTER."

On Friday night, Chamberlain renounced his office as Prime Minister and First Lord of the Treasury. Chief warmonger Churchill became Prime Minister. It is further reported that Churchill is said to have asked all Ministers to remain at their posts for the time being. Thus, the most extreme warmonger usurped all political power. The umbrella and prayer book carrying Chamberlain attempted at all times to play the role of an honorable man. The British Cabinet is now headed by an exponent of plutocracy, which since time immemorial has promoted a brutal war of destruction against the German People."

I did not notice anyone showing outward signs of excitement about the invasions by German troops. Things calmly went on as before. Exuberance was confined to the news media. The radio broadcast special bulletins every few hours, preceded by fanfare and followed many times by the national anthems, the "England Song" or other appropriate music. A number of new songs were used as signature tunes to identify individual bulletins. For France, it was "The Watch on the Rhine" and later the new

"Song of France." For Greece, it was the "Balkan Song." The Lutine Bell rang to indicate the sinking of enemy vessels. Other special announcements were preceded by Liszt's "Preludes."

Newspaper headlines:

May 12

"MAXIMUM SENTENCES OF PENAL SERVITUDE FOR CRIMINALS LISTENING TO FOREIGN RADIO STATIONS. " (Note: Offenders were sentenced to 5 to 6 years in a maximum security prison and in some cases they were sentenced to death.)

May 18

"OUR TROOPS IN BRUSSELS. BELGIAN GOVERNMENT FLEES TO OSTENDE."

"The documentary entitled "The Momentous Battle of Decision in the West" will be shown in special performances and at special prices. Admission: Adults 40 pfennig, children and soldiers half-price, 20 pfennig."

On May 21, an announcement proclaimed that pregnant women would receive additional <u>daily</u> food rations: 1 liter of milk, 5.2 ounces of semolina or pasta, for up to 6 months after delivery or for as long as the mother breast-feeds the baby. A doctor's certificate was required.

In addition to the normal <u>monthly</u> rations, they were to receive 12.2 ounces of butter, 8.75 ounces of cheese or 1 pound of cottage cheese, 4.2 ounces of synthetic honey, 0.75 ounces of cocoa powder, 8 pounds 14 ounces of bread or 4 pounds of flour, 1 pound of children's starch products, 2 pounds of meat, 3/4 liter of milk a day and extra soap.

May 22

"ON ENGLAND'S DOORSTEP. THE CHANNEL HAS BEEN REACHED. WHEN IT COMES TO RUNNING AWAY, THE ENGLISH ARE ALWAYS THE FIRST, THAT IS THE BRITISH FIGHTING TACTIC."

On May 24, there was a distribution of three eggs per person.

In addition, it was proclaimed that bells made of bronze and parts of buildings made of copper must be delivered to collection centers. The obligation to deliver also applied to private owners of church bells. Bells weighing less than 20 pounds or those used for signaling purposes were exempt.

At noon on May 28, following the special announcement about the capitulation of the Belgian Army over all German radio stations, the "Song of France" was heard for the first time. The text was written by Heinrich Anacker and the music was composed by the composer of the "England Song," Herms Niel.

New announcements came over the radio: "The Commander in Chief of the French Army, General Prioux, was captured!

Number of prisoners incalculable. British units in process of complete dissolution.

Rescue fleet destroyed."

May 26

"Calais has fallen."

May 28

"Belgium has capitulated unconditionally. King Leopold stays."

May 29

"We regret to announce that Prince William of Prussia has been killed in action."

June 4

"German troops enter Dunkirk. Thousands (of British and French) taken prisoner."

The Fuehrer ordered bells to be rung and flags to be flown in celebration of Germany's victory in Flanders.

I cannot recall a single comment about the offensive by anyone I knew, except my teacher and our headmistress. In fact, people of my acquaintance did not even talk about the war. We were so saturated with news reports that we were glad to talk about things not connected with the war. This does not mean to say that we ignored current events completely but they were not the major topic of our conversations. It does not preclude that there were many people who did feel elated and excited about the news from the fronts. As one victory announcement chased another, those of our neighbors and acquaintances who were Nazi sympathizers or more looked smug and let events speak for themselves. Occasionally, in public, I caught complimentary comments about the Fuehrer, his policies and victories.

Even the reports about the bombing of Freiburg in May by enemy planes did not change anything. Much was made in the media of the raid in which 23 civilians were reported killed, most of them children. Apparently, a school or school yard was hit. We, Mama and others in our circle, assumed that the pilots had been aiming for some military target nearby and missed. We all agreed that errors happen during a war on both sides. What else were we to expect or what did the government expect? It was war. One had to take whatever happened. Berliners were sober and realistic about the situation. It was terrible that children were killed and there was sympathetic empathy but also unsentimental acceptance of that which could not be changed. We attached no blame to the attackers.

From the newspapers:

June 6

"BELLS RING FROM EVERY CHURCH TOWER

Greater Germany puts out flags to honor her soldiers.

Berlin one sea of flags."

On June 14, it was proclaimed that flags were to be flown for three days. Our newspaper stated:

"On the occasion of the great victory won by German troops in France, which was crowned today by the entrance into Paris, as well as on the occasion of the victorious conclusion of the heroic fight in Norway, the Fuehrer ordered that as of today, and for the duration of

348

three days, flags are to be displayed in all of Germany to honor our soldiers."

Throughout the early summer days of 1940, I expected to hear at any moment that the Fuehrer had ordered the invasion of England. Rumors circulated as to the plans the Fuehrer had for England once he occupied it and how he would reeducate the British to fit into his schemes. I remember hearing details but cannot recall them with any certainty. I was, therefore, astonished that the Fuehrer made no move. After Dunkirk, I was sure that the Fuehrer would follow hard on the heels of the fleeing expeditionary force across the channel. Nothing happened. This gave rise to all sorts of stories. For instance, it was said that the Fuehrer had premonitions or visions warning him not to invade England. Meanwhile, the hate campaign against Britain continued.

On June 22, the Fuehrer spoke in the Reichstag and said that there was no reason for the war to continue. The Fuehrer offered peace to England. "Therefore, if the war continues, England is to blame," he exclaimed. The British rejected the Fuehrer's peace offer.

The Fuehrer was obviously annoyed and angry that his peace offer was not accepted and vowed that in consequence he would fight to the bitter end. England and France had rejected the Fuehrer's hand of peace. In doing so, they had thrown down the gauntlet and Germany had picked it up. The government denied that the Fuehrer would make yet another peace offer to France.

At this Reichstag session, the Fuehrer promoted Hermann Goering to Reichsmarshall. Goering, always a flashy dresser, began carrying a fancy marshal's baton and wearing a cape. The latter was probably due to the fact that he had become quite stout. The cape was more flattering to his full figure than a coat.

349

Goering was the only top Nazi who enjoyed a certain popularity among the populace and who was openly flamboyant. Of course, no ordinary German knew what he or the other *"Bonzen"* (a derogatory name for power and/or money hungry party bureaucrats) were really like. None of the top Nazi leaders allowed anyone to get close to them but kept people at a distance.

News teams accompanied the advancing troops into the Netherlands, Belgium and France. On newsreels, I saw thousands of bombs falling on Rotterdam, as well as paratroopers jumping and descending on the city. I watched German troops taking Brussels, artillery firing, machine guns barking, soldiers running and throwing hand grenades and bombs whistling down and exploding. I saw Belgian, Dutch, French and British prisoners of war sitting by the wayside awaiting transportation to POW camps and the retreating expeditionary force at Dunkirk, with countless abandoned vehicles and weapons. There was the break-through into France and the German victory at Sedan, which was reminiscent of WWI for many who had fought there. Thousands of Allied troops were trapped at Dunkirk facing the sea with the German Army at their back. Not all of them got away. As I recall, there were no pictures of wounded or dead Germans.

The Blitz continued. Norway capitulated and Paris was occupied. Films showed German troops marching down the Champs Elysees, through the Arc de Triomphe, all the while stepping out smartly. The German flag was raised over Versailles and France was forced to surrender. The Fuehrer gloated with satisfaction. He had humiliated the French as they humiliated the Germans in 1918. The French were forced to sign the armistice in the same Wagon Lit coach at Compiegne in which the Germans had signed in 1918. We were told to "Fly the flags. Ring the bells."

Father never put a flag out because his balcony faced the yard. Mama had a very small flag and only put it out when the papers specifically ordered flags to be flown by everyone.

And so, on June 28, the flags flew and the bells rang out all over Germany. A victory parade, the first since 1871 following the defeat of the French in the Franco-Prussian War, passed through the Brandenburg Gate. Throngs of Berliners, who had been given the day off, turned out to watch and cheer. BDM members carpeted the streets with flowers and flower petals.

I did not see it since I did not go into town to take part in the celebrations. Father and Mother were not inclined to do so and Mama was so antiwar and anti-Hitler that she would not participate in anything connected with the regime.

The radio covered the events live and later on we saw it all in the movies. The newspaper next morning brought pages of pictures of cheering, enthusiastic, smiling crowds, with HJ and BDM members shouting "Heil Hitler!"

At this particular time, I was most interested in the fact that it was summer and vacation time. School was out! In the spring, I had my medical at Scherl and was notified that I would be sent to the Brenner Pass in the Alps for six weeks. It sounded great and I was looking forward to it. Then came the let down. A family conference decided it was too risky to let me travel that far through the western parts of Germany which were subject to enemy air attacks. Perhaps the train would be bombed. Mama was in favor of my going but everybody else was against it. She was outnumbered.

So, Mama and I went to Balz instead. For the first week or so, we stayed with Aunt Lotte. However, she received a letter that her sister was coming and we made arrangements to move

351

into the inn next to the bakery, about a mile or so east of Aunt Lotte's house.

The couple who owned the inn, Mr. and Mrs. Ziegler, were in their mid to late 50s at that time and their three sons were in the Army. The heir to the property (the inn and the hereditary farm) was a widower with two small children, both under the age of 7. Another son owned a farm approximately 2 miles away. The inn, a large building, had at one time been the local manor house. In the early 1800s, Queen Louise of Prussia spent the night there on her way to East Prussia to meet Napoleon. The house was badly in need of repairs and renovation. On the west side of the house, steps from a terrace led into what had once been a formal garden but which was then just an overgrown copse. The terrace steps had begun to crumble, moss grew between the flagstones and the big flower urns stood empty.

The north side of the garden bordered the road, the south side a meadow and the west side a potato field ending at a small pond. I liked to walk along the edge of the potato field early in the morning and watch small frogs jump into the furrows. I picked them up, collected them in my apron, carried them to the pond and watched them jump in. The pond was also full of leeches. I was warned about how they leech on to people and suck blood so I was careful never to step into the water.

I spent most of the time amusing myself by reading, sitting on the terrace, singing songs, making up stories and acting them out to the music I sang or hummed. We took our usual walks to the local lakes, visited Aunt Lotte, wrote postcards, walked to Vietz or bought delicious wild blueberry and sour cherry cake at the bakery. We enjoyed good and plentiful food like homemade sausages, smoked ham, pork, brick oven baked rye bread, fresh butter and beef. Since we lived on meager rations in town and eggs were also strictly rationed, it was a treat to feast on

352

scrambled eggs with smoked bacon. Mama, concerned about my health, made me drink half a gallon of milk a day. However, she boiled it first because the milk was not pasteurized and she was afraid tuberculosis germs might be transmitted from a cow. I hated the taste of it and have never liked milk since then.

The summer was lovely, although unusually hot and dry. But one morning, I woke up to a strange sight. Mama was sleeping under an open umbrella. It had started to rain during the night and was still raining, one of those steady soft country rains, and it was raining through the ceiling. The floor was covered with pots and pans to catch the drips. The scene reminded me immediately of Spitzweg's painting, "The Poor Poet."

Much to my delight, Vicki turned up unexpectedly. I don't know if she had ever ventured this deep into the country before. One night, just after we had gone to bed, she created quite a commotion. She burst into our room, very upset, to report that she had found a big green grasshopper in her room. She refused to go back until we chased it out.

A couple of nights later we heard Vicki scream. We rushed into her room and found her sitting in bed, her sheets pulled over her head, pointing to a bat that was flying around the room. She was terrified that the bat would get into her hair. It took some time to chase the bat out of the window with a broom. I am sure the bat was more scared than Vicki. There was never a dull moment with Vicki around and I was sorry when she left after only a week.

Our stay this time was only four weeks, and toward the middle of August, Mama and I returned to Berlin.

Newspaper announcements:
July 26, 1940
Extra ration: 3.5 ounces of butter.

Enemy of the People executed.

Otto S. broke into 20 locked cars during blackout.

Cigarettes rationed. Smokers receive ration cards.

Railroads were used primarily for troop transports and supply shipments for the armed forces. The result was a shortage of good trains to supply Berlin with victuals. Streetcars were utilized at night to transport food, mainly potatoes into the city.

School started a few days after our return to Berlin and it was back to routine for me. I had always loved school but my homeroom teacher was the reason I began to dislike it.

We followed current events daily. Miss Kunz happily dwelled on events that had taken place during our holidays, particularly the reports about our U-boats sinking many British ships, destroying 200,000 tons of shipping in three days at the end of July, as well as additional tonnage since then, or so we were told.

The Luftwaffe had been flying sorties of a blitz nature against London since the beginning of July, pounding the city along with other targets in Britain night after night.

On the other hand, the RAF bombed a great number of German towns during July and the beginning of August.

By the time we had returned from our summer vacation, many soldiers stationed in countries now occupied by German troops were coming home on leave. All of them arrived bearing gifts, items which had completely disappeared from the shelves of our shops and department stores, such as luxury lingerie, silk stockings, silk scarves, perfumes, perfumed soaps, lipsticks, costume jewelry from France, chocolates from Belgium, furs

354

from Norway, cocoa from Holland, ham and butter from Denmark and coffee. We envied everybody who was the recipient of such luxuries.

Kurt was in the Army. At first he was stationed near Berlin while receiving his basic training. In the summer of 1940, his unit was transferred to France to the outskirts of Paris. One day, we received a small parcel from Kurt and we were very excited when we opened it. It contained two pairs of silk stockings and a lipstick for Mama and a pretty pair of pajamas for me. The pajamas were made of white moire taffeta with alternating pastel pink, blue and green stripes. I loved them but alas, they were too small. I could not wear them but I kept them just to look at. I have no idea what happened to them. I guess they ended up as an exchange item for coffee or food.

When Kurt came home on leave, the conversation at one point turned to all the goodies that were being sent, shipped and brought home by members of the German armed forces. Kurt told us that the officers had cornered the market. For one thing, they had more money than the enlisted men. For another, they made sure that the troops were kept working late so they hardly ever had a chance to go into town while the shops were open. The officers, of course, could go almost any time. Besides, the officers had the opportunity to ship large items and quantities of goods to Germany without using normal channels, with no questions asked. Kurt reported that the ordinary soldiers were very sour about it.

Our headmistress and Miss Kunz asked and encouraged us to write to members of the armed forces. We were to address our letter simply "To an Unknown Soldier" and choose the destination, either France, Belgium, Holland, Norway, Denmark and, later, Russia. I addressed my letter to France and one day I received a reply from a young man named Heinz. He was from

Frankfurt/Main and 24 years old. In civilian life, he was a baker and his widowed mother lived in Frankfurt. I was a terrible letter writer. I can't say that his letters were very interesting, either. Our correspondence dragged on but he never mentioned anything about Paris or what he was doing in his time off. I sent the occasional parcel with cigarettes, cookies and whatever else was available that a serviceman might find useful. Of course, I also wrote to Kurt and to Uncle Herbert and sent them small parcels. Later on, I acquired another pen pal, Robert, who wrote polite, formal and impersonal letters. I never found out much about him. Judging by his style of writing, I thought he was older than Heinz.

Hitler Youth were busy once again going door to door, collecting scrap metal, rags, old papers, wood glue, paint, old clothing and shoes. By this time, we had nothing left to contribute.

HJ boys were called upon for war service, acting as couriers distributing propaganda material, doing odd jobs, and being watchmen at party offices. The boys also worked as messengers and mail carriers for police departments, post offices and fire departments. They distributed ration cards and during blackouts they helped people find their way home from railroad stations. The boys cleared snow from roads and pavements, sanded icy streets and delivered goods to retail shops and factories.

As the time for the potato harvest drew near, we were told that the RAF was dropping potato beetles to destroy our potato harvest. HJ boys were sent into the fields to search for the little pests and destroy them.

During the harvest, many Berlin HJ and BDM members were drafted to work on farms. They were also detailed to help mothers with small children, work in old age homes and kindergartens, in civilian and military hospitals, and first aid stations. These jobs were considered Honorable War Duties and taken very seriously.

Berlin had been attacked on August 14 while we were still in the country. But we returned before August 20 when Berlin was attacked again. The raid started at 12:20 a.m. and the all clear sounded at 2:23 a.m. I was, of course, fast asleep when the alarm came. It took me a few minutes to wake up, orient myself and get dressed. Mama was ready before I was and urged me to hurry into the basement shelter. I was very drowsy and tried to sleep but I was not very successful because everyone was talking. After a little while, the antiaircraft guns started firing. I tried to guess where the planes were but I did not hear any bomb detonations nearby. It sounded as if the planes were not directly overhead. Although it was a long raid, I heard that the bomb damage in Berlin was slight because the British planes dropped more leaflets than bombs. Naturally, I would have liked to see a leaflet but as soon as it was known that they had been dropped the HJ and other organizations were on the streets in force to capture the leaflets almost before they hit the ground. It was strictly prohibited to pick them up, read them and keep them. It was considered treason if one was caught with enemy publications.

The next day, the news report on the radio said, "Bomber units flew another terror attack against the Reich capital. The combined efforts by air defenses prevented a systematic attack and the enemy air gangsters dropped their explosives and fire bombs aimlessly onto several parts of town. There were casualties and damage on apartment houses in working class districts."

On my way to school the following morning, and on subsequent mornings following air raids, I noticed a number of boys walking slowly, eyes to the ground, scanning the pavement and the road. I asked one what he was doing and he said that he was looking for antiaircraft and bomb shrapnel. They were difficult to spot because the metal was grey and blended in with the grey pavements and with the gravel between streetcar tracks. It was the latest and most interesting item to collect. I started looking myself and was thrilled when I found a couple of pieces.

Another sought after souvenir for kids were English fire bomb remnants after they had exploded. These bombs resembled a thick stick. They were 6 sided and about 3 feet long, with a small head containing explosives and a long tail made of highly polished aluminum. The latter part was what was usually found, somewhat warped and discolored in places by the impact, the explosion and fire. I had one. I did not find it but asked an air raid warden for it after a demonstration.

Undetonated fire bombs were used by the air raid wardens in their demonstrations of how to deal with bombs if found and how to put out fires caused by them. Their mechanism was simple, actually quite primitive. The heavy head had to strike almost head-on in order to explode on impact and it caused a relatively small fire. However, if the fire was not discovered quickly, it could spread and develop into a serious blaze. Wardens made rounds during raids and a thorough search followed the all clear. If a fire was discovered, wardens and tenants tried to put it out.

Early in the war when the damage caused by enemy planes was insignificant, the fire brigade responded to calls from private residences and apartment houses if no priorities prevented the response. Industrial concerns, factories, government buildings and hospitals were first on the priority list. Later on, when damage was substantial and extensive, we were on our own. Outside help was seldom, if ever, available or only after a considerable time. Ambulances raced through the night to bombed sites during raids and were at times hit themselves by bombs. I heard of a number of these incidents from people who had been eyewitnesses or whose relatives told them about it. It was sad but that was war.

In order to minimize the danger of our windows being blown out, we crisscrossed them with tape and opened them before going to the shelter.

Britain, we were told by our government, was in bad shape. Their troops trained with broomsticks instead of guns, which was pathetic and ridiculous. The British air force was practically nonexistent. Germany controlled and was master of the skies. Not in my book. Mama said, "Just wait and see, who laughs last laughs best." Right at the beginning of the war, Goering had boasted loudly that his name would be Meyer (a common name and also the name of a big chain of liquor stores whose slogan was "No party without Meyer") if even as much as one single enemy plane ever reached Berlin. Well, it did and not only one. Goering was instantly referred to as Meyer.

On the mornings following air raids, we found out what had been hit: Siemens, extensive fires in Moabit and Wedding, hits near the Lehrter Bahnhof and so on. Next came the news reports that acknowledged the fact that Berlin had been attacked but minimized or did not mention damage or casualties. Instead, the newscasters dwelt at length on the air raids the Luftwaffe made on London.

On bright, moonlit nights we felt pretty safe and sure that we would be able to get a good night's sleep. During the first couple of years, the fierce fire from the antiaircraft guns called *Flieger Abwehr Kanone,* or flak, could be heard as soon as enemy planes appeared over the city. We were able to guess how far the enemy planes were from our neighborhood, when they were overhead and when they left by the volume of sound. The flak bellowed for as long as an enemy aircraft was over greater Berlin. Once the planes passed the Brunswick/Hannover area, our all clear sounded.

The next air raid on Berlin, during the night of August 25-26, was different. This time more than just a few fire bombs and leaflets came down. There were 81 planes that dropped a total of 22 tons of bombs, many of which hit the northern boroughs of Reinickendorf, Pankow and Lichtenberg.

Headline: Enemy planes flew over Berlin.

During the night of August 25-26 enemy planes flew over the Greater Berlin city area and dropped fire bombs on two suburbs. One of the aircrafts was shot down on its return flight.

Then, during the raid on August 28, bombs hit close to our area for the first time and resulted in casualties. Several houses in the Kottbusser Strasse, on the Kottbusser Damm, and the Kottbusser Bridge were hit. It was reported that 10 people were dead and 20 injured. The papers made a lot of the fact that these were working class neighborhoods and civilians had been killed. It was something of a sensation, since none of us had ever seen actual bomb damage, and hundreds of people flocked to see the bombed sites, Father and I among them. This was very atypical for Father, but these were atypical times and atypical happenings. It is really strange how calm one can remain viewing the scene of destruction and death. The reaction usually sets in later as does the fact that this sort of thing can happen to you at any time.

Because only apartment houses were damaged and destroyed, it was a great opportunity for the propaganda machine

360

to kick in and go to town. The victims were all buried at the same time in the St. James' Cemetery near the Hermannplatz following a well publicized memorial service which was attended, in addition to the bereaved families, by numerous high party officials and the local population.

Newspaper headlines:
August 28
> Six hours alarm in London. England admits: Germany bombs only military targets.

Churchill's lies about the bombing of the Reich capital, Berlin.

August 15
> From Narvic to the Pyrenees: German front of facts. In three days England lost 317 airplanes but they still delude themselves by lying and broadcasting victory reports.

August 18
> Total Blockade of England.

Germany begins the total blockade of England. Total victory on the seas around England.

> A crazy act of villainy: Bombs fall on Goethe's garden house in Weimar.

During the month of August, we heard that the Luftwaffe continued heavy attacks on London, the West End in particular. Fires raged and damage was substantial. It was reported that on

August 8, 800 German planes raided London. Newsreels showed aerial pictures of London under attack, bombs released from planes hurtling down and exploding, clouds of smoke rising and countless fires burning. The Fuehrer announced an all out war on British cities in reprisal for the RAF bombings of German cities.

The movie *"Jud Suess"* premiered on August 20. One morning our class was taken to the cinema to watch a special performance of this movie together with other schoolchildren. I did not want to see it because I heard that it contained a torture scene and the heroine, played by Christina Soederbaum, committed suicide. (Christina Soederbaum committed suicide by drowning in a number of films and was consequently nicknamed "Reich water corpse.") I did not like this type of movie. I did not like unhappy endings. Also, I did not like the idea of torture. Therefore, I was not at all happy but very tense in anticipation of what I was going to be forced to see. When it came to the torture scene, I lowered my head and pressed my hands over my ears until I was sure it was over.

This film was another tool to intensify anti-Semitic sentiments. Over the years, I had already heard enough about the Jews being to blame for everything that had gone wrong in Germany economically, politically and otherwise after WWI. This film cast the Jews again, and more so, in the role of criminals, usurers and sex fiends. It came across very clearly and emphatically that the heroine hated Jews.

Newspapers printed the following headlines and stories, with some photographs, during this period of 1940:
Caption under photos of British children being evacuated to the U.S.A.:

"Children of plutocrats are evacuated to the U.S.A. Working class children must stay in England."

August 29

Last night British planes systematically attacked residential quarters in the Reich capital. High explosive and fire bombs were dropped, killing and wounding many civilians, causing fires and other damage.

August 30

Disgusting travesty was witnessed by 4 million Berliners. The attack on Berlin residential areas is falsified by Churchill into "a successful attack on military targets."
Photo of destroyed living room at the Kottbusser Tor and four photos of bomb damage on the Kottbusser Damm.

August 31

During the night, British planes continued their attack on Berlin and other targets in the Reich. A number of bombs fell in center city and on working class residential areas.

September 1-10
Nightly air raids on Berlin.

September 7

Last night, enemy planes again attacked the Reich capital. Casualties and damage were caused by indiscriminate bombing of nonmilitary targets in center city. The Luftwaffe has now begun to attack London with strong forces. Last night, dock installations in East London were attacked with high power explosive and fire bombs. Fires started. Conflagrations were observed in the docks and at the oil supply depot at Thameshaven.

English Royal Family flees to Canada.

September 8
Senseless night attack by British aircraft on Berlin. Berlin-Wedding bombed, no military objects hit.
Again, senseless bombing of Berlin by British bandits.

September 27
Churchill fantasizes about his successes over Berlin. Night and day, heavy attacks flown against all parts of England. Schools start on time after nocturnal raid.

October 2
Attack on Berlin working class district.
What Churchill plans to bomb in Berlin.

October 4
Aimless bombing of Berlin residential areas. (Photos showed destroyed apartment houses in East Berlin.)

364

From September 1 through 11, the RAF attacked Berlin almost daily with some raids being heavier than others and there were more fires. The attacks continued less frequently into November and, by the end of 1940, 27 night attacks had taken place. We had a breathing space after December.

It became a novelty to have one or two nights without an air raid. I was quite astonished to wake up some mornings realizing I had had a night of undisturbed sleep. The current joke advised people to go to bed early to get as much sleep as possible before an air raid. When they came into the cellar and said, "Good Morning," it meant they had slept. If they said, "Good evening," they had not slept but if they said, "Heil Hitler!" it meant they had always been asleep.

The Fuehrer spoke on September 4. The audience was made up of nurses, social workers and women. At the time, I did not know, but found out later, that when the Fuehrer spoke the people who filled the Sportpalast did not come of their own accord, singly and voluntarily. They came by order and in groups from factories, hospitals and other organizations. The reason for this particular speech was the opening of the Winter Aid Campaign. The Fuehrer said that although the British had bombed German cities he, the Fuehrer, had refrained from bombing Britain in the hope that the British would stop this "mischief." "But Herr Churchill has interpreted my gesture as a sign of weakness," he said. "Now we will bomb British cities night after night. For every 2 or 3 thousand tons of bombs dropped by the RAF, we will drop 150, 230, 300 or 400 tons a night." Shouts and applause interrupted him at this point. He continued, "When they declare that they will increase their attacks on our cities, we will raze their cities to the ground. We will stop the handiwork of these air pirates, so help us God."

Of course, we had begun to make jokes about the Fuehrer and Goering, pardon, Herr Meyer. The Fuehrer emphatically stated that in reprisal for air raids on German cities his air force, the Luftwaffe, would erase British cities from the map. We remembered these words later on when most German cities lay in ruins. Our comment: Hitler lost his eraser and Churchill found it.

On September 11, it was reported that Buckingham Palace was hit by German bombs. The raids on England and London continued, with London hit hard. Newspapers and the "Illustrated," a magazine I read, featured stories and pages of photos showing Londoners bedding down with blankets on the concrete floor of tube station platforms every night for weeks on end. Every inch of space was filled with men, women and children of all ages.

Miss Kunz enthusiastically showed us these pictures, smirking about the "scared British." Mama's comment was: "Just wait! The English have not finished with us yet. They haven't even started. It is abominable to take malicious pleasure when people are under attack and ridicule them for seeking what shelter they can." People in Berlin did not shelter in the U-Bahn because the U-Bahn in Berlin is not built as deep as in some other cities.

An air raid which took place during the night September 23-24 lasted four hours. Again, the industrial north of the city was the target. Railroad stations received hits but I didn't know how severe the damage was. I did not see it myself. The damage was probably repaired in record time.

The longest air raid so far occurred on the night of September 25-26. It lasted from 11 p.m. until 4 a.m. I recall very clearly looking at the clock in the kitchen when we were ready to go into the basement. Most air raids started around 11 or 11:30

p.m. We could almost set our alarm clocks to wake us before the sirens sounded. The British were very punctual.

As the number of raids increased, I lost a lot of sleep. I began to go to bed earlier. I found it hard to wake up when the alarm went off because I was in the deepest phase of sleep. I felt like a zombie. I often put my clothes on backwards and my feet into the wrong shoes taking longer to get ready than necessary while Mama stood over me urging me to hurry and antiaircraft guns could be heard firing in the distance.

I mentioned that a number of partitions in the basement had been removed in order to make room for an air raid shelter. People had brought chairs and benches and picked a spot. Here we spent many a night sitting up and talking or trying to sleep while above us bombers unloaded their cargo and antiaircraft batteries tried to defend the air space over the city. Conversation in the shelter often centered around food, on the air raids, on the damage done, listening to and commenting on the antiaircraft fire, the bomb explosions and guessing how far away they might be. A number of people did not talk and they tried to sleep.

Any time of year, the basement was cool and slightly damp. I wore warm clothes, socks and boots and wrapped myself in a blanket. Nevertheless, after hours of sitting still, the dampness got the better of me. I was very cold and clammy in spite of the warm clothes, the blanket and stamping my feet. It was almost impossible to sleep sitting up. Once I made it back into bed, it took a while to get warm and fall asleep. It was tiresome because school still started at 8 a.m.

Some people brought thermos flasks with hot drinks and snacks into the shelter. It was quite interesting. Here were people who, although they had lived in the same building for years, decades, even 50 years, had only a nodding acquaintance with each other. Now they were all stuck together in the small cellar for hours.

Our neighbor, Mr. Wagner, was a fun person with stories to tell. He reminisced about his life prior to WWI. It was fascinating. He described all sorts of things, food in particular. This was a favorite topic since we were short of food. I can still hear him telling us that you could purchase a *prix fixe* dinner (soup, roast with two vegetables, rolls, butter, coffee and dessert) for 50 pfennig. When one bought two large white herrings, the fishmonger threw in three small ones for free and so on. Mr. Wagner's reminiscences turned our thoughts to all the wonderful things that were no longer available and made us forget or at least ignore what was happening in the skies over the city at that moment.

Mr. Wagner had started to come to the basement only recently. His wife, whom I had never seen, suffered from depression or so Mama told me. Mrs. Wagner never went out so he did everything. He shopped. He cooked. He took care of her. He was always friendly, courteous and cheerful. He had stayed upstairs with her during air raids. Then one day, he received a directive ordering him to take his wife to an institution. If I remember rightly, it was Ploetzensee. I knew that Ploetzensee was a mental institution. If children wanted to deride someone they sang, "You are crazy, kid, you belong in Ploetzensee where all the crazy people are." He was very upset and tried in vain to keep her at home. She had never done anyone any harm. He was not permitted to do so and he was not allowed to visit her.

Within two months a notice appeared on our building's bulletin board announcing Mrs. Wagner's death. Poor Mr. Wagner was crying when next we met him. He had been married for 50 years. His wife's death was a tremendous shock to him. We felt sorry for him.

Rumors circulated that an increasing number of institutionalized mentally ill people died shortly after being transferred to different institutions, always without knowledge or consent of the family. It was rumored that they were "helped" into the hereafter.

The death notices received by relatives of mentally ill patients read as follows, "We regret to inform you that your wife (husband, son, daughter) who was recently transferred to (name of institution) by ministerial order, unexpectedly died on (date) of (cause of death). Unfortunately, all our medical efforts were without success."

At the end of September, it was announced that children under 14 would be evacuated. That left me out. I talked with my classmates about it. We wanted to be evacuated because we thought it was exciting, like going on a long vacation to a place we had not been before. But, we were too old. We felt left out and resented it to a certain degree.

Once more, a big drive was on for raw materials, including scrap metal, old newspapers and bones. All iron fences and such had long been dismantled. Church bells had been melted down and even the metal tips atop flag poles had been collected. Again, we were urged and required to collect more scrap metal items from people's homes such as pots and pans, old irons or other metal items that might still be stored in basements. After the first round of collecting from family, friends and neighbors a long time ago, not a piece of scrap metal was left in anybody's household, certainly not mine. I refused to go door-to-door collecting. All children everywhere had to collect and there were no sources left.

The pressure to produce continued and I began to worry. The teacher appointed to be in charge of this operation set up a table in the school yard during our break. We lined up and delivered whatever we had. The items were weighed and the amount entered in a book, as well as in individual booklets each child had been given. I was afraid I would have only a row of goose eggs under my name. That would be very bad indeed. However, help was near.

I left home at 7:20 every morning and walked approximately four blocks to the streetcar. Occasionally, I walked with Mr. Becker. The Beckers, a couple in their 50s, had an apartment on the third floor and I liked them. Mr. Becker was wounded in WWI and, as a result, he walked with a limp. He was an engineer but I don't know what kind. On our walk, we talked mainly about school and current events. Mr. Becker was an ardent anti-Nazi and Hitler hater. He felt free to express his caustic criticism of the regime to me but never while we were on the streetcar.

One morning, I mentioned my problem and my inability to find any more scrap metal. I said I was afraid that I would get into trouble for not delivering anything. Much to my astonishment and delight, Mr. Becker replied, "Don't you worry about it anymore. I can help you." From then on, once or even twice a week, he told me to open my briefcase and dropped some neatly wrapped rolls of aluminum and brass discs into it. They were obviously discards from some work process in his factory. At first, I was a little apprehensive about delivering these items to the teacher and thought he might want to know where I got them but he never asked. In fact, I did so well that I was awarded a prize, a book, for being the best scrap metal collector in the school. I do not remember the title of the book and lost it later in the war.

Listening to foreign radio stations constituted treason and entailed severe punishment including the death penalty. Nevertheless, Mama and some of her friends listened to the BBC broadcasts. They had to be extremely circumspect and did not dare breathe a word to anyone. Much later Mama explained, "I could not tell you. You were only a child and very guileless. You were subjected to propaganda at school. Your high school teachers were 'brown.' It was too dangerous. You might inadvertently have said something which revealed that I listened to the BBC. That would have had dire consequences not only for me but for all of us."

Mama hid the radio in the oven and so she had to put her head into the oven every time she listened. The BBC used Beethoven's "boom-boom, boom-boom" from his Fifth Symphony as its signature, very impressive but also very dangerous. This particular sound carried like nothing else even at the lowest volume. It could be detected from afar. One of Mama's friends listened, too. One night, her husband came home on leave unexpectedly. As he walked along the deserted street at about 11 p.m. and approached his apartment house, he heard the faint but unmistakable sound of Beethoven's Fifth. "Someone is listening to the British," he thought. His horror was real when he found it was his wife.

A poster at the time proclaimed the following message:
YOU ARE A TRAITOR!
IF YOU LISTEN TO ENEMY BROADCASTS
IF YOU BELIEVE ENEMY PROPAGANDA
IF YOU SPREAD ENEMY NEWS
IF YOU FOLLOW ENEMY INSTRUCTIONS
IF YOU COME TO TERMS WITH THE ENEMY
EVEN IF YOU HIDE BEHIND THE MASK OF AN HONEST
MAN AND PRETEND
TO BE A FRIEND OF MANKIND, YOU WILL NOT ELUDE
US.
WE WILL ACT FAST AND WITHOUT FAIL!
TRAITORS BELONG ON THE GALLOWS!

Inevitably upon returning from school, I recounted the day's events to Mama and she immediately countered with criticism and comments. Our talks provided an outlet for her hatred for the Fuehrer. She was able to voice her complaints, criticisms and counteract the propaganda I was fed without fear of reprisal. Mama was very outspoken and would otherwise probably have been provoked or tempted to say something politically incorrect to the wrong person and come to a bad end. All of us developed what was called the "German Look," which was to look over your shoulder and scan the vicinity before speaking. Several people in the neighborhood and a few acquaintances were suspect. They were not party members but strong supporters of the Fuehrer. Caution was definitely called for.

Mama's next door neighbors were a middle-aged, childless couple, not native born Berliners. We were on speaking terms and once in a great while I visited them. The woman's sister worked in a large butcher shop in another part of town. Now and then when she visited, she was caught by an air raid and stayed until it was over. On several occasions, she brought goodies to the shelter that were out of reach of ordinary mortals. For instance, one night she unpacked two large bunches of enormous blue grapes. She, her sister and brother-in-law proceeded to eat them. I thought it was not very nice of them to eat the grapes in front of everyone without sharing. She was showing off how well she was doing and what the right connections could do for a person. Working in any kind of business certainly helped to supplement the meager rations and made it possible to obtain luxuries. Working in a big grocery or butcher store guaranteed it.

However, wheeling and dealing was not without risk. Punishments for people caught in black market activities were severe, ranging from years of hard labor to concentration camp to death. Nevertheless, people engaged in it despite the danger.

On the night of October 3, we had another raid which lasted until 4 a.m.

Newspapers and broadcasts on October 10 informed us that Germans troops were moving along the Danube in the direction of Romania and on October 12 we heard that the troops had entered Bucharest. Another news item informed us that St. Paul's Cathedral in London had been hit by German bombs.

On October 28, Italy attacked Greece.

During the summer and fall, the daughters of Mama's Frankfurt cousins frequently visited Berlin. One cousin, Brigitte, had a boyfriend, Helmut, whose parents lived in Berlin. Helmut was an army lieutenant stationed near Berlin. Once, when he was on weekend leave, I was invited to a small party. I can still see Brigitte and Helmut dancing, looking into each other's eyes, very much in love. They became engaged and a December wedding was planned.

By now, most able men in the appropriate age brackets had been called up, leaving jobs vacant. Women, who had heretofore been encouraged to consider marriage and motherhood as the only worthwhile and sole career in life, were more than ever needed to fill job vacancies. The most urgent need was for farm workers. To fill the gap, the government issued a new directive, namely that those leaving school must serve one year in the country helping farmers. I viewed this so-called Land Year with trepidation. We already had the Duty Year. Now it seemed that another year was to be spent on a farm. I did not want to serve either one.

The Land Year had to be served in whole or in part in addition to the Duty Year at age 14, when most girls graduated from grade school, or upon leaving school. Land Year girls lived in camps. They worked for farmers in the morning and spent the rest of the day at camp.

373

The newspaper reported:

September 7: "Last night enemy planes again attacked the Reich capital causing casualties and damage by indiscriminate bombing of non-military targets in center city. The Luftwaffe has begun heavy raids on London. Last night dock installations in East London were attacked with high explosive and fire bombs resulting in widespread fires."

My life continued much as usual. School, homework, movies, visits to Oma's on the 12th as well as on each first and third Sunday of each month to see Papa. On the first Sunday in November, I happened to go into Oma's bedroom and was astonished to see a baby carriage. I did not say anything to her or ask about it. In the afternoon, I visited Aunt Martha and mentioned it. She said, "Well, maybe you will have a little sister or brother." Although I had been to Papa's home on a number of occasions, I had not been there in recent months. On November 12, my next visit, Oma told me that Papa was not coming because he was visiting Aunt Elsbeth in the hospital. She had had a baby girl that very day. What a surprise and most extraordinary event for me. The baby was named Gertraud.

In class on Monday morning before the first period, I told my friend, Lydia, about the baby. Most of the students in my class (both in elementary and high school) were only children. So, this was exciting. The news spread and was relayed to Miss Kunz, who acknowledged it with a perfunctory smile. I do not recall if she made any comment.

The following period was math with Miss Fischer. One of the girls said, "Miss Fischer, Gisela has had a little sister." Miss

Fischer, who also taught biology, looked distinctly embarrassed and said, "Well, Gisela, then you know all about it." That sentence covered our sex education. I, of course, was as ignorant as I had been before. My teachers knew nothing of my circumstances at home.

Two weeks later, I was invited to Papa's apartment. Aunt Elsbeth was home from the hospital with the baby. When I arrived, everyone else was there too: Oma, Aunt Frieda, Uncle Willie, Aunt Elsbeth's parents, her brother and his wife. The baby was cute and had lots of dark hair. It all seemed to be a bit much for Aunt Elsbeth who was lying on the sofa looking pale and tired.

I felt strange and after a while I started to cry. I could not stop. I cannot explain why I cried. I did not feel jealous because I never had a close relationship with Papa that would be threatened by the baby. I felt awful because I did not know why I was crying. No one paid attention to me but there was nowhere to hide. Finally, Papa took me into the bedroom, sat me on his lap and said, "Don't cry, you will always be my big girl." Whatever that was supposed to mean. He probably did not know what else to say. He never hugged or kissed me, complimented me on anything or showed any physical affection. I finally managed to control myself and went home.

From that time on, I went to Papa's place rather than to Oma's to visit him. Legally, once I was 14 years old, the obligatory visits came to an end. Now I went because the baby was an attraction. I still visited on Sunday mornings and we took Gertraud for a walk, with me pushing her pram. Men never pushed prams in those days. One Sunday, Papa and I stopped in front of a store window. An elderly couple walked by and gave me a very disapproving, raised eyebrow look. Obviously, they assumed that the baby was mine and here I was, looking like a child myself. I thought it amusing.

The invitation to Brigitte and Helmut's wedding arrived. It was to take place on December 20, at 2 p.m. in the Evangelical Church, Ferbelliner Platz. Only Mama and I accepted.

At the appointed hour on the wedding day, the guests were seated in the pews. The organ played softly. The organ played for a long time but the bridal couple did not arrive. Minutes ticked away, half an hour went by, the guests grew restless. Then the air raid sirens sounded. We had to go into the church basement and wait for the all clear. It came over an hour later. Soon afterwards, the bridal couple showed up. They had been unable to find a taxi before 2 o'clock and were further delayed by the air raid. The ceremony could now be performed. When Brigitte started up the aisle, her veil caught on the rough red carpeting and I was asked to carry it during the procession into and out of the church. In spite of the delays, it turned out to be a very nice wedding. The ladies wore long dresses and carried long stemmed roses. I wore my confirmation dress. Brigitte looked charming. Helmut looked handsome and smart.

The reception was held at a nearby restaurant. Weddings warranted extra rations. The meal was a treat for everyone except for me. I did not feel well. I felt nauseated and itchy. Later, I was diagnosed with a slight case of jaundice. Sadly, I watched everyone enjoying soup, Wiener schnitzel with roast potatoes, fresh mixed vegetables, rolls and butter, wine and the special wedding gateau with mock whipped cream and real coffee.

It was after 11 p.m. when the party broke up. Unable to find a taxi, Mama and I took the U-Bahn home. Standing on the platform of the Kottbusser Damm station where we had to change trains, we realized that it was a few minutes past midnight. My 15th birthday. Mama hugged me and said, "Congratulations."

Over a year later, Brigitte gave birth to a boy during a particularly heavy air raid. Not too long afterwards, Helmut was killed in action.

1941

January	Hitler offers Mussolini help in Albania and Greece. Italians lose Tobruk to British.
February 6	British take Benghazi. Formation of Africa Corps under General Rommel.
February 14	Rommel arrives in Tripoli to reverse setbacks. Bulgaria is occupied and joins Axis.
March 8	Martial law declared in Holland.
March 13	Secret edict by Nazis for invasion of Russia.
April 6	Germans invade Yugoslavia and Greece.
April 9	Greek line breaks and Germans are in Thessalonika.
April 17	Belgrade falls.
April 27	Greece collapses and its government flees to Crete.
May 6	Stalin becomes premier in Russia.
May 10	Hess flies to Scotland and the official Nazi explanation is that he lost his mind. He is replaced by Bormann. The *Bismarck* is sunk.
June 1	Invasion of Crete.
June 11	German troops move on Soviet border.

June 16	U.S.A. closes consulates in Germany.
June 19	Germany and Italy expel U.S. consuls.
June 21	German troops into Russia.
July	Germany and Italy divide Yugoslavia, with plans for Croatia to become independent.
July 23	Germans bomb Moscow.
August 5	In Russia, Smolensk falls.
August 24	Euthanasia Program suspended.
September 1	Jews must wear Star of David.
September	Germans shell Leningrad and Volga Germans are exiled to Siberia.
September 9	British, Canadian and Norwegian troops land in Spitzbergen. They destroy coal mines. Spanish "Blue Division" to fight at Leningrad. Crimea is cut off.
October 1	Jews are no longer allowed to emigrate.
October	Red army counterattacks in Ukraine.
October 10	Reds halt Germans outside Moscow.
October 16	Germans take Odessa.
October 21	The execution of 50 French hostages is in retaliation for the killing of one German officer.
October 25	Charkov falls.
November	Germans and Rumanians win Sebastopol.
November 17	Soviets make gains. The cold weather in Russia is deadly to Germans.
November 19	British attack and move 130 miles into Libya.
December 5	German troops are outside Moscow. Soviets counterattack.

December 7	The attack of Pearl Harbor by the Japanese.
December 11	U.S.A. enters the war.
December 16	Hitler sacks von Brauchitsch and assumes supreme command of the army himself.
December 20	Germans 20 miles outside Moscow. Bitter cold halts the advance.
December 21	The author's 16th birthday.

Whenever I visited Oma, Opa was there. He usually sat on a chair in the kitchen. He was very quiet and did not say or do much. Sometimes, when I was very young, Opa and I played ball. The ball was pink on one side, turquoise on the other and had a golden-yellow band around the middle. I threw the ball to Opa and he tossed it back to me over a distance of 3 or 4 feet. Just a very gentle game. I cannot remember anything else about him.

I visited Oma on the first Sunday in January and Opa was not sitting in the kitchen. He was sick in bed, which was very unusual. I went into the bedroom to say hello. Apparently, he had not been well for the past week. I don't think anybody told me what was wrong with him, only that he did not feel well. Therefore, I was quite unprepared and very shocked a few days later when I received the formal printed announcement of his death in the mail. Opa died on January 15.

It was and still is customary in Germany to mail death notices. These are printed on white paper with a black border and the envelopes are also black bordered. Nowadays, grey often replaces black. Newspapers did not automatically publish obituaries but the family could choose to pay for an announcement. Contents and size were the choice of the family.

Aunt Marga was taking me to the State Theater on the evening of the day I received the news about Opa's passing. Aunt Marga managed to obtain tickets to the theater even though they were hard to come by because they were in great demand. I suppose everybody wanted to escape from the real world if only for a couple of hours. I was very fortunate. I was able to attend many plays and see many famous actors on stage in performances of "Falstaff" or "Merry Wives of Windsor," "Turandot," "The Broken Jug" with Emil Jannings, "Iphigenie on Taurus" and more.

My confirmation dress had been changed into a dress suitable to wear to concerts or to the theater. The bodice was altered from black to a combination of black and aqua taffeta, with applique lace covering the transition from one color to the other. On this particular evening, I wore this dress. I clearly remember standing in front of the hall mirror combing my hair and thinking of Opa. It was the very first time someone in my immediate family had died and I was quite shaken. For the first time, I would have to go to a funeral. Later, at the theater, I could not concentrate on the performance.

We had no funeral homes in Berlin, only funeral directors, whose storefront office was usually connected to a showroom with coffins. The body was not embalmed and it was taken in the casket to the cemetery. Each cemetery had a small building, consisting of a chapel and a basement, where the body rested until the funeral. Viewing was not customary. If anyone wished to take a last look at the deceased, he or she might do so in the basement prior to the service. Then the coffin was closed and brought up by lift to the chapel for the memorial service, which was followed either by interment or the coffin was again lowered into the basement and taken to a crematorium.

Opa's funeral took place on January 18 at 2 p.m. Needless to say, I slept badly the night before. I had been trying to find a way to avoid attending the funeral. I broached the subject with Father. He was quite firm, insisting that it was my duty and it was expected of me to attend. I begged him to come with me but he declined.

At 1:30 p.m., wearing dark clothing, carrying a spray of evergreen and mimosa, I set out for the cemetery. It had snowed again during the night and it was bitter cold. Members of the Home Guard were clearing the wide sidewalk in front of one of our big movie theaters. As I walked by, one of them said to another, "Look! She is going to Grandma's birthday party," and they all laughed. I was already in such a nervous state by then that this set me off. I began to giggle and could not stop. I was terrified. I thought I would not be able to control myself by the time I reached the cemetery.

When I approached the cemetery gate, I saw Aunt Gertrud, Aunt Frieda, Oma, Papa and Aunt Elsbeth waiting for me. Aunt Gertrud even hugged me. I had to bite my lips so as not to giggle all the way to the chapel. To my dismay, I discovered that I had to sit in the front row. Even though the coffin was closed, I had never been this close to one, never mind one containing a body. I felt most uncomfortable and tried very hard to concentrate on something sad and on Opa. The choir sang "Holy, holy, holy, Lord God Almighty," one of my favorite hymns, and I began to feel calmer.

After the service, we followed the coffin to the grave site where the pastor pronounced the final blessing. One by one, we stepped up to the open grave and threw in a handful of earth. I stood in the receiving line with the family while the mourners filed by expressing their condolences. I cannot recall whether or not the mourners and the family went to a restaurant or to Oma's apartment for the traditional repast provided after a funeral. I went home. I was much relieved that my ordeal was over but it bothered me for a long time. I felt guilty about having had such a nervous reaction quite unsuitable for the occasion.

Winter continued cold, snowy and with bitter east winds blowing. Mama put blankets halfway over the kitchen window and stuffed newspapers in between the double windows. We huddled around the kitchen stove because we did not have enough fuel to heat another room.

One afternoon in late January or February, Vicki turned up unexpectedly, much to my delight. I had not seen her in ages.

384

Vicki's visits were always fun. She was vivacious, like a breath of fresh air. This time, she was in uniform and looked very smart. She had joined the Women's Auxiliary Army and was stationed in Norway. It was entertaining to hear Vicki relate her adventures. She attended many parties and, quite obviously, she was having a great time. Considering her personality and charisma, I was not surprised. I do not recall details of the conversation but remember one remark. I guess Mama and Vicki were talking about age and Vicki said, "Well, you realize that you are getting older when your boyfriends are getting younger."

Mama had made some new friends. Alma lived at the upper end of our street. She had no children and her husband served in the same unit with Kurt. Franziska lived in Tempelhof with her 5-year-old boy. Then there was Fanny, a dressmaker. Her mother lived in Bad Flinsberg in the Isergebirge near the Silesian/Czech border.

The film "Carl Peters," the story of a German colonial pioneer, premiered in Berlin on March 21. *"Ohm Krueger"* was first shown on April 4 and was the story of the Boer War. I did not see either one but read the programs and heard that both movies were extremely anti-British. The British were portrayed as insufferable and insensitive brutes responsible for starving innocent women and children to death. I agreed that their treatment of the Boers was abominable.

Meanwhile, the war in the Balkans had not gone well for the Italians. We joked, "What is the Italian Step?" Answer: "One step forward, three steps back." It seemed that the Italians needed help and it came on December 13 when the German Army moved in to stabilize the situation until the German campaign in Greece got under way on April 6. Then things changed rapidly on the Greek front. It looked like another blitz. Miss Kunz instructed us to write a paper on the Greek campaign, due two months hence. "Collect newspaper articles about the campaign and make the report into something special," she instructed us.

I was less than enthused about yet another current event assignment. What a bore. Therefore, I simply pushed it into the back of my mind and forgot about it for the time being. By this time, I was thoroughly disenchanted with Miss Kunz. She always had her favorites in class. I still received my usual "satisfactory" grade irrespective of my efforts.

We began reading the *"Nibelungenlied"* (an epic written around the year 1205 by an unknown poet) in German class. Most of us were familiar with it or at least with the story. I had received a beautiful book of German sagas when I was younger and had read the stories of Siegfried, Lohengrin, Parcival, the Holy Grail and more. However, now we did not simply read the *"Nibelungenlied."* Miss Kunz had us dissect each verse grammatically. I did not mind doing this for the first few verses but as days and weeks went by, it became exceedingly dreary and boring. I began to dread German class and to this day I cannot bear to think of the *"Nibelungenlied."* The mere mention of it makes me shudder.

On May 10, it was officially announced that the German battleship *Bismarck* had been sunk. German losses were hardly ever publicized, only when it was absolutely necessary or served some specific purpose for the regime. I suppose a loss of this magnitude could not be ignored and swept under the carpet. After all, the relatives of over a thousand men talk and news of their loved ones' death spreads, so the name of the ship on which they served becomes known. Most families also published obituaries.

I recalled the stories we had read in class describing WWI naval battles and what happened when a ship was hit and caught fire. The metal surface became red hot, impossible to walk on and men were trapped in the engine room. The crew was covered in oil and ran out screaming, like living torches. The wounded burned while lying on the hot metal decks and men jumped overboard screaming. It was the embodiment of Dante's inferno. It was horrible. The images haunted me and recalling them made my skin crawl.

These memories surfaced now and I not only suffered with the German crew but also with the enemy for whom I felt no hatred. It was clear to me that they were human, like our men, and suffered just the same. They too had wives, children, parents, sisters and brothers at home.

Most of my teachers throughout my school years were women, almost all of them middle-aged or older. WWI had deprived them of husbands. Every time we read stories about WWI or we were told about the war, I thought about all the young men who had been killed. Slaughtered is a better word for what happened. Every time I saw rows upon rows of crosses on military cemeteries, I thought about how each one had a mother or a wife and children. For every man killed, there was a girl who would never have a husband and a family or he left a widow and fatherless children.

One fine day in May, I was stunned to learn that Rudolf Hess, of all people, had taken off for Scotland. Hess was the deputy of the Fuehrer who, in Hitler's name, had the power to decide all questions of the Nazi Party but not government or leadership. He was also entitled to attend all cabinet sessions. It was simply unbelievable and left me and everyone else wondering what on earth was going on. How had he managed to get away? Most of all why? The explanation given was that Hess had lost his mind. It was also announced that Hess was replaced by Bormann.

Almost immediately, another Weiss Ferdl story made the rounds. Weiss Ferdl, a Bavarian comedian and film actor, regularly appeared on the variety stage. Stories about political jokes he made reached us from time to time. It was rumored but not officially confirmed that he had been incarcerated for some of them. On this occasion Weiss Ferdl, supposedly, appeared on stage carrying a toy plane under his arm. The audience roared. He held up his hand asking for silence. When it was quiet, he simply said, "I'm not a Hess, I am a Bavarian." This brought the house down.

One of the German States is called Hessen and the people living there are called Hesse (singular) or Hessen (plural). Weiss Ferdl, speaking in his Bavarian accent, would say Hess rather than Hesse.

On Monday, June 23, the newspaper headlines were:

According to plan and successful! The combat in the east
Simultaneous air strikes against England and Alexandria!
World reaction to the Fuehrer's action!
Germany looks to her soldiers
Churchill admits concordance with Moscow
Army and Air Force fight
Forward without respite!

We had followed the growing tensions between Germany and Russia for months. Nevertheless, the outbreak of hostilities came as a shock. Hopes that the war would end now, or at least within a reasonable time, vanished. My family's comments were gloomy. Father recalled Napoleon's defeat and predicted the same fate for the Fuehrer's foolhardy endeavor. Kurt was transferred to the middle sector of the Russian front. Uncle Herbert and my pen pals Heinz and Robert were in the east, too.

In school, the anticommunist slogan once again faced the class. Miss Kunz read "Abandon Hope All Ye Who Enter Here" to us in German class. I dreaded these readings and had nightmares about what I heard. There were detailed descriptions of purges when innocent pedestrians were indiscriminately rounded up like cattle in the street and thrown into jail for no other reason than to fill the prisons. To force confessions of imaginary treasonable crimes, prisoners were tortured, had their nails pulled off and burning cigarettes were stubbed out on girls' chests. Torture continued until the victim broke down and signed the phony confession that was his, or her, death warrant and all of this was without trial or recourse. It was horrible and monstrous. It terrified me. I was deeply disturbed and scared. The thought of Soviet Russia filled me with terror.

Whenever we read books about purges in Russia, and other war related incidents, it affected me deeply. I did not look on these things as a spectator but imagined myself in the place of the victim in that particular situation and felt the fear, the hopelessness, the anxiety, the loneliness and the terror. I realized the helplessness of an individual vis-a-vis brute, merciless force. It scared the hell out of me to imagine being defenseless against the regime that was in power. I knew the danger around me in my own country, embodied by the powerful and ruthless Gestapo.

However, life went on. Needlework in my later elementary school years included learning many embroidery stitches which we utilized by making a gym sack. Hemming with drawn thread work and how to apply a perfect patch was also taught and mastered, as well as darning. In high school, needlework classes included knitting a short sleeved sweater, creating its pattern by using a variety of stitches, sewing an apron with pockets and embroidering it, and making a dress with decorative embroidery of our own design. I cannot remember the apron but I do remember the dress. It was beige. I embroidered it in a cross-stitch design of little hearts set in a kind of scroll pattern. It was not very imaginative because I was not interested in it and made up the simplest thing I could think of. As a result, I received another "satisfactory" mark.

Algebra and I did not get along. I simply could not get the hang of it and, consequently, I hated it. Finally, Aunt Marga talked to Mr. Lambert and he agreed to tutor me in math and algebra. Once or twice a week after school, I walked to his apartment and he struggled to enlighten me. It was a long time later, in fact about six weeks before I graduated, that the proverbial penny finally dropped. Now I was fascinated by the logic of math. Alas, it was a little late in the day and too late to change my grade from "satisfactory" to "good" or better.

New subjects added to our curriculum this year were shorthand, typing and home economics. Home economics were taught in another school equipped with kitchen facilities. The walk to the other building became an enjoyable break.

Food shortages did not make it easy to create tasty dishes from practically nothing. Nevertheless, our teacher was excellent. The very first thing we made was semolina lemon soup. After we finished cooking or while a dish was in the oven, we were instructed on how to set a table. Then we ate what we had cooked or baked and the teacher took turns sitting at our tables. We were shown the proper way to clean up and wash the dishes: glasses first, and so on. We kept a record of recipes, which included the cost of each ingredient. I enjoyed this class very much.

I learned many things that stayed with me over the years. I learned about nutrition and vitamins. Our teacher taught us how to avoid destroying the natural vitamins in vegetables by steaming them rather than cooking them in water. We learned how to peel apples and potatoes in the most economical way, wasting practically nothing, and much more.

Home economics included instructions in how to take care of babies. We practiced diapering on a large doll.

The war made grocery shopping a chore. Mother was now over 70 years old. She found it impossible to stand in line because of her back. Yet that is what one had to do day in and day out at the greengrocers and various other shops in order to get what was available and to what one was entitled. Mama and Mother were registered at different shops of their personal preference. Mama did double duty by queuing up at her shops and then at Mother's shops. She usually stood in line three and four hours a day. I was used to Mama being at home when I returned from school. Now I arrived home to find the apartment empty at times. This upset me a lot. I cannot explain why but it did. I hated to come home and not find Mama there.

"Combat Spoilage! Now more than ever!" exhorted posters from the advertising columns and in food stores, as well as in newspaper ads, to remind us not to waste a thing. I did not pay attention to the running of the household and I assumed that food scraps were still collected to feed pigs. I know we were very careful with what we had. Most people in large cities had to get by solely on their rations and that was not easy. A tip I read in the newspaper: use a small amount of water to absorb whatever fat was left in the frying pan and pour it into your vegetables or gravy before washing the pan.

Our life was pretty humdrum during the week. For me, it was school until 2 p.m. And after 3 p.m. until supper time, I did my homework, many times even after supper. Mama was always busy shopping for food. In the evenings, we sat around reading, listening to the radio that, apart from news and special news bulletins, brought mostly musical programs like "Music in the

391

Morning," "Musical Pastime," "Harbor Concert," "Light Fare," and "Afternoon Pastime." Sunday morning offerings included classical and chamber music, along with a program called "The Treasure Trove." Sunday afternoon hours were devoted to the Request Concerts. In order to have their request chosen, people resorted to tricks. Birth announcements almost guaranteed selection. I have never heard of so many newborn babies weighing 10, 12 and even 13 pounds. Mama and I found it very amusing and laughed about it.

On weekends, I generally visited Aunt Martha and Oma. Occasionally, I spent an afternoon or evening with Dieter and his mother. I also wrote letters to Kurt, Uncle Herbert, Heinz and Robert.

These rather routine activities were interspersed with a few highlights, like a variety show at the Admiralspalast, the Wintergarten or the Scala. I was fortunate enough to obtain tickets for a number of musicals. I enjoyed them enormously. I was quite stagestruck but never dreamed of doing anything about it or asking for voice lessons. I must have felt that it was quite impossible to realize my dreams. The stage was still not held in very high esteem, classical theater aside, and variety artists were viewed with suspicion by older people like Father and Mother. I knew they would never be in favor of my entertaining thoughts about a stage career.

However, I did insist on attending a ballet school. I loved the national dances of different countries, most of all the Czardas. I dearly wished for a Hungarian costume: a pair of shiny red boots, a voluminous white pleated skirt and a headdress with colored ribbons streaming from it. Alas, it was a dream that could not be realized. For a while, I had trouble with acrobatics but I persevered and was thrilled when I succeeded in doing splits and tumbles.

Now and then, Mama and I went to Kempinski's Haus Vaterland at the Potsdamer Platz. I had been there a few times before the war with Aunt Martha when I was quite small. On these occasions, we only visited the Rhine Terraces and I had not seen the whole establishment until Mama took me. Haus Vaterland opened in the early afternoon and remained open until midnight or later. I am not sure if there was an admission fee.

Upon entering, we checked our coats. The Rhine Terrace was a long room furnished with tables, covered with white tablecloths, and red plush upholstered chairs. About midway in the room was a dance floor. Here an orchestra played and after awhile magicians, singers, jugglers, comedians and acrobats entertained while patrons enjoyed their afternoon coffee. There was no dancing on weekday afternoons, only at night. Afternoon customers were required to leave before the evening activities.

At the far end, wall to wall and ceiling to floor, glass separated the room from the landscape which gave the room its name. It was intended that the patrons imagined themselves standing in a vineyard above the Rhine looking down on the river at a place called Bingen. Close to the glass was soil planted with artificial vines. Below, the miniature, lifelike Rhine flowed around the castle of the Cat and Mouse situated on its little island in the middle of the stream. Alongside the river, close to the water's edge, tiny trains traveled, while small boats, barges and steamers moved sedately up and down the stream. The sun smiled from a cloudless blue sky and birds sang in the vineyard. During intermission, the sky paled, clouded over and turned grey. The sun disappeared. The birds stopped singing. It grew darker. Rolls of distant thunder could be heard coming steadily nearer until finally the storm was overhead. Lightning illuminated the landscape. It began to rain, gently at first, increasing in intensity along with the approaching storm. Water poured down inside the glass partition. Lights came on in the houses, on the boats and on the trains. Eventually the storm abated, thunder turned into mere rumbling and the rain subsided. It grew lighter, the sun reappeared and the birds resumed their singing. Intermission was over.

Haus Vaterland accommodated two additional large restaurants: the Palm Court and the Grinzing. The Palm Court was circular, decorated in white, red and gold with columns fashioned to look like palm tree trunks supporting the upper level. Here, too, an orchestra played. The upstairs gallery afforded patrons an excellent view of the dance floor, which was also used for presentations of the same entertainment offered in the Rhine Terrace.

The Grinzing imitated a garden restaurant in the well-known Viennese suburb, Grinzing, famous for its Schrammel musicians and the new wines of the season, the *Heurigen*. Lattice ceilings and walls were entwined with vine leaves and grapes. Vine covered lattice also separated the tables and at the end of the room, behind glass, was a view of Vienna by night. In contrast to the Rhine scenery, this view was not animated nor did it change in any way.

Situated on different floors were a number of bars. The entrance to the Spanish Bodega, for instance, was in the shape of a huge wine barrel. Inside, patrons sat on small barrels around larger barrels. The decor was Spanish and the musicians, attired in Spanish costumes, played classical guitar music. The waitresses wore Andalusian dresses.

In contrast, the narrow Hamburg ship's galley sported port holes overlooking a mock of the Elbe estuary near Hamburg. Freighters and steamers could be observed as they slowly passed by. An accordion player entertained patrons with sailor songs typical of Hamburg and the North Sea coast. Regional food and drink was served by waiters wearing sailor suits.

My favorite was the Hungarian Puszta Inn. On the outside, it looked like a lonely whitewashed farmhouse with a thatched roof. A fence, with sunflowers growing alongside, separated the farmhouse from the seemingly endless expanse of the Puszta. Close to the fence stood a distinctively Hungarian well. A gypsy band in costume entertained with fiery czardas and romantic gypsy music.

An African Safari Lodge, located on the top floor, boasted gazelle, lion and tiger skins with stuffed animal heads on the walls.

For as long as Haus Vaterland remained open, and before it was reduced to a heap of rubble, it was a fun place to visit.

Mama and I stood outside Haus Vaterland one Saturday in April. We had spent the afternoon at the Rhine Terrace. It was early yet, too early to go home. We wondered what to do and decided to visit a nearby café. The café was crowded but we were lucky to find a table. A few minutes later, the waitress ushered in a soldier to share our table. It is customary to share tables when a restaurant or café is crowded. The man was tall, slim and good looking. He smiled, we smiled and he tried to talk to us. This proved to be almost impossible because he did not speak more than a half dozen words of German.

He was a Spaniard, a member of the Spanish Blue Division, made up of volunteers who fought against Russia with the Germans. We struggled for a while until a gentleman at the next table put down his newspaper and politely offered his services as an interpreter. He spoke Spanish fluently and soon the men were engrossed in conversation. The gentleman told us that the Spaniard (I cannot remember his name), aged 32, was from Madrid where, until he volunteered to fight the communists, he had worked at the ABC newspaper in some editing capacity. He was wounded in Russia and was recuperating at a military convalescent home in a Berlin suburb. More smiles all around. After we finished our ersatz coffee, we shook hands. With the help of our interpreter, we wished the Spanish gentleman luck and went home.

Aunt Marga, who frequently went on Sunday excursions, took me to Hoppegarten one early summer Sunday to watch the horse races. I was thrilled. It was my first time at a racecourse. I loved the horses, the crowds, the jockeys in their colors, along with the tension and excitement before the start, during and at the end of each race. Standing on the platform of the S-Bahn station waiting for our train, I could think of nothing else but that I would love to be a jockey.

As I mentioned earlier, Aunt Marga often managed to obtain tickets for the State Theater. Getting the tickets was a question of connections, which people called "Vitamin C." One needed connections to acquire items, such as coffee. Berliners are very fond of their coffee and it was one of the things really missed. "Vitamin C" enabled some lucky people to come into possession of small quantities. Aunt Marga managed to do so, as well as obtain tickets from time to time.

Stockings, or rather the lack of them, became a problem. We spent hours darning the ones we had. Runs were a particular bother. Soon a new business flourished: picking up runs in stockings. The drawback apart from the expense was that the stockings had to be taken to the shop and picked up. Besides, so many women were in need of this service that soon the stores could not cope with the volume of work. We were, therefore, very happy when the little hooks used by the repair shops appeared on the market. Much of my spare time was now occupied repairing runs for Mama, my aunts and myself.

Aunt Martha, an accomplished seamstress, was a genius and, at the same time, a glutton for punishment. She spent hours fiddling around with materials and patterns to see how she could make a new dress from two older ones or from leftover cloth. She was apt to choose patterns which involved an inordinate amount of intricate, time-consuming work. For instance, this summer several of my dresses had a bodice made of net or tulle. Aunt Martha spent hours sewing narrow strips of the dress material into tubes, turned them inside out, and applied them either vertically at narrow intervals or in a lattice pattern over the net.

My term paper on the Greek campaign was almost due. I began to worry. I had not collected any newspapers, I had not made any notes, and I had not wasted one thought on the project. It was due in two weeks. Frantically, I visited neighbors, friends and relatives but nobody had old papers. After I had exhausted these sources, I approached a few of my classmates. I was very fortunate because one of them was willing to lend her papers to me. I breathed a sigh of relief and set to work. I had no time nor did I feel inclined to spend any on devising a really original way of writing and presenting this paper. But I knew I had to make some effort. So I hit on the idea of writing the essay in Gothic style calligraphy. This, I did, all 23 pages of it. My grade was the usual "satisfactory." After this I gave up trying to obtain higher grades in Miss Kunz's classes altogether.

One of my classmates, Barbara, lived in Britz. Many times we met at my streetcar stop where she changed cars. This gave us an opportunity to talk. She told me that her sister was engaged to an SS man and later on recounted all about the wedding. One morning in early summer, we were waiting for our streetcar when a soldier got off another car accompanied by a member of the Royal Air Force, obviously a prisoner of war, who had lost an arm. We stood on the platform with them. We did not speak. They did not speak. It was the first Englishman I had seen in person and the only time I saw an Allied prisoner of war.

I do not recall the exact date our holidays started, probably in the middle or at the end of June. Father, Mother and I went to Balz. Mama joined us later. It was the best place to go. We stayed again at the Ziegler's, enjoyed the peaceful nights and appreciated the good food. Everything tasted heavenly. Mrs. Ziegler served scrambled eggs and bacon, an easy and fast to prepare meal, almost every day for either lunch or supper. After my first yen for eggs had been satisfied, I had to force myself to down them. I could hardly bring myself to watch when Mrs. Ziegler commenced to break 12 eggs into a frying pan full of chopped bacon. I wished fervently for some way to save these meals so I could spread them over the rest of the year.

Old Mr. Ziegler and his wife ran the farm as best they could with one horse, the help of a Duty Year girl and a Labor Service maid. Every morning at 8 a.m. sharp, the maid rode into the yard on her bicycle. I saw very little of her. She was put to work in the stable and in the field until she left at 5 p.m.

The Labor Service Camp was in Vietz. Mama and I walked by one day. I got uptight just looking at the girls in their cornflower blue work dresses. On weekends, they wore a khaki suit, white blouse, Nordic pin, hat, khaki stockings and brogue. The leaders did not work on the farms. They ran the camp. I heard that they were former BDM leaders. They looked like an advertisement for proper Nazi women with no make-up, hair pulled straight back and twisted into a bun or cut short and straight. Some of them, but by no means all so I heard, were nasty. If one fell foul of them or they took a dislike to someone, they gave that person a really tough time. They had absolute jurisdiction over the camp. This made me shudder more than anything, even though I knew that not all of them were mean.

I was reminded of a commemorative article by the Reich Leadership of the party's women's labor service, published in the National Socialist press in February 1934: "The camps must be of a certain primitivity. The girls must get used to the straw mattress and simple bathroom facilities. The girls must get used to doing without every kind of beauty and personal hygiene products in order to toughen them up. This will result in toughening across the board and will foster the development of a certain frontline spirit. The girl's mother instinct, which National Socialism otherwise encourages, must temporarily recede into the background. The camps serve the purpose of training the girl in self-discipline, sobriety, obedience, endurance and stringency against self. The girl must adjust to become a rank and file soldier."

Labor Service girls spent the summer months in the country but, after the harvest, were required to serve the remaining time in the War Auxiliary Service to do social work, to work as conductresses on streetcars and buses and, if lucky, to work in army offices. However, many girls were employed in armament factories. They were paid 1.70 marks a day. Some were even called upon to man antiaircraft guns.

I saw quite a lot of Doris, the Duty Year girl at the Ziegler's, who was about my age. She had left school at age 14. She worked around the house, the kitchen and in the inn. Although the inn was open all day, almost no one ever came in until the evening and on weekends. Rows upon rows of liquor bottles, mostly liqueurs, stood behind the bar. I was fascinated by a particular bottle because its contents glowed in poisonous looking fluorescent green and yellow.

Doris and I were alone in the kitchen one afternoon when a couple of village boys walked into the bar. They ordered two Magenbitters, a liqueur by Mampe used mainly as a remedy for an upset stomach. At least, that is what Father used it for on rare occasions. After they had paid 15 pfennigs each for the drinks, the boys turned and left. Doris called after them, "What about your drinks?" They laughed and replied, "They are for you two." I had not had a liqueur before, only malt beer, Berliner Weisse (wheaten ale) and wine mixed with water. I tasted the liqueur and liked it. I thought it was delicious. Doris did not want hers, because she was afraid Mrs. Ziegler would disapprove if she found out, so she gave it to me. As expected, the unaccustomed beverage went to my head. When Father and Mother returned from their walk, I went straight to bed although it was only 5:30 p.m. and slept through until the next morning.

Two weeks later, Mother and Father returned to Berlin. Mama arrived the day before they left to stay for the rest of my vacation.

We fell into our usual routine. Mama sat on the terrace reading and I played in the garden. We walked to the lakes and to Aunt Lotte's and to Vietz. Uncle Otto, although 45 years old, had also been called up. Vietz was a funny little country town. Among the few shops in the town square was a small shoe store. I discovered the cutest sandals in the window. They were made of thin leather straps in white, red, blue and green. I fell in love with them at first sight and wanted them very badly. However, they were beyond my reach since it required a special No. 2 purchase permit to buy them. I did not have a hope in the world to get one. All I could do was stand at the window and gaze longingly at the sandals.

Once I accompanied Mr. Ziegler on the wagon to one of his distant fields. I helped with the hay. A couple of days later the horse, the only one they were allowed to have, was sick. This was serious. The horse suffered from colic. The vet came and I was fascinated to see him push his arm up to his shoulder into the horse's behind. I don't know if he prescribed any medicine but the horse had to be walked. I watched Mr. Ziegler lead the horse around in a circle for a while and then I volunteered to relieve him. My offer was gratefully accepted because it freed him to take care of other chores. At first it was fun but after three hours it became a bore to walk around in a circle. Luckily, the horse recovered.

One morning, I awoke with a pain in my chest. At first I did not think anything of it but as the morning progressed it became more and more difficult and very painful to breathe. By 10 a.m. I could only take rapid shallow breaths. I could not straighten up and it was difficult and painful to walk. Every movement hurt. I was afraid to tell Mama. Slowly and carefully, I made my way out of the farmyard until I reached a haystack by the edge of a field. Here I gingerly lowered myself onto an old garden chair someone had left long ago. The sun was warm and I sat motionless for a long time. I was scared. I thought I was going to die. I did not want to die. I was too young to die. Hours later I realized that breathing had become a little easier. I made it back to lunch and took a nap afterwards. By the next morning, I was fine. I have no idea what caused my distress.

For some time now, Poles had been recruited to Germany to work, mostly on farms. A Polish boy joined the Ziegler household. The boy was about my age, 15 or 16. He was blond and blue eyed. He worked around the house on time-consuming tasks which freed Mrs. Ziegler to do other more urgent things. For instance, the boy took red currants off their stems, peeled potatoes and fed the chickens. I had not met many foreigners before and I was curious. I also felt sorry for him. Mama said it was a crime to take a child away from his family and his country. So I went and helped take the stems off the currants and tried to talk to him. I asked him his name. It was Jaroslaw. I pointed to different things and told him the German name for them and he told me the Polish one. Jaroslaw was quiet and unhappy. He was homesick and had no one to talk to. No one on the farm spoke Polish. He had his own room and got the same food as everyone else. The Zieglers did not overwork him and was he never ill-treated.

Sundays were days of rest and Mr. Ziegler did not work in the fields. Only necessary chores were completed. Doris and Jaroslaw had the day off. Jaroslaw went out to meet other Poles who worked on neighboring farms. One Monday morning, a policeman appeared at the inn and demanded to see Jaroslaw. The policeman, Mr. Ziegler and Jaroslaw stood in the yard while the former explained that Jaroslaw had been at a meeting with other Poles. Foreigners congregating in large numbers, Poles in this case, was unlawful and highly suspicious. He tried to question Jaroslaw about his movements the previous day. Jaroslaw was scared and did not respond to the questions, which he probably did not understand.

After a few minutes, the policeman grew angry, began to shout and at one point hit the boy and kicked him in the behind. Mama, who happened to be in the kitchen, saw this, ran out and remonstrated the policeman. I followed. She said, "It's all very well to question the boy but there is no need to hit him or kick him. He is only a child. It is uncalled for. You should be ashamed of yourself." The policeman told Mama to keep out of it. He left shortly thereafter. Mama carried on for some time about the brutality of the police. Mr. and Mr. Ziegler agreed with Mama but were scared because they were responsible for the boy and his actions.

The two Ziegler grandchildren, age 6 and 4, were mostly left to their own devices. I liked to play with them and tell them stories. They loved it. The little girl was ready to start school and I sang a little ditty to them, "I saw 40 little girls on their way to school." Once I started, they could not get enough of it. I had to repeat and repeat the song until it came out of my ears. In the country, the school year started in early August. The first school day arrived and I walked the little girl to school. She did not receive a *Schultuete* like the kids in town. The schoolhouse stood next to the church within sight of the inn and was a one room school. The schoolhouse served a double purpose. It provided teaching space, as well as housing for the teacher and his family. I met the teacher, introduced myself and asked if I might be allowed into the classroom to watch. I was very disappointed that the answer was "No."

Although I looked at the red brick church every day and had made a nice colored pencil drawing of it, it never occurred to me to attend Sunday Services. I regret this omission.

Vietz and Balz were located along the No. 1 highway which led to East Prussia. It was only an ordinary country road, one lane each way with no center markings. This summer, long military convoys moved east daily and few went west. When I was around, I watched the columns and waved. Every night, I heard the rumbling of wheels and the hum of motors for hours as long convoys snaked to the front. Most troop movements took place at night.

The uneventful, leisurely weeks passed by until vacation time came to an end and we returned to Berlin, school, air raids and shortages.

Hitler himself reminded us frequently that the Reich was God's chosen nation and he, Hitler, the savior who would deliver the world from the curse of communism. Hitler and Germany were the only barrier, "the knights in shining armor," who prevented the red hordes from sweeping over all of Europe.

Since the beginning of the Russian campaign, special news reports followed each other in quick succession announcing rapid progress and victories. Newsreels from the front showed columns of infantry smiling and marching along unpaved roads, ankle deep in dust, far into Russia. Often they had to march more than 40 kilometers a day carrying full gear in temperatures higher than those in Germany, often soaring to 104 degrees Fahrenheit. The soldiers' faces were deeply tanned. When they took off their caps or their steel helmets, their foreheads were white in stark contrast to the rest of their faces. I felt sorry for the infantry and their poor feet. The roads in Russia were almost exclusively dirt roads. In summer, the dust was several inches deep. When it rained, it turned into deep, deep mud. Horses, people and vehicles got stuck in it. All Russian railroad tracks had to be changed to the German rail gauge by the Corps of Engineers to facilitate smooth supply lines.

We were told repeatedly and continuously that our troops would take Moscow before winter set in. The Russian campaign would be another blitz, over before we knew it. But, contrary to the boasts and the fanfare, this did not come to pass. The Luftwaffe bombed Moscow and the artillery shelled Leningrad. The Army cut off the Crimea and surrounded Odessa but they did not take Moscow.

Earlier in the year, Father brought up the subject of my future. That is, what did I want to do when I left school. This embarrassed me. I found it hard to talk about my future simply because I had no idea what I wanted to do. I had toyed with the idea of becoming a landscape architect. I loved botany and biology. Then there was chemistry. I could picture myself in a white lab coat doing research.

But now it was fall and my future plans became more pertinent. I would graduate in the spring and although I did not know what I wanted to do, I knew exactly what I did not want to do. I still did not want to go into the Land Army. I knew that there was really nothing I could do if I received a call-up notice. To refuse was unthinkable. I began to sleep badly. If only there was something, anything, that would keep me out of those dreaded services. I knew that if I was caught in the net and forced into the Labor Service I would not survive. I was convinced of it. It was as simple as that. I was not a group person and I was no match for Nazi leaders. The very idea that I would be at their mercy was more than I could stand. I became nervous and depressed. I had nightmares. I worried. I fretted. I was afraid. I had to wait and see.

Miss Kunz accompanied our class to a school hostel somewhere in Brandenburg in September. It was a small old town of red brick buildings by a canal. It looked very rural, old fashioned and backward. We did not see much of the town because we went immediately to the hostel and spent all our time there. We took long nature walks and observed plants and insects and took notes. A couple of days after our arrival, Miss Kunz informed us that British planes had dropped leaflets during the night. We were to comb the woods in search of any leaflets which might have landed in the forest. We spent all morning and all afternoon walking at a snail's pace, almost shoulder to shoulder, through the undergrowth. One girl found a leaflet but before she had time to look at it, and before anyone else could catch a glimpse of it, Miss Kunz confiscated it. The following day, we were to occupy ourselves in the same fashion. I decided that this was not for me. I could not imagine anything more boring. I asked permission to stay at the home and help dig up potatoes in the adjoining field. Permission was granted. I spent a very pleasant afternoon in the garden helping a Yugoslav prisoner of war digging up potatoes. We worked silently. He could not speak German and I could not speak whatever language it was that he spoke. He looked very foreign to me. I climbed a fruit tree, sat on a branch and ate some apples. On the whole, a very satisfying afternoon away from Miss Kunz.

I mentioned before that it was difficult to get new shoes. We had to apply for a permit and the applications were mostly denied. However, people are resourceful and never more so than when necessity dictates it. A new fashion item appeared in the shops: Shoes with wooden soles. The solid, one piece soles were curved somewhat like Dutch clogs. The uppers were of man-made material. I was delighted when Aunt Marga came home with a pair for me, tan lace up, trimmed in red. I was very happy and proud. I wore the shoes right away. A short time later, someone had the bright idea to make the soles from individual slats. It made walking easier because they bent with the foot. I had a pair of those as well. I needed shoes badly because I kept growing out of the ones I had.

One morning our teacher entered our classroom for the first period still wearing her coat. She announced that we were going out. How exciting! Miss Kunz would not say where we were going. We walked toward center city, quite some distance from our school. Finally, surprise, surprise, we found ourselves at the Wilhelmplatz opposite the Reich Chancery. We were not the first to arrive but joined a great many schoolchildren and were told to stand facing the Chancery close to those already in place. More children arrived, filling the square to capacity.

The day was overcast with a low cloud ceiling and shortly after we arrived it began to drizzle. Nobody had an umbrella but by now we were packed in so tightly that only our shoulders and heads were exposed to the rain. We still had no idea why we were there. To pass the time, we talked and sang a little. Mostly we just stood, shifting our weight from one leg to the other, stamping our feet to keep warm. Minutes stretched into half hours, into hours. We were bored, cold, wet and hungry. Of course, we kept wondering why we were there and what it was all about. No one knew and the teachers would not answer our questions either because they did not know or else they were not supposed to tell us. I believe the former to be the case.

We stood facing the Chancery and after we had been there for some time we noticed a number of Spaniards standing along the Chancery wall. We knew they were Spaniards because they wore the khaki uniforms and red berets, familiar to us. At one point, we noticed the youths move to the curb, come to attention and salute as a big black limousine drove by. Then they assumed their former position, leaning against the wall. About an hour later, we were told to go home. We had stood for three and a half hours in the rain.

I had no money for the U-Bahn and decided to walk over to the Mohrenstrasse and call on Aunt Marga at G'sellius. It was lunch time. She took me for a hot drink at a café and gave me money for the fare home.

The following morning before class, we were all talking about it. The newspapers reported that hundreds of schoolchildren, cheering and waving enthusiastically, welcomed the leader of the Spanish Fascist Youth Organization as he drove to the Chancery to meet the Fuehrer. The mystery was solved and we knew the reason we had been taken to the Wilhelmplatz. It was a joke, because we had been completely ignorant as to why we had been standing for three and a half hours in the rain. We had not cheered and we had not been enthusiastic. Of course,

407

Miss Kunz had an explanation: we were not told what was going on for security reasons. We did not believe her, at least I did not believe her and a few others did not either. Our comments to her were not complimentary to say the least. Comments among ourselves were even less so.

A police decree was issued: "As of September 19, 1941, the yellow Star of David must be worn on the left breast by all Jews six years and older. The meaning of this order is clear."

Once, and it was the only time since Jewish people were forced to wear the Star of David, I saw a Jewish person. Mama was at the box office of the cinema. While I was waiting, I noticed a couple walk by. If it had not been for the star, I and nobody else would have known they were Jewish. I thought it must be awful to be marked like this. It seemed to me like being branded. Mama, who had been very upset when we first saw the signs at the box office and later at restaurants "Jews not welcome," remarked that it must be a sad life for them without cinemas, theaters or restaurants to go to and to be recognized every time they went out. She said it was a crime, a crime that would not go unpunished.

An ironclad saving program was advocated and enforced as of November 14. Every German was encouraged and expected to save three to six marks a week. The sum saved was income tax exempt and would earn a high interest rate thus yielding a favorable return after the successful conclusion of the war. "After all," so the instructions went, "we have shortages, therefore nothing to spend money on, so save." Inducted soldiers were made to sign participation forms and others, already in the forces, also had to take part in the program.

I still corresponded with Kurt, Uncle Herbert and my two pen pals. One day, I came home from school and found another letter from Heinz. I began reading it and soon went into

408

hysterics. He said that he thought I was a very nice girl. He hoped to meet me some day and when the war was over he wanted us to get married and open a bakery. I found this to be hilariously funny and laughed my head off until Father came into the room and demanded to know what was going on. In between fits of laughter I told him. After I had calmed down, I was sorry I had been so silly. Heinz was a decent guy and obviously quite serious. But I was only a 15-year-old schoolgirl and I hastened to write and remind him of it.

The reader must realize that things were very different in those days. Girls of 15 were barely considered adults. I was sheltered from real life and knew very little of the real world. I had always gone to a girl's school. Apart from the boys among my playmates, I had no contact with boys of my age socially. Young men older than myself were in the forces. Boys did not interest me at that time. Of course, I thought of marrying but that was a long way off in the future and I did not waste time on speculating whom I would marry. One day, I would somehow meet a young man. In spite of all the Nazi regulations, I would fall in love and marry. I read many novels and saw movies but that was the extent to which I was involved with romance. All fictional.

Air raids began again in October causing more damage. They were worse than before. Raid frequency increased to such an extent that I never got enough sleep but I still had to be in school at 8 a.m. Mama became increasingly nervous. She now thought it wiser for me to return to Father and Mother, whose apartment was on the first floor and had heavy outside shutters.

From the beginning of the attack on Russia in the summer of 1941 until the end of 1941, there were 109 RAF attacks on Berlin. How did all this affect Berliners? We stood up to it. We did not lose our sense of humor, a very caustic down-to-earth brand of humor, often directed at the regime. After all, did we have a choice? What good was it to make things worse by fighting city hall when you knew you could not possibly win. We went about our business calmly and, with a big pinch of resignation, accepted the inevitable. Instead of saying *"Auf Wiedersehen,"* which means "see you again," we cautioned, "See that you are left over, survive." Someone put a sign on the skeletal remains of a warehouse that read, "Open day and night."

Every morning after an air raid we talked about it and tried to find out in as much detail as possible where the bombs had hit and damage caused. We tried to get in touch with friends and relatives to see if they were okay.

Our social life was severely curtailed due to the ever present possibility of air raids. Nobody wanted to be caught away from home during a raid. Now we only visited or were visited on weekend afternoons. Movies became more popular than ever. They afforded us a few hours of escape from grim realities. Most films were pure entertainment and not war related.

The senior class at school performed Mozart's "Bastian and Bastienne" in our assembly room one Saturday afternoon. I invited Dieter to come along. It was a wonderful production and the costumes were pretty. Dieter had never been to a theater that I know of so it was something new and different for him and we both enjoyed the performance.

Days and weeks passed. October arrived and with it the news that the Soviets were putting up stiff resistance and continued to hold the German troops within sight of Moscow, about 20 miles outside the city. But, so we were told, this was only a temporary delay. The Army would take Moscow before winter came. However, the Army did not advance and the Army did not take Moscow. Winter comes early to Russia, much earlier than to Germany. This year, winter came with a vengeance. Rumors, well founded, had it that our troops were not issued any additional clothing to combat cold weather. No extra underwear, no scarves, no gloves or ear muffs, no extra socks. Watching the newsreel, we could see for ourselves that the soldiers wore their normal uniforms, with no scarves, gloves or ear muffs.

Incidents of frostbite took on enormous and alarming proportions. Rumors were further substantiated by official appeals for winter clothing for the troops in Russia. Women were urged to knit gloves, socks and scarves and mail them to soldiers at the Eastern Front or take the items to collection centers, which would forward them to the front. I did not knit anything simply because I could not get any knitting materials and we owned no handknitted garments that could be unraveled. I have no recollection if and what we gave or if anyone came to collect door-to-door. I do know that we sent gloves and scarves to Kurt. Oma knitted things for Uncle Herbert. She still had a supply of wool.

We were amazed to hear and read that some items were stolen from the collection centers even though punishment for stealing was severe. Several people were sentenced to death and executed. I read in the papers about a couple who had stolen a fur coat. They received the death sentence, which was carried out almost immediately.

Advent arrived and, with it, traditional advent wreaths and candles. However, December 7 was a black day, because of Pearl Harbor. Soon thereafter we were at war with America. The news was received with dismay by Father and Mother, Mama and, with grim foreboding, by everyone in my circle. The older people recalled vividly what had happened after America entered into WWI. Secretly, I hoped that the Americans would do something fast and end the war before it lasted much longer. My family was sick of it.

411

At the same time, complaining could not help and could get us into trouble, perhaps executed. I heard a rumor and rumors were usually based on fact that a person living a couple of blocks away in our neighborhood had been arrested for saying, "I wish this bloody war was over." Very unfortunate. The person had been extremely careless, since statements like this were taboo. They undermined morale. People who displayed defeatist attitudes were sent to concentration camps. I was shocked when I heard it and talked to Mama about it. It seemed a high price to pay for such a small offense. Caution was called for. I was even more careful about what I said in public and what I said to whom in private. The "German Look" became second nature. Posters on the walls everywhere reminded us that "THE ENEMY IS LISTENING." At the same time, they reminded me of our enemies within.

We warned each other about potentially dangerous people, party members and supporters. The warnings ended with: "Be careful, you don't want to end up in Oranienburg." Nobody I knew personally was ever arrested, although I knew some people who were dangerously outspoken in their criticisms of the Fuehrer and the war as time went on. Mama, in particular, was.

As the year 1941 drew to a close, my future was still uncertain. I was graduating in the Spring of 1942. At one time, there was talk of a teacher shortage and the need for recruiting young people into the teaching profession. I volunteered but my teacher and the headmistress decided I would not be suitable. Teachers could recommend or not recommend people for jobs or training for professions.

Winter Solstice, December 21, was intended to be a Yule celebration but nobody I knew celebrated it. We all celebrated Christmas. Solstice, with anonymous gift exchanges, was celebrated by HJ and BDM. Schools were encouraged to do so but it never took off.

This year, Miss Fischer suggested an anonymous gift exchange. We drew names out of a hat and brought a gift for the person whose name we had drawn. It was my bad luck that I drew the teacher's name. I was not very happy about it at all.

On the occasion of a teacher's birthday, some children brought small gifts. In 1940, Aunt Marga had insisted that I mail a book to Miss Kunz as a birthday present. Her birthday, I think, was in September. I had not wanted to do it but my aunt persisted. I still recall how reluctantly I made my way to the post office with the parcel. No one can imagine my dismay when Miss Kunz walked into class the day after her birthday and announced to everyone present that I had sent her an expensive book. She said this was absolutely out of line and made me walk up to her desk where she handed me the book, including the wrapping. I was humiliated and burned with shame and indignation. Naturally I told Aunt Marga about this dreadful incident. She wrote a letter to Miss Kunz. I have no idea what she wrote and we never spoke of it again.

I certainly did not want a repetition of that experience. Therefore, I did not tell anybody anything about this year's gift exchange. I simply asked Father for a few pennies and bought three pencils, a pencil sharpener and an eraser because Miss Fischer always lost or mislaid hers. I wrapped the items in colored tissue paper to resemble vegetables. My classmates, who knew that I had drawn Miss Fischer's name, were curious as to what her present would be and crowded around her table when she opened it. They and Miss Fischer were disappointed. By coincidence, Miss Fischer had drawn my name and I received a small notebook. It had a red wooden cover with a spray of white flowers painted on it. I copied poetry and aphorisms in it. I still have it.

December 21 was my 16th birthday.

1942

January 29	German and Italians reconnoiter in Benghazi, Libya, North Africa.
February 8	Albert Speer replaces Fritz Todd as Minister of Armaments and Munitions.
February 24	von Papen escapes an assassination attempt.
March 1	Russians launch counterattack in Crimea. German losses are 1.5 million.
March 7	Belgians deported to Germany to work.
April 24	Exeter bombed.
April 28	Luebeck in flames, with heavy damage.
May	Rommel advances on Tobruk.
May 8	German offensive in the oil region of the Caucasus is unsuccessful. Charkov attacked by Reds, with heavy losses.
May 30	Cologne is raided by 1,000 bombers, which drop 2,000 tons of bombs.
August 26	Soviet air raids on Danzig, Berlin and Stettin.
September 3	Stalingrad city line pierced by Germans.
September 7	Reds push back Germans at Stalingrad.
October	Canterbury bombed in the biggest day raid to date.

November 19	Soviets launch counteroffensive at Stalingrad. Four days later, the Soviets close the ring around Stalingrad and trap the German Sixth Army.
November 23	Soviets drive German troops 15 miles back at Don. British break through at El Alamein and Rommel retreats.
December 21	The author's 17th birthday.

The new year dawned. We were at war with the United States. I wondered what difference this would make. We had spent a quiet New Year's Eve at Aunt Martha's and an equally quiet New Year's Day.

The Americans were somewhat of a mystery to me. We had not learned anything about U.S. history and we did not spend any significant time studying the physical geography of that country. Once we were shown a documentary about America. "Why does the Statue of Liberty turn her back on America?" the commentator asked, pointing to the statue. This and a scene showing men pouring milk from huge cans into the gutter stuck in my mind. Apparently, they were dairy farmers protesting low milk prices. The commentators pointed to the waste of it, that the men showed no concern and destroyed the milk rather than use it or give it away. Bad point for U.S. capitalism. The rest of the film was in the same vein, showing unemployment lines, soup kitchens, slums and so forth, with biting anticapitalist narration.

The winter was very cold, as usual. Once again, Mama put blankets in front of the windows and we huddled around the stove. Reports from the Russian front mentioned temperatures of minus 31 to 40 degrees Fahrenheit and the appeals for winter clothing for the troops in the east continued. The soldiers who fought in Russia that winter (1941-42) were decorated with a special medal, the East Medal or Russian Front Medal (*Ost Medaille*), which came to be known as the "Frozen Meat Medal."

The Fourth Reich Clothing Card was issued. The soap we were able to buy now was something like a pumice stone. It was green, gritty and abrasive. To top it off, soap was very scarce.

Magda's birthday fell on a Saturday. Mama and I called in the afternoon and joined a number of ladies for ersatz coffee and cake. There were flowers everywhere. A particularly lovely bouquet of pale pink carnations stood on a small table between the windows. I walked over to admire them and enjoy their fragrance but when I came closer I discovered that they were artificial. The blooms looked so real that they fooled everyone. Apparently, a shop at the Doenhoffplatz specialized in silk flowers. After seeing this bouquet, I made a point of visiting the establishment the following Saturday and was amazed. The window looked like that of a florist shop filled with fresh flowers. They were the most stunning silk flowers I had ever seen.

Shortly after we had arrived, the doorbell rang. Magda went to open the door and we heard her shout for joy because her husband stood outside, on leave from the Eastern Front. Naturally, all the guests departed within a few minutes.

We celebrated Mama's birthday on January 13 with the usual open house. Most of her friends came for ersatz coffee and supper. My aunts and I even managed to find some of the dark red, almost black, carnations she liked so much.

My days and nights passed with school, homework and air raids. People in the shelter talked about raids, reports about raids on other German cities, bomb damage, and friends or relatives who were bombed out or had been killed or wounded.

Cologne was attacked almost every night over a long period of time. My math teacher told us about the owner of a butcher store who generously provided refreshments for the tenants who lived in his apartment house. The tenants decided to show their appreciation by having a party during the next raid, complete with wine and a dozen long stemmed red roses for the lady. The wine was cooling, the roses ready but the British did not play ball. The night passed peacefully. Everything was ready the following night: the wine was cool, the roses stood in a vase. Nothing happened. This went on for several more nights. The roses finally wilted. My teacher did not know if the party ever took place. We thought this was very funny.

Raids on Berlin became much heavier. More people were bombed out of their homes and left with nothing but the clothes they wore. In order to avoid this situation, we packed suitcases with clothing, as well as other essentials and deposited them with friends. They in turn deposited things with us. Aunt Marga, unbeknown to me, took some things to Aunt Lotte in Balz. I found out, after the fact, that she had included the new seal coat she had given me at Christmas, which I had only worn twice, as well as my confirmation necklace, a lovely amethyst ring and Mother's amber jewelry. Later in the year, I begged her to go or let me go to bring the suitcases back. She refused. I never had a chance to go and the items were lost.

It was a dreary winter. Thank goodness, the movies were a welcome, though very temporary, escape. Books helped me a great deal by transporting me into a world of adventure, peace and romance. To a certain extent, the radio did the same. Apart from news, evening programs provided light popular or light classical music, as well as selections of operetta and opera music. I loved those but, as they usually came on after 9 p.m., I only managed to hear part of them. We went to bed early and I could not disturb Father and Mother by playing the radio too late.

The most popular radio program remained the Sunday request program. The program actually resulted in an honest to goodness romance that was later made into a movie. During the 1936 Olympic Games, a young couple met. Somehow, they were separated and lost touch. The young man was now in the forces and sent in a request for the girl he met so long ago. She responded, they were reunited and subsequently they married. I

419

don't know if they survived the war. It would be interesting to find out.

Restaurants and cafés were still open. On weekends, bands played and dancing was permitted. One evening, Mama and I met some friends at the Odeon Café in the Hasenheide. I felt quite grown-up. It was the first time I had been there at night. The café had a colored glass dance floor illuminated from below. On another occasion, one Sunday evening, we went to a Berlin Kindl Restaurant. It was very crowded. People wanted to hear music, dance and forget the war. Much to my amazement, a young man asked me to dance. I was so taken by surprise that I just sat there and looked at Mama because I was at a loss as to what to do. Mama nodded and motioned me to get up and dance. I was very self-conscious and ill at ease. I could not think of anything to say. I was glad when the dance was over and that I was not asked again.

On our way home, Mama remarked that it was time I took dancing lessons. In the fall, she enrolled me in Keller's Ballroom Dancing School. I did not want to go alone and asked Kirsten to join me. One Sunday afternoon, Kirsten and I made our way to the dance studio. Rows of chairs lined the ballroom walls. Boys sat on one side, girls on the other. First the teacher and her partner demonstrated the steps and then the pupils practiced the steps separately. Afterwards, the boys chose girls as partners. I enjoyed the dancing but I had no idea what to say to the boys and they were equally tongue-tied. We did not have time to socialize because everybody left for home as soon as the lessons were over. There was a dance party at the end of the course. Kirsten's and my partner asked us out for coffee afterwards. We went to Kirsten's home and to mine to ask permission to go out. Then the four of us walked to a café. It was very crowded but we did manage to squeeze in. Over a cup of ersatz coffee, we spent an hour or so in conversation, somewhat forced and labored because none of us had any experience in socializing with the opposite sex. I was relieved when the boys escorted us to our respective apartment house doors, although I was flattered to have been asked out.

Soon afterwards, directives were issued prohibiting public dances. It stated that people at home should not enjoy dancing while men were fighting at the front. No allowances were made for those soldiers on leave who would have dearly loved some lighthearted entertainment to forget, for a little while, that they had to return to the front and face death.

The end of my school days was in sight and Aunt Marga was making plans for me. She enrolled me in a business college for two years because students were exempt from service. When Papa heard of it, he balked. He wanted me to be apprenticed to a flower shop and train to become a florist. I loved flowers but was not interested in becoming a florist. I was not consulted. A battle of wills raged. Aunt Marga and Father against Papa. Papa was adamantly opposed to my going to school because it meant that he must pay support for another two years, which was only one mark a day. Mama had never asked for an increase and Papa had never offered one. It was pathetic. Papa even came to see Father to remonstrate him but Father gave him a piece of his mind and told him in no uncertain terms what he thought of him for trying to deprive his daughter of the opportunity for additional education.

However, Papa did not give up. He went to see my headmistress. Much to my amazement I was called to her office one morning and there he was. The headmistress said, "I understand you are to go to business college. This means your father would be forced to pay support for another two years. That's unreasonable. I think it is also unreasonable that in addition he will have to pay your tuition." I was standing in front of her desk shaking in my shoes. I was very upset that Papa had come to see this woman. But I spoke up and told her that the part about Papa paying tuition for me was not true. The tuition had already been paid in full and he was not expected to contribute. This took the wind out of her sails. She was obviously surprised and Papa was embarrassed. She dismissed me. I returned to my classroom, quite angry.

I very much wanted to go to the college because it meant two years of safety from the dreaded Labor Service. However, I could not do so without Papa's consent. I went to see him on the following Sunday to try and change his mind. I spent the whole Sunday afternoon sitting on the couch with him, pleading and asking for his consent. It was in vain. I left quite late and in tears. I was exasperated.

Then I received a letter from my official guardian asking me to come to his office in the Neukoelln City Hall. I had never met the man before and this remained the only time I did. During our interview, he asked me whether or not I wanted to attend the college. I answered in the affirmative. Obviously, Papa had also been to see him, hoping he would side with him. However, Papa came up against unexpected opposition. My guardian, like Father, told Papa he could not believe that a father would deprive his daughter of the opportunity for further education. After that dressing down, Papa relented and came to see Father in order to give his consent. Unfortunately, it was too late. The registration deadline had expired. Aunt Marga had been obliged to cancel my registration. It was irreversible. My place had already been given to someone else.

As a result, the danger of being drafted into the Labor Service loomed larger than ever. How could I escape? What could I do? Aunt Marga was the bearer of good news. She had found out that a youth apprenticed to a publishing house was excused from compulsory services for the duration of the apprenticeship. This was one of a very few exceptions.

So far, I had not contemplated working in an office but this was no longer a consideration. The important factor was that if I was successful in obtaining a place as an apprentice I would be safe for a few years. Fortunately, Kurt and Mama both had worked for the Scherl Publishing House. Kurt, though in the Army, was considered to be on an indefinite leave of absence and thus technically still an employee. This put me in an advantageous position and I hastened to submit my application for an apprenticeship. I was accepted. What a relief. I prayed fervently that the war would be over within two years.

I was still taking ballet classes and was thrilled with the progress I was making. Someone told me about another dancing school and one night I took a trip across town to see what it was like. I felt very brave. The school was a lot classier and much more professional than the one I attended. For the first hour we did nothing but exercises, pulling and stretching, mostly in pairs. It was extremely strenuous. Afterwards, my knees were shaking so badly, I had to sit down while changing my clothes. I was very sore the next day. Unfortunately, the school was too far from home and I did not want to be caught away from home in an air raid. At the same time, Mama was pressuring me to quit dancing. She was worried that I might become sick, that I might catch tuberculosis because I did not get enough sleep. She fretted that I had to work hard at school, did not have enough food and was underweight. This combination could be dangerous to my health, she reasoned, because I was only 16, and overtaxing myself by doing such strenuous exercises. I resisted but finally the decision was taken out of my hands when dancing schools were ordered to close. They were considered nonessential.

423

On every possible occasion, such as January 30, April 20, *Heldengedenktag, Totensonntag* and Mothers Day, we had assembly and listened to many patriotic speeches by our headmistress, the Fuehrer, the Youth Leader and the Minister of Education. There were also readings from "politically correct" books which I don't remember because I tuned out. We learned poems and songs suitable for each occasion. Each class contributed to the program which began or finished with the singing of the national anthems. In our class, one girl was especially good at reciting poetry and was usually chosen to appear on stage.

Another girl, who sat behind me, also loved to recite. Lisa was the only girl in our class who was not a native of Berlin. She was born and spent the first years of her life somewhere in Southern Germany. She still spoke with an accent, the leftover of a regional dialect. She was one of the girls our teacher picked on. Miss Kunz had an unkind way of putting people down, primarily the few girls she disliked. For example, once she reduced a girl to tears and pleading for another chance after being bitingly criticized for a poorly done test.

At one time, Lisa confessed in class to her ambition and dream to become an actress. The first time she mentioned this, Miss Kunz practically guffawed. "What, with your accent?" she sneered. Lisa had tears in her eyes as she sat down. Lisa and I were friends. We talked a lot and I felt empathy for her because of the way she was treated. After this incident, Lisa confided that she was taking elocution lessons from the mother of a well-known child star movie actor. I was awed. Her diction improved by leaps and bounds. Early in 1942, she auditioned for one of two openings at the famous Burg Theater in Vienna and was accepted as a pupil in their theater school. Very impressive. Somehow, it became known in class. I know Lisa did not tell

Miss Kunz but when Miss Kunz heard about it she asked her to reenact the scene she had done at the audition. It was the deathbed scene from "Hannele's Ascension" by Gerhard Hauptmann.

Lisa related that applicants were called onto an empty stage. The famous actor director of the Burg Theater and the other judges sat in the dark theater while the stage was bathed in stark white light. Applicants wore neither costumes nor make-up. In the play, Hannele clutches at her throat as she is dying and when Lisa clutched at her throat she broke the string of pearls she was wearing. Lisa knew she must not let this distract her. Ignoring the pearls which cascaded and rolled all over the bare stage, she carried on. Now she reenacted the scene for us in class. She was marvelous. She had us on the edge of our seats and in tears. Miss Kunz was literally speechless. When she came to, she smiled and made some insidious remark about how much Lisa's diction had improved or something of that nature.

Early in 1942, my class began thinking about a way to celebrate our graduation. Miss Kunz was consulted. She suggested that we have a party on a Saturday afternoon after school because most girls lived considerable distances from school and it would be impossible for them to return again later on the same day. We agreed to the plan and picked a date in February.

Then we brainstormed about the type of party to have. We eventually decided upon a pantomime shadow show. A large white cloth was to be stretched across the front of the room with enough space behind it for the performers and two strong spotlights. I wanted to take an active part but for a while I was at a loss as to what I could contribute. An incident in class gave me an idea.

425

Shortly before our rehearsals got under way, Miss Kunz upbraided us one morning for the sloppy way we extended the German Greeting "Heil Hitler!" when she entered the room. She instructed us to mend our ways and demonstrated how to salute: stand up straight, raise our arm straight and look sharp, instead of slouching. I decided that my contribution to the party would be a little sketch about this incident. It gave me an opportunity to ridicule her with my portrayal of her and overacting her "Heil Hitler!" example.

Refreshments were to be offered after the entertainment and we were asked to contribute to the buffet. This was a problem for me. We only had our rations, as did many others, and they had been cut a number of times already. Mother found it hard to make ends meet and was hard put to spare anything. In the end, after agonizing over the situation, we settled on baking a Bundt cake made from farina, flour, two tablespoons of fat, a little sugar, egg substitute, lemon peel, lemon juice and baking powder.

Many interesting recipes were devised by inventive and creative women. Cakes and dishes were tasty although they contained hardly any or no fat or meat at all. It certainly was very healthy fare by today's standards. All the same, we would have dearly loved to eat rich pastries with whipped cream. We reminisced about peacetime goodies and drooled while talking about prewar food.

Our party came off well. It proved to be a welcome interlude, a little diversity, fun and excitement in our otherwise depressing and drab everyday wartime existence. I did my sketch. The girls liked it and I derived a lot of satisfaction from it. The highlight of the entertainment was Lisa who enacted Gretchen's "mad" scene from Goethe's *Faust*.

426

Although distracted to a certain extent by preparing for our party, I was very much aware of the approaching finals coming up in March. We were all worried about the exams. Nature came to our rescue and intervened in the form of a measles epidemic. Our school closed down two weeks early and finals were canceled.

I think it was early March when I noticed something going on at our old playground. A few trucks were parked in the street and men worked behind the fence. From Mama's apartment window, I saw them dig up the entire lot. The men wore broad striped black and white prison clothes and matching caps. Mama found out that the lot was being converted into a water reservoir and that the men were concentration camp prisoners. One day after school, I saw some of them so close that I could have touched them. They were loading their shovels onto a truck under the supervision of an armed guard. They were fairly young men and they appeared normal. Their coloring was good and they did not look emaciated, sick or starved. I assumed that they were political prisoners from Oranienburg where political prisoners, so rumor had it, were kept. I think they had red patches on their jackets.

April 1 found me at 8 a.m., together with a dozen or so other girls and boys, in the Personnel Department of the Scherl Publishing Company. I was nervous. After keeping us waiting for a while, each of us was assigned to a department. I was assigned to the "The Gazebo," Scherl's oldest magazine. "The Gazebo," though no longer published due to wartime paper shortages, was allowed to exist because one of its original attractions and main selling point had been a life insurance policy that came with the subscription. It paid death benefits even for war related deaths.

427

"The Gazebo" occupied a four story former apartment house in the Kochstrasse, part of the city block that was the Scherl complex. Scherl's newest edifice was at the intersection of Kochstrasse and Zimmerstrasse, the same site where, in the 1960s, Axel Springer built his publishing house right on the detested wall and in defiance of it.

In the entrance hall of our building was the Commissioner's cubicle. His name was Mr. Klutzke. He was a proper Prussian, a former noncommissioned officer complete with slicked down black hair and a mustache. He dressed impeccably and never smiled. He remained completely impersonal and, as far as I could tell, had no sense of humor whatsoever. He performed numerous functions, including that of being on duty well before office hours to check employees in.

Our working hours were 8 a.m. to 5 p.m. Mr. Klutzke stood outside his cubicle and, although he knew all of us well and by name, we had to show him our identification cards. If a person was late, even one minute by his clock, the identification card had to be surrendered. Mr. Klutzke attached a slip noting the time of arrival and forwarded it by messenger to the personnel department. The culprit picked the card up when leaving the premises at 5 p.m. We also had to show our card after coming back from lunch if we left the premises. Mr. Klutzke was at his post to make sure nobody left the house until the second hand of his big wall clock reached the full hour of 5 p.m. Usually I waited for this to happen while standing on the bottom step of the stairs, poised to race out of the door so I could catch the first train after 5 at the Kochstrasse U-Bahn station, just below the spot which later became Checkpoint Charlie.

At "The Gazebo," a complete organization in itself, I was to spend approximately two months in each department and learn all aspects of office procedure. First, I was assigned to the registration department on the second floor.

I was introduced to my fellow workers: Miss Krause, Mr. Sander, Mrs. Werner and Marianne, a lovely young lady of 18. I hung up my coat and donned my new duster which we were required to wear. The color was optional but navy blue was the only one available when I bought mine. I was shown to a table in the far corner near the back window of a large room which spanned the entire depth of the building. Marianne brought several long boxes filled with thin yellow paper slips, which were 3 inches by 5 inches and additional piles of slips held together with rubber bands. The slips were numbered in the right hand top corner running from 100,000s up to 2 million. Each slip bore the name and address of the insured. Handwritten notations in red and black ink indicated if death benefits or payments for an injury had been made, to whom and when. It was my job to reinsert the slips into their proper place in the filing boxes, a deadly dull occupation. I was not used to sitting in one place for hours on end, certainly not from 8 a.m. to 5 p.m. It was not only hard on me mentally but physically on a certain part of my anatomy. I was miserable. However, when I considered the alternatives, I was gratefully miserable.

Miss Krause occupied a desk at the window on the street side of the room. She always wore a washed out beige overall, had short straight salt-and-pepper colored hair, smoked and was a party member. In time, I found out that she had ordered a VW and was paying five marks every week toward her car. She even had an order number which meant that she had paid at least 75 percent of the purchase price. She was confident that Hitler was going to win the war and that her car would be delivered to her soon afterwards. Her colleagues laughed about it behind her back.

429

Lunchtime was a very welcome break and Marianne took me to the staff canteen. The afternoon seemed endless. I looked at my watch every few minutes but the hands crawled around its face at a snail's pace. The first days were simply torture. I hated every minute but again I thought of the alternative and was grateful.

Later that week, a little elderly hunchbacked lady, Adele, joined our department and was put to the same donkey work as I was. I felt sorry for her. It was hard on her back having to sit in the same position all day. We both grumbled to each other. She was an ardent foe of Adolf Hitler and whispered snide remarks to me every time Miss Krause extolled the Fuehrer's virtues.

Marianne and I quickly became friends. Marianne was blond, blue eyed and tall. We usually spent our half hour lunchtime together. Scherl, like all large firms, had a subsidized canteen, where most employees took their meals. In order to reach the canteen we did not have to leave the building but walked across attics, up and down flights of stairs, through a big printing shop and other offices. Marianne lived in the Borough of Kreuzberg so on many mornings I took the U-Bahn, got off at the station close to her home, met her and walked with her to the office. We talked about everything: family, movies and movie stars, girl talk, about getting married and so forth. I remember her describing the kind of wedding dress she would like to wear: lace with a full skirt made with layers of frills. Personally, I did not think this would be a good style for her because she was not petite but leaned toward statuesque. I've wondered if she ever had a dress like that.

We also grumbled about the war, food shortages, that there was nothing much in way of consumer goods to be found in the shops, air raids and so on. Most of the time, if she was not walking, we traveled home together. Marianne was the one who told me to be careful because many plainclothes Gestapo officers were infiltrating public transportation and generally mixing with crowds, listening to what people were saying. Anyone being overheard voicing a politically incorrect remark was arrested. Consequently, we only talked about the weather and entirely personal subjects. I often scrutinized my fellow passengers' faces trying to guess which one of the men might be a Gestapo agent.

After I had slaved over my yellow slips for seemingly endless weeks, I was given other jobs to do, such as writing the notations on the slips to indicate address changes, that the person was deceased or that benefits were paid.

My pay was 40 marks a month for the first six months. Thereafter, it was 60 marks a month for the next twelve months and I received 80 marks a month during the last six months of the apprenticeship.

We had a day off on Easter Monday and on May 1, still an official holiday. I was ecstatic. It was a spell of freedom. A happy escape from the office and I made the most of it by visiting the zoo, the Tiergarten and going to a show.

Every time Marianne or I were sent on an errand to another part of the Scherl complex or were on the way to the canteen, we passed through the photographic department. We slowed down to look at the photos of the latest heroes who had been awarded the Knight's Cross. The department superimposed the decoration onto a studio photo of the recipient and the fresh prints were pinned up to dry. Marianne and I did not care why these men had been decorated. We picked out and admired the most handsome guys, usually fighter pilots and U-boat captains. Now and then we asked for a copy of the photo to take home.

The North African campaign and General Rommel captured my interest. From what I heard, saw on the newsreels and read in the papers, Rommel was extremely well liked by his troops and very popular with people at home. He was often shown surrounded by his staff and smiling members of the Africa Corps. Once I saw a scene demonstrating how hot it was in North Africa. A reporter wiped oil onto a flat section of a tank, then broke and fried an egg on it. I thought that was neat. Later on, one of the photographers at Scherl who had been there told me that part of the panzer was preheated with a blow torch to make sure the egg fried nicely for the cameras. I felt let down and cheated.

Part and parcel of my apprenticeship was simultaneous attendance at a business school twice a week from 8 a.m. until noon. I liked that a lot. The subjects taught were bookkeeping, shorthand, typing (I had already learned the latter two in high school), business German, business correspondence, German and math. All apprentices were required to attend and I met several other girls from Scherl. After school, instead of using public transportation to return to the office, we walked. It took a lot longer. I enjoyed the fresh air and freedom it afforded. One girl, Ursula, invited me to her home a number of times and we occasionally went to the movies together. Unfortunately, she did not live very close to me.

As the war went on, conditions deteriorated. Our potato ration was 1 to 1 1/2 pounds per person per week during the first half of 1942. Fruits, vegetables and potatoes were scarce in the summer this year and our meat ration had been cut from 16 ounces to 13 ounces and fat was cut to 7 ounces a week. Lines at the various stores were long and the women complained. Stores had even fewer goods on display. Almost every item one wanted to buy required a permit, such as pots and pans, sieves, thermos flasks, pails, flatware, dishes, flashlights, towels and bed linen. We were told, "this is the time to show community spirit. If your

pots and pans are worn out, organize community kitchens."
Clothing rations were cut in half. Barter ads appeared in the
papers because money no longer had buying power. Without a
permit, there was only one way to obtain scarce consumer goods:
one had to have connections or "Vitamin C." Mama had no
connections at all. Aunt Marga had some connections and she
had access to books. Occasionally, she brought home the odd
quarter pound of real coffee.

Trading on the black market was dangerous. Punishment was
swift and severe. In April, an intensive campaign was under way
to stamp out black market activities. Daily papers published
reports of trials and consequent death penalties being passed on
black marketeers. The reports stated simply that (name of
person) had been arrested for black marketeering, tried,
convicted, sentenced and executed. The culprits came from all
walks of life. They were farmers, cattle dealers, butchers, hotel
owners, civil servants, people who had stolen ration cards,
printers who had printed counterfeit ration cards mainly for their
own use, textile merchants and so on.

For example, on May 23, a court in Weimar tried a married
couple, textile merchants from Erfurt, who were accused of
exchanging secondhand articles of clothing for food. The man
was sentenced to death, the woman to eight years of hard labor.
A butcher in a small town just outside Berlin, "aided and abetted
by a number of farmers," had killed cattle, enough that,
according to the prosecutor, 187,000 people were deprived of
their weekly 13 ounces of meat ration. The butcher was
sentenced to death. After a couple of months, reports of black
market perpetrator trials ceased. The population had received a
drastic warning. But we knew, by word of mouth, which was the
way real news spread in those days, that Nazis felt safe and were

safe from prosecution in these and other matters. This did nothing to enhance their popularity and we grumbled a lot.

The following joke was making the rounds: a man was walking along a street at night when the air raid alarm went off. He ducked into the nearest basement which happened to be Goering's. On the way down, so he told his friends later, he slipped on bricks of butter which covered the passage floor and, if he had not grabbed and held onto rows of salamis hanging from the ceiling, he would have slid right into innumerable sides of beef and come to serious harm.

It became almost impossible to get anything repaired. Repairmen were either in the forces or had been drafted into armament plants. The few places that were still in operation had to give priority to soldiers on leave and people working in war related industries. Here too, "Vitamin C" helped to get things done. Those who were in a position to supply some scarce commodity were "in." Repair shops and shoemakers opened their businesses only for a few hours a week. Lines formed long before the shops opened.

Some time in 1940, I had a slight toothache. Aunt Marga, who had discovered an excellent dentist, made an appointment for me. I had not seen a dentist since I was nine years old. The examination showed that most of my back teeth needed fillings, deep fillings. No novocaine or any other kind of painkiller was available. I figuratively had to grit my teeth and bear it. Dr. Lange did not finish a tooth in one session. It took several visits before he put the final filling in and on the last visit he polished it. He was a perfectionist. In later years, other dentists remarked on and admired his work. However, at the time I did not relish my visits to his office. One day, after a particularly painful session, he said, "You will have to suffer a lot more than this before you become a grandmother." Some consolation.

The way Dr. Lange met his wife, Sibylle, was quite interesting. Sibylle's family lived in Brueckenberg in the Riesengebirge in Silesia. She and her sister, Andrea, were on a visit to relatives in Berlin when Andrea developed a bad toothache. Sibylle accompanied her to Dr. Lange's, who had just started his practice. He was using a room in his mother's apartment, which served simultaneously as treatment and waiting room. While he was working on Andrea, he kept stealing glances at Sibylle, who was sitting at the other end of the room reading a magazine. On the sisters' next visit, he asked Sibylle for a date and eventually they married.

Their wedding took place in the famous church *Wang* in Brueckenberg in the winter. The church *Wang* was a Norwegian Stave church made entirely of wood. All the pieces are fitted together without using nails or pins.

The bridal couple went to church in a horse drawn sleigh. The bride wore a white fur jacket over her dress. I thought this was very romantic.

This summer, Aunt Marga and I traveled to Brueckenberg for our vacation. Sibylle's parents, Mr. and Mrs. Huber, still lived in Brueckenberg and owned a guest house. A butcher store took up the first floor. Brueckenberg was beautiful, quiet and peaceful. It was situated in the highest part of the Riesengebirge almost at the foot of its highest mountain, the Schneekoppe, which was clearly visible and within walking distance.

Aunt Marga and I had a lovely time. We visited the local beauty spots, looked at the famous church *Wang*, took afternoon ersatz coffee in the garden of any of the many cafés. Luscious red currant cakes were served, since red currants were in season and plentiful. The nights were tranquil and I slept like a baby.

One day, we decided to climb to the top of the Schneekoppe. We started out after breakfast but it was noon by the time we reached the summit. We had taken the steeper, faster approach because it afforded spectacular views into Czechoslovakia. The restaurant on the mountain top offered rest and light refreshments before we descended once more to Brueckenberg.

The following day, Aunt Marga persuaded me to see a doctor. She insisted. She felt that I should have a medical in view of the strains and stresses of our lives in Berlin, as well as the poor nourishment. The doctor found that I had an irregular and accelerated heartbeat. He ordered rest, "Sit in a deck chair in the shade and don't move out of the garden for a week." He also wrote a certificate to be mailed to Berlin stating that I was unwell, which extended my vacation by a couple of weeks. When I saw him again, my condition had improved. I was allowed to go for walks but only on level ground and not uphill.

We spent several mornings at the municipal swimming pool close to our guest house. Although the doctor had forbidden me to swim, I could sit at the side of the pool and dangle my feet in the water. Most mornings, a young couple with a 7- or 8-month-old baby visited the pool. Both were tall and blond and the young man was obviously on leave. I suspected and heard it whispered that he was in the SS. She looked like an ideal German Nazi woman: hair pulled straight back into a bun at the nape of the neck, blue eyes and well built.

The couple was determined to take the baby into the pool but, instead of introducing the child gradually to the new element at the shallow end of the pool, they went right away into deep water. The little boy was terrified and screamed and screamed when they dunked him. The parents became very exasperated. The young father obviously felt that it was a disgrace that the son of an SS man behaved this way. He was very determined, dipping the boy into the water again and again. The poor little guy screamed until he had no voice left and could only hiccup pitifully. Only then did the couple give up and leave. They looked quite put out.

The guests at the pool were upset by this performance. Nobody dared to interfere in spite of the child's obvious distress and terror because the father was SS and the couple had never spoken to anybody by the pool. They took no notice of other people, looked aloof and unapproachable. I hated to think of the little boy's future. Normally, people were not that reticent in voicing their disapproval but the SS connection proved to be a powerful deterrent.

We enjoyed our stay with the Huber's enormously. They were a lovely couple and Mrs. Huber was a wonderful cook. Meals were served by a maid in our room. I especially savored her delectable cabbage salad. Finely shredded cabbage was blanched for two or three minutes, then mixed with a dressing of water, vinegar, sugar, salt, pepper and chopped, fried smoked bacon. It was served cold.

I was lucky to have the extra vacation. I needed it. The days passed quickly. All too soon, it was time to say good-bye and return to the city.

In Berlin, life went on pretty much in the same way. However, Papa had acquired a garden. A large open area not too far from his home had been divided into plots and allotted to people for growing vegetables. I do not know how these allotments were made. I suppose people applied for them but there must have been many more applicants than plots. Anyway, Papa had one. He was now working 84 hours a week and only had every other Sunday off and, on alternate weeks, Saturday afternoon. He spent all his spare time gardening.

Even before this, Papa was always busy. He had many hobbies like breeding canaries, learning how to fly a glider and cut-out work with plywood. He made flower cribs, lampshades, magazine racks and more. He was also adept at photography. He took, developed, enlarged and colored his photographs. I never saw him idle. Now he was gardening and experimenting with smoking fish when he managed to get some while on vacation at the Baltic Sea. He also baked cakes, fancy ones, and tried his hand at many other crafts.

One Sunday, I decided to ride Kurt's bicycle to Papa's plot. It was a long ride, clear to the other side of the city and I had never gone on a bike ride in Berlin. The only time I used a bike was in Balz during our vacations. Because of the war and it being Sunday, there was hardly any traffic apart from the streetcars. In the evening, on my way home, I ran down a little hunchbacked woman. When she saw me coming, she stepped into the road, she dithered back and forth and could not make up her mind which way to go. I dithered with her in order to avoid hitting her but in the end we collided. Both of us landed on the pavement. I was petrified that I had caused her bodily harm but she was very sweet and after dusting each other off I continued home, knees shaking. I never biked to Weissensee again.

I cannot recall whether Kurt came on leave this summer or not. I know he came one summer, either in 1942 or in 1943. In Kurt's unit, leave was granted in alphabetical order. Kurt was unlucky because his last name began with the letter "U." As a result of this unfortunate circumstance, he repeatedly lost his turn when soldiers were transferred to his outfit whose names began with letters preceding "U". In all fairness, they should have joined the end of the line but then nothing was fair and they were inevitably pushed in ahead of Kurt. He told us that a lot of soldiers in his unit used every possible ruse to get leave. The guy who owned the pub, for instance, told his wife to send him a telegram announcing the birth of a baby boy. He had nerve. All his comrades knew, because he had told them, that his wife was

438

unable to have any more children. Others had telegrams sent about a death or serious illness of immediate family members. They got away with a lot because I am sure the army could neither spare time nor manpower to check up on every telegram.

From the beginning of the Russian campaign, Kurt had been at the Eastern front. He was with a maintenance/repair unit for panzers and was always just a few kilometers behind the front lines. He came on leave infrequently, unexpectedly, thin, tired and hungry. Before soldiers coming on leave from Russia entered Germany, they were checked for lice. All the soldiers had lice. They had to go through the delousing procedure not once but three times. Once when Kurt came on leave, he brought home a frontline soldier's care package, given to him at the border. It contained a can of sunflower oil, chocolate and some other food items. It was not much but helped to stretch our meager rations to feed Kurt adequately. This was important because following each air raid, he expected to have breakfast. He explained that, "Each morning, reveille is followed by breakfast." We had never heard of sunflower oil or used it before but I baked a wonderful cake with it.

It was fascinating to listen to Kurt. He told us that his outfit worked from dawn until dusk when darkness made work impossible. It was, of course, forbidden to have lights or fires after dark. The field kitchens did not move close to the front; consequently, his outfit hardly ever had a hot meal. This was a real hardship during the long and extremely cold winter months. They had to fend for themselves, build fires and melt snow for water while daylight lasted in order to have something hot to drink in the subzero temperatures of the Russian winter.

Kurt was in the middle sector of the front and in Ukraine. When the weather became too inclement for the troops to camp out, they were billeted with Russian peasants. The peasants lived

439

in small, one room log cabins that boasted one door and one very tiny window with blind glass. The window was never opened and had not been opened since it was originally installed. Not only did the peasants and their children live in this room but also the livestock, including goats, chickens, pigs, dogs, cats and vermin. One corner was taken up by a huge tile stove with straw on top. There the whole family slept, fully dressed in their sheepskin coats. They wore the coats with the fur on the outside in summer, and turned the fur to the inside in winter. A wooden table was fixed permanently to the hard stamped clay dirt floor in the center of the room. In the winter, no one ventured outside for anything. The hut lacked running water and sanitary facilities. Kurt said the stench that met him on entering made him wretch but he had to endure it because outside he would have frozen to death.

He told us of two or three day furloughs spent in Charkov and Kiev, described the cities and brought back cookies from Charkov, which were good. He told us how, when they first entered Ukraine, the peasants and the population in general had been very friendly. People welcomed the German troops and hoped for freedom and independence from the Soviets.

Each time Kurt arrived home, great joy reigned for a few days but it was short-lived. As the days wore on, his face grew longer, his demeanor more and more morose. He sat around, brooding and listless, aware only of the diminishing time he had left, hating the thought of having to return to the front. We tried to encourage him to enjoy every minute, to think of how much time he had left rather than how little but I guess it was not in his nature to feel that way. I cannot say that I blamed him. Of course, he was also worried about us because we were no longer safe.

Living in a big city like Berlin, we were much worse off for food than people in smaller towns and in the country. We and many other city dwellers were very unlucky in that we had to exist solely on our rations which were, at best, inadequate. People were very fortunate if they had relatives in the country or had a garden where they could grow vegetables, fruit and perhaps even keep a couple of chickens and raise rabbits.

When Kurt came on leave, it was time for me to take a few days off "sick" and make a quick trip to Balz. I packed a suitcase with clothing that I had outgrown and other garments Mama, my aunts and Mother no longer needed and visited the Ziegler family. On one of our vacations there, Mama and I had walked a couple of kilometers to the farm of the Ziegler's second son and made the acquaintance of his wife, parents-in-law and children. The parents-in-law and the wife were running the farm while the young man was in the army. I was very fond of the grandmother. By now it was difficult to get clothing and they were very glad to give me much needed food in exchange for the items I brought.

On my return, my suitcase was packed with lard, butter, homemade sausage, bacon and a freshly killed chicken. The children loved my visits. They were left on their own most of the time because none of the adults had time to spend with them. They did not leave me alone for a minute. Before they went to school, in the afternoon when they came home, after supper, all evening I played with them, sang to them and told them stories. When I went to bed, they crawled in with me and I kept on telling stories until they finally fell asleep at 11 p.m. or much later. I was quite hoarse by then but I did not mind; in fact, I enjoyed it. I could only stay two days because I had to make some excuse at school or work for my absence and three days were the most we were allowed to take off without a doctor's certificate.

441

On my last trip, the grandmother was sitting in the kitchen one morning peeling potatoes. Her basket was almost empty. I gallantly offered to go into the basement to fill it up. I felt sorry for her because she was old and still had to work hard. It was a large wire basket. After I had filled it, it must have weighed at least 45 pounds. I lifted it the wrong way and I felt a stab just as if a very fine needle was being pushed into my lower back. It only lasted a second. I delivered the potatoes to Grandma. An hour later, I was bent over at an angle of 90 degrees and could not straighten up. I tried to lie on my bed until it was time for me to catch my train. The station was an hour's walk away and I had to carry the heavy suitcase. I was lucky because the neighbor's boy offered to accompany me part of the way and put the suitcase on his bicycle.

In the train, I had a compartment to myself. I spent over an hour gingerly straightening out on the wooden seat. We had arranged that Kurt should meet me at the Schlesischer Bahnhof. Kurt was there but my train was late. Kurt decided that he had time to run to the kiosk for cigarettes. Of course, the train pulled in while he was away and it only stopped for two minutes. I looked out of the window and when I did not see him I stayed on and got off at the next station which was closer to the U-Bahn. It was agony, struggling down two long flights of stairs with my suitcase and, upon arriving at my destination, up two flights of stairs back to street level. Then I had to walk three blocks uphill and climb four flights of stairs. I was almost crying with pain but my ordeal was not yet over. I had to go downstairs once more and walk two and a half blocks to Father and Mother's apartment before I could collapse.

I was in bed for three days. The doctor came and prescribed mustard plasters. I could not move and it took several more days before I was able to return to work.

442

I no longer saw much of the kids I used to play with, except Dieter. I still dropped in on him and sometimes he came to see me. I do not remember what the girls or Guenter were doing. Peter was still in school and Martin was an apprentice in an aircraft factory. Hannelore's older sister was engaged to an SS man and later married him. When I met Hannelore in the street one day, she told me that her sister was going to a Lebensborn home for expectant mothers. All wives of SS men stayed in such homes until after their babies were born and were well looked after. Later Hannelore told me that her sister had a boy. After the dancing classes ended, I also lost touch with Kirsten, my school friend.

Beginning in January and for months on end, we were exhorted to make greater efforts and more sacrifices because the "total war" demanded it. More and more people were drafted from nonessential jobs into war related industries. More foreign workers were shipped in. Working hours increased and workers were told that two people must do the work of three. Our circle of friends and acquaintances became increasingly depressed, downhearted and dissatisfied.

A directive was issued on July 30: "An employee must accept any kind of work he/she is given and is obligated to perform it. He/she cannot refuse or delay whatever work may be referred to him/her, including extra hours, night, Sunday and holiday shifts. He/she cannot in violation of his/her duty stay away from work without a valid excuse or repeatedly be late for work without valid reason or leave his/her job. Offenses are punishable by fines, or imprisonment for two years, for staying away from work a couple of times without valid excuse or for loafing on the job. Two or three times late is punishable by two to three years in jail." People, who after a 14 hour day felt incapable of working additional overtime, were sentenced to one year in jail.

Fortune-telling had been outlawed. By now, it was even more dangerous to practice it. Nevertheless, in times of stress and calamity, people turn to religion and superstition. Clandestine fortune-telling flourished. Somehow Mama learned to read cards, just for fun. She wrote the meaning on each card to help her memorize it. She read cards for her own entertainment.

A rather strange thing happened. During spring and early summer, the same sequence showed up almost every time she spread out her cards: a death in the family of a young man and a journey. At first, she did not mention it to me but, when this recurred time after time, she told me about it. From now on I watched and, sure enough, saw it for myself. Mama said, "Nonsense," trying to make light of it, "this is just a game and a coincidence. I don't believe in it anyway. Besides, we do not have any young men in our family." Then she gathered up her cards and firmly deposited them in a drawer.

We did not mention the subject again and forgot about it until a few weeks later when Mama received a postcard. It was from Aunt Lotte in Balz informing us that her son, Hans, was dead. She asked if Mama would come to the funeral and Mama went. When she returned, I heard the sad story of how Hans, barely 19, had met his untimely end. Hans had been drafted into the army at 18 and was stationed in a small garrison. He came down with a fever, a very sore throat and swollen glands. His unit had no doctor, only a medical orderly who ignored Hans when he reported sick. The fever rose, the throat got worse. A week later, the medical orderly finally thought it was time to call a doctor but by then it was too late. Hans had diphtheria and he died the following day. After he was dead, Hans received plenty of attention. When his body was sent home, 18 of his comrades were detailed to accompany it to Balz, where Aunt Lotte had to accommodate and feed them until after the funeral. The funeral procession walked a mile to the cemetery where Hans was buried with military honors. The soldiers fired three shots over the open grave.

Mama and I were up in arms about the army's negligence and that this death could easily have been avoided. However, being upset about it did not change anything. It just made us more aware of some of the things that were going on.

Hans' father, Uncle Otto, had been called up a few years earlier and never came back. I don't know what happened to him. Eventually Gerhard, the youngest son, was also caught up in the war machine and never heard of again. Aunt Lotte was forcibly evacuated from her home and lost her little property when the Russians advanced. She was not able to return after the war because the territory east of the river Oder was ceded to Poland and all Germans were evicted.

I was still writing letters to Kurt, Uncle Herbert, Heinz, whom we had nicknamed "Faithful Heinz," and Robert.

In September, the directives issued in July were reinforced. It was specified that "no worker can change his/her place of work for higher pay without permission from the local employment office. An employee cannot refuse but must accept any work he/she is assigned and must do it." If anybody resisted these directives it meant arrest, prison, concentration camp or death. Shifts were increased to 12 and 14 hours or 84 hours a week with one day off every two weeks.

As of October 17, an ordinance made it possible for soldiers to marry in absentia. The prospective bridegroom was required, in the presence of his Battalion Commander, to sign a formal declaration of his intent to marry. This action led to marriage, provided that within the ensuing six months the prospective bride, at her local civic registry office, officially agreed to the marriage. If the soldier was killed in action or was declared missing during this interim, the marriage took place anyway. The date of the marriage was the day the soldier submitted his declaration.

At times, I would run into Mr. Becker. He was as outspoken as ever about the regime and the Fuehrer. He asked if Aunt Marga could get him a copy of *"Mein Kampf"* because he wanted to compare the later edition to the original version to see what changes had been made. Aunt Marga was able to obtain the book for him. I never found out what he discovered, if anything.

Strange as it may seem, we were not made to read *"Mein Kampf"* in school. In fact, I have never read it in its entirety. In the late 1970s, an acquaintance presented me with a copy and I started reading it but never finished, mainly because I was too busy with other activities.

During WWI, casualty lists were published daily. Such lists were not posted now. We did not see German casualties in the newsreels. We saw only enemy dead, wounded and prisoners of war. Occasionally, a few shots would include a German soldier with a bandage but still up, about and smiling. Goebbels visited military hospitals at Christmas but I do not recall seeing his visits on newsreel. Older people, in particular, remembered WWI and everyone knew that where there is war there are casualties. Therefore, it was a given that German forces suffered casualties and the death announcements in the papers became more numerous as time went on.

Late in 1941 or early in 1942, Uncle Herbert was wounded at the Russian front. Aunt Gertrud was informed much later, after her husband was finally transferred to a military hospital in

Germany. Uncle Herbert had 58 shrapnel pieces in his back from the neck down to his toes. One knee and one hip were shattered. The injuries to his knee and hip would not have been as permanent and incapacitating as they turned out to be had he received immediate medical attention.

Unfortunately, care given to casualties was not always the best. Because of a shortage of doctors, the wounded frequently received only the most rudimentary first aid often given by inadequately trained orderlies. The consequences of such initial neglect were infections and septicemia. There were no antibiotics. By the time the patient finally reached a doctor and/or hospital, it was usually too late. To avoid gangrene, if it had not already set in as in cases of severe frostbite for instance, amputations were called for. Amputations were frequently performed as a preventative measure when it was impossible to get the patient moved to adequate medical facilities within a short time. I saw a great number of convalescing soldiers who were missing arms and legs.

When Uncle Herbert was struck down, he was evacuated from the front line to Poland where he spent a full month without medical attention lying on the straw covered floor of a barn with no plumbing facilities. Eventually, he was brought to a military hospital in Germany. By then, his wounds were badly infected. He almost lost his leg and he was lucky the doctors in Germany were able to save it. He was delirious for weeks and his leg was swollen to three times its size. Pus drained from the window in the cast which covered him up to his chest. While he was running a high temperature, he was told that he was allowed to eat anything he fancied. This was really a joke because in his condition he had no appetite whatsoever. Once the fever was down and he was hungry he was put on the usual hospital diet which, I am sure, was a far cry from "whatever you fancy."

447

Uncle Herbert recovered and was invalided out of the army. His hip and knee remained stiff. One piece of shrapnel had severed the lateral ankle ligaments so he could no longer raise his foot. But, he was luckier than thousands of others.

Mama and her friends discussed casualties. At the same time Mama, Magda and their friends were angry. They complained to each other about able-bodied Nazis who managed to stay home and out of the services or, if they were in the army, remained either in Germany or well behind the front lines.

I also heard that some soldiers shot themselves in order to be repatriated and invalided out of the army. It was known as a "Repatriation Shot." They would shoot through a loaf of *Kommissbrot* (heavy black bread, an army staple), usually aiming for their foot. The problem was how to get rid of the bread once they fired the shot. Anyone caught was executed.

The news that women were being mobilized to serve in the armed forces shocked me profoundly. I prayed harder and harder for the end of the war. In one short year, my apprenticeship would be over and then the specter of the Labor Service and now, in addition, that of the Armed Forces loomed large and threatening. I heard that at this time the land army girls were sent to the country to do farm work during the summer. The remainder of the year was served in a factory, as street car conductors or other war work where required. Some girls upon reaching the age of eighteen were drafted right into the Army, bypassing the Labor Service. This was no consolation to me. I would turn 18 in December, four months before the end of my apprenticeship.

Every day, Mama spent hours standing in line for food. She often came home disgruntled and told me how the women grumbled, though carefully and in whispers, while waiting. It was hard for women to feed their families, especially when even

448

potatoes were rationed to four and a half pounds per week and we only got one egg a month. Weekly rations had been cut again.

In April, the bread ration was reduced to 10 ounces per day and the meat ration to 10 ounces per week. The quality of butter was awful. I saw it. It looked disgusting, full of dark blue and green spots. I also tasted it and it was inedible. Women complained loudly and openly. The government had to come up with some reason for the reduced rations, which subsequently was published in the papers and broadcast on the radio. According to the government, the reason for reductions was because Germany had to feed so many other countries, there were not enough farm workers and production was down, and the potato crop had frozen during the previous terrible winter. The government did not replace the inedible butter. It seemed that Berlin was always at the end of the supply line and usually got the wrong end of the stick, not the best quality nor quantity.

Meanwhile, I learned a new craft of how to make bags out of paper string. String made from fibers had long been displaced by string made from paper. Now someone had come up with the idea of weaving bags with it. It required a round frame and nails placed at half inch intervals around the outer edge. The string was stretched between opposite nails and weaving began in the middle where all strings crossed. Two round parts were joined with a straight piece to give the bag depth, leaving an opening at the top. Plaited string formed the two handles. To make the bag more attractive, we used whatever colored yarns we could find to alternate with the string. It was fun to do and for a while the bags were popular until even paper string became scarce.

Shoes were harder to get now. Adults were lucky if they were able to obtain a permit every two or three years. Applicants had to state on the application how many pairs of shoes they owned and how old and in what state of repair these were. Spot checks were made to see if the applicant had filled in the form truthfully. If not, he or she was punished.

My problem was that I still outgrew my shoes. At one point, Aunt Marga gave me a new pair of shoes she had stashed away since the 1920s or very early 1930s. They were of fine calf leather, light beige but of a style and with heels of a bygone era. I balked and would not wear them.

This Christmas was less festive than the last. We still had trees but it was almost impossible to find candles. We kept ours from year to year and lit them for only a few minutes on Christmas Eve, the two Christmas days and on New Year's Eve. Papa had electric ones.

A special distribution of additional victuals for Christmas was as follows: 1 pound of flour, 7 ounces of meat, 4 ounces of butter, 2 ounces of cheese, 8 ounces of sugar, 4 ounces of dried peas or lentils, 4 ounces of candy, 1.6 ounces of coffee and half a bottle of liquor for adults. Children under 18 received a quarter pound of candy in lieu of liquor. Workers in heavy industries, night shift workers and those working extra long hours received one bottle of liquor instead of half a bottle and, in addition, one bottle of wine.

The Hitler Youth was busy making and repairing toys for Christmas fairs. The WHW sold lovely wooden miniature toys. Everybody loved them and, in Berlin alone, four and a half million pieces were sold. There were 10 different items: a house, a farmer's wife, a goose, a tree, a rocking horse, a small train engine, a hobby horse, a whistle with a bird on it, a toy soldier and a cannon which could actually shoot. The proceeds went to the Mother and Child Welfare Organization.

The December 25 issue of our newspaper included a supplement featuring articles about Albrecht Duerer and photographs of his work *"Holy Night."*

450

On December 21, I was 17 years old.

By now, we were seriously worried about Kurt. We knew he was in or near Stalingrad. My pen pals were also on the Eastern front. I hoped that they would not be caught but the news was frightening.

Magda came to see Mama while I was there. She was extremely upset and cried. She had received a letter from her husband and gave it to us to read. Leo wrote that conditions in Stalingrad were desperate. The troops were running out of ammunition and were without shelter and food. There were no medical supplies. Without the issuance of extra clothing, soldiers were freezing and a great many suffered severe frostbite. They were starving. Leo wrote that he hoped to get his letter out of Stalingrad by the last military plane, which was scheduled to leave that day transporting wounded out of the city. This was the last time Magda heard from Leo. After the war, she made extensive and exhaustive inquiries for years, but to no avail. She never found out what happened to her husband. Finally, he was declared dead.

For the first time, the family did not get together on New Year's Eve. There was nothing to celebrate. Food was scarce and the news was depressing. Everybody I knew wanted peace and, if they did not pray for it, they hoped for it. Peace to me was just a word. I had no conception of what it might mean, what it would be like. I knew for certain that Germany would not win the war but I could not imagine how the end would come. At this time, I kept a diary. On New Year's Day I wrote in it, "What will 1943 have in store for us? Hopefully the peace we long for."

451

1943

January 18	Russians relieve Leningrad after 18 months siege.
January 31	The German Sixth Army surrenders at Stalingrad.
February	Count Ciano ousted by Mussolini. RAF bombs Berlin with 2,900 tons of bombs in half an hour.
March 6	RAF planes bomb Essen and Krupp.
March 10	Hitler recalls Rommel.
June 1	Sicily taken by Allies.
July 12	Anti-Nazi opposition establishes National Conference for Free Germany.
July 25	Mussolini is arrested and under house arrest. Badoglio (1871-1956) who affects Italy's change to the side of the Allies, takes over Italian government.
July 28	Hamburg is devastated. Seven square miles burn and are flattened in firestorm of 15,000 degrees Fahrenheit. Approximately 80 percent of Hamburg is destroyed and 30,000 are dead.
September 8	Hitler occupies north and central Italy.
September 12	Mussolini is rescued from house arrest by special commando unit of the SS.

October 13	Italy declares war on Germany.
December 21	The author's 18th birthday.
December 26	*Scharnhorst* sunk in Arctic.
December 31	Heavy air raid on Berlin.

Until some time in 1942, I had worried about the possibility that Germany might win the war. Now, I was certain that Germany would lose the war. Although I had a good idea of what life, and my life, would have been if the Fuehrer prevailed, I had no conception of what it might be like after the Allies won. A "joke" made the rounds: "Enjoy the war, peace might be awful." This expression seemed to fit the situation.

The plight at the eastern front grew more and more desperate. The Soviets were on the move and gaining ground. The siege of Leningrad had lasted 18 months but now the city was relieved by Soviet troops. Of course, our official bulletins never mentioned the word retreat. "Straightening or adjusting the front lines," "regrouping" or similar phrases were used.

The critical conditions at Stalingrad overshadowed everything else. The news, doled out to us sparingly, was grim and was getting worse with every passing day. Mama and her lady friends met, commiserated with each other and shared their anxieties about the fate of their husbands who were all in Stalingrad. News reports were full of praise for the Sixth Army, extolling the men as "brave and courageous, fighting against overwhelming enemy forces." I was certain that they were doomed. They had no ammunition, no winter clothes, no food and no medical supplies. I felt oppressed by all these thoughts, as though I was carrying a heavy weight on my shoulders. I felt acutely the hopelessness and harshness of their plight of being trapped with no way out. In public, people spoke in whispers about Stalingrad. We sympathized with all who had relatives there.

We worried about Kurt. Every day that went by without a letter from him added to our anxiety. It was a long time before we heard from him but it turned out that he had been lucky. His panzer repair unit was just outside the Stalingrad city limits. His unit was withdrawn literally moments before the Soviets closed the ring and encircled the city. I also wondered about my two pen pals because I had not heard from either of them for a considerable time. As it turned out, I never heard from them again.

In 1940, special victory news bulletins had followed each other at short intervals and fanfare blared practically without ceasing. In 1941, 65 such special announcements aired and there were 19 in 1942. Only two special announcements were made in 1943. Then the sound of fanfare ceased.

For some time, all kinds of foreigners, including Russian men and women, had been brought to work in Germany, mostly in armament factories. Our food rations had been cut again and by now were quite small. I am sure those workers received less than we did. The Russians fashioned small wooden toys and on weekends they went door to door selling these or begging for food in exchange.

None came to Mama's or Father and Mother's apartment building but they did come to Aunt Martha's once when I was there. She either bought two toys from them or gave them food in exchange. One item was a wooden disk. Four small chickens sat on the perimeter, facing in, each with a string attached to its beak. All strings were fed through a hole in the middle, gathered and threaded through a big wooden bead suspended about 6 or 8 inches below. When one swung the bead, the chickens pecked.

The other toy was a wooden snake made up of individual segments which allowed for certain snakelike movements. We felt very sorry for those workers, so far from home. Mama heard from someone who had firsthand knowledge that the Russian women were abused by their guards and sexually molested. Mama told me about it when we happened to walk past some prefabs near the Tempelhof airport that housed Russian women.

456

Mama was upset, called it a disgrace and was highly vocal in her condemnation of the ill treatment but there was nothing she could do about it.

My reactions to what was taking place around me and to what I experienced were completely emotional. By 1943 and from then on, when situations threatened me personally, my feelings were of a deep down fear, settling in the pit of my stomach. My mouth went dry. I was enveloped in a claustrophobic grip. Even more than before, I felt helpless and hopeless.

Air raids on Berlin continued. January 30, the 10th anniversary of the Fuehrer's ascent to power was marked with special speeches by Goering and Goebbels. As Goering was about to speak, the air raid sirens sounded the alarm and the same thing happened when Goebbels was about to launch forth later in the day, a rather comical coincidence. Our Fuehrer did not speak this year.

Our main concern remained the Stalingrad crisis. I could not understand why General von Paulus did not retreat or rather that he had not retreated while retreat was still possible. I could only surmise that he was forced to hold out by orders from the Fuehrer. It seemed to me to be madness. I was unable to keep from thinking about the desperate plight of the troops there. Freezing temperatures in Berlin seemed mild compared to the Russian winter in Stalingrad.

On January 31, the government finally announced that the Sixth Army had been forced to surrender. The news was received with relief. We did not know how high the casualty figures were at the time but we guessed that thousands of surviving soldiers must be prisoners. At last the fighting was over, although the prospect of captivity in Russia was in no way reassuring. The government decreed three days of public mourning. Flags flew at half-mast and the radio broadcast only serious classical music. I found out after the war that there were approximately 90,000 survivors of the original 300,000 men in the Sixth Army. They became prisoners of war and, out of the roughly 90,000, only about 5,000 came home eventually, many of them years after the war.

News headlines:
February 2
Stalingrad held under the command of General Field Marshall Paulus to the last shot.
Encircling tactics of the Bolshevists on the Don front and in the area of Wornelsch unsuccessful.

February 4 newspapers reported:
German sacrifice in Stalingrad.
Example and obligation for the nation.
The Sixth army fought to the last bullet.

When Kurt was on leave, he told us how he and his comrades were shocked by and disgusted to see the way Russian prisoners of war were treated by their guards. The prisoners did not receive food and they were starving. To amuse themselves, their guards occasionally threw a few crusts of bread into their ranks just to see the prisoners scramble and fight for them. The guards laughed and hit the prisoners with their rifle butts. Apart from shouting at the guards to stop, Kurt and his comrades were helpless. They could not interfere without risking a court martial or being shot. Mama commented, "How can people be so inhumane? Well, just wait and see what happens when the tide turns." I thought with trepidation of the fate awaiting German prisoners, and possibly us, at the hands of the Soviets.

News from Italy was almost as bad as news from the east. Mussolini ousted Count Ciano. On the whole, the opinion about the Italians held by most people whom I knew was not high. After all, didn't Germany have to bail them out when they messed up in the Balkans? They were looked down upon and ridiculed as "the spaghetti and macaroni eaters." Because they had been turncoats in WWI when things began to get tough and the winds of war changed, no one was surprised that it was happening again. People shrugged because it was more or less what one would expect from the Italians. History repeated itself. The funny thing was that Italy had always been the favorite destination for vacationing Germans in peacetime.

As of February 4, all militarily nonessential industries and all restaurants were closed. Cultural life largely halted, in part because people were too tired to go anywhere and they used what little free time they had to rest.

Schoolboys and members of the HJ were drafted to serve as flak helpers after February. The boys were used to replace soldiers who were needed at the front. Although the boys belonged officially to the HJ, they wore air force and navy uniforms. The boys received a pay of 50 pfennig a day. Mama was disgusted. "These boys are only children," she said. I agreed with her.

One day, I don't recall what day of the week it was, Mother was reading the newspaper by the kitchen window and Father was also in the kitchen. They were talking about the announcement that the siblings Scholl had been executed on February 22 for treason. Father said that they had conspired against the Reich and were caught doing so. I did not hear more details other than that they were students and had lived in

Munich. Years later, I found out that they had been tortured and that the girl made her way to the scaffold on crutches to be beheaded. How they must have suffered. I thought how brave they were or rather how brave they had been.

From 1933 to 1945, regular, special and Volk courts imposed 16,000 death sentences. Between 1941 and 1945, there were 15,000 and more than two-thirds were carried out. The death penalty before 1933 was reserved for three types of crimes. By 1943-1944, it was for 40 types of crimes and misdemeanors. There were no pretrial procedures. Offenders were sentenced immediately with no recourse. During the war, a malicious gossip law was in effect. The penalty for anti-Hitler jokes was death.

These are some of the jokes I heard and repeated during the war:

Before the war and after being unemployed for a long time, a man finally gets a job in a vacuum cleaner factory. He decides that his wife should have one and begins stealing a different part each week. When he has all the parts, he spends one Sunday putting them together. But no matter how many ways he tries, it always turns out to be a machine gun.

Hermann Goering enters Hitler's office. "Good morning, my Fuehrer." Hitler looks up and an expression of alarm spreads over his face. "Hermann, are you sick? You do not look like yourself, what is wrong?" "I am fine, my Fuehrer," replies Goering. Hitler, after staring for a moment, relaxes. "I know what's wrong," he says, "you are not wearing your medals!" "Good gracious," Goering splutters, "I must have left them on my pyjamas!"

460

Hitler, Goering and Goebbels are driving across the country. While passing through a village, a dog runs in front of their car, is struck and killed. They stop to ask who the dog belonged to and are told it belonged to a particularly obnoxious farmer. There was great consternation: who will tell the farmer about his dog?! Finally, Hitler and Goering say, "Joseph, you have the gift of the gab, you go and tell him." Goebbels limps up to the farmhouse and enters. Time ticks by. He is gone for a long time. Hitler and Goering are alarmed. What is happening? Finally, after a long wait, they see Goebbels come out of the house staggering under a load of smoked sausages, sides of bacon and ham. "What happened? You were gone for ages, we were worried that you had come to harm, perhaps the farmer beat you or worse. Now here you are, loaded down with food. What happened?" "Well," says Goebbels smiling, "I knocked on the door and, when the farmer opened it, I simply said, 'Heil Hitler! The dog is dead!' Whereupon the farmer insisted on showering me with gifts."

Hitler, Goering and Goebbels are in an airplane. The plane has no facilities. Hitler is hard-pressed to go to the bathroom. What to do? Finally, he cannot wait any longer. Goering and Goebbels suggest, "Use your hat!" Hitler uses his hat and throws it out of the window after he has finished. Shortly thereafter, the plane lands and the three continue their journey by car. Not too far from the airport, they see a crowd of people in a field shouting, jumping, throwing their hats and caps into the air, embracing each other. Hitler, Goering and Goebbels are curious. What is going on? Goebbels is told to go and investigate. He approaches the outer edges of the

461

crowd and asks a man, "Why the excitement?" "Hitler is dead!" "How do you know?" Goebbels asks. "We found his brain!" replies the man smiling broadly.

Weiss Ferdl walks onto the stage holding three photos, one each of Hitler, Goering and Goebbels. He stands for a long time contemplating the pictures in silence. The audience snickers. Finally he turns to the audience and says, "I can't make up my mind. Shall I hang them or line them up against the wall?"

The curtain opens on Weiss Ferdl, who stands on the stage with two pigs and a piglet. People laugh. Weiss Ferdl says: "Let me introduce the Mann family: this is baby Mann, this is Frau Mann, and this is Her(r)mann."

Hitler, Goering and Goebbels are in a plane. They discuss their individual popularity. Goebbels says, "I will make myself popular if I throw down petrol coupons." Goering goes one better, "I will be more popular if I throw down food coupons." The Fuehrer wants to outdo his friends. "I will be even more popular," he boasts. "I will throw down petrol, food and clothing coupons." "Wrong," says the pilot, "I will be the most popular if I throw the three of you down."

Hitler, Goering and Goebbels are flying in an airplane. The airplane crashes. All three are killed. Who is saved? The German people.

A little boy comes into a butcher shop. The butcher's wife asks him, "What can I get for you?" "5 pounds of Goebbels meat," replies the boy. The butcher's wife is horrified. She excuses herself and rushes into the back of the shop where she tells her husband, "That little boy who just came in wants 5 pounds of Goebbels meat.

What shall I do?" "Simply give him 2 pounds of bones and 3 pounds of snout," answers her husband.

A goat and a snail meet and chat. The goat is very derisive about the snail's slow pace. "I can beat you any time," boasts the goat. "Is that so," says the snail, "let's have a race and see who wins!" The goat laughs, "This is no contest. I can win this race lying down!" They start the race and, surprisingly, the snail arrives first at the finish line. The snail waits for the goat. The goat turns up three days later. "What happened?" inquires the snail. "You boasted so much and now you are late." "Well," says the goat, "while I was on my way I grumbled, was arrested and thrown in jail for three days." "Ha," gloats the snail, "now you have found out the hard way: you must never grumble, you must crawl."

Hitler, Goering and Goebbels are in the country and see a skunk running away from them, taking shelter in a small hut. Goebbels says, "Let's have a bet as to who can stay in the hut with the skunk the longest." They decide that Goering has to go first. He comes out after a minute. Goebbels is next and he manages to stay in for 5 minutes. Now it's Hitler's turn. The Fuehrer goes into the hut. After 10 seconds, the skunk runs out.

Goebbels dies and goes to heaven. God meets him at the Pearly Gates and welcomes him. Goering dies and God meets him halfway between His throne and the Pearly Gates. Hitler dies and, when he arrives in heaven, God remains seated. Goebbels and Goering are astounded. Hitler is outraged. "You got up and came to meet Goebbels at the gates, you met Goering halfway. Now that I come, the most important, the greatest of them all, you stay put? Why did you not come to meet me?" God smiles and says: "I must remain seated. If I get up, I know you will sit down on my throne."

After the failed attempt on Hitler's life on July 20, 1944, some people raised their arm in the Nazi salute and murmured, "Schade!" (What a pity!)

People discuss what they are going to do after the war. One man says, "After the war I am going to tour Germany on my bicycle." "And what will you do in the afternoon," asks his friend.

An American, a Frenchman and a Berliner meet after the war. "When I stand on top of the Empire State building, I can see the whole of New York," boasts the American. "Ha, I do not have to go that far," scoffs the Frenchman. "The Eiffel Tower is high enough to afford me a view of all Paris." "You guys have to take a lot of trouble," says the Berliner. "I only have to step onto my kitchen chair and I can survey all of Berlin."

In April 1945, a woman comes to the vet with her brown dachshund. "Doctor," she says, "my dog is very sick, he cannot stop shaking." "This is very common," replies the vet. "all brown dogs are shaking nowadays."

I never heard a single joke about Himmler. Nobody made jokes about him, I think, because of who he was.

On March 7 there was a distribution of previously ordered frozen produce: one package of either fruit or vegetables.

I do not recall the date of the first day raid on Berlin but day raids began and, as time went on, occurred with increasing frequency. We learned that when the enemy planes approached a certain area, heading for Berlin, a cuckoo sound was superimposed over the current radio program. Now even Father and Mother turned the radio on during the day to be forewarned about raids. Once we heard the cuckoo, we prepared to go to the shelter because the siren sounded within two to five minutes.

The boroughs of Wilmersdorf and Berlin-Mitte were "block bombed." It is called block bombing when bomber units fly in formation and continually drop bombs onto a specific area, causing bomb craters every few yards. The Roman Catholic Cathedral, St. Hedwig, and four other churches received hits. The raid resulted in 1,700 casualties. At the time it happened, I did not know the casualty figures because they were not published.

In March, the RAF dropped 2,900 tons of bombs on Berlin within half an hour. It became difficult to tell the old from the new bomb damage. I could only recognize the new damage if I had seen a house there the day before and the next morning it was a heap of rubble. Mama and I reflected on one of the Fuehrer's pronouncements just before he came to power: "Give me ten years and you will not recognize Germany!" How prophetic! How true!

On April 1, I had an awful shock. An official letter arrived for me. It was a summons and I was to present myself at 8 a.m. on a certain day at the Neukoelln City Hall for the purpose of a medical prior to being inducted into the Labor Service. I trembled. I was frightened, terribly frightened. I had heard about these medicals for the army and for the Labor Service. I gathered that the girls had to strip completely and line up for the male doctors, who inspected and examined them in front of everyone. I shuddered. The very thought of it was horrifying and humiliating. I panicked but I had to face the fact that I must go to

City Hall. I had no choice. If I did not show up, it would mean dire consequences.

After I had spent several sleepless nights, the dreaded day dawned. Needless to say, I could not swallow a bite of breakfast. With butterflies in my stomach and shaking in my shoes, I walked to City Hall, forcing myself to take one step at a time. In the corridor outside the specified room, I waited with many other girls. My anxiety mounted. Eventually my name was called. My knees felt so weak that I could hardly walk to the registration desk. The clerk checked my name, address, date of birth and asked me where I worked. I explained that I was an apprentice at the Scherl Publishing House and showed them my contract. After perusing my papers, the clerk announced that I was exempt from call-up and the medical examination. I could go. I almost fainted with relief and was out of the building as fast as my legs could carry me. "Thank God!" I repeated over and over again. "Thank God! Let the war be over before they get me."

Heavy raids on Berlin took place on the nights of April 27-28 and 28-29. The zoo was hit and many animals perished. I heard that a number of poisonous and nonpoisonous snakes had escaped from the aquarium. I did not make a special trip to see the damage. The zoo was, of course, closed and from the outside it was difficult to estimate the extent of the destruction. Berliners were very upset. They loved animals and the Zoological Gardens were a very popular place to visit. I did wonder how the zoo managed to feed all the animals.

My friend Dieter was ready for his confirmation and I was invited. Together with his mother and his Aunt Lotte, I attended the service and the small, quiet celebration afterwards. It remained the only social event of the year for me. In fact, I had no social life. I did not know any young people and had been out of touch with my former playmates for some time.

During April and May, reports from Africa, as well as the news from the Russian front, could not ignore the progress made by the Allies and the Soviets. Although Rommel had rallied in the spring in Africa, he was subsequently forced to retreat as the Allies increased in strength and gained more and more ground. As a result, Rommel was recalled by the Fuehrer.

The Fuehrer and Mussolini met in Salzburg on April 11 to discuss the lost cause and, on May 12, the Italians and the Germans capitulated in North Africa. 150,000 members of the Africa Corps were taken prisoner by the Allies. However, Rommel's popularity did not diminish and people did not blame him for the defeat of the Africa Corps. It was obvious to us that he could not hold out against the combined Allied forces. Conversations centered around these events, as well as on the destruction of the huge Mohne and Eder dams by bombs on May 17. The newspapers admitted that there were casualties.

More air raids on Berlin followed during May, June and July and raids on the industrial Ruhr increased.

Work continued but I was no longer in the registration department. I had moved on to correspondence, mailing and statistics. The new law drafting women into the armed forces caught up with a girl in statistics, Monika, who was a couple of years older than myself. She received her call-up papers and had to join the Army. I prayed that the war would come to a sudden end, any end, before I could be called up.

One Sunday, late in the afternoon, I walked along Tauentzienstrasse and toward the Wittenbergplazt U-Bahn station. It was a warm day but the sun was getting low in the west. The street was empty. I was wearing a white floral dress and red sandals with wooden slat soles. The slight breeze felt like a cool caress on my bare arms. I was lonely. I cannot remember where I had been or why I had come to the west end

467

on that particular day. Now the emptiness of the street made me think of the emptiness of my life and of the future. The future was blank. My imagination failed to conjure up images. I could not envision anything beyond that day or night. I lived from day to day without the certainty of a future. For a short time right there, I felt a vacuum and had great apprehension as to what would fill it. The feelings lasted a few moments but they were indelibly etched into my mind. Even today, I can see the blue sky and the reddish sunshine on the tops of buildings in front of me. I can still feel the pavement beneath my feet, the warm breeze and my utter loneliness.

Early in July, Father and Mother went to Balz for a vacation so Aunt Marga and I stayed in their apartment. One day, Aunt Marga brought home two large baskets of black, sour cherries that someone had given her. These cherries are too tart to eat and are used for cakes, syrup and jam. I decided to make and bottle cherry juice. I organized bottles, spent two hours pitting the cherries, boiled the juice with the small amount of sugar at my disposal and filled the bottles.

When I checked them a few days later, I noticed tiny bubbles in one of them. I opened it. Wow! It was like opening a bottle of champagne that had been vigorously shaken. The dark red juice exploded out of the bottle all over me and the kitchen staining my pale peach colored silk dress, the kitchen walls, ceiling and curtains. What a mess. I ripped off my dress and dunked it into the zinc tub filled with cold water which stood by the kitchen sink. Since the beginning of the war, we had been instructed and encouraged to have some large containers of water standing by at all times so we would not be without water should there be an interruption of service. Now it came in handy and saved my dress from ruin. The stains had no time to set in. The rest of the bottled juice turned out okay.

468

Massive attacks on Hamburg over a period of several days and nights transformed the city into a burned-out wasteland. A sea of flames stretched for 7 square miles and a fire storm raged with temperatures of 15,000 degrees Fahrenheit, destroying 80 percent of the city and killing 30,000 civilians. At the time it happened, we had no knowledge of the number of casualties but the severity of the raids and damage could not be denied. I heard people talk about it, in particular, those who had relatives and friends in Hamburg. Fire engines from Berlin and other cities raced to assist the Hamburg fire fighters. News spread and this could not be kept secret. When the Berlin fire fighters returned, they talked and gave graphic descriptions of the devastation and the casualties they had encountered.

We commented: "Hitler lost his eraser, the Allies found it." This was a reference to his statement that his air force would erase the British cities from the map. However, German cities were now experiencing a lot of eraser application.

News about air raids and damage in other cities and towns filtered through by networking. Friends and relatives learned a lot about what was going on in various places. In this way, I was apprised of details that were not reported in the newspapers. Unfortunately, I had to rely on secondhand and thirdhand reports since my family had no connections or relatives in other large cities. All our friends were Berliners whose families also lived in Berlin.

On August 14, there was a distribution of one pound of fresh tomatoes.

Father, Mother and I still did not go into the basement during air raids. We felt quite safe in our first floor apartment because the windows were covered on the outside by heavy storm blinds. They kept out light and sound and now protected the windows, which we opened during an air raid to save them from being broken by a possible nearby explosion. We remained in the apartment but took a few precautions. For some considerable time, in fact, all through the previous winter, I had gone to bed fully dressed. I wore everything: stockings, socks, underwear, dress and cardigan. My boots stood ready by my bed and my scarf, hat and coat lay on a chair next to it. Although Father and Mother got up and sat in the living room when the alarm sounded, I stayed in bed, turned over and went back to sleep. The detonations sounded like distant thunder in my dreams. When the detonations came closer, Father and Mother insisted that I get up and put on my shoes and coat.

This continued until the nights of August 22 and 23 when the siren wailed at about 11 p.m. The interval between the time the alarm was sounded and the arrival of the bombers over the city was now shorter than before. Only a few minutes elapsed before I heard antiaircraft guns barking and the hum of airplane engines followed by bomb explosions. On this particular night, it sounded as though a great number of planes were over the city with very little antiaircraft fire. I heard the droning of the bombers' engines, and numerous detonations, some quite close. I got up, put on my boots and my coat and went into the kitchen. I was somewhat anxious because of some papers I kept in my purse.

I was thinking. All along jokes about the Nazi trio, Hitler, Goering and Goebbels, circulated. Naturally, one would only pass the jokes on to people of whom one was sure. A number of politically incorrect jokes were on paper and I had copies in my purse. One was an imaginary speech made by the Fuehrer which began: "Now that Russia has become part the of Reich,

Roosevelt has offered the United States of America to Germany as a German colony. We must be concerned earlier than ever about the welfare of our Volk comrades everywhere. For this reason, I am opening the Winter Assistance Program in May to ensure that our Volk comrades in Siberia will receive their gifts in time for Christmas." It went on in that vein, making the Fuehrer look ridiculous.

The other joke was a piece of 8 by 8 inch paper divided into four squares, each with the drawing of the face and the shoulders of a different national: a Greek, and three others. When the paper was folded a certain way, the Fuehrer's face appeared. Unfortunately, I cannot recall the story or joke that went with it, only that it was derogatory and alluded to the fact that all these countries had been swallowed up by the insatiable Fuehrer or phrases more strongly worded to that effect. I had also written sundry other jokes on paper in order to memorize them. They now burned a hole in my purse while I thought of the implications should anything happen to our building and the papers were found on my person.

Just then, I became aware of a most peculiar noise which grew louder and louder. It was a whining sound and I was not sure if it was some kind of new bomb or an aircraft in trouble. I decided that it was the latter and I held my breath. The sound increased and came uncomfortably close. I wondered if the plane would hit our house when suddenly there was an explosion followed by silence.

That made up my mind for me. I turned on the gas stove, lit a match and regretfully burned the jokes, watching the paper curl and turn to ashes in a saucepan. I felt very relieved because I had saved myself and my family from possible disaster.

The morning paper reported that an enemy plane crashed into a square less than a kilometer from our house.

At work, my colleagues and I discussed the recent raids and I learned that the Borough of Steglitz, badly hit during the first raid, was hit again the following night. The damage was said to be considerable. Phosphor bombs had caused extensive fires. The fires still burned two days later, for as soon as the phosphor was dry it reignited.

Marianne and I decided to take a look. After work, we traveled by streetcar and bus to Steglitz, where we walked down the Schloss Strasse, one of the borough's main business and shopping thoroughfares. We were forced to walk in the middle of the road because the buildings on each side were either burned-out or had collapsed across the sidewalks. Some were still on fire. We walked two kilometers before turning back, gaping at the ruins and the damage. The sight left us speechless. It was awesome.

Injuries caused by phosphor were particularly nasty, so I heard. A couple of days later, I saw this for myself when a man got onto the U-Bahn train and sat opposite me. His face was dreadfully disfigured by what I assumed to be phosphor burns. I did not want to stare but could hardly take my eyes off him. It made my stomach turn and his purple-red, raw face haunted me for a long time.

The paper on August 25 said: "Greater Berlin's air defense success: 60 four-engine enemy bombers destroyed during terror attack. Night terror attack on Berlin. The enemy paid a high price for the latest terror attack on the area of the Reich capital."

472

August 25

Numerous units of enemy planes attempted a concentrated heavy attack on the Reich capital during the night of Monday to Tuesday. Significant numbers of enemy bombers were intercepted by night fighter planes and caught by spotlights before reaching the city limits over Berlin itself, thus preventing the execution of a concerted, coordinated attack. The enemy dropped high explosive and incendiary bombs indiscriminately and aimlessly on residential areas of the city resulting in damage to public buildings. There were casualties, dead and injured. According to a preliminary confirmation, 60 enemy planes were shot down."

August 27

Civilians are instructed to go immediately to the cellar when the alarm sounds. Don't wait for the anti-aircraft guns to start firing.

Counterfeit food coupons, dropped by the enemy, must be surrendered immediately!

August 28

Berlin declared air raid disaster area.

These heavy raids convinced Father and Mother that, henceforth, it would be advisable to join the other tenants in the air raid shelter. As soon as the siren sounded, we made our way downstairs. Mr. Becker had rigged up a radio with earphones and placed it on a small table. Sitting in the basement for hours was very dull. I asked permission to join Mr. Becker, who was kind enough to share the earphones with me. We had one each. The announcements gave us a good idea of what was going on outside. I learned the direction from which the enemy planes approached, when they actually crossed the Berlin city limits, what districts they were headed for and bombed, and when they turned to leave. Once the planes reached the Hannover/Brunswick air space, it meant that the all clear would sound within 60 seconds. As soon as I heard this announcement, I was up and away. By the time I reached our apartment door, the siren wailed. When the siren stopped one minute later, I was already undressed and in bed.

Many times we had two air raids a night, one following the other at approximately a one to two hour interval. I got really mad when this happened. For one thing, I had just managed to get warm. Now I was obliged not only to get up once more but to get fully dressed because after the first raid I undressed and got into my pajamas.

At first, raids occurred only at night. We especially expected attacks on nights when there was a low cloud ceiling, with no moon or stars. I usually went to bed at 10 p.m. and was fast asleep as soon as my head hit the pillow. When the unmelodic howl of the siren penetrated my dreams, it took me a while to realize that I must get up. I had to be called repeatedly. As time went on, I became adept at getting dressed very quickly, a habit that has stayed with me.

At the beginning of the war, the alarm was sounded early enough for people to have a reasonable amount of time to get up, dress and make their way into the shelter or walk to a nearby bunker before the first enemy plane reached the city limits. We usually met other people on the stairs and within a few minutes of entering the shelter, everyone had settled down in their chairs. Conversation picked up where they had left off the time before. We talked about family, weather and recipes. There was discussion about what had been bombed during previous raids, attacks on other cities and public transportation. Politics were never discussed. After a while, unless someone asked me something and I was included in the conversation, I tried to sleep. It was not easy to do so sitting up, with people very close to me talking. Most of the time, my attempts failed. The unheated cellar tended to be cool and damp. Although I wore long jogging pants, socks over my stockings, boots, a scarf and a hat, the dampness crept surely and steadily into my bones, in spite of stamping my feet intermittently to keep them warm. I was too tired to read. Besides, the light provided by a single low watt bulb suspended from the ceiling in the middle of the shelter was insufficient. Some people remained quiet for the duration of the raid. They huddled in their chairs, closed their eyes and never took part in conversations.

Usually the talking continued until the antiaircraft guns began to bellow and everyone stopped to listen to what was happening outside. Our attention focused on the sounds, judging by their volume if and when enemy planes were approaching our area. Soon the detonation of bombs became as clearly audible as the antiaircraft fire. Depending on how far away the bombs hit, their explosions drowned out the sound of the guns. If a bomb came down very close to us, I heard a whistling sound and held my breath. Fortunately, this did not happen too often in the initial stages of the war. The British flew nuisance raids dropping mostly leaflets and fire bombs, which caused little damage. The first real bomb sites were objects of great interest and curiosity. Many people made a point of going to see them.

Every house had an air raid warden whose duty it was to patrol the building during an air raid, to check for damage, to organize people to put out any fires, to check that fire fighting supplies were placed and maintained at strategic points throughout the building and to make sure that people came into the shelter and stayed there until the all clear sounded. Buckets of water and buckets of sand were placed on each stair landing. The water was renewed at intervals. People also filled their bath tubs, wash tubs, basins and tea kettles in case the water supply was cut off. We knew that we had to rely mainly on our own efforts to contain fires and deal with emergencies resulting from a hit. The fire brigade could not be called. Their services were reserved for essential, war related industries, factories, installations, government buildings, public utility plants and hospitals. In the case of injuries, ambulances came to pick up casualties even while the raid was still in progress. Ambulances were sometimes hit by bombs or falling buildings.

During every air raid, we were all in imminent danger of death but I did not think about it. I could not imagine that it could happen to me. I did not dwell on the possibility during the raid and I was not afraid. Had I been examined by a doctor at the time, I do not think that he would have noticed an accelerated pulse or heart rate. Air raids happened and were part of my everyday life. I did not get upset about it. I can honestly say this and mean it because I have experienced fear and know the symptoms. I had none of them during air raids, ever.

However, there was one thing that bothered me. I became increasingly aware of the fact that, should our building receive a direct hit and we were buried alive under a huge pile of rubble, no one would come to dig us out, maybe not even to check if anyone was alive under the ruins. I imagined being trapped and knowing that people on the street went about their business. Their duty was to go to work. The idea that people were left to die like that frustrated me beyond measure and gave me claustrophobia just thinking about it. Early on in the war, the home guard was employed to clear rubble and free people trapped under collapsed buildings. As the war continued, the damage became too extensive and widespread. Help grew scarce and was almost nonexistent. More and more buildings were hit and there were fewer resources to rescue victims. Many times people were trapped under collapsed buildings for days.

My concerns were well-founded. I heard stories, told by friends and relatives, about people buried under their houses who suffocated. There were also reports of people being found alive a week or two weeks after being buried under rubble. The stories frightened me but I only thought about this after an air raid was over. During the air raid, I was busy listening to the radio and the noises outside.

Often I passed by bomb sites where a handful of home guards, who were elderly men, were trying to shift mountains of rubble using shovels. Although some time ago the walls between apartment houses had been broken through to create escape routes from one building to another, more likely than not the emergency exits were blocked when a blast occurred. I also heard of a new type of bomb, an air mine. It created great suction rather than a blast and tore peoples' lungs to pieces, while making intense heat. A house on the corner of Herrfurth Platz and Schillerpromenade was hit by such an air mine. Apparently, the heat inside the basement measured in excess of 2732 Fahrenheit. After more than a week, rescuers reached the cellar where they found tiny shrunken, burnt to a cinder, unrecognizable corpses. In another part of town, a couple was discovered sitting in their cellar. They were dead, the tops of their heads blown or sucked off. These were not isolated incidents.

Another heavy raid followed on September 4. The RAF dropped 500 tons of explosives per minute.

Working people were no longer allowed to leave the city. However, government offices and workers were surreptitiously relocated to other parts of the country. When the population became aware of this, anger grew and they expressed their discontent. As a result, the evacuation of government offices was discontinued. A new directive stated that work was to be carried on in Berlin for as long as possible.

At the same time, due to the continuing intense air attacks, Goebbels, the regional party leader of Berlin, made speeches and issued press releases strenuously urging women and children and old people to leave the city. As a result of constant publicity and pressure about voluntary evacuation, approximately 1 million people left Berlin within three months. Schools were closed, another measure to force people out of town.

Suddenly, Italy was no longer Germany's ally. Consequently, German troops occupied Northern Italy on September 8. This was followed by the news, broadcast with much fanfare, that Mussolini had been rescued by German commandos. Mussolini had been arrested at the end of July by the Italians and was held under house arrest until his rescue. At the time of his capture, he was replaced as head of state by Badoglio. The Fuehrer had ordered the rescue operation, which was carried out in great secrecy and was crowned by success. It was hard for us to decide whether this was good news or bad news.

On the Eastern front, German troops were forced to retreat from their positions. However, these facts were couched in terms like, "The Army withdrew in order to straighten the front or in order to eliminate bottle necks." A positive slant was supposed to offset the negative facts. Letters to the front and letters from soldiers became subject to censorship.

A poster appeared late in the war and it read "Our walls break but not our hearts."

Reported in the newspaper:
October 3
Severe defense strikes against U.S. bombers, 20 planes shot down.

Summer turned into autumn. Father and Mother's approaching Golden Wedding anniversary on October 7 was an event I had long anticipated.

Father and Mother had been married in the Parish Church of Muellrose. Mother wore a black dress, the traditional myrtle wreath and a veil and she carried a bouquet. It was not unusual for brides to wear black, particularly in the country. Father wore tails and a top hat. The bridal couple were driven to church in an open horse drawn carriage. According to custom, local children stretched ribbons across the street forcing the carriage to a halt. The bridegroom had to pay toll by throwing coins and candy before the children removed the ribbon barrier. This was repeated numerous times along the way. It was great fun for the children, who made the most of it. The wedding ceremony was followed by a reception at the Linden Inn on the Market Square.

In spite of the war, with its depressing news and shortages, we were determined to celebrate this special day. A 50th anniversary entitled one to extra food rations. For a maximum of 12 people, including the hosts, extra rations were 4 ounces of meat, 1.75 ounces of butter, 7 ounces of flour or bread and 3.5 ounces of sugar per person. There was also some coffee but I don't know how much.

We were able to order a gateau and could plan afternoon coffee, with REAL coffee, and dinner for the family and close friends. Aunt Marga had taken the day off to organize the affair. I also asked some time in advance if I could take the day off but my request was turned down. Normally, I was timid but I felt this occasion warranted rebellion against Scherl. I decided, in spite of my conscience, to be brave and play truant. I was not going to be cheated out of this special day's celebration. Therefore, on October 7, I telephoned the office and told them that I was sick and could not come to work. Then I firmly put the matter out of my mind. The sky was blue, the sun was shining. It was a picture perfect, delightfully lovely and mild autumn day.

Before noon, Father and Mother received callers, among them a city representative conveying congratulations from the mayor. He presented them with a commemorative citation. Neighbors and acquaintances brought or sent flowers, so many that we soon ran out of vases. The callers were offered sherry and cookies.

In the afternoon, the guests arrived in time for coffee, the traditional home baked plum cake and a really luscious gateau. The afternoon passed quickly and my aunts set the table for dinner. Uncle Gustav opened the champagne and proposed a toast. Everybody sang "Happy Anniversary" and insisted that Father and Mother kiss. They obliged and we applauded. Naturally, Father replied to the toast. He was good at this type of thing and he also proposed a toast to Kurt and Uwe who were in the forces, hence absent from the party.

After dinner, at the request of the guests, I did my best impersonation of the famous film star, Zarah Leander, by singing a few songs in her style and deep voice. We drank more wine and Father smoked a good cigar. I regret that I do not have a photograph to serve as a tangible memento of this special day.

News from the various fronts continued to be bad. On October 13, Italy declared war on Germany. We had expected it. It was almost a joke, though we did not dare to laugh.

We were informed that we would no longer receive clothing coupons. Henceforth, these were reserved strictly for children and people who were bombed out. Potato rations were reduced from 5 to 4 and then to 3 pounds. Meat rations were reduced.

October 15

It is now permitted to heat apartments in Berlin.

Air raids intensified considerably during the following months. Exceptionally heavy raids took place on the nights of November 18-19, 22-23 and 23-24, with between 450 and 650 bombers taking part in each raid. Fires raged and fire fighters from as far away as Hamburg and Breslau were ordered into the city. To help clear the streets of rubble, 50,000 members of the armed forces were brought in. These attacks left 2,966 dead, 68,262 buildings destroyed, 5,837 badly damaged and over 6,000 others partially damaged, leaving 400,000 people homeless.

Mama's friend, who lived in Tempelhof, and her 8-year-old son perished in one of these raids.

The Berlin Zoo, or, to give it its proper name, The Berlin Zoological Gardens, officially opened on August 1, 1844. It was Germany's first and the world's ninth zoo. By 1939, the Berlin Zoo was the most outstanding one in the world, with approximately 4,000 mammals and birds. The equally famous aquarium housed more than 750 species of reptiles, amphibians, fish and invertebrates. In all, there were 8,300 inhabitants of the aquarium.

Within a few hours, the work of a 100 years was destroyed. The Berlin Zoo was again bombed during heavy bombing raids on the nights of November 22-23, 1943, January 29-30, 1944 and the last days of 1945. These raids saw the end of the old, famous Berlin Zoo. Only 91 animals survived.

Highly concentrated attacks continued. Target areas were government buildings, center city and districts with the highest density of civilian population, that included Neukoelln.

In the basement, I listened to the radio with Mr. Becker. I clearly remember the sound of exploding bombs coming closer and the whistling noise a bomb makes when it is near. I was told that you do not actually hear the bomb that hits you because the sound travels away from it. One of them was so noisy, I was sure it would hit right next to us. The explosion shook the foundations of our building. The lights went out but flickered on a couple of seconds later. The air was filled with dust and fine particles of mortar making the room look foggy. Everybody coughed but nobody was hurt. This bomb hit two houses away and another bomb hit my old school.

One morning, following a heavy raid, Mrs. Werner did not show up for work at "The Gazebo." She telephoned to say that she had been bombed out. She returned to work a couple of days later and told us what had happened. She had spent the evening with friends and was detained at their place for the duration of the raid. It was dark when she arrived at her street and she almost stumbled into a large bomb crater in front of the ruins that had been her home. A home guard shouted a warning, grabbed her arm and prevented her from falling in.

In spite of these devastating raids, many evacuees began returning to the city. Why would they come back at a time like this? They were Berliners and they were homesick. They loved

Berlin. I know because I felt the same way about my hometown. Besides, evacuees were not welcome in many of the areas to which they were sent. People in rural parts of Germany, who had never suffered air attacks, were very contemptuous of city people. They talked about them until the country people themselves, on a visit to a big city, experienced raids. Even a very light raid sent them packing the next morning. But Berliners wanted to come home in spite of it all. The situation demanded measures which would stop evacuees from returning to the city. One attempt was that Berlin's schools remained closed.

I mentioned before that I did not have a social life. I did not know any young people and I was out of touch with all my former playmates. The boys, except Dieter, were in the forces. Apart from the usual visits to relatives and Mama's friends, the radio and the movies, there was no social life. Understandably, I was excited when a drama group for young people was formed at Scherl and I joined. An actor had been engaged to work with us. At our first session, he asked us to imagine a very comical incident and laugh. Another time he said, "Act out the following scene: Upon entering a room in a house or an apartment you discover a body. How would you act or react?" Of course, everyone had to come up with a different reaction. While I was awaiting my turn, others acted out several of my ideas so each time I had to think up something else. Finally, I decided that I would come into the room, take one look at the body, look shocked and run away.

In subsequent sessions, the gentleman suggested a plot for a sketch. The dialogue was made up by each player, impromptu, along the lines of the plot which concerned a family with teenage children. I was cast as one of the daughters. I don't remember the plot but at one point I was to come in while the family was sitting at the dinner table and give a rather enthusiastic, impassioned account about something to do with the Hitler Youth. This was so alien to my feelings that I could not get into it at all. I struggled through a couple of rehearsals but it was no good. I declared I was not right for this particular part and it was given to someone else. The role of a housekeeper was created for me. I played it with gusto because her character was one of outspokenness, with a sarcastic and caustic Berlin sense of humor. At the beginning of December, we performed the play at the employees' Christmas party. I invited Dieter. The director of personnel was very taken with my performance and called me "a natural." I was flushed and excited. I loved being part of this activity but, unfortunately, it was discontinued.

Like many teenagers, I was stagestruck. I loved going to the theater, preferably musicals, and longed to be on stage. Once, Marianne told me that the Admiralspalast Theater was holding auditions. I wanted to go very badly but was timid. She said one of the tests was for a person to walk across a large empty dance floor. She said, "You have the right figure, why don't you try?" We discussed what I should wear and Marianne said that I looked very nice in my winter coat. Silly, it was summer and my winter things were in mothballs. Besides, I could not very well turn up in a fur trimmed coat in July. Nothing came of it in the end because I was afraid to take time off from work for the audition.

The continuing heavy air raids proved to be very trying and brought Mama to the brink of a nervous breakdown. She decided to pay an extended visit to her friend, Leni. Leni had moved to Silesia where she lived with her mother. Mama stayed in Bad Flinsberg until shortly before Christmas and then returned to Berlin.

Between November 18 and December 3, the RAF flew the heaviest series of attacks against Berlin yet. The western and center parts of the city suffered the worst damage. Casualties were 2,700 dead and 250,000 homeless. The traffic system was damaged but still functioning. Highly concentrated attacks on Berlin continued throughout the month of December.

The media reported "the Wednesday evening bombing of Berlin included air mines, phosphor canisters, explosive and fire bombs. Enemy planes stayed well above the thick cloud cover. The attack killed the defenseless, our loved ones, murdered and maimed women and children."

Once again, Christmas time was upon us, preceded on December 21 by my 18th birthday. I have no recollection of what I did on that day. I know I did not have a party or the usual open house. It was so close to Christmas and nobody had the time. This was the most depressing Christmas yet for me. Outwardly, we continued to do all the seasonal things. We had our Advent Wreath and we had Christmas trees. Nevertheless, the real spirit of Christmas eluded me.

On December 26, Second Christmas Day, the German battleship *Scharnhorst* was sunk in the Arctic. I do not remember whether or not we heard about it that day but it had to be reported. It could not be swept under the carpet.

It was New Year's Eve 1943. What a New Year's Eve it turned out to be! This year we had fireworks, all right. More than 2,000 Allied bombers attacked Berlin and dropped 2,240 tons of bombs, creating an inferno that was seen 200 miles away. Fire engines from distant cities rushed to the aid of Berlin fire fighters.

Mama had come to hate air raids. They really got to her and she was increasingly shaken by them. Mama spent New Year's Eve with us at Father and Mother's apartment. When the alarm sounded, we went into the basement together. The raids at Christmas and New Years' proved to be the last straw for her.

Most people stayed calm during raids. If they were afraid, there was no outward sign of it. I know this because I saw everybody for hours while in the shelters. Mama had been calm during the first war years but now she was a nervous wreck. This night, as soon as the first bombs fell, she began to shake. She did not shake a little, she shook like the proverbial leaf. I had never seen anything like it and I have never seen anything like it since. I could not stop looking at her. She was a pitiful sight. Her face quivered and her whole body shook uncontrollably. Beads of perspiration glistened on her forehead and her hands shook so much, she could not use a hankie to wipe them away. Mama was near collapsing.

The following day I found her packing. "I cannot take this," she said, "I cannot stay in Berlin any longer. I am going to Bad Flinsberg."

However, Father and Mother remonstrated her because she had been away for a long time and had left me "alone" in Berlin. They thought it was her motherly duty to stay with her daughter but Mama was adamant. She would leave. She was going to leave. After a lengthy discussion, she decided that instead of going to Bad Flinsberg, she would go to Frankfurt/Oder and stay with Aunt Klinger, Mother's sister, who owned a small house in Frankfurt's historic district. She would find a way for me to join her.

1944

January 4	Soviets cross the Polish border.
January 20	The RAF drops 2,300 tons of bombs on Berlin. One week later, 1,400 U.S. planes attack the city.
January 21	On second day of U.S. air raids on Berlin, 2,000 bombers drop 8,000 tons of bombs.
January 22	Allies are on Italian mainland.
February	Count Ciano shot for treason on Mussolini's orders. Hitler invades Hungary.
April	Soviets take Odessa.
June 5	Rommel on leave in Germany. The Allies are in Rome.
June 6	The Allies land in Normandy.
June 12	Hitler's revenge: First V1 rockets hit London.
June 21	Major daytime raid on Berlin.
June 22	Assassination plot on Hitler revealed.
June 25	Goebbels at Sportspalast asks: "Do you want total war?"
July 18	The Soviets reach border of East Prussia.
July 20	The Soviets launch major drive in Ukraine.
July 25	The Americans are in Paris.

August 8	The plotters of attempt on Hitler's life are executed.
September	Americans are in Brussels and Antwerp, Belgium, as well as Holland. Soviets are in Greece and the U.S. troops are five miles inside Germany.
September 1	The Warsaw uprising. Theaters and schools in Berlin are closed.
September 8	V2 rockets launched against London.
September 25	Teenagers and old men are called up into Volkssturm, or People's Army.
October 2	Warsaw uprising is squashed.
October 7	Allies are in Greece and Albania. It's proclaimed that women must work. There is a severe cut in bread ration. It is now prohibited for more than two people to congregate in public. Three or more are subject to arrest.
October 14	Forced by Hitler, Rommel commits suicide. There is a State funeral.
October 21	Aachen occupied by U.S. troops.
November 18	The Allies are in the Saar basin.
November 12	The Tirpitz is sunk.
December 2	Patton breaks through Siegfried line in the Saar.
December 16	Germans counterattack in Ardennes, France until December 24 and the fight becomes known as the Battle of the Bulge. German counteroffensive fails.
December 21	The author's 19th birthday.

Mama left for Frankfurt/Oder after New Year's to stay with Aunt Klinger but before she left, she paid a visit to the personnel department at Scherl. We were aware that by now new ordinances, prohibiting working people to leave the city, were in force and I could not simply pack up and go. I needed permission. Scherl maintained a small branch office in Frankfurt and Mama requested that I be transferred to that office. Scherl refused because I had yet to finish my apprenticeship. They said their branch office was too small and could not offer me the training necessary to complete my contract and sit for the examination.

We needed to find another solution. Mama maintained, "Who cares about the apprenticeship? What good is it if you are dead or maimed? Who cares about what happens after the war? Who knows what will happen then?" Father and Aunt Marga, however, were of the opinion that it would be better for me to stay and take the exam in April. I personally wanted to leave because I wanted a change. I besieged the personnel office to grant me a transfer but it was refused.

The solution Mama and I came up with was that, although I was not allowed to leave Berlin permanently, no one could prevent me from leaving every night and returning in the morning. Therefore, I would take a train to Frankfurt every evening and return to Berlin the following morning.

From then on, I rushed to the Friedrichstrasse station after work to catch the "Orient Express." On its way to Prague, Vienna, Budapest and, I think, Istanbul, the train's first stop was Frankfurt/Oder.

The express train originated at the Zoo station. When it arrived at Friedrichstrasse, it was already packed. At first, I attempted to board in the usual way, through a door. This proved to be quite impossible as passengers practically fell out of the train when the doors opened. Next, I looked for open windows and was successful in being hauled up and into the train through one of them.

For as long as I traveled to Frankfurt, I never entered that train through a door. It was all right, though, people always helped me to climb in and I wore sweat pants because it was winter. I never had a seat but I did not care. It should have been only a one hour trip to Frankfurt. In reality, the trip took from one and a half hours, if I was lucky, to three hours or more for the distance of 60 miles. On numerous occasions, the train stopped and sat in the middle of nowhere for a long time before resuming its journey.

Every morning, I rose at 5:30 a.m. The express was scheduled to arrive at 6:58 a.m. and depart at 7:00 a.m. It was never on time and the delays were considerable. The first few days, I waited hours. I noticed that a frontline furlough express pulled into the station at 7:03 a.m. and left at precisely 7:05. This train was run for the sole purpose of transporting soldiers on leave from the Eastern front back to Germany and Berlin.

After I had seen this train arrive and depart on time while I stood on the platform waiting for "my" train, I decided that I could not afford anymore to wait and arrive hours late at the office every day. I would get into trouble if I did not make it to the office as close to 8 a.m. as possible. I had already seen raised eyebrows when I arrived around noon a couple of times. I figured that I would have to board the military train surreptitiously, in order to get to the office on time. On the following morning when the train pulled in, I kept my eye on the military guard and the stationmaster. As soon as their backs were turned, I quickly climbed aboard. I became very adept at it, although always apprehensive about being caught.

490

The express was almost empty and no matter which compartment I entered, the men were very glad of my company and helped me hide from the guards behind their coats, which hung in the corners. Once I even hid on the luggage rack, covered with coats. It was amusing.

A couple of times, the guard caught me. He checked my papers and pointed out that civilians were not permitted to travel on this train and I must disembark at the next stop. I apologized and promised to get out. The next stop was Friedrichstrasse where I wanted to get off anyway. Although I was not in any danger, I still did not like to be caught and I was always a little nervous.

I had to work on Saturdays until 2 p.m. Until it was time for my train, I visited Father and Mother. Now and then, I stayed in town. On the Sundays I spent in Frankfurt, I met my second cousin, Regina. She was a few years older than I, much more worldly and sophisticated. We usually went to a café. Even though there was no longer dancing or any music the cafés were crowded, nevertheless. The majority of patrons were soldiers stationed in Frankfurt or convalescing in local military hospitals. If we had coupons to spare, we splurged them on a piece of pastry. Customers shared tables. One Sunday, we met two pleasant young sergeants and enjoyed talking with them. We even went for a little walk together. I had quite a crush on one of them. I mentioned during our conversation that I came home from Berlin every night. For a while, I hoped that he would be at the train station to meet me and was disappointed when he was not.

Aunt Klinger was a very pleasant old lady and Mama relaxed because, so far, Frankfurt had not been attacked. My day was long, beginning at 5:30 a.m., and most of the time I did not get home until 8 p.m. or later. Apart from eating supper, talking

491

to Mama and Aunt Klinger and maybe reading for a while, there was nothing to do in the evenings. Consequently, I went to bed early. It was great being able to sleep undisturbed through the night but this happy state of affairs was rudely interrupted and my sojourn in Frankfurt came abruptly to an end.

One night, Frankfurt was attacked by American bombers who targeted the railway station. I was sleeping like a log when the alarm sounded. I ignored it. Mama and Aunt Klinger were up in a jiffy. Mama stood by my bed urging me to get up and get dressed so we could go to the shelter, since Aunt Klinger's house had no basement. We came out of our little house to see numerous "Christmas trees" hanging in the sky, lighting up the night almost to daylight brightness. "Christmas trees" were a type of flare dropped by bombers to illuminate the area to be bombed. The flares allowed the pilots to more or less see the target. The air was filled with the droning of plane engines and antiaircraft barking. Almost immediately, I heard bombs whistling down and exploding close by.

Mama was frantic. In the morning, she was packed and ready to leave for Bad Flinsberg and nothing would stop her. I did not blame her. However, much as she wanted, she could not leave immediately because the railroad station and the tracks had been hit. We were stuck in Frankfurt until the damage was repaired. Three days later, train service resumed and Mama left for Flinsberg. I packed up, too, and moved back to Berlin. Now that Mama was no longer in Frankfurt, there was no reason for me to stay.

I never returned to Frankfurt and I never saw Aunt Klinger again. Sometime in the spring of 1945, she turned up at Father's apartment in Berlin in a deplorable state: disheveled, dirty, full of lice and half starved. She had walked the 60 miles from Frankfurt to Berlin. On the way, she was raped by the side of the road by several Russian soldiers. She was 79 years old at the time.

At work, I was transferred to the accounting department. I made friends with Hilde, Eva and Ellen. Hilde lived with her parents in Britz. She was engaged and her fiancee was in the army. Eva was also engaged but wore no engagement ring. In Germany, a couple wore their wedding rings, bought at the time of engagement, on the ring finger of their left hand. During the wedding ceremony, this ring was moved to the ring finger of the right hand. Eva told me that she and her fiancé had been unable to marry. They were forbidden to do so because of some medical problem in her fiancé's family. He fell under the laws concerning hereditary health and diseased offspring so they just lived together.

My office was on the third floor. The window at the back of the room overlooked a courtyard. It afforded a view into a print shop housed in a yellow brick building. One day, much to our amazement, Italian prisoners of war appeared at Scherl and two of them worked in this particular print shop. One came regularly to the window, looked over at our office, smiled, waved and clowned around. It was funny and broke the monotony of our very boring work. We smiled and waved back. We nicknamed him "Macaroni." Soon he was joined by a fellow prisoner, a good-looking, more serious young man.

Since day raids were becoming common place, the management decided that in order to protect office equipment, which could not be replaced, we must take it into the shelter. As soon as the siren sounded, we covered our typewriters and adding machines and lugged them into the basement. The machines were heavy and cumbersome to carry down and up four flights of stairs. I had the bright idea that the Italians should carry the machines for us. I went over to the print shop and asked the master in charge for permission. It was granted.

The next time, and from then on, when the alarm sounded the two men presented themselves in our office. After depositing the machines in the basement, the prisoners had to report to their guard for the duration of the raid. But they came back when the raid was over. Macaroni was all smiles. His friend volunteered to carry my typewriter. I found out that his name was Gino. Both of them were from Palermo. A lot of gesticulating and mimicking was necessary in order to communicate. No one in our department spoke Italian. We had so much fun that we almost looked forward to hearing the siren.

I always made Gino stop halfway to the basement on one of the landings where he could rest the machine on the wide windowsill. One day I asked, "Do you speak English?" Gino smiled and said, "Yes." The following day, Gino passed me a note. He had learned English at school. From that time on, we exchanged notes every time there was an air raid. Several weeks later, Gino's note said, "I wish I could be with you in a gondola in Venice. Perhaps we will be one day." After I read it, he kissed my hand. How romantic. Somebody told me that it was possible for Italian prisoners to leave their camp for a few hours if a German vouched for them. I thought it might be nice to invite Gino out somewhere. I asked Aunt Martha if she would vouch for him and if I could bring him to her apartment one Sunday for coffee. She would not hear of it and did not want the responsibility, she did not want to deal with the authorities, she was afraid.

During a night raid, "The Gazebo" building was hit and damaged to the extent that we could no longer work there. We were moved to the fourth floor of the new building on the corner of Koch and Zimmerstrasse. I did not see Gino again for some time.

I was still attending business school twice a week. Naturally, between classes, I talked with my classmates about the current situation. The Soviets were advancing. We speculated on how long it would take for them to reach Berlin. We did not like the prospect. One of the girls said, "My mother said if the Russians come into Berlin, she will turn on the gas and kill herself." It was strange. We could talk and remain outwardly very calm, almost as though we were talking about the weather. Looks, however, were deceiving. Inside we were frightened. I know I was. I had heard from Kurt how the German Army treated Russian prisoners of war and, in some areas of Russia, the civilian population. I heard how badly Russian women in Germany were abused. I was under no delusion as to what might be in store for us. The outlook was dismal to say the least.

Among ourselves, family and close friends, we constantly criticized the Fuehrer for starting the war, for going into Russia, for not learning from Napoleon's fate, for ransacking occupied countries, for the shortages, for just about everything. Complaining and criticizing got it off our chest but did not change anything. I felt apprehensive but, for the time being, I tried to put it out of my mind as much as possible and live from day to day. Propaganda continued and our Fuehrer still claimed that victory would be his.

Meanwhile, at the movies, entertaining films and musicals filled the bill such as: "The Great Love," "Request Concert," "Vienna Blood," and "Women are Better Diplomats." "The Great Love" was one of, I think, only two or three films in which the story took place in the present. A popular singer meets an air force officer in an air raid shelter. She falls in love and then worries about him when he is ordered to the front.

495

My apprenticeship neared its completion. The examination was scheduled for April. On the appointed day, I reported to the Berlin Chamber of Commerce at 8 a.m. for the four hour test. We were divided into two groups, and one group took Part I while the other group took Part II. We were just halfway into the test when the sirens announced the imminent arrival of foreign visitors. We trooped into the shelter and were instructed not to talk about the exam. Nevertheless, a small group of kids from each group huddled together and exchanged information. I was not among them. Approximately two hours later, we resumed the test. The grades one could earn were simple: "Good," "Satisfactory" and "Fail." My grade was "Good." I remained in the employ of the Scherl Publishing Company and at "The Gazebo" as a regular employee. My pay was increased from 80 marks to 110 marks a month.

I cannot recall the prices of that time so I cannot say what buying power my money had. It was not much but I had no expenses, since I lived at home. What I earned was sufficient to cover my fares and lunches. The rest was my pocket money.

April

This is a reply received in answer to an application for a new frying pan: "I regret I cannot approve your application for a permit to purchase a new frying pan. Safeguarding war material requirements and the full engagement of the German economy for the total war demands now more than ever that everyone must severely modify his needs and lifestyle. I ask you to take this fact into consideration and put even legitimate wishes on the back burner for the time being. An appeal against this decision at this time, has no prospects of success."

❖　❖　❖

Air raid intensity abated for a few weeks. A number of nuisance raids, when few planes kept coming in relays and staying over the city for as long as possible without causing much damage, were more annoying than anything else. Meanwhile, the media constantly hinted about the Fuehrer's revenge, the terrible revenge he was planning to take on Britain. I could not imagine what it would be. A few neighbors were talking about it when Mama and I met them in the staircase. They were very confident that our Fuehrer really had something so powerful up his sleeve that it would make everything all right and ensure German victory. I was speechless for more reasons than one. I could not believe that anyone could be stupid enough to believe anything the media and Fuehrer said or that anything he could do would make Germany win the war. As far as I was concerned, it was obvious that the war was lost.

Life went on. Work was boring but not demanding. If I did not bag my lunch, I went to a pub across the street. It was a change from the canteen and the pub served quite a decent "free" meal, which required no food coupons. It was usually a cabbage, vegetable or bean soup. Occasionally, I took my sandwich up onto the roof when the weather permitted. Sometimes, Mr. Sander from the registration department joined me, as he did on April 4, which was a lovely, sunny and mild day, with a little wind. We sat and talked about the date, 4/4/44. He remarked that it was an important date for stamp collectors. He also told me that his son was in a military hospital in Silesia.

A few weeks later, we went up to the roof following an air raid. Suddenly, we saw leaflets floating down. I had heard in the course of the past years that planes occasionally dropped leaflets. I was anxious and curious to see one. We watched but, although thousands of leaflets fluttered by, not even one landed on our

497

roof. Many came tantalizingly near, close but not close enough for us to catch even when we leaned far over the railing. I noticed numerous HJ boys and men in civilian clothes in the street snatching up the papers before any pedestrian had a chance to pick them up. In retrospect, I think we were lucky that we did not get a leaflet. It might have cost us dearly.

During the last week of April, I went to Bad Flinsberg to visit Mama for a week and I loved it. Flinsberg, nestled among pine covered hills, was beautiful and so peaceful. Leni's mother was a darling and I loved her. My room in Leni's mother's house overlooked a garden where a small brook meandered, splashing and gurgling over rocks, lulling me to sleep once I got used to its sound. No siren disturbed my sleep. It was heavenly.

Bad Flinsberg was, as the word "Bad" indicates, a spa. Most of the villas had been guest houses but had been requisitioned by the government to serve as convalescence homes for members of the armed forces. The place was swarming with men in uniform.

By now, Mama had a job because a new directive made it compulsory for women to work. She was engaged by the Post Office to deliver telegrams in Bad Flinsberg and the surrounding area. Mama loved walking and enjoyed going all over town, to neighboring villages and to outlying farms. Most mornings and sometimes in the afternoons, I accompanied her on her rounds.

One day, when I was walking through the town alone, I noticed a soldier following me down the street. He was tall, dark and handsome. The next day, Mama told me that the young man had asked her if she knew me because he wanted to meet me. Mama was well-known in town as a result of her job. He was from Vienna, convalescing in Bad Flinsberg after being wounded at the Russian front and contracting malaria. Mama introduced us. His name was Steffan and he was 32 years old. His father had been killed in WWI and his mother lived in

Vienna. Before the war, Steffan had lived and worked in Munich as an architect. From then on, I saw him every day and we went for walks. In Germany, when people go for a walk they almost always have a destination in mind, usually a café, a restaurant, a place of special interest or a vista.

We spent most evenings after supper at one of the local inns. They were always crowded, smoky and noisy. We talked but he did most of the talking. I was ill at ease. I had never had dates before and did not know how to cope with it. I liked Steffan but I did not feel romantic about him. He was the perfect gentleman and had a charming accent.

My vacation was short and early in May I returned to Berlin. Steffan asked if he could write to me. I said yes. I was a terrible letter writer and wrote mostly about the weather, not at all what the poor guy wanted to hear. He even told me that he was not interested in meteorological reports from Berlin. He telephoned a couple of times. Then he wrote that in June he would be given two weeks' leave prior to returning to his unit at the Eastern front. He wanted to see me and asked if he could come to Berlin after visiting his mother in Vienna.

Steffan arrived in Berlin on the day the Fuehrer's long promised retribution began. Rockets had been launched against England. I can still see the headlines of the newspapers displayed on the newsstands at the station. I went to meet Steffan's train but I insisted that Father come along. Mama was in Flinsberg and I was staying with Father and Mother so we gave Steffan the key to Mama's apartment. Steffan brought me a number of small gifts: Viennese confiture, chocolates and a couple of other items that were scarce. On weekdays, Father took Steffan sight-seeing. After work and on the weekend, I took over. Once we went to the movies and he took me out to dinner a few times.

499

At that time, I was shy, not outgoing and not used to male company. I felt tongue-tied and did not know what to talk about. He was most solicitous. It was obvious that he was in love with me. However, I was not in love with him and did nothing to give him the idea that I reciprocated his feelings. I think that was the reason I avoided being alone with him. Strange as it may seem, I did not even want to be kissed. I told the girls at the office about him and they were bursting with curiosity. After work on Monday, they insisted on seeing Steffan and followed me to the Doenhoffplatz where I had arranged to meet him.

The following day, the girls were very enthusiastic. They thought Steffan was handsome and asked what was the matter with me. Why was I not in love with him? I did not know. Steffan left on June 19. I went to the station and I took Father along. It was a rather subdued farewell. Steffan was sad. I was relieved. Mama was upset because she was very fond of Steffan. She told me that he had asked her permission to propose and had hoped to get engaged to me while he was in Berlin. I suspected something like this and was reluctant to give him an opportunity to speak. I did not want to hurt his feelings, especially since he had to return to the front.

Steffan was a disappointed young man when he left, Mama told me. I still corresponded with him and our correspondence dragged on for some months. It stopped somewhere around or after Christmas and I never heard from him again.

So far, I had been very lucky in avoiding call-up but for how much longer? I was 18. I thought of Monika, who had worked with me in the Statistics Department and had been drafted into the Army. When she came on leave for the first time after her basic training, she visited the office. Monika had a much more robust nature than I, was self-confident and not easily floored. However, she said that she had a very hard time adjusting to the army. The one thing that kept her going when she felt really unhappy and homesick was the advice an uncle had given her. "When you feel really bad," he said, "just imagine people without their clothes on."

During a lecture given by a particularly obnoxious sergeant, she suddenly remembered this and burst out laughing and could not stop. The sergeant demanded to know what was so funny. Of course, Monika could not tell him. As a punishment, she had to scrub the dining room floor with a very small nailbrush in spite of the fact that her arm was swollen to twice its size and she was burning up with fever following a "full house" of inoculations.

The thought of having to go into the army was a constant nightmare. I knew that I could not cope with people like the sergeant. Besides, I had heard Kurt talk about the obnoxious methods used by army sergeants and the often uncalled for harsh treatments dished out to recruits and privates. Subordinates were at their mercy. I was sick with apprehension whenever I thought about it, which by now, I did frequently.

Some headlines and reports from June 7:
THE FREEDOM OF EUROPA IS AT STAKE
THE REICH PRESS SECRETARY COMMENTS ON
THE INVASION

At the request of the German News Agency, the Reich Press Secretary, Dr. Dietrich, issued the following public statement: "This morning our opponents in the west, by orders of Moscow, have begun their bloody sacrifice, something they had been reluctant to do for a long time. The frequently predicted attack on the freedom of Europe by the Western sympathizers of bolshevism has begun. We must prepare a warm welcome for them. Germany is conscious of the significance of the hour. She (Germany) will fight with all her strength and passionate determination to preserve Europe, its culture and the life of its people from the assault of barbarism."

One example of the many obituaries which appeared in our newspaper:

"We were grievously shocked by the sad news that
our dearly beloved son, a dear brother, cousin,
nephew and grandson,
wearer of the Iron Cross Second Class
(the German equivalent of Purple Heart),
was killed in action on the Eastern front shortly before his 20th birthday.
He is mourned in deepest sorrow by his parents (names of parents), family and friends."

Earlier during the war, at school, we had learned to make masks. These masks were to be carried at all times just in case one was needed during or after an air raid as a smoke protector. If possible, they were to be soaked in water before use. The pattern for the masks was published in the newspapers. We started with pliable wire placing the middle of the piece over the bridge of the nose, molding it from there to follow the contours of the face toward the ears and down to cover the mouth, ending slightly below the chin. The ends of the wire were twisted together carefully so as not to have sharp ends. The wire frame itself was wrapped with layers of gauze bandages and then the entire shape was covered with several layers of gauze and a final covering of heavier material. I used red satin remnants from one of my dresses. At each side of the mask, I attached ribbons so it could be securely tied at the back of the head. After learning how to produce a mask, I made one for each family member and a few for friends.

Two days after Steffan left, June 21, we awoke to a perfect summer day. The temperature was around 72 degrees Fahrenheit with a slight breeze. The sun beamed from a deep blue cloudless sky. I walked to the office with Marianne. It was so beautiful that we hated to go inside. At 10:45 the alarm sounded. Together with the other employees, I went into the shelter situated under the main office building. We sat around and chatted until we heard numerous detonations nearby. I heard bombs whistling down and many seemed to explode simultaneously. The building shook, the lights flickered and went out. Flashlights were switched on and the air raid wardens came through to check for damage. Thick smoke began filtering into the shelter. It grew steadily thicker and we quickly donned our masks after soaking them in one of many barrels of water which stood in the corners of the room. During this air raid, the mask came in handy. We returned to our seats and waited. Everyone remained calm. There was no panic, no screaming, no hysterics, no outward sign of fear. We waited for instructions. After a while, emergency lights came on.

Masks and smoke made it impossible to talk. We had no idea what was going on outside. It seemed as though the bombing had stopped but the all clear had not yet sounded when a number of people came through the opening in the wall leading to the adjacent building. They were dirty, covered in white dust, some bleeding and staggering, but calm. One of them was the personnel director who had liked my acting. He looked frightful and very pale and had a bloodstained bandage around his head. Someone asked him what happened and he told us that there had been a number of hits on the Scherl complex. People were injured and one of the two exits of our shelter was blocked by

503

debris. A few minutes later, air raid wardens appeared with flashlights and directed us to the only exit that was open. We filed out slowly and orderly without any pushing or shoving.

It had been dark in the basement with only dim emergency lighting. Now, as I stepped out into the open air, a scene met my eyes that could easily fit the description of Armageddon. For one thing, it was even darker outside than in the basement. Gone was the sun, the cloudless sky, the summer day. The sky was black. The entire area for as far as I could see was blanketed by thick black smoke, daylight couldn't penetrate. The only illumination came from the fires all around us. Everything everywhere was ablaze. Huge orange-yellow flames wantonly licked at buildings or what was left of them, like tongues stretching skyward, some changing color into blues, greens and whites as they fed on various substances. The pub across the street was also hit and burning. I was stunned. My heart thumped as I stood there surveying this chaotic scene. Far to the west on the horizon, miles away, I detected a narrow strip of light sky.

Planes, flying in formation, had carpet bombed the inner city, leaving bomb craters every few yards. All around Scherl's main building, huge rolls of newsprint were stored, covered with tarpaulin. These caught fire but, because the newsprint was very tightly rolled, it smoldered rather than burst into flames and created the thick smoke that had seeped into our shelter.

The all clear sounded one and a half hours after the alarm. The actual bombing lasted only 45 minutes. Our Scherl in-house fire fighters, official wardens and first aid people were busy. Fire hoses lay all over on the sidewalks. I stood around for a while, stunned. Then I asked a fireman if I could help but I was told to go home.

I did not attempt to go to the U-Bahn station. Instead, I walked through the inferno. It was very quiet, with any sounds muffled, fires crackled. Pedestrians gaped at the damage but kept walking. I progressed slowly, taking in the sights along the way. Bomb craters were every few yards and enormous piles of rubble that two hours ago had been buildings. For a long time, the scene did not change. I felt nothing. I moved like a robot. Gradually, I emerged into daylight and arrived home at 3:30 p.m. Father and Mother were happy to see me in one piece and wanted to know what had happened. I managed to tell them. I could not eat the lunch they served me. Suddenly, I felt drained, completely spent and exhausted. I lay down on the sofa and fell asleep.

By the next morning, I was fine and I walked to Scherl. The smoke had cleared but the landscape was one of complete devastation. I walked along a route I had known like the back of my hand and did not recognize anything. The streets were covered with big chunks of buildings, bricks and beams. I had to climb over them. One place turned out to be the Moritzplatz but at first, I did not know it. The remains of a streetcar crushed by a huge section of a building stood among the debris like a strange monument in a post-Armageddon landscape.

"The Gazebo" building and almost all the other buildings in the area were damaged beyond recognition. The main edifice was burned out but because it was a modern, concrete structure, the staircases and floors had remained intact. I walked up to our floor to look at what was left. I was amazed. Everything was gone. Nothing remained of the solid wooden desks and other heavy office furniture. In their place, a quarter of an inch of white ash covered the floor. Here and there, I spotted small blobs of metal about the size of a large fist. These were the typewriters and adding machines. Here and there, stood a lonely teapot, a cup and a saucer. I touched one and it disintegrated instantly. Ashes to ashes. The heat must have been tremendous.

Other employees arrived. We stood around talking. I learned that one of the shelters in our complex took a hit. It was located under a courtyard covered only by a thin layer of concrete. Most of the casualties occurred there with eight killed and about 150 injured, some seriously. I did not know any of the people personally except for the executive whom I had seen in the air raid shelter. We wondered what, if anything, we could or should do but were told to go home and come back in a couple of days.

On Thursday, June 22, the media reported: "New terror attack on Berlin. Densely populated residential areas hit, cultural sites destroyed."

"During the morning hours of June 21, American air gangsters led a new terror attack against the Reich capital. Numerous bombers flew over the area of greater Berlin under partially cloudy skies and, obviously for pure terrorist purposes, dropped large quantities of explosive and fire bombs on various parts of the city. Again, mostly densely populated residential areas were hit causing damage and casualties among the population. Once again, churches, cultural sites, as well as historic buildings, of the Reich capital numbered among the targets of their attack. Fighter planes and antiaircraft guns met the enemy terror pilots with determined opposition. Numerous hits were observed over the city itself."

The June 21 attack on Berlin involved 2,500 U.S. bombers and fighter planes. The area where I had been was systematically carpet bombed.

The newspaper report is incorrect as far as the weather is concerned. There were no clouds in the sky that morning. I think the papers always liked to stress that the bombers reached Berlin in a cowardly manner, using clouds as cover.

Although our newspapers were full of derogatory articles and hate propaganda, I seldom heard it repeated in

506

conversations. My experience was that people I knew did not express hatred of the Poles, the British, the French or the Americans. The Russians were feared more and more as time went on, as the fortunes of war turned against Germany. The Americans, after they entered the war, were regarded as potential conquerors by virtue of their victories in WWI. It was strange but even after the terrible air raids on Berlin and those we heard of on Hamburg, Luebeck, Rostock and other cities, I heard no hate expressed for our adversaries. Early on in the war, "brown" people made sarcastic and disparaging comments about the Allied Forces combined with predictions of how they would lose the war. They were confident in the abilities of Fuehrer to deal with them. These were remarks I overheard in public places and were not made by anyone in my immediate circle.

We had hardly recovered from the big raid on June 21 when it was announced that Goebbels was to speak at the Sportpalast on June 25. I heard part of this broadcast on the radio and I saw it on newsreel afterwards. If I remember rightly, it was a Sunday. Mama turned the radio on because she was curious to hear what outrageous remarks he would make.

Incidentally, the Sportpalast had long ago been nicknamed "Goebbels' Pantomime and Vaudeville Theater" and "Little Clubfoot's Comedy Stage." The Sportpalast was filled to the last seat by an enthusiastic crowd or so the commentator informed us. Goebbels' speech lead up to and culminated in the shouted question: "DO YOU WANT TOTAL WAR?" The answer came back: "YES." There was "Heil!" shouting and clapping. Mama was beside herself and turned the radio off. She made dire predictions as to the consequences of this reckless commitment. Wasn't the war total enough yet? Was not the writing on the wall? What else were these criminals letting us in for? What else was to follow? Mama scoffed, "Idiots! They'll soon find out the

507

hard way what total war is but we are the ones who will suffer. The Nazis who started this will make sure that they are okay." I agreed with her.

We found out later that on this occasion, as on previous ones, the people who filled the Sportpalast had not gone there of their own volition. They had been drafted. This time, all off duty employees of the BVG and off duty personnel from factories and other government offices were told to assemble at various places and were taken to the Sportpalast. SS presence was prominent. Everyone present was expected to shout the politically correct, "YES."

We were ordinary people. We were very upset and feared the consequences of such a provocative demonstration. Mama said she feared that this acclamation would be totally misunderstood and misinterpreted abroad, where people would get the impression that all Germans were behind the "Yes."

A few days later, all teenagers at Scherl were issued grey jump suits, picks and shovels. We were divided into groups and assigned specific jobs. Some groups picked bricks from the ruins around the corner in the Jerusalember Strasse. Boys loaded the bricks onto wheelbarrows and pushed them to my group in the Kochstrasse. We cleaned the mortar from the bricks.

I sat on the rubble and chipped away, glad to be out in the open and not having to work in the office. I got dirty and tired but I did not mind. I had to meet a quota. The clean bricks were counted and loaded onto wheelbarrows by the Italian prisoners of war and taken into the building where other groups bricked up the windows, leaving room for only a small pane of glass.

Macaroni and Gino were engaged in this work but I did not have an opportunity to talk to them. Our jobs were not without danger. Several youngsters who were working on the rubble in the Jerusalemer Strasse collapsed and had to be rushed to hospital. They had been sitting close to a damaged gas line and inhaled enough gas to poison them.

On July 20, it was reported that a bomb had exploded at the Fuehrer's headquarters, that the Fuehrer was injured and that he would address the nation later in the day. Apparently, his injuries were slight. I could not detect any reaction in public. The people I knew talked about it in hushed voices. Almost immediately, somebody told me about the new greeting: You raise your arm in the Hitler salute but instead of saying, "Heil Hitler!" you murmur, "Schade!" (What a pity!).

Numerous acquaintances expressed the view, in strict confidence and in private, that it was too bad the assassination attempt had gone wrong. I felt deeply for the men who had risked their lives and were now imprisoned. I knew they were doomed to die and I hated to think of the kind of treatment they were receiving at the hands of the SS and Gestapo. Their trial was a farce. It was not a fair trial but no one expected it to be, least of all the accused. The judges were abominable, shouting insults at the prisoners and depriving them of all human dignity. On August 8, the conspirators were executed. The Fuehrer went on the air and informed his listeners that Stauffenberg, the man who had actually placed the bomb in the Fuehrer's headquarters, was dead. I mourned him and the others. I know I was not the only one.

The news about the attempt on the Fuehrer's life was overshadowed to a great extent by reports that Soviet troops had reached the borders of East Prussia. Also on July 25, the Americans entered Paris. This news was far less disturbing than the news from the Eastern front.

Meanwhile, V2 rockets were launched amid much publicity. The V2 was the second stage of the Fuehrer's long prophesied revenge. I did not believe for a minute that this would make any difference to the outcome of the war. In fact, I hoped that it would not.

I continued cleaning bricks. Finally, when the cleaning up was almost complete, we were called to the lobby. I had no idea why we were to report but found on arrival that a number of tables had been set up, each manned by a recruiter. When my turn came, the man interviewing me asked my name, address, date of birth and so on. From the information in front of him, he could easily determine where I lived in relation to the jobs he had to fill. Nevertheless, he assigned me to work in a factory clear across town in the north of Berlin. I do not recall the address but I think it was in Wedding. I protested and asked if I could work nearer to my home. The answer was a categorical, "No, you have to go to where you are sent." The minor official was flaunting his authority. My working hours were 6 a.m. to 6 p.m., with half an hour for lunch. It took me almost an hour to get to work.

The factory manufactured detonation devices for artillery shells. On my first day at the factory, I was taken to a large hall full of machinery and introduced to the master. After a curt "Heil Hitler!" he in turn called one of the section chiefs, who led me to my place of work: a stool in a long row of other stools at a counter occupied mostly by women and a few older men past military age. In front of me was a machine, next to it a lamp with a magnifying glass, a small measuring device consisting of an oblong piece of metal with two round indentures, and a large container full of tiny metal cylinders.

My chief explained the work process, "You pick up a cylinder with the tweezers, put it into the machine, pull down the polishing arm and hold it down for a few seconds while the machine rotates and polishes part of the cylinder. You lift the polishing arm, take out the cylinder with your tweezers and look at it under the magnifier to see if it is nice and shiny. Next, you insert it in the No. 1 hole. If it fits, it is okay, if it does not fit, the cylinder is too large. You must polish it again to whittle it down to size. If it fits and is loose, it is too small. In that case, try it in the No. 2 hole. If it fits, it goes into the tin and will be collected for the next procedure. If, however, it is too small, then it is a reject and goes into the can marked 'rejects'." He told me that I would have a couple of days to get used to it. After that, I was expected to polish 40 cylinders a minute.

It was extremely tedious work and hard on me. I was not used to sitting and staying in the same position, hunched over for 12 hours. The master stood at one end of the hall surveying his domain. He was in his 40s, blond and about 5 feet 5 inches. He scowled most of the time. He also made rounds to inspect and repair machines that broke down. He watched how many times and for how long people went to the bathroom. I went often because I needed to get up and stretch since I ached all over. I was reprimanded for it. I hated every minute I had to spend in this place. I swore that for every day I was forced to work at this job, I would take a week's vacation after the war. So far I have not kept the promise I made to myself.

It only took a couple of days to find out that my chief, a thin, elderly Berliner with sparse black hair streaked with grey, was anti-Nazi. He was a former Social Democrat. In a conspiratorial whisper, he told me political jokes, made derogatory remarks about the war, the regime, the Fuehrer, the Nazis in the factory and the master. I was a little apprehensive in case someone overhead us. However, there was no way the other workers and I could have a conversation. We sat close to each other yet far enough apart to make conversation over the noise of the machines impossible without shouting, which would have attracted the master's attention who watched us diligently. One had to be careful of people like the master. They were encouraged, by the regime and backed by law, to report on workers who slacked off, did not fulfil their quotas or came to work late. The only person with whom I could talk was the chief. He constantly moved along the rows of workers in his section, stopping here and there for a comment or a camouflaged chat.

An acquaintance, whom we ran into at times at one of Mama's friend's apartment, was dangerous. He was a party member and boasted in Mama's and my presence that he had reported people to the Gestapo. He said that he had denounced any employee who was late for work by five minutes on more than two occasions. He held some minor executive position but I don't know the firm for which he worked. He was not called up because he was a Nazi, which says a lot about him.

Years later, I heard that when the Russians entered Berlin and searched every house, they found him shaking in his boots, huddled in the basement. The officer in charge of the search party poked him with his gun and said, "You, young man. Why not in Army?" He feebly gestured and answered, "My heart, my heart." He was scared to death and later committed suicide. At least, he had the guts to do that. Most other Nazis did not. After the war, they pretended to be " innocent" and denied being Nazis. It made me sick. That is why I left Germany at the earliest possible moment. I could not stomach those kind of people.

On September 25, it was announced that teenage boys 16 years of age and old men up to age 65 were to be drafted into the Volkssturm, the People's Army. More women were compelled to work and the bread ration was severely cut.

Mama was still in Bad Flinsberg. She sometimes delivered telegrams to a factory, which had been relocated from Berlin, to a neighboring village and found out that they had an opening for a secretary. I went to Flinsberg on a weekend, was interviewed and got the job. However, I needed permission from the employment office to change jobs and leave Berlin. I discovered that, although my factory would not give employees time off for personal reasons, employees were entitled to go to the employment office. By now, I was really motivated to try everything in order to leave the factory and Berlin. I hardly ever met my quota of cylinders and I worried because I had so many rejects. This could easily be construed as sabotage if it went on for too long. Therefore, every morning at 8 a.m. I visited the employment office. I was lucky because I had a sympathetic case worker. I told her that I was practically alone in Berlin and wanted to join my mother in Bad Flinsberg. She was sympathetic but unable to issue the required permit unless I could be exchanged. Only an even exchange was permissible: a factory worker for a factory worker.

Once more, I had incredible good fortune. After I wrote to the plant, I was informed that one of the factory women was most anxious to return to her home in Berlin. Everyone agreed to the switch. The employment office added its stamp of approval to the required and desired permit. I was free to leave Berlin.

Within a week, I traveled to Hirschberg, where I changed trains to go to Greiffenberg and from there, onto a diminutive local train, which took me via Friedeberg to Bad Flinsberg. Mama made arrangements for us to have a furnished room at a farmhouse located near the railway station.

By now it was fall and I reported for work at 7 a.m. one morning after a lovely one hour walk downhill. I was shown into a large, clean hall with long tables and big windows. It was quiet. There were no machines. I had to work with some kind of metal pieces made of aluminum and brass. I had no idea how these items were used. I had to sort them into boxes. Mr. Koch, the master in charge of factory operations, was a tall, good-looking man with curly blond hair and blue eyes in his mid-30s. He had a pretty wife and two cute children. He was not in the army because of medical reasons. Mr. Koch made rounds and inspected the work. He told me that I would have to stay in the factory for a week before I could be transferred to the office.

It worked out just as the master predicted. A week later, I started work as secretary to the plant manager, Mr. Polz. He was a short, slim, dark haired man of unremarkable features. He was a party member and ardent Hitlerite but he was not nasty. He had a sense of humor, was easy to work for and treated his employees with respect. He was in no way inhumane to the Polish and Russian workers assigned to the plant. He was strict but fair. On the other hand, he was full of "our wonderful Fuehrer." His wife was equally enthused about Adolf. They both took great pride in telling everyone repeatedly that their 4-year-old son had started to give the Hitler salute at the tender age of nine months. The boy accompanied his mother when she visited her husband at the office. When he opened the door, and before he stepped over the threshold, his little arm was raised and he shouted "Heil Hitler!" It was very comical and sad at the same time. The poor little guy did not know what it meant.

Our office was small. Apart from Mr. Polz's office and a small anteroom, there was only one other room. Two large desks stood side by side facing two other desks. Mr. Koch and the plant engineer, Mr. Voss, sat at the desks nearest the window. The other two were occupied by Mrs. Richter and a younger woman, Mrs. Liebig, a newlywed whose husband was at the front.

I shared the outer office with a veteran, Mr. Winter, who was invalided out of the army because he had lost an arm. He had no time for our Fuehrer. We exchanged many jokes and sarcastic comments about the Polzes and their little Nazi. We were careful to do so only when we were alone. Although we had no quarrel with Mr. Polz and got along fine, we would not trust a party member. After the war, Mr. Polz called on Aunt Marga to find out how he could get in touch with me. He wanted me to sign an affidavit, no less, to the effect that he had not been a party member. Needless to say, my aunt did not give him my address.

Working hours were from 7 a.m. to 6 p.m. We had half an hour for lunch, which we ate in the plant canteen. The Polish and Russian workers also ate in the canteen but at separate tables and they did not get the same food we did. Fraternization between us and the foreign workers was not permitted. From what I saw, their food was appetizing and plentiful. They looked well, clean and were not ill-treated in any way. They had a spokesman who presented any grievances to Mr. Polz, who looked into them.

The plant's first aid, or sick bay, was presided over by an registered nurse. She was in her 50s, about 5 foot 6 inches, blue eyed with a lovely complexion, and masses of white hair worn in a French knot. She was a countess from one of the Baltic states and she hated the Russians passionately. She held them responsible for the loss of her family, her estates and her country. She spoke Russian, Polish, English, French, German and her own language, Latvian. I found her fascinating, although her hatred of everything Russian was all consuming and made her bitter. I got to know her quite well. She invited me a number of times to tea at her apartment, which was furnished in part with period furniture she had managed to save.

Field Marshal Rommel, popular even after defeat in North Africa, made news again. Some time earlier, it was reported that he had been seriously wounded by machine gun fire from the enemy fighters while driving near Lisieux, France. Following his discharge from hospital, he convalesced at his home in Southern

Germany. On October 14, a special news bulletin informed us that Rommel had succumbed to his injuries but that "his heart had always belonged to the Fuehrer." Rommel would be given a hero's state funeral. Somber music followed the announcement.

I was shocked, as were my colleagues. We talked at length about Rommel's life and death. I saw the newsreel of the funeral and it was grandiose. The nation grieved. Rommel had been the most popular general in the German army. There was never a hint or a rumor that Rommel's death was not from natural causes. It was only revealed after the war that he had been forced to commit suicide by order of the Fuehrer. What a travesty his wife and son had to go through attending the state funeral.

Life settled into a routine. I rose at 5:30 a.m. and walked to work. At 6 p.m., I started for home. On Saturdays, we worked only until 1 p.m. On my way home, I passed through a village where a farm right by the road kept three geese plus a gander, a singularly vicious fowl. I was afraid of him. As soon as I approached, he flapped his wings, stretched out his long neck, hissed and waddled toward me as fast as he could. He attacked me by pulling back his neck and stabbing at me. Fortunately, I carried my leather brief case and used it as a shield. It took a beating. I always walked slowly lest the gander would think I was scared and attack more fiercely.

The farmhouse we lived in accommodated the stable under the same roof. Soon we became aware of another kind of "livestock." A few minutes after we went to bed and turned the lights off, scurrying feet and rustling sounds disturbed our slumber. The mouse soccer team arrived for its nightly game. Next to our tile stove stood a box filled with coke. The mice managed to maneuver a number of pieces out of the box. Under the beds, they commenced to play a long, drawn out and noisy game. Mama put the light on and said " pssst." All became quiet as the mice ran away. We crunched up paper and stuffed it into the mouse hole. Lights out. In no time, the mice were back in force, shoving and pushing the paper until they dislodged it. What a racket. The soccer game recommenced with vigor. For a few days, when I was home sick with a sore throat, I borrowed our landlord's cat thinking it would chase the mice away. No such luck. The soccer tournaments continued. Finally, in desperation, Mama broke a glass and shoved the pieces into the mouse hole. It had the desired effect. The games were over.

On Saturday afternoons, I accompanied Mama on her rounds. On one occasion, we visited a farm on a hillside and were invited for coffee and sandwiches. The daughter of the house had been married the week before and her wedding dress was hanging in the kitchen. It was made of lace, with a voluminous frilled skirt and was similar to the type of dress my friend Marianne had envisioned for herself. Mama leaned over and whispered, "Gisela, you could have a dress like that if you wanted to." I did not.

One Saturday, I happened to pass the church just as a bridal couple entered it. I decided to go in. The bride wore a plain grey suit, a myrtle wreath and a veil. The bridegroom was in uniform. It was a very simple ceremony.

On clear nights, I observed Venus and the moon. They were in close proximity to each other, a lovely sight over and against the black silhouettes of the mountains in the dark, still night. The only sounds were of leaves dropping, wind rustling in the trees and, occasionally, an owl hooting and a dog barking.

Many mornings, hoar frost covered every tree, branch, twig, bushes and grasses, transforming the landscape into a glittering fairyland, sparkling like diamonds in the pale winter sunshine. Later it snowed and the farmers used their sleighs. I was thrilled to be invited for a sleigh ride one Saturday afternoon. It was exhilarating to glide along to the jingle of harness bells.

Mrs. Richter, her 6-year-old daughter Gudrun and I decided to go sledding on a clear and sunny Sunday afternoon. Other people had the same idea. We joined the crowd and made our way up a mountain path pulling our sleds behind us. While we climbed, those who had gone up earlier, came sailing past on their sleds yelling and laughing. It was very cold but after climbing steadily for almost three hours we experienced a wonderful feeling of achievement once we reached the top. We glowed from exertion and cold but felt very happy. We rested for a few minutes to catch our breath. It was too cold to linger longer. I mounted my sled, Mrs. Richter and her daughter sat on theirs and we pushed off. The descent was fast. It only took 15 minutes but it was an exhilarating ride and well worth the effort.

Our factory supervisor was also the local ski instructor. On Sundays, he arranged ski outings. So, I borrowed a pair of simple wooden skis and practiced that Friday and Saturday night on the slope outside the farmhouse where we lived. Every time I slid down the gentle incline to the edge of the brook at the bottom, I fell. Invariably. On Saturday morning, I went to work on skis. It was fun but harder than I had imagined coming back uphill. The gander attacked me, as usual.

Sunday after lunch, I set off for the meeting place. I was supposed to be there by 1 p.m. but I was a few minutes late. Everybody had gone except a girl who arrived almost at the same time as I did. She happened to be the ski instructor's daughter. She said, "We have missed them but we might catch up with them." Little did she know I had never skied before and I did not enlighten her. Off we went. I copied everything she did, sidestepping, herringbone stepping and so on. I was not as fast as she was but did a pretty good job keeping up with her. Whether or not we were too far behind or whether the others had taken a different route than originally planned, we never did catch up with them. Once we reached a certain plateau, we began our downhill run. I followed her although I had no idea how to turn either left or right or how to stop. The terrain was formidable and varied from steep slopes to a narrow, bumpy path through a forest. I kept my knees slightly bent and loose, like shock absorbers while bouncing along. Finally, we crossed a huge meadow and she stopped. To my amazement, considering my previous experience outside the house, I did not fall once and survived the whole course in great shape. The only way I knew how to stop now was to let myself fall into the snow and that is what I did. It has remained my one and only skiing experience.

Goerlitz was within easy reach of Bad Flinsberg and I visited Aunt Gertrud and Uncle Herbert when I could. Uncle Herbert showed me around town. Goerlitz was an interesting old city with a number of ancient buildings, such as the town hall, dating back to 1546. I had not seen Uncle Herbert since the wedding. His knee and hip were stiff as a result of his injuries. Numerous pieces of shrapnel remained imbedded in his back, too close to the spine to be removed and he walked with a cane. Sometimes Aunt Gertrud and I went to look at the shops, had coffee somewhere or went to the movies. We got along well. On my last visit in December, Uncle Herbert's sister dropped in while Aunt Gertrud was busy cutting out a dress. She asked, "Is this dress for before or after?" "After," said Aunt Gertrud. It turned out that at long last she was expecting a baby. She was very happy but what a time to have a baby!

Mrs. Liebig at my office was in seventh heaven when her husband came on leave. She took three days off and, afterwards, she and her husband came to the office so we could meet him.

519

She was very proud of him. He was good-looking, pleasant and polite. I wonder if he survived.

I was homesick for Berlin. I loved Berlin and longed to return. The other Berliners at the plant were equally homesick and looked forward to going home for the holidays. On the day before Christmas Eve, we boarded the train to Greiffenberg where we caught the express to Berlin. The train was overcrowded and I had to stand for the entire six hour trip but I did not care. I was so excited it choked me. For a while, I talked to a young forester, resplendent in his green uniform. Unfortunately, he got off at the second stop. For the rest of the trip, I counted every milestone along the route. It was very late when the train pulled into the Goerlitzer Bahnhof. It did not matter. I was home again. I felt like bursting into song, one from a musical that went something like, "Folks, it is simply grand to be back in Berlin."

My Christmas was very quiet and subdued, due not only to the circumstances brought on by the war but also because Mother was ill. She was in bed suffering from an infection of the gall bladder. I had never known her to be sick. I hated to see her so listless.

On the First Christmas Day, I visited Oma and Aunt Frieda and told them about my visits to Goerlitz. On the Second Christmas Day, I visited Papa. Traudchen was now a cute four year old. Papa took a number of photos and a home movie.

I did not have to return to Bad Flinsberg immediately. This gave me an opportunity to visit Scherl and say "hello" to my former colleagues who were installed in the lobby of a building in the Zimmer Strasse. It was crowded and dark, not at all cheerful. They were pleased to see me, especially Marianne. Mrs. Heller, the head of statistics, was eager to chat and tell me that she was expecting a baby in late spring. She was 40 or 41 years old. Although she was pleased she was also apprehensive. No wonder. I must say I was sorry for her and I worried about how she would fare, what with the war, the Soviets making progress into Germany and air raids day and night. I would like to know how she made out and what happened to her.

I found out that one of the girls I knew had been called up into the Labor Service. She was sent to the country for the summer where she was worked off her feet. The remaining eight months she worked as a street car conductress. Food was bad and insufficient, hours very long and there was never enough sleep. I was distressed to hear that she had caught tuberculosis and was quite ill. The prognosis was that given time, rest and plenty of good food, she would recover. This was a prescription that was almost impossible to fill under the circumstances. She had been a very lovely and vibrant girl.

I did not find out anything about Monika, who was in the Army. Apparently, nothing bad had happened to her as far as anybody knew.

I spent a quiet New Year's Eve and left on New Year's Day. I said good-bye to Mother. I kissed her and told her to get well. I was worried about her, but not unduly so. I felt sure she would recover.

1945

Back in Bad Flinsberg, snow lay deep in the valley and on the mountains. It was cold and snowed frequently. When I left the house at 6 o'clock in the morning, it was still dark. The stars twinkled but the snow made it light enough to see. Walking downhill was not hard, although I had to take big steps because the snow came to my knees in most places. I had to be at work at 7 a.m. and it took me the full hour to get there. Returning home, uphill, took much longer.

Work was routine. We did it because it was there to do and was expected of us. But we did not do much and our hearts were not in it. There seemed to be no point to it. The news from the fronts was dismal. The Soviets advanced steadily, though slowly. Fighting was fierce along the entire Eastern front. The German Army put up stiff resistance to stem the Soviet troops. In the west, the Allies made progress. That was okay with me. I was not concerned about that but I was very much concerned about the Russians. I was not the only one. When the Soviets crossed into Germany, it was disturbing but not unexpected news.

Letters from Berlin were equally disconcerting. Mother was still sick and very weak. She could not eat anything. Air raids continued day and night. On Sunday evening, January 28, we received a phone call from Aunt Marga. Mother had died that afternoon. Aunt Marga told us how she had tried to make Mother eat a little soup and custard at noon. She did take a few spoons full. In the afternoon, Mother simply fell asleep and slipped away peacefully.

The funeral was to be on February 2. I could not go. I had just come back from Berlin and the death of a grandmother did not warrant permission to take time off. On Saturday morning, I sat in the office and cried at the time the funeral took place in Berlin. I loved Mother dearly. Later, news reached us of the extremely heavy air raids Berlin suffered on that day. Aunt Marga told me on the phone that the procession had just arrived at the grave site and the pastor was about to intone prayers when the sirens sounded. Most mourners turned and rushed to the cemetery exit some distance from the grave. Only Father, my aunts, uncle and a few brave souls stayed until the blessing was pronounced, somewhat hastily, and the coffin lowered into the ground. It was one of the heaviest raids the city experienced. After the all clear, the company of mourners made their way from the shelters near the cemetery to Father's apartment for refreshments.

Berlin was bombed that day by 900 U.S. planes, which dropped 2,000 tons of bombs. Damage was considerable, with 22,000 dead.

The Fuehrer had the audacity to make a speech on the anniversary of his coming to power on January 30. It was unbelievable. He was still ranting and shouting about winning the war. He said the war "will not end until Germany wins." How could anyone in their right mind believe it? It was too ridiculous. The Russians had taken Koenigsberg in East Prussia and had reached the Oder at Frankfurt, 60 miles from Berlin.

We were somewhat off the beaten track and isolated in Bad Flinsberg. There was only the small railroad to Friedeberg, where another train connected with the main line in Greiffenberg. No major roads lead through Bad Flinsberg.

Therefore, we did not see the stream of refugees from the east heading west, fleeing from the Soviets. Radio and newspapers provided only scant news as to what was really going on. Nothing was said about the evacuation of the civilian population. What we heard about this was always by word of mouth and rumors. However, refugee farmers with horse drawn wagons had come to Bad Flinsberg in late October or early in November. They were transitory and stayed only one or two nights. Mama traded my Bavarian linen dirndl dress for lard. The farmers had barrels of it and had packed eggs in the lard so they would not break. I do not remember from where they had come.

One Friday, young Mrs. Liebig announced that a store in Friedeberg was selling shoes without permits. Saturday after work, Mrs. Liebig, Mrs. Richter and I took the train to Friedeberg. It was true and we were able to purchase shoes. Quite elated and excited, we returned to the station.

Our train was standing on the track but was not scheduled to leave for some time. We settled into our seats and chatted. Across the aisle from us sat a young woman. Her head was turned toward the window and after a little while we noticed that she was crying silently. Tears streamed down her face. Her eyes were red and puffy. We exchanged glances and crossed over to ask if we could be of any help. What was wrong? She told us her story. She was married, living in Oppeln and had a 4-year-old daughter. She had been notified that her husband had been killed in action. The Soviets were steadily advancing on Oppeln. Two weeks later, she was bathing her little girl when there was a loud knock on the door. Upon opening the door, she was confronted by several SS men who brusquely announced that the town was being evacuated. She must be out of the apartment in 20 minutes. Here she was with a child in the bathtub. She quickly dried and dressed the child, threw a few things into a suitcase and snatched a blanket.

Off they went to the train station and were stuffed with other people onto an already overcrowded goods train bound for Breslau. The refugees were without food. The only water available came from the train engine. In Breslau, everyone had to disembark and wait for a train that would take them further into Germany. The station was packed with refugees. Nobody knew when and from which platform the next train or trains would be leaving. As she stood waiting, she noticed a young woman next to her who held a big feather pillow covered by another feather pillow obviously wrapped around a small baby. They stood for hours. Finally, she remarked, "Your baby is exceptionally good. So quiet all this time." The young woman thought the baby was sleeping. She took a peek and found to her horror that the pillow was empty. Apparently, the baby had slipped out as she made her way up and down the stairs from one platform to another. The young mother became hysterical and began pushing her way through the crowds in the hope of finding her baby. It was surely a futile search. The crowds were so dense that any small baby falling down would be trampled to death without anyone ever knowing what they stepped on.

Soon afterwards, a public announcement informed people that a train was pulling in on another platform. Everyone shoved and pushed with their luggage toward the stairs. The woman from Oppeln was carrying a suitcase and holding the 4-year-old by the hand. In addition, she had a purse and a small case. The crush and pushing of the crowd was tremendous, with everyone wanting to get onto the train. Eventually, the little girl was wrenched from her side. There was no way she could turn and go back. Anyone who fell was trampled down, unable to get up. She panicked and she was frantic. She looked everywhere.

A railway employee told her of an entire platform where bodies of people who had died or had been crushed to death were laid out. Her child was not among them. When we met her, she was making the rounds of every Red Cross station, hospital, orphanage and refugee center in the hope of finding her child. We tried to be supportive, hugged her and tried to kindle some hope in her but, in our hearts, we felt that her search would be in vain. We cried with her while parting and wished her luck. Our joy about our new shoes evaporated and my heart was heavy.

The news became worse. Mrs. Richter and Mrs. Liebig were worried sick about their husbands. I was worried about Kurt at the front and everybody in Berlin. I was frightened of the Soviets and extremely nervous. No one was interested in doing any work. We just sat around pretending, talked, listened to the radio and to rumors which were coming in fast. The stories about the Soviets raping women did nothing to put my mind at rest. I slept poorly.

Then, faint at first, but gradually increasing in volume over the succeeding days, I heard artillery fire. Our windows first began to vibrate, then to rattle. I could hardly sleep at night. I was jittery and I wanted to get away. Officially, we were not allowed to leave but by now I no longer cared. I did not want to wait until the Soviets arrived. I did not want to be raped. Mama was quite unperturbed. She loved Flinsberg and hated the idea of leaving. She minimized the dangers threatening us from the Russians. I badgered her every day and pleaded until, finally, I prevailed. I think by that time she was scared, too.

We decided on Saturday night to leave on Monday morning so Sunday we packed. Unfortunately, we had brought a lot of things to Flinsberg, including my Olympia portable typewriter, photo albums, keepsakes, books and a lot of clothing. We could only take two suitcases each and had to leave much behind.

Monday morning, I dressed in two of everything: sweat pants, stockings, socks and boots, underwear, two dresses, a winter coat and a fur coat. It was uncomfortable but it was the only way to carry more clothing.

Our train was scheduled to depart at 8 a.m. The hour came and went, so did 9 a.m. and 10 a.m. It was cold and I was anxious. I simply had to get away from the sound of the artillery and from the Soviets. We stood on the platform but it was too cold and we went into the crowded waiting room to get warm, then out again. I had butterflies in my stomach. I wanted to get away. Suppose someone saw me or someone came looking for me. I had not gone to work and left no message. If I was caught, I could go to prison, if I was lucky. This preyed on my mind. And here I was, stuck. Shortly after 11:30 a.m., the train arrived, huffing and puffing uphill. The main line was already cut off. We could no longer go down to Friedeberg, hence to Greiffenberg. This train went to Zittau, not far from Flinsberg.

We might as well have walked for the progress we made. It took us 12 hours to cover a distance of not more than 25 or 30 miles, across the mountain and away from the fighting. When one is fleeing, delays are nerve-racking. A young air force officer started a conversation with me as soon as the train left Bad Flinsberg. We spent most of the time together standing on the outside platform. His name was Andreas and he was on his way to report back from leave. He was taller than I, had dark blond hair and was nice looking, polite and easy to talk to.

Our little train discharged all passengers somewhere during the night. From then on, things are a little hazy. I was overtired. We changed trains. Andreas left us at some point. We exchanged addresses.

I cannot recall exactly where we finally disembarked but it was a small town. I found out the next morning that we were close to where the river Spree began: a small spring trickling downwards, growing along the way until, after flowing through Berlin, it pours itself into the Havel. I stood in the forest listening to the murmuring spring. I was very homesick. I felt lost, uprooted and homeless, a feeling that has stayed with me ever since.

We took a room in a small hotel and at night we sat in the lounge with other guests. Little lamps with rose colored silk shades placed throughout the room cast soft light. We even danced to the music from a record player. Public dancing was prohibited but we could label this a private party. I was sad. I had no peace of mind and everything was so very uncertain. Where were we going? Where would we sleep next time? Where would we end up? What was happening in Berlin?

We moved on. Westbound trains were overcrowded with refugees. I observed troop trains going east and trains with wounded going west. We heard stories of escapes and more accounts of people being forced out of homes by the SS only hours before the Soviets arrived. People looked distraught, disheveled, disturbed and depressed. It was miserable. After traveling for a couple of days, Mama and I arrived in Saxony. We were dirty, hungry and exhausted from lack of sleep. We had not been out of our multilayered clothing for days and we longed to have a bath.

We got off in Eilenburg. There must have been a refugee center at the station because Mama was given the address of people who were willing to take in refugees. From then on, we stayed in various private homes. I can only say that the hospitality of people in Saxony overwhelmed me. They opened their homes to complete strangers, made us feel at home, were sympathetic and fed us. They were generous and gracious. We stayed with a lovely family in Eilenburg for a night and one night in Weissenfels. These small towns had never been attacked from the air and spent the war in relative peace and quiet. They were surrounded by farms so most people had gardens or relatives and friends in the country who helped out with food.

We pressed on. By now, strict regulations were in effect allowing people to travel only short distances. Passengers could only travel three stations without a permit. Therefore, we bought tickets and at the third stop we disembarked and purchased another ticket. Now and then, we managed to get back onto the same train if it stopped long enough. Mostly we had to get off, skip a train and continue on the next one.

One day, we boarded a train bound for Nordhausen in the Harz mountains. For once, we had seats. Our fellow travelers were friendly. When it was time for us to purchase another ticket, Mama decided that we should skip a train and have lunch before continuing our journey. A couple in our compartment suggested that we should leave our luggage on the train. They would deposit it in the luggage department in Nordhausen, which was also their destination. They were staying at such and such a hotel. We could come and collect the luggage receipts when we arrived. Mama agreed. We said good-bye, got off the train, walked out of the station and down the main street to the first hotel, quite close to the station.

The time was 11 a.m. and the dining room was not yet open. We went to the restroom, washed our faces, combed our hair, and walked up and down the street. It was one of those pale sunny prespring days with a fresh breeze blowing. We did not walk far, returned to the hotel and took our seats in the dining room. Lunch would be served in half an hour, at noon. More people came. The room filled up and I could hear dishes clattering, a promising sound.

Suddenly, sirens wailed. What a surprise. We trooped into the basement. I did not like it because it was too crowded. I went back upstairs and stood in the entrance hall which was tiled and had a very nice double door with large beveled glass insets. After about 15 minutes, I heard planes. I stepped outside, looked up and I saw six planes in formation of threes passing overhead. Simultaneously, I heard whistling noises. I quickly ducked back inside and crouched in the corner behind the door. The whistling grew louder still until it ended in deafening detonations. The building shook. Glass tinkled as it splintered and flew all over the hall. Then it was quiet. A few minutes later, the all clear sounded. The dining room was a shambles, glass shards covered tables and floors. I don't know what happened to our lunch. I cannot recall whether we ate or not. The town was in a tither. This was the first time they had been bombed. We were very close to the station, which was hit. The tracks were the obvious target, not necessarily the station building.

Nobody knew if or when there would be another train, but we had to get to Nordhausen to get our luggage. At about 3 o'clock in the afternoon Mama decided we should walk to the next railroad station some eight miles away. We set off along the road and later along the rail tracks. It was not too bad but after four miles the heel of my boot came off. This made walking extremely uncomfortable. Luckily, at the next station we found out that there would be a train, sometime. It did come several hours later and we finally arrived in Nordhausen at midnight. We could not retrieve our luggage without the receipts so we walked through the dark, sleeping town until we located the hotel where our acquaintances were staying. Everything was dark and quiet in the hotel, the door was locked. It was 1 a.m. Mama called their name repeatedly, hoping their room faced the street. Finally, when we were about to give up, a window opened and they threw the receipts down. Mama and I went in search of a hotel but at this late hour, it was impossible to find one. Nothing was open. We returned to the station where we spent the night in the waiting room. First thing in the morning, we picked up our luggage and were lucky enough to catch a train to Saalfeld.

Saalfeld in Thuringia, on the river Saale, is an old city with a burg (a burg is a castle, stronghold or fortress) dating back to the 10th century. Just outside Saalfeld are the famous Feengrotten, caverns with naturally colored rock formations. In 1680, Saalfeld became the capital of the Duchy Saxony-Saalfeld.

Mama and I spent three days in a small hotel, which was the maximum time allowed. The sheets were not clean and this made me feel icky. The sheets were not dirty but it was obvious that they had been slept in more than once. I suppose the shortage of soap necessitated this economy measure.

The main industrial concern in Saalfeld was the big Mauxion chocolate factory, a well-known, high quality brand. The biggest and best hotel in town was the Mauxion Hotel, where we stayed for the next three days. It was a first class hotel. The furnishings were luxurious, the carpets thick and plush, the armchairs deep and comfortable. Original oil paintings in heavily gilded frames graced the walls and the staircase. Bell boys wore uniforms and white gloves. Guests still dressed for dinner, although no longer in evening gowns but in elegant afternoon dresses and suits. The waiters, attired impeccably in tails, provided excellent service. In spite of the hopeless situation and the uncertainty of the future, this hotel kept up its standards.

At dinner we sat in deep armchairs at round tables set with faultlessly pressed clean linen tablecloths and napkins, silver flatware and bone china. What little food there was, was served with style and grace. There might only be half a potato, some kind of meat concoction and a few vegetables but the food was offered and presented on a large silver platter with all the flourish of a gourmet meal. Even though our stomach still called for food when we rose from the table, our spirits had been refreshed and uplifted by this wonderfully elegant atmosphere. It was an oasis in the desert of the war.

Mama and I visited the Feengrotten, walked around town, sat in the hotel lobby, read books and wondered what to do next. Regretfully, we had to leave the Mauxion Hotel and move to a smaller one after our three allotted days were up.

By now, we needed money and new food coupons. We were also tired of staying in hotels and having to move every three days.

I am not sure if we were entitled to new ration cards and money now that we had a Saalfeld address. Weekly rations for adults were 4.38 ounces of fat, 8.75 ounces of meat and 3.72 pounds of bread. In any case, we went to the refugee center at the town hall and Mama was offered furnished rooms in private houses. We had to split up but it was okay since we were fairly close to each other. Mama also found out that local military hospitals desperately needed blood donors. Blood donors received extra food rations so Mama gave blood. She did not allow me to do so.

My landlords, a nice middle-aged couple, lived in a two story house located in a narrow lane leading through a pass in a hill with just enough room for a few houses along one side of the road. Behind the houses and on the opposite side of the road, the ground rose, sloping almost vertically to a height of approximately 35 to 45 feet. It was sparsely wooded. At this time of year, the trees were still bare.

On Sunday, my landlady invited me to dinner. We had a roast, red cabbage, Thuringian dumplings and gravy. I had heard about these dumplings because they were famous but had never eaten any. They were absolutely delicious.

One sunny morning, the alarm sounded. When I heard the steady drone of airplane engines overhead, I went outside and looked up. What I beheld amazed me. The sky was filled with four-engine bombers flying in formation. I could not see the first formations anymore, they had already passed almost out of sight. I began counting planes as far as I could see. By the time the last planes had gone, I had counted 900 planes, not including those further to my right and further to my left that were obstructed from view by the hill. I estimated that there must be 1,400 or 1,700 planes on their way, presumably, to bomb one of the larger cities in Saxony like Leipzig or Dresden. They were flying east but, I thought, were too far south to be heading for Berlin, which lay to the northeast. My throat went dry when I thought of the people who were alive at this moment but would be dead within the hour.

After the planes passed, there was a lull. A few moments later, however, two planes came into view passing directly overhead. As I watched, something was ejected from one of the planes. I saw two trails of white smoke and heard the familiar whistling sound. I ran into the house and thought for sure that it would receive a direct hit. Nothing happened. The whistling stopped. There was no explosion. Complete silence reigned.

My hosts and I talked about it later with some neighbors. The conclusion we reached was that the planes had discarded some empty fuel containers or perhaps bombs that failed to detonate, although I could not imagine why only two bombs should have been released so far from their target area. Also, I did not know if bombs trailed white smoke. No matter, we were very happy that whatever it was did not hit us and did not explode.

I am not sure how long we stayed in Saalfeld altogether. I have no idea what date it was when we arrived or the date we left. I was terribly homesick. I wanted to go back to Berlin or at least closer to Berlin. Mama had no desire to go into Berlin but she agreed to move closer to the city.

Traveling was becoming more of a problem. Trains were no longer running as regularly as before and we needed a permit if we did not want to rush out all the time to get new tickets. However, apart from the railroads, there was now another form of transportation available to civilians. At the main intersection in Saalfeld, a military police check point halted all military traffic. Civilians lined up with their luggage and waited for a vehicle going to or near their destination. If there was room to accommodate extra passengers, the civilians were given a ride.

Early one morning, Mama and I joined the line. Before long, a tractor towing two small trucks stopped. They were bound for Fuerstenwalde just east of Berlin. They were SS. Together, with a number of other civilians, we got into the second truck. Two private cars, which were out of gas, were added and towed. We left town heading towards Gera. On approaching the town, we noticed numerous columns of smoke ahead to the right and left of us. Our driver asked a passing motorcyclist what was going on and was told that American fighter planes were shooting up everything that moved along the roads. A second bit of information seemed to be of greater importance: a tanker truck was a few kilometers further up the road and actually had fuel. Our driver looked for a suitable place to park along the single lane country road. When we came to a small copse, he pulled up onto the shoulder. He and his co-driver unhooked the tractor and took off to find the gasoline truck. The only other soldier, a corporal, stayed behind.

All of us disembarked, spread our coats on the ground, enjoyed the pale sunshine and ate breakfast. As usual, I was wearing my two winter coats. I took off the fur coat and sat on it. The corporal sat next to me. We talked idly while awaiting the return of our tractor. Conversational efforts were somewhat vague because our attention was constantly diverted by airplane noises of American fighters still circling over the area. Now and then, we heard sporadic gunfire and detected new smoke columns. The new ones were darker and thicker, while the older ones faded as the fires diminished. In spite of this, we felt quite safe and unconcerned. The trees, still bare, provided a little camouflage.

Suddenly, the droning took on an intense and ominous sound. It seemed that the planes had made a decision. They were in formation and goal oriented. Their target, it turned out, was our vehicles. The noise grew louder and shriller as the planes swooped low. I sat and stared in the direction from which they were coming. I would have stayed there, rooted to the spot if the corporal had not jumped up, grabbed my hand, yanked me to my feet and dragged me across the road. We leaped over the ditch into the undergrowth where he threw me to the ground hitting it himself at the same time. Even before we hit the ground, the machine-gun bullets whistled over us. The planes screamed upwards, circled, viewed the scene, regrouped and swept into another attack.

There were eight planes. None of our four vehicles had burst into flames. I imagine the pilots thought they had missed their target so they attacked again. The machine-guns barked. Still, none of the vehicles caught fire as they expected. The pilots were unaware that there was not a drop of gas in the tanks so, consequently, there was no explosion. The pilots must have been quite miffed and puzzled by this apparent lack of success. They attacked five times before finally giving up.

We waited until the noise of their engines diminished in the distance and it became silent once more. We got up, dusted our clothes off and made our way back to the road. So did the other people who had run in the opposite direction. Being civilians who had never been attacked by planes, we had no idea which way to run. We just ran. Only the corporal had run in the direction from which the attackers came, to be out of the reach of strafing bullets. The others had been in greater danger. I was fearing what I might find, fearing that Mama had been hit, fearing to find dead and wounded. By some miracle, no one was hurt. What a relief this was. One woman, in particular, had every reason to be thankful. It sounds unbelievable, but one bullet took off the heel of one of her shoes and another the feather on her hat but she was unhurt. Mama told me later that a boy, about 8 years old, lay next to her on the ground. He buried his head in his arms and prayed out loud, "Dear Lord, protect us all. Dear Lord, protect us," while sweat streamed down his face. We were greatly relieved that no one was killed or wounded.

On inspection, I found that my fur coat, the one I had been sitting on, was riddled with bullet holes. Then I noticed that the truck that we had traveled in was also shot full of holes, as were the other vehicles. The particular small area where I had been sitting in the truck while traveling, and would have sat if I had remained in the truck instead of sitting by the road, had seventeen bullet holes in it. Next, we inspected our luggage. Mama and I carried our suitcases to the edge of a nearby field. Every garment we unfolded and held up practically blew away in the breeze, completely shot to pieces. I still have my hymn book, with one corner shot off. We abandoned two suitcases and my coat.

About an hour later, our tractor returned. We had been worrying and wondering if they too had been attacked and hit. Luckily, they had found the tank truck and refueled. The journey could continue but it was no longer feasible to tow the trucks and cars, since they were shot. What to do with the civilians? The sergeant in charge decided that he could only take two people and picked Mama and myself. The other travelers were in groups of more than two. They grumbled but nothing could be done. It was very crowded in the cab. Mama and I practically sat on each other's lap but we did not mind.

While we were riding along, the guys told us how they had ended up in the SS. Originally, they had been an air force unit. On the morning of Himmler's birthday, and they did not even know it was his birthday, they were informed that as of that time they were SS. Goering had presented this air force unit to Himmler as a birthday gift. These men did not look like the typical SS types. We had already wondered about that. They hated being SS but what could they do? They were on their way to Fuerstenwalde to the SS headquarters.

We were now approaching the Leipzig area. We had no radio and no idea what was happening. We drove on. Late in the afternoon, with the sun low in the west, we entered a village that seemed to be in great agitation. People stood around in groups talking, something that was most unusual because no more than two people were allowed to congregate in public under threat of arrest for sedition. Something had to be going on. As we passed through the village, a man, who introduced himself as the mayor, jumped onto our running board. He said that the Americans were less than a kilometer from this village and advancing toward Leipzig to close the encirclement of the city. The situation was tense. The mayor stayed on the running board directing the driver to the only route that offered a chance of escape. He wished us luck and hopped off.

Our driver hit the gas pedal. At top speed, we went over fields and meadows in the direction that would allow us to slip through the last loophole of the encircling U.S. troops. I clearly recall the hazy reddish tint of the late afternoon sun, the urgency in the mayor's voice, the intensity of the driver trying to coax maximum speed from the engine, employing all his skills to transverse over unusually rough terrain, to avoid being sighted and, in all probability, fired upon by the Americans. It was strangely exciting though fraught with danger, perhaps because of it. I felt none of the fear I had felt when we were fleeing from Flinsberg. The Americans did not elicit fear like the Soviets. However, all I could think was that I did not want to be caught in the company of SS even though they were not the real thing. The Americans would only see the insignia. The SS had a bad reputation and I did not want anyone to think that I had in any way been associated with them.

Somehow, we made it. We kept driving into the falling shadows, into the night. We did not stop. We reached the vicinity of Berlin in the early morning hours. The driver said he could not take us any further and let us off in Michendorf, some 12 or 15 kilometers south of Potsdam.

Michendorf is close to Werder. Werder and the surrounding countryside, southwest of Berlin, is famous for its fruit orchards. Every spring, Berliners flock to see the blossoms and sit in garden restaurants under the flowering trees.

We found the local inn, and even at that ungodly hour, were fortunate to secure a room. In the morning, we found that the place was full of refugees. We had nothing to do but sit and speculate about the situation. We were eager for news. It seemed that the Americans were making progress. The Russians were closing in on Berlin and were very close to Berlin's eastern suburbs. At night, we sat in the large room, which had formerly served as a banquet and dance hall, and sampled the fruit wine produced in this area. It flowed freely. There were no restrictions and the innkeeper opened his cellar. Why keep it for the Soviets? We all had some, enough to relax but not to intoxicate. Nobody got drunk.

A day or two later, I stood at the edge of the orchard looking north. It was another sunny spring day with a high, pale blue sky, muted sunshine, still a little cool. The land there is flat so it was possible see for miles. I saw the panorama of Potsdam as though in miniature. Planes were attacking Potsdam. On that and the following day, British planes bombed the city, killing 5,000.White plumes of smoke like geysers rose as the bombs hit and exploded, a strange and horrifying sight. I turned away and spent the day doing nothing, speculating as to what would happen next and what was going on. Nobody wanted to be alone. Company provided comfort, strangers though we might be to one another. The wine was still flowing but did not result in merriment. We were too subdued to make our gathering a party. I was frightened, restless and insecure.

It was a strange time. I lost count of the days, of the date, of what day of the week it was. I was so close to Berlin. So close and yet so far. I had escaped from the Soviets and did not want to be caught by them now. But the pull to go into the city was strong. Mama and I had lost most of our clothing due to the fighter attack. It was getting warmer and our winter clothes were too heavy. I wanted to replenish what we had. Mama refused to go and tried to dissuade me but I was adamant.

The following day, I boarded the suburban train into Berlin. My heart was beating fast. What would I find? I arrived late in the afternoon, on what had been a warm, sunny spring day. The sun was descending in a pinkish haze. The S-Bahn was still running and I observed trains going in the opposite direction passing the one I was on. When I emerged from the station, I saw streetcars chugging along. Shops were open and shoppers were about. Lights in some stores were lit and people were walking along the street. I was the only one who was running. I was in a hurry. Although the street scene looked normal, it was anything but. Looks were deceiving, for quite clearly I recognized the sound of artillery, distant enough to be muted but nevertheless unmistakable and constant. The Soviets were bombarding the eastern suburbs. Berlin was not declared an "Open City."

Father and Aunt Marga were astonished. They were happy to see me but they were also concerned. I told them that Mama and I were fine, we were in Michendorf. I simply wanted to pick up some clothes and leave. Aunt Marga was flustered. She had packed our clothes into suitcases, taken them to their storage unit in the basement and used them as a platform upon which she made beds for herself and Father, ready to occupy once the fighting began. How was I to get out of town? It was now half past five and soon it would be dark. I could not catch a train and it was dangerous to be on the streets.

Aunt Marga handed me a letter from Andreas and he had enclosed a photo. I showed it to Aunt Marga and told her that I really liked this guy. He told me where he was stationed but that had been two months ago and that area was no longer under German control. God only knew where he was by then. I thought it unlikely that I would hear from him again and I was right. At present, my main concern was how to get out of Berlin.

I was desperate, my mind was working overtime, trying to think of a way to get back to Michendorf, out of Berlin and away from the Soviets. I remembered that Kurt's bicycle was in the

541

basement and decided I would use it. Aunt Marga was upset because I tore part of their arrangement apart in order to reach the bike which was hanging, or standing, at the back of the cubicle. I got it out and the tires looked okay. I pumped some more air into them and was ready to leave. I was unable to find my clothing. Aunt Marga gave me a small heel of bread and put it into a shopping net which I hung on the handlebar. Father was very worried. He pleaded, "Don't go. The home guard will stop you. They confiscate bikes. They won't let you pass. You will get lost and won't be able to come back." However, I was determined to leave. I hugged Father, said good-bye to Aunt Marga and hoped they would be all right. I had no map. I only knew the direction I had to go: south. I could think of nothing but how to get out of Berlin.

The Hermannstrasse went south so I biked along the Hermannstrasse through Britz and Mariendorf, going as straight south as possible. I was the only bicyclist on the road and there was no other traffic, only a few pedestrians. After a while, I reached a crossroad, just outside the city limit. The road was chock full of army vehicles: trucks, cars, lorries, motorbikes, all facing west. They were not moving at that moment and it was an enormous traffic jam. Obviously, this was the place to turn west and I did. It became impossible to ride the bike so I walked. Soldiers called to me and asked where I was going. I stopped and asked the occupant of a car if he had a map and could tell me how to get to Michendorf.

The young man, a lieutenant, got out and told me that he and his unit were heading for the very same place. "Too bad," he said, "if you did not have the bike I could give you a ride." Quick as a flash I replied, "Could we put the bike on one of the lorries?" He said he would see about it, walked back to a lorry and, sure enough, they could accommodate the bike. The car was small and the backseat full of luggage and all sorts of things. Beside the officer was his driver. The only way he explained, somewhat embarrassed, was for me to sit on his lap. He told me during the ride that he had only recently been promoted in the field. Apparently, his unit sustained heavy losses on the Eastern front, including most of its officers.

It took quite a while before the column moved on. It had rained and the road, a dirt road full of potholes, had turned to deep mud, which caused numerous vehicles to get stuck, causing the jam. By now, it was dark and it took hours, driving at a crawl, to reach Michendorf.

We arrived at about 1 a.m. People at the inn were still up, sitting around, drinking wine, imbibing somewhat more freely. They were in quite a hilarious mood and singing. Mama was happy and very relieved to see me. My rescuer and I were invited to have a glass of wine. He drank it standing up, then excused himself to see to his men.

The army unit camped in tents in the field near the inn. The following morning, we stood around watching what the soldiers were doing. We heard no news as to what was happening. I told everybody how I found things in Berlin. We were downhearted. What would happen next?

The next day, the unit received orders to move on, west. Mama, I and other civilian refugees went along with them. We were able to ride in the lorries. The convoy set off along a country road toward the river Havel, which we reached at about 1:30 or 2 p.m. There were no bridges, just a small ferry that could take only one truck and a motorcycle at a time. The line of vehicles stretched from the river's edge for simply miles along the road. We were held up for hours, advancing only one car length at a snail's pace. Nevertheless, the soldiers were in fairly good humor. They had loaded up with supplies from army food depots that were about to be blown up. One lorry harbored a few live chickens. As soon as a hen laid an egg, a shout went up. Egg flip (raw eggs beaten up with hard liqueur sugar and cream) was manufactured on the spot, distributed and consumed. For once, we had no food problems. We had bread, canned meat and sardines. We were happy and satisfied with what we were given.

We had started out in the morning and now it was late afternoon. As the day progressed, we grew weary and tired. It was trying to be held up for so long by such an insignificant obstacle because we wanted to get to the other side fast. We worried what progress the Soviets were making during the time we were waiting.

The sun was low. I was sitting in the cab of a truck which had no windshield. It had been blown out or shot out a long time ago, somewhere east of Berlin. The driver, an Austrian named Poldi, in his middle or late 40s, was dozing. The column of vehicles moved again. When Poldi did not respond immediately, he was rudely awakened by a military policeman and came out of a dead sleep, waking up with a start. The sun was in his eyes. His foot hit the gas pedal before he had time to know what he was doing and he lost control of the vehicle. We careened from one side of the road to the other and, lurching forward, hit a telegraph pole with enough force to knock it down. I feared we were in trouble. Military police reappeared almost instantly. However, the situation was so chaotic that, luckily, Poldi got off with a severe dressing down. The fact that the traffic started to move again probably had a lot to do with it. We crept nearer to the ferry. Eventually, at dusk, we were ferried across the narrow river.

A few miles further west, we made camp in some woods. Tents were erected and Mama and I had one to ourselves but that was all we had. There were no blankets, no straw and no groundsheets. We slept in our clothes on the bare ground, which in April was still cold and damp, but thank God we had a tent. Although nights were anything but comfortable, we were grateful to be relatively safe and that we had food. During the following days, there was nothing for us to do. We waited around, talked to other refugees and watched the troops. They were checking their gear, their vehicles and making small adjustments and repairs. In short, they were killing time while waiting. We were all waiting for orders, for gasoline, for whatever came next. I talked a lot to Poldi, who took a fatherly interest in me. He told me how much he hated the army and that he had been drafted early on in the war because of his previous political associations as an active Social Democrat. He was persecuted by the Nazis and even served a prison term for his political convictions.

One day, I managed to find a bowl and hot water and was able to wash my hair for the first time in many weeks. I felt really awful because I had not been out of my clothes for days and nights on end. I managed to soap down completely in the tent with the flaps down and Mama standing guard outside. It felt great. I did the same for her later on. We had, of course, no facilities. Fortunately, the woods and the undergrowth provided sufficient privacy but it was somewhat unnerving when one is in the immediate vicinity of over 100 men.

We ate with the troops who were good enough to share what they had. I had not eaten this well since before the war. Nevertheless, we were growing concerned when days went by and nothing happened and there were no orders to move on. We had no news of the war, either, but we were certain that the Russian Army was not standing still. We had been in this place for five or six days when an air force unit pulled into the woods and camped alongside our army unit. Two days later, Mama heard that the air force unit had orders to move on. She said, "We will go with them." Poldi was glad we were able to move on. At least, we would be getting further away from the Soviets. I was worried that he might not make it and hated to think of him being a prisoner of war of the Soviets. It should not happen to an anti-Nazi.

After lunch, we pulled out. Late in the afternoon, we attempted to enter a small town but it was impossible because the road was blocked by abandoned vehicles. Our unit followed suit and abandoned theirs. We continued on foot. The sun was low, about to set and the air had that warm glow which made window panes look like molten gold. The streets were jammed with civilians, troops and . . . Americans. What a strange sight and stranger atmosphere.

The war was not yet over. The German soldiers were for the most part unarmed. Sidewalks and gutters were littered with guns, rifles, submachine guns, ammunition, steel helmets, pistols, revolvers and other army equipment. I even saw a Nazi party button. No one took any notice. We simply stepped over them as we made our way through town. The only noise I heard was that of shoes and boots crunching on the pavement. Everyone was intent on going somewhere. There was no time for talk. Now and then I saw Americans, the first I had ever seen, wearing battle dress, steel helmets, guns, bayonets and ammunition belts. They were picking up souvenirs. A couple of them passed close to us. One of them grabbed Mama's wrist and took her watch as he did with every civilian he passed. This was war. He was not doing anything wrong.

The town (it may have been Strelau) was near the banks of the river Elbe. Apparently, and I heard and saw the evidence, the Americans were on the opposite bank. They came over in motor boats to look around, collected souvenirs and returned across the river to their units. They would not advance further but awaited the arrival of the Soviets on our side of the Elbe. U.S. and Soviet troops met at the river Elbe on April 25.

Mama and I, together with just about everyone else, walked through and out of town for several kilometers until we reached a village directly behind the Elbe dike. The village was deserted. The inhabitants had been evacuated or had fled. Someone directed us to the schoolhouse. Here the classrooms, empty of furniture, served as a shelter. We bedded down for the night on the floor, packed in closely together. I could not sleep for hours. No one slept much and we were all up at dawn. Mama and I washed, combed, straightened our clothes as best we could and ate some of our provisions, although I cannot recall what these were. Then we were on our way to the river.

First, we walked out of the village and along the base of the dike. More and more people joined us. After a while, we climbed up onto the dike, which was wide and flat like a road on top. I had noticed people on the dike from way off but once up there I had a better picture. The entire dike ahead of us, was occupied by German soldiers, civilians and vehicles. Every space along the water's edge was crowded with people. Long stone moles reached into the river at intervals of approximately 75 yards. Ahead of us the river curved slightly to the right. There was no bridge in sight. It became impossible to walk along the dike because it was too crowded. We climbed down to the edge of the water to a spot where a large barge rested at the end of a mole.

We talked to the soldiers who camped there. We tried to find out what was going on. Why were we all waiting here? No one knew. How far was it to the nearest bridge? No idea. How far to the next town? Which was the next town? Hamburg? How far was it to Hamburg? A very long way. Why didn't anyone move on? There were no answers. We stayed. We had nowhere to go.

There was plenty of food. Every unit had loaded up with whatever rations army storehouses were giving away before being blown up. They traded this for that. Some had cases of margarine, others had meat, coffee, chocolate, soap, cigarettes and so on. The day was clear, sunny and cool. At night, we slept in one of the trucks. We were fortunate because most people slept on the ground.

We were up at daybreak. It was eerie. There were thousands of people on that dike and by the river but it was very, very quiet. There were no raised voices, just a murmur, which was uncanny. Everything was hushed. Foreboding filled the air like a tangible. Almost the first thing we heard was that during the night the Soviets had reached the villages behind the dike. They had celebrated and were now sleeping it off.

I grew anxious, nervous and apprehensive. What now? Somehow I felt safer being out in the open. I can't explain why. What kind of security was that? While we had been with the army unit, I was able to discard my old heelless boots and had acquired a pair of army boots. They were the smallest size available but still three sizes too big and wide. I had also been able to replace my fur coat with a rabbit fur jacket, white with brown spots. I carried a backpack and a suitcase. Mama had one suitcase and a handbag. Mama was not feeling well. She had caught a chill while we were camping and was running a temperature.

By noon, nothing had happened. There was no sign of Russians. We were hungry so many groups lit fires and began cooking. Our group had pork chops, thick beautiful center cut pork chops such as I had not seen for years. They smelled heavenly as they fried in lots of butter. The pork chops sizzled and were done to perfection, ready to be devoured. Just then movement spread through the crowd. We looked up and saw a number of Russians standing on the dike. That did it. The guy who had been frying the chops threw them, along with the frying pan, into the river and extinguished the fire. Nobody wanted to eat. We had lost our appetite. The appearance of the Russians drove every other thought from my mind. As soon as the initial shock wore off, people took action. Many soldiers stripped to their underwear, covered themselves from head to toe with a thick layer of margarine, walked to the head of the mole and jumped into the water. The river was wide, the current fast and swift, the water extremely cold. They swam. The current carried them along. How many of them made it to the other side I do not know.

Slowly, the Russians who had stood on the dike surveying the scene descended. They moved in our direction, advancing slowly. One was an officer, resplendent in an immaculately tailored dress uniform with polished leather webbing, red and pale blue epaulettes and a red star on his cap. He wore a leather pouch, containing maps and pens. He was armed with a revolver or pistol. He wore brown leather boots with smooth, shiny shafts. All eyes were upon him. He was accompanied by four soldiers armed with rifles and sten guns or light submachine guns. They, too, wore dress uniforms, not battle dress.

The Russian officer stopped in front of me. I was face to face with the feared foe. I felt my heart thumping and my knees getting weak. Everyone stood absolutely still while he surveyed the scene calmly, with the confident air of a conqueror, like a field marshal surveying a battlefield after victory. The spell was broken when someone asked, "What shall we do?" His manner was at once grandiose and patronizing. He replied that all German soldiers were prisoners. The civilians were free to go wherever they pleased. They were free to return to the land behind the dike, he gestured, or go across the river and he pointed to the other side of the Elbe.

I looked toward the dike and saw other Soviets ordering the German soldiers to line up. The German soldiers around us were told to join them. One of the guys near us got up to leave. We had talked a lot to him. He was devastated. He asked me for my scarf which I gave to him. A captain to whom I had been talking the previous afternoon also had to go. He, too, was crushed. He gave me a Red Cross pin saying, "Perhaps this will come in handy. For what it is worth, it may provide a small measure of protection. Wear it. Perhaps the Russians will respect it and the wearer thinking you are a nurse." I was sad to see them go, even though they were strangers. Their fate, and that of all the other soldiers, was nothing to look forward to. I looked after them until they were lost in the crowd and I could no longer see the guy waving my scarf. Some civilians also decided to return inland and began moving that way. I saw many civilians climb into the barge at the end of our mole. Mama and I walked down the mole and waited our turn.

Mama and I clambered quickly up and into the barge which filled up fast. A tall middle-aged man, wearing the peaked cap of the railroad uniform, seemed to take charge. The railroad guy waved his arms to those still on shore shouting, "No more! No more! It is too full already!" The railroad man and another man found two long poles and tried to maneuver the barge into the river. They were inexperienced. In fact, they had only the faintest idea of how to go about it. In addition, they were extremely nervous and anxious to get away from this shore, away from the Soviets. Many people in the boat shouted directions, well meant but completely useless advice. The boat was too heavy and overloaded. Two men and two poles were insufficient to accomplish anything against the strong current.

Besides, nobody was cool, calm and collected. The situation did not make for cool heads and coordinated efforts. Slowly, the barge nosed away from the mole but as soon as we made a little headway, with about half the boat past the head of the mole, the current pushed the head around it and into the section of water between this mole and the next one. The men kept maneuvering the heavy barge until it was at the inside head of the next mole. Again, their efforts to nose it into the current failed. We rounded the head of the next mole and were pushed into the next section. This happened a couple more times and now we were only 300 yards from where we had started three and a half hours before. The men were tired, not only of pushing but of the unsolicited advice shouted at them by their increasingly nervous passengers. To top it all, the last attempt to get into the current cost one of the precious poles. It broke and now it was impossible to budge the overloaded barge. We were stuck.

Everyone was talking at the same time, trying to figure out a way to get going again when someone pointed to shore and all eyes turned that way. We fell silent. Coming down the mole were the same Soviet soldiers and the same officer whom we had met three and half hours ago. Only now, they did not look quite so cool. It was obvious they had been drinking and were the worse for it. The officer jumped onto the rim of the barge close to the railroad guy. Somebody tried to explain the situation to the officer but he cut him short, pointed at the railroad guy's cap, and said, "Swastika! You Nazi officer!" With that he pulled his pistol, ready to shoot. Everybody in the barge began to scream and the guy tried to explain he was with the railroad and the cap was part of his uniform.

I was sitting quietly against the side of the boat watching when a young woman got up, walked past me, climbed onto the rim of the barge and jumped ashore. The argument at the other end of the barge continued. I looked to see where the woman was going and realized that she was heading toward the next mole where half a dozen people stood waiting for a boat that was coming across from the opposite shore. I thought, if she can do it, so can I. I whispered to Mama, who was shivering with fever, what I was about to do. I got up, climbed onto the rim and jumped off. The soldiers who had accompanied the officer and were standing by the water's edge did not take any notice. I walked along the edge of the water toward the other mole.

After about 40 yards or so, I suddenly had a funny feeling and looked back over my shoulder. To my horror, I saw that two young Soviet soldiers were following me. One carried a rifle, the other a sten gun or submachine gun at the ready. Just then, I had reached a point where I either had to walk several yards back toward the shore to avoid the water or walk through the water. The choice was to stay dry, risk being caught by the Soviets and miss the boat, or plunge into the water and try to get away. In either case, I could not escape bullets should they decide to shoot. I had come this far and was not about to give up. I plunged into the water. It came up to my waist and was icy. It filled my big army boots making it hard to keep walking but I was determined. I did not look back again but plodded on aware that any moment could be my last. But all remained quiet, there was no shout for me to stop. Nothing happened.

In spite of the cold water and the coolness of the evening, I was sweating profusely when I made it to the mole just in time to get into the boat. They had seen me and waited for me. Now they pushed off at once. The men who rowed the boat were German air force soldiers taken prisoners by the Americans. I have no idea who gave them permission to ferry us across, if they had decided to do this on their own initiative or at the behest of the Americans. We did not talk. It was almost dusk when I stepped

552

ashore on the other side. The ground was soggy and muddy. Together with the other passengers, I made my way up the embankment to a house. The house was deserted. Its owners had been evacuated or had fled. Furniture stood on the grass, drawers pulled open, their contents spilled. I followed the woman from the barge into the house.

By now I was shaking with cold. My clothes were dripping and my boots were full of water. Sleeping men occupied the beds, obviously soldiers who had swam across. One room was empty, we went in and closed the door. We were anxious to get out of our cold, wet things. I only had a backpack but it contained underwear and a dress. We stripped off our jackets, coats, boots, sweat pants. We were standing in our underwear when the door was kicked open.

Five or six very tall American soldiers filled the doorway and stalked into the room. In full battle dress, armed to the teeth and wearing steel helmets, they looked extremely menacing to me. I tried to say something in English but my mind went blank. I could only stare and think, "Oh, my God! I got away from the Russians and now what will these soldiers do to me." The woman seemed to feel equally threatened and kept saying in German, "Leave! Leave! We want to change our clothes." When the Americans looked more menacing and made some gestures that could easily be interpreted in a certain way, she said in English, "I am sick, I am ill." Whereupon I came to, nodded and repeated what she had said. Anything! I did not care. Just to make these soldiers leave. They did. Reluctantly and looking somewhat mystified, they shuffled out of the room. She slammed the door behind them. We both collapsed onto the floor and breathed a sigh of relief. After a few minutes we recovered, quickly got out of our wet clothes, dried ourselves as best we could, dressed and left the house. I don't know where she went after that.

I walked down to the river to see if Mama had been lucky enough to get away. The rowboat arrived a few minutes later. Much to my relief, Mama was on it but she was very sick. She was shivering and was extremely agitated. She practically collapsed when she saw me. "Thank God!" she exclaimed and began to cry. She told me that she had not noticed me getting out the of barge. The Russians had finally left the railroad guy alone but took his cap and threw it into the river. She watched as the Russians took a girl away who wore a rabbit skin jacket just like mine. They took her off the boat, dragging her inland. Mama thought it was me and was sick with fear.

By now it was pitch dark. We began walking along the road and were picked up a few minutes later by an American Army truck, which drove us to the next village where we were told to spend the night in a schoolhouse. In the morning, together with six other people, we started walking. We were stopped a couple of times by American patrols. I tried to remember my school English. The second time was in some small village and the soldiers asked would we mind if they could take some photos. Our group posed for them and with them. We must have looked a sight in our odd clothing and with our bundles. By late afternoon, we reached another village and decided to stay. Mama talked to the innkeepers and they allowed us to sleep in one of the downstairs restaurant rooms on sofas.

On the following day, I think, we reached the city of Salzwedel. Mama asked around and I guess it was the refugee center that directed us to a very friendly childless couple in their early 50s who took us in.

For the first time in weeks, I undressed, bathed and slept in a bed. Mama was still sick, still had a fever and stayed in bed for a

554

week. I did not have the flu but the tensions and stress of the past weeks took their toll. Once I was out of danger, I came down with a fever and felt ill. When I was feeling better, our host took me for a walk through town. The streets were crowded. The park, too, was full of people who sat in the sun talking. I had not seen people congregate like this since before the war. It was a very strange, peculiar atmosphere. For me, the war was over. But I had no idea what had happened during the past days nor what was going on now. A day or so later, we heard that the war was officially over. Germany had surrendered unconditionally. This was it. I had no feelings about it other than "Thank God! The nightmare is over."

We were in Salzwedel for 10 days, and I liked it. I wanted to stay. Mama said, "We are leaving. I have heard that the Soviets are going to occupy this area." We left. There was no railroad service so we walked until we came to Celle.

Soon after we passed the city limit, Mama knocked on the door of a large house and asked the lady if she would take us in. She was a spinster and the daughter of a clergyman. She was in her 60s, devout and kind. She already had four or five refugees staying in her house. She invited us for dinner and we had goulash. It was very tasty: in fact, it was delicious. Later I found out that it was made with horse meat. I wonder if I would have eaten the stew had I known it was horse meat. It tasted like beef, only sweeter.

I wanted to stay in Celle. After three months on the road, I was tired of being homeless, of walking without knowing where we would be at night, where our next meal was coming from, where we would find a place to sleep. Actually, I had no cause for complaints. Mama took care of everything. I don't know what I would have done without her. I suppose I would have had to pull myself together and taken care of myself. Anyway, I cried. I said I did not want to go on. Mama tried to persuade me to go further south to where the Americans were. British troops occupied the area where Celle was located. Finally, she relented. Perhaps she, too, was tired.

The refugee center issued us with papers classifying us as refugees, which entitled us to accommodation and food stamps. This was very important because we had lost our papers. After I had left the barge, the Russian soldiers ripped open all the luggage and what they did not want they threw into the river, including Mama's purse which contained our papers. Mama had managed to save a suitcase. It was not discovered because she sat on it. The refugee center provided us with accommodation and two or three weeks later we moved to the other side of town.

At last, I began to realize that the war was over.

The Fuehrer's 1,000-Year Reich had come to an end.

I had lived through these 1,000 years and I had survived.

Epilogue

The war was over. It was finally over. I was exhausted, not physically but emotionally. The strain of the past months took its toll. But it was May, it was spring, the sky was blue, the sun was shining, the trees wore their first fresh green, the birds were singing the flowers were blooming and I was young.

We stayed with the dear little old lady for a couple of weeks. Her house had a large garden. A brick wall, which boasted a little square building with a patio on its top, was at the bottom of the garden and separated it from a public walkway. I spent most of my time sitting on the patio reading and writing in my diary, watching people go by and daydreaming.

Mama and I ventured into town occasionally, mainly in order to make sure we received ration cards. For some reason, we could not stay where we were and Mama applied for other accommodations. Local residents had to give up spare rooms due to the influx of refugees into the area. We moved to the west side of town to a modern three story apartment building. The woman who owned the house, Mrs. Lindner, was an elderly widow and lived on the top floor. We were assigned a furnished room in the second floor apartment with Mrs. Kolwitz and her daughter, Sigrid, who was my age. Sigrid and her mother occupied one bedroom, a young man occupied the living room and we were given the other bedroom. The first floor apartment was occupied by a couple and their daughter.

Life was different. It was strange. The cities were devastated by the bombs and the fighting. There was no rail service, no telephone service, no postal service and industries were idle. Most of the infrastructure was destroyed.

I had virtually nothing to wear. My lovely black and white woolen dress needed to be cleaned but there were no dry cleaners. I washed it in cold water and it shrunk two sizes. Besides, it was now too warm to wear a woolen dress. The army boots were far too large for me. Mama traded them in for food at some point. Soon Mama befriended a refugee couple in our neighborhood and the woman gave me a dress and a pair of tennis shoes. The dress was silk, patterned all over with a small floral design in several shades of purple and white. It was full of small holes but they were almost invisible because the pattern camouflaged them. The tennis shoes were rust colored, more than a size too large and also sported a couple of holes. However, these modest gifts were a blessing.

Our food rations were smaller than the ones we received before the end of the war. Food stores only opened when they received goods. They distributed them and closed until the next delivery.

Sigrid and a friend, Paula, started work at the large airfield outside town shortly before we moved in. I went along with them one day to inquire about a job and I was hired. Every morning at 8 a.m., we were picked up by a lorry and taken to the airfield. The airfield was occupied by approximately 800 RAF personnel, including officers. Paula worked in the officer's quarters and Sigrid worked in the laundry. I was assigned to the airmen's mess hall in the large modern and beautifully equipped cook house. I arrived every morning after breakfast had ended and found that several baking sheets of fried eggs, bacon or sausages were left over. I was allowed to help myself to these leftovers.

My duties, and those of several other girls, consisted of collecting the condiments and jam dishes from the tables, cleaning the tables and sweeping the floor. We filled salt and pepper shakers, sugar bowls and replenished the jam. By the time we finished, it was lunch time and we helped to serve. Taking our places behind a service counter, we dished out food into the airmen's mess kits as they filed past. Most of the time I served dessert, usually baked or steamed pudding, sheet cake or fruit and custard. We soon had favorites among the airmen, whom we saw twice a day, and gave them extra big helpings. Some looked very surprised at the size of the portion and had no idea why they were so lucky. We did not talk to the airmen and they did not talk to us.

General Montgomery had issued a nonfraternization order: members of the British Occupation Forces were not allowed to talk to Germans. Germans were not allowed to talk to the British. Of course, the personnel with whom we worked had to communicate with us. I was one of only five girls on the airfield who spoke English. I had not used my school English for three years but I managed and was very popular because of it.

Our mess sergeant often stopped and chatted with me as did Jimmy, the tea maker, a tall slim guy from Southampton. Jimmy wore the khaki uniform and beret of the Army Catering Corps. He loved to clown around. Every time he came into the cook house carrying pails of milk, he put them down, raised his right arm and shouted, "Heil Hitler!" I can't say that I found it too hilarious but he was so comical that I could not help laughing.

559

Another regular visitor to the cook house was the mailman, also named Jimmy. I guess he was in his late 40s. He was short, dark haired with thick eyebrows, blue eyes and he smoked a pipe.

One day I was serving coffee. The mess sergeant stood close by and, after a while, he said to me, "See the corporal you just poured coffee for? That was his third refill." I looked puzzled. The sergeant continued, "Thing is, this guy does not drink coffee!"

After lunch, I went into the kitchen to eat. I could eat all I wanted and it was wonderful. The food was so good. I ate things I had not seen for years like pineapple, peaches, jam, puddings and more. I particularly remember one meal. The huge cookers were used to prepare boiled beef and carrots. The beef was of the finest quality, tenderloin tips. I ate three deep soup bowls full of beef and carrots followed by two bowls of cling peach halves. I think only a person who has gone without proper food for a very long time can understand how wonderful this meal was to me. When the lunch period was over, the other girls and I cleaned up the dining hall the same way we had done in the morning after breakfast.

Unfortunately, Mama could not partake of these culinary delights. We were not allowed to take anything off the airfield. At the gate house, before boarding our lorry to go back into town, everyone's purse was checked and we were subject to spot-check body searches by female air force personnel.

Almost every day, between meal times, morning or afternoon, several airmen came into the mess hall to talk to me. They were nervous because of the nonfrat order; nevertheless, they came to have a brief chat. They invariably brought me chocolate bars, soap, chewing gum, cigarettes. Each time I refused, saying, "Sorry, I'm not allowed to take things home from here." It was sad because these items were currency on the flourishing black market where they could be translated into food and other necessities.

Even though I refused to accept gifts, that did not mean that the other girls did the same. Every evening, as soon as we were on the lorry and out of the gate, Paula said, "Here, hold my bag open," and she began "unpacking" herself. From somewhere on her body, she produced cakes of soap, bars of chocolate and packets of cigarettes. I marveled because she wore a tight fitting skirt, a more or less see-through navy voile blouse and no stockings. It was a complete mystery to me where she hid these items. I could never detect a bulge on her body.

Sigrid also managed to smuggle things home, mainly bacon. Mama smelled the bacon cooking on numerous occasions and said, "Sigrid manages to bring home the bacon, how about you? Can you do it?" I asked Sigrid and I found out that every day one airman spent a couple of hours in a basement room slicing bacon for 800 men. Strange as it may seem, his name was also Jimmy. Sigrid went to see him while he was thus occupied and asked, "Jimmy, may I have some bacon, please?" Jimmy would say, "I have to go somewhere for 10 minutes," and left the room. Sigrid helped herself and departed before Jimmy returned. One day, I descended into the basement to see Jimmy who, upon my request, promptly departed on his 10 minute errand. I quickly wrapped up a good pound and a half of bacon in some wax paper and left.

On this particular day, I was wearing my woolen dress which fitted me like a second skin. I positioned the wax paper containing the somewhat flattened out bacon around my waist just before I went to the gate where we waited for our lorry to pick us up. I was nervous when I entered the guardhouse and showed my bag for inspection, fearing that I might be called in for a body search.

All went well and I went outside to wait. I stood along a wall inside the gate. There was no shade. The sun was bright, slanting almost horizontally onto my stomach. The temperature was in the high 70s and the lorry was late. Minutes ticked by and it was warm. More minutes elapsed and it got warmer. I grew more nervous and my temperature went up. I was perspiring and not only from the heat. My bacon, exposed to the sun and my body heat, began to exude an enticing aroma. If I could smell it, someone else might, too. I was most uncomfortable, I was very nervous and the lorry was very late. The 15 or 20 minutes I waited seemed like an eternity. Finally, the vehicle arrived and gratefully I climbed aboard. Mama received her bacon but only this one time. I simply could not subject myself to such an ordeal again.

Mama and I were concerned about what was happening in Berlin and about our family. We worried about Kurt, I thought of Steffan, Oma, Papa and Traudchen. We heard that Hitler was dead but I cannot remember when. Mama was happy, except for the fact that he had not been killed years ago.

One of our lorry drivers was a young man called Neil, a 32-year-old Londoner. He looked a lot like Burt Lancaster. One day he boarded the lorry but not as a driver. He was going into town and the girls were teasing him, saying, "Neil has a girlfriend. He is going on a date." At that time all British personnel were required to be armed when they left the base. They carried rifles or sten guns and Neil had a sten gun. By now, a route with several pickup and drop off stops had been established. Sigrid, Paula and I were able to get off very close to our apartment. I had not been home for more than five minutes when somebody noticed that Neil was walking up and down the street outside our apartment house. I heard later that the people in the first floor apartment had become quite agitated seeing an armed soldier repeatedly passing by their window.

I went downstairs and said "Hello," to Neil. He admitted that he had come into town specifically to see me. I invited him in and we spent the evening with Mama, drinking tea. He asked if he could come again and I said yes. Neil came to visit once or twice a week after that.

Airmen still came to the mess hall bearing gifts. I mentioned this to Jimmy, the tea maker, and he suggested that I should give him the stuff. He and Jimmy, the mailman, went to the *Naafi (*a military social club*)* in town several times a week and would bring me my presents. Of course, we could not meet openly in the street. Therefore, we arranged to meet under a railroad bridge on a street leading into town that was usually empty of pedestrians and traffic in the evenings. I took a big shopping bag and when we met I opened it and the two men dropped chocolate, cigarettes and soap into it. It worked well. After a while, Mama suggested that I invite them for a cup of tea. They were very happy to accept. It was a change from the *Naafi* and, from then, on they visited more often. They also came along whenever Neil visited. We played cards and talked.

At that time, there was nothing going on. No cinemas, no television, no dances, no theater, nothing. Mama and I went for walks on weekends when I was off. We had a few new acquaintances. Mama made friends easily. She was also friendly with our landlady, Mrs. Lindner, and soon we spent time visiting her, as well.

When the post office began functioning again, in August 1945, I wrote to Steffan's mother, Mrs. Holst, in Vienna. She replied that Steffan had not come home and that he was reported missing. I visited Vienna in 1960 and called on her. She was a delightful old-fashioned Viennese lady in her 70s. She even wore black lace up boots. She told me that Steffan had been on leave in April 1945. At that time, many soldiers on leave made a point of not returning to their units. They went into hiding. The punishment for those who were caught was death. They were deserters and, therefore, traitors. Mrs. Holst had pleaded with him to go into hiding. However, he declined and was never heard from again. I am still very sad about it.

I am not sure when I moved out and Mama moved upstairs to Mrs. Lindner's apartment. It was a much better arrangement for us. I had a room some distance from Mama with Mrs. Braun, who had no children. She was in her 40s and owned a dog. I occupied her spare bedroom. Celle had suffered only one air raid toward the end of the war and a few windows in the house were broken, including the two top panes in my room. Other than that the apartment was immaculate. If I came in out of the rain, I had to take off my shoes at the apartment door. Whenever she had visitors, she put newspapers or cardboard under their feet before they sat down.

Mrs. Braun's husband was missing in action. They had owned and operated a small business but I cannot recall what it was. The business ceased to operate some time after her husband was called up and Mrs. Braun obtained a cushy office job in the local barracks. She often entertained me with reminiscences of the great times she had during the war. She attended parties at the barracks, where the liquor was flowing and food was plentiful. She did not experience shortages of any kind during the war. Now many of her former friends supplied her with more than the bare necessities. Her dog ate better than I did. She never shared anything with me.

Mama admired the beautiful lace curtains in the windows of a neighbor's house. She met the owner and complimented her on her window treatments. The woman told her that her husband, an officer, had been stationed in Riga, Latvia for a while. She visited him for an extended time and they lived in a requisitioned villa. When she left, she packed up everything that was not nailed down, including the lace curtains, and had it all shipped to Germany by the army. Mama was angry about the way Germans behaved in occupied countries.

Walking through a small park in the center of Celle was quite an experience for a while. It was where the black market flourished. I remember walking through the park on a winter evening, carrying my briefcase. A man sidled up to me and whispered, "What have you got?" I said, "Nothing." "Well, then what are you doing here?" he said rather disgustedly. I did not have anything to trade but occasionally we had cigarettes, which were currency. Mama handled the trading. Money was not worth the paper it was printed on. In Berlin, things were much worse, so I was told by my aunts later on. Years later, when I got married, I remembered Aunt Martha's lovely bone china, which was a hand painted dinner service for 18, including all the serving dishes with lids. I wrote and asked her about it. She replied that right after the war she had traded it away for three loaves of bread.

Late in the fall, Jimmy, the mailman, told me that the RAF Police were looking for a secretary/interpreter. I applied and got the job. It was with a War Crimes Unit and was run by a Sergeant. Three other noncommissioned officers worked with him. We had two displaced men and an ex-concentration camp inmate as interpreters, who accompanied the sergeants when they conducted investigations. The ex-prisoner was Jewish and had been in the concentration camp at Bergen-Belsen until he was liberated by the British.

I realized that taking this job was a mistake because I left the flesh pots of the airfield behind. At the RAF police, I was only provided with a light lunch and nothing else. No one offered me bars of soap, chocolate or cigarettes. Once in a while, men in my department gave me a bar of chocolate but that was all. I was always hungry and drank innumerable cups of tea with a lot of milk and sugar to banish hunger pangs.

It was in Celle that I first heard of the concentration camp called Bergen-Belsen and of the horrible things that had taken place there. Now I heard more. The prison attached to our building housed the notorious "Beast of Belsen," a woman who had tortured and killed inmates. I was told that she had lampshades made from human skin. I found this horribly revolting. I found it impossible to believe that a person could do that to another person. The men in my office talked and laughed about the fact that she requested male visitors. It was obvious she wanted to get pregnant because pregnant women were not executed and she was pretty sure she would receive a death sentence. Our department was not involved in this investigation but one day when two our corporals had to go into the prison they took me along and I had a look at the beast through the glass inset in her prison cell. She was a very ordinary looking woman.

Naturally, all the Nazis were lying low. They had thrown away their party buttons and pretended to know nothing about anything. They were acting like innocent little lambs. I was a stranger in this town and did not know who had been a Nazi and who had not. However, I only needed a few minutes of conversation with a person to know if they had or had not been "brown."

Work at the War Crimes Unit was interesting. Most of the information came from rumors and informers.

Two significant cases were investigated by our unit. The first case involved political prisoners. A number of citizens reported that at the time the town suffered its only air raid, on Sunday, April 8, a train with concentration camp prisoners stood on a side line near the station. The station was the target of the attack. When the bombs began to fall and explode, the terrified prisoners jumped from the train and ran. They were, of course, easily recognizable because they wore prison garb: wide striped black and white pants and jackets. After the raid was over, auxiliary policemen were required to report to the police chief. They were told that dangerous criminals had escaped from the prison train and must be recaptured. Arms were issued and the hunt began.

Information trickled in pointing to people who were involved in the affair. Eventually, the suspects were questioned and arrested. One by one, they were brought from the prison to our office and interrogated. I sat at my desk and listened to the proceedings. When needed, I served as the interpreter.

The story as it emerged was that during that Sunday night following the air raid, the policemen, under the direction of the police chief, went in search of the prisoners. Some prisoners sat near the train or under it, waiting. Others had run from the train to seek cover. When sighted, they were challenged and taken into custody. If the prisoners did not stop, shots were fired. A number of prisoners were wounded or killed on sight, despite the fact that they were stationary.

The prisoners were German political prisoners. This was born out by the insignia on their jackets which marked them as such. The police chief maintained and emphasized to the auxiliary police that these prisoners were dangerous criminals, possibly murderers who must be apprehended at all cost.

One of the men arrested by the British Intelligence was in his 60s. He was bewildered by the proceedings and told us that he had been drafted into the auxiliary police. During his interrogation, he stated that on this particular Sunday he was called out to hunt these prisoners down. He was told that they were dangerous criminals, many of them murderers. During his search, he came upon two prisoners who, upon being challenged, fled. He fired, shot and killed both of them. He was shocked when he was told by the RAF sergeant that these men were unarmed German political prisoners and that, according to international law, he had committed murder and was a war criminal. The thought had never occurred to him. He mentioned that, at the time, he was unhappy about the fact that he had actually killed the men but felt that, in view of what he had been told, he was protecting his community and his family from dangerous criminals. He was deeply affected by the revelation and became very depressed. He was a nice, simple, honest, law-abiding man and citizen. He was not a Nazi.

One morning upon arriving at the office, I was told that the old man had hanged himself during the night. His conscience had troubled him so much about what he had done that he could not bear it. I was left alone to wait for his daughter and break the news to her. It was one of the saddest, most difficult things I ever had to do. I did not know what to say. No words of comfort came to mind. The poor woman was devastated. I felt extremely sad for her.

While this investigation proceeded, information regarding another case came to light involving the murder of a British prisoner of war. Following extensive inquiries, the driver of the military vehicle used to transport the POW was apprehended. He stated that he had been chauffeuring an SS officer when they came upon an army unit that was taking a British Air Force officer to a POW camp. The SS officer demanded that the POW be handed over to his custody. Reluctantly, the army officer complied and the POW climbed into the SS man's vehicle. They drove through a wooded area and the SS officer spoke to the

British officer in English. The driver spoke only German and did not understand what was said. The SS officer ordered the driver to stop, saying that the Englishman had to go "to the bathroom." The POW got out of the vehicle and, followed by the SS officer, walked into the woods. Shortly thereafter, the driver had heard a shot. The SS officer returned and explained that the Englishman tried to escape and he had to shoot him.

The driver helped to bury the body. Now he led the RAF police to the site and the body was exhumed. The postmortem revealed that the POW had been shot in the face at short range. Part of his spine and his lower jaw, which clearly showed that the bullet entered from the front and exited at the back, reposed in a square tin canister on my desk for several months.

The perpetrator who shot the British officer was subsequently apprehended, incarcerated and frequently interrogated. He had joined the Nazis and the SS in the 1920s, before Hitler came to power. As I listened to him, I became more and more infuriated by his arrogance and demeanor. One day while I was interpreting, I became so angry that I gave him a piece of my mind. Of course, he had to listen but it really did not make any difference. The words rolled off him like water off a duck's back but I felt better after letting off steam.

Eventually, he wrote a confession. He wrote it in German script, which people in my office could not read so I translated it. The trial took place in Hannover and I was ordered to attend. During the trial, I waited in a waiting room until I was called. Then I took the stand, swore on a Bible that the evidence I was about to give would be the truth, the whole truth and nothing but the truth. There was something in the oath at the beginning about omnipotent and omniscient. I practiced the pronunciation beforehand so as to do it correctly in court. I was handed the original confession and asked to read it out loud one sentence at a time. After I read, the court interpreter repeated the same sentence from my translation to make sure the translation was correct. It was. Then I left the court. The SS officer was convicted, sentenced to death and executed.

Sometime in 1946, a couple of sergeants and one or two of our interpreters from our department had to go to Berlin for some reason although I cannot remember why. They took Father's address and said they would try to visit. I was very excited when they returned. They brought a suitcase full of clothes, as well as a photo of Father and Aunt Marga. I was very happy and they were ecstatic to know that Mama and I were all right. Things in Berlin had been terrible and were still far from good.

After I had left Berlin in April and the fighting began, Father and Aunt Marga spent 11 days and nights in the basement in the dark, with all the other tenants, without electricity or flashlights. After the bombardment, which took out most of the wall of our living room, Soviet troops searched the house repeatedly because some ruthless SS troops and Volkssturm still put up resistance. After a while, the Soviets allowed a few tenants to go upstairs to check the house and their apartments. Mr. Becker and another tenant, a former schoolmate of Mama's who lived in the next building, were among them. While they were upstairs and unbeknown to them, a number of German soldiers entered the building and opened fire on the Soviets when they emerged from the basement. Consequently, the Soviets shot every civilian and German soldier on sight. Unfortunately, Mr. Becker and the other man were shot. At the time, no one in the basement knew what had happened. After a considerable time, someone else was allowed upstairs and found their bodies hanging over the bannister. I felt it was a grave injustice of fate that Mr. Becker was killed.

Soviet searches continued for days. They entered the basement and shined their flashlights into everyone's face. The first troops that were thrown into the battle of Berlin were Mongolian. They had not been granted leave for three or four years. They were considered expendable, uncivilized and wild. Our neighbor, a war widow in her 30s, was raped on her kitchen table. A widow in her late 50s was also raped. Parents hid their daughters by rolling them in blankets and sitting on them.

One woman was afraid and became hysterical because her husband was a party member. She killed her child and then she jumped from a balcony to her death. By the time the fighting was over, 11 people were buried in our apartment house yard.

Soviet troops occupied the first and second floor of the building, including our apartment. These men had no knowledge of indoor plumbing. They washed potatoes in the toilet, flushed it and then wondered what happened to the potatoes. The apartment was a mess after they left.

The troops looted, raped and pilfered. Radio cars with loudspeakers blaring drove through the streets warning people to stay in hiding until these troops were withdrawn from the city. They left dragging everything imaginable with them on trucks, even rows of seats from cinemas. As a result of the rapes, incidents of venereal disease rose.

During the bombardment of Berlin, many people had taken refuge in the subway tunnels. When the first Soviet troops reached the subway terminals, they used them to escape detection. When the SS realized what was happening, they flooded the subway by blowing up water mains. In the process, thousands of civilians, old people, women and children, drowned. Later on, ex-Nazis were put to work cleaning up the mess. For years afterwards, the U-Bahn tunnels retained a dank smell. It smelled when I was there in 1947. In some stations, it lingered longer and I still detected it on a visit in 1953.

Berlin's infrastructure was destroyed. There was no gas, no electricity and no food. The water was contaminated. A typhoid and dysentery epidemic raged in Berlin. When I visited Mother's grave for the first time, I noticed that practically all the graves near her and beyond were those of people who died within days of each other, including entire families. My friend Ursula, I found out later, fell victim to this disease. She was 19 years old.

People had to fetch water from special distributing centers every day. One day, Aunt Martha went to fetch the water. When she returned home, she found that Uncle Gustav had passed away. There were no resources available for burials and she was lucky that she found a coffin. However, there were no nails. She had to go around and ask people for nails.

At this time, Aunt Marga suffered a nervous breakdown. Our dear Dr. Baumann walked half an hour each way every day to make a house call, although he himself was not well, and saved her life.

Berlin casualties from air raids alone were approximately 600,000. It was the most bombed city in Germany with 6,340 acres destroyed and 47 percent of the dwellings destroyed and/or uninhabitable. Harry Hopkins, a personal friend of Franklin D. Roosevelt, on his way to Moscow on May 25, 1945 commented, "Berlin is a second Carthage."

All the rubble from the Berlin ruins was later sorted through by hand for usable bricks. The rest was carted away by the so called *"Truemmerfrauen,"* or wreckage women, who worked at this backbreaking job for 57 pfennig per hour. My former school friend, Kirsten, worked as a wreckage woman for a while because there was no other work available. A little later, the pay was increased to 61 pfennig an hour. Today, two hills in Berlin bear witness to their labors. One hill, called the Insulaner, has a observatory on its summit.

Here and there, we heard about and saw returning German soldiers. One of our neighbor's husband came home one day and jubilation reigned. She played the piano for hours in celebration. Later on, I saw a few soldiers return who had been prisoners of the Russians. I could not believe that they were actually young men, probably not even 35 years old, mostly younger. They looked like 70, emaciated, sick and broken.

So far, we had not heard from Kurt. When we did, we were told that he had been wounded and had been in a military hospital for some time and a convalescent home afterwards. Apparently, he had been hit by shrapnel that almost severed his left hand. He could count himself extremely lucky that the doctor who treated him did not amputate but did everything he could to save the hand. It never functioned normally again. Kurt wore a bandage or a support and suffered discomfort and pain from it most of his life.

Mama's apartment was badly bomb damaged. Homeless people had been quartered in the apartment but were gone by the time Kurt returned.

After things settled down a little, we found out how Germany had been divided by the Allies into different occupation zones. Refugees were anxious to return home but Mama was not keen on returning to Berlin. Berlin was divided into four sectors: British, French, American and Russian. However, Berlin was isolated from the British, American and French Zones of Germany because it was situated in the middle of the Russian occupation zone, like an island in a red sea. Access routes were established but the situation was very unnatural. The border between the Russian, British, French and American Zones was open. There were no demarcation lines or, at most, very improvised ones and some check points. The border was patrolled on each side, more so on the Soviet side. Soon people began crossing back and forth, taking a chance that they would not be caught. It was called black crossing and the chance included the risk of being shot on sight. In the beginning, it was fairly easy to cross. As time went on, the demarcation and fortification of the border increased making crossing more difficult and dangerous. Many people were shot.

At some point, an Inter-Zonal train to Berlin was established.

I felt uprooted. I did not want to return to Berlin because I did not like being surrounded by Soviets and I did not like the thought of a divided city. For many years after the war, even as

575

late as the 1970s, I had nightmares about being captured by the Soviets. Now I really was at a loss about what to do next. It is always difficult in a new place to get to know the locals and, as a refugee, I had little chance of gaining entry into their community. I had no contact with them other than Mrs. Braun, Mrs. Lindner and Sigrid's mother. However, they had no social life, either, and were not involved in any activities. I led a day-to-day survival existence and I felt suspended in a kind of limbo. What next? I was very interested in everything British so I began reading British newspapers and magazines. England was fascinating because it was so very different from Nazi Germany. But again, I felt I did not belong. I was German, not British. I was uncomfortable with many Germans because of the immediate past and also because I did not want to be associated with people who had in any way been tainted with brown. I was not very happy.

There was not much to do for fun in my spare time. I took English literature lessons from a retired professor to improve my English.

The Allies realized after a while that it was impossible, even ridiculous, to keep up the nonfraternization law and it was rescinded. British troops held dances in various places so I went with Sigrid and Paula to some of them. I was taken to some of the British movie shows that were put on for the troops. I heard the latest musical hits and saw a number of movies including "Rebecca."

I celebrated my 21st birthday on December 21, 1946. My one and only present was three apples. Everyone was nice but it was not a special day.

That winter was fierce. I spent the evenings with Mama, sitting around the stove in Mrs. Lindner's kitchen, and went back home at 9 p.m. before the curfew started. My room was extremely cold. It could not be heated and two panes at the top of the windows were missing. Cardboard replaced them. I went to bed dressed in pajamas, socks, a cardigan, scarf, dressing gown and a hat. I wrapped myself in a blanket up to my armpits and slept under a feather bed. Some time later, I moved back to Mama's place.

In Spring 1947, I ventured to Berlin on the Inter-Zonal train because I was afraid to try to cross the border illegally. The train was very crowded. I stood on the platform of the carriage for the entire trip, with many other people. One of them was holding a huge basket containing some evil smelling homemade cheese right under my nose. It was horrible. At the check point between the British and the Russian Zones, we were ordered to disembark with our luggage. We had to line up under the auspices of armed Russian soldiers and proceed through a hut where some Russians sat at tables and checked our papers. They made us open our luggage before they allowed us to board the train again. It took three hours or longer before the train was able to resume its journey.

Berlin was drab. I could not believe the damage I saw, although by now it had been tidied up to a certain extent. People looked haggard and worn out. I did not stay very long but picked up some more of my belongings and returned to Celle.

The winter of 1945/46 and the winter of 1946/47 were terrible. Temperatures dropped well below zero. We received only a minute ration of coal, insufficient to heat the apartment. Mrs. Lindner had another woman and her daughter staying with her. All of us huddled around a small potbelly stove in the kitchen. Electricity was only available for a short time every day and evening. We sat by the light of one or two candles.

The bread we were issued was weird. I don't know of what it was made. I would not be surprised if it contained wood shavings. It was also very wet and we placed the slices on top of the stove until they dried out and were at least edible, though not palatable.

Many people went into the countryside and bartered with the farmers. We did not go because we had nothing with which to barter. I heard stories about farmers getting rich by selling food on the black market. A joke at the time was that farmers covered the floors of their cow sheds with oriental rugs. Another one went like this: A pastor preached one Sunday morning in his country church. He was upset because he had found out that a city woman had come to the village and given her wedding ring to a farmer in exchange for a small amount of food. The pastor was appalled and appealed to the farmer to return the ring. He said, "Simply place the ring in the collection plate." When the collection plate was emptied, eight wedding rings rolled out.

When an opportunity to go to England presented itself I took it and left Germany in December 1947.

I lived in a business girls' residence on Southampton Row in London where I met and made friends with a number of girls.

For holidays, I received invitations from the girls' parents, although they had never met me. In the summer, I was invited to spend a week with my friend Grace's parents in Hereford. Her mother called some of Grace's girlfriends and asked them to come and meet me. One of them, Phyllis Morris, invited me to her home for tea on the following Tuesday. I met her outside the post office where she worked and we rode our bicycles to her house.

This is an essay I wrote later for my English class at Pennsylvania State University in 1987:

Tea with the Enemy

We parked our bikes in the garden and entered the house by the back door. It was very quiet, the kitchen empty. Sunshine streamed through the window where a solitary fly buzzed frantically in an attempt to find a way out. Had it not been for the tea kettle humming softly on the stove, I would have thought nobody was at home.

"Come on," Phyllis prodded me ahead of her into the dining room.

Her parents and her younger sister, Vivien, were seated at the beautifully set tea table. Silver on white linen complimented the bone china, reflecting the pastel shades of the fresh flower centerpiece.

"Hello, everybody," said Phyllis, "here we are. This is Gisela, Grace's friend."

Looking back so many years, I cannot recall much of the conversation during our meal. But the atmosphere became friendly and relaxed. Everyone was trying to put me at ease and make me feel at home. At that time, I was almost painfully shy and timid when meeting strangers. No doubt my hosts noticed it.

I do remember, however, Mr. Morris saying, "I have an old German Bible and a pair of Leica binoculars. After tea, I would like to show them to you. You might find them interesting.

"First I want to show her the garden and my room," announced Vivien.

"Yes, we want to go into the garden before it starts getting dark," added Mrs. Morris. "If you all help clear the table, it will be a great time-saver." A few minutes later, we trooped into the garden where I admired the really beautiful roses. "Roses flourish especially well here," remarked Mr. Morris. "I think it is due mainly to the climate and the almost complete absence of pests." Later, I was shown the rest of the house. In his upstairs study, Mr. Morris produced the Bible and the binoculars.

"An elderly German lady I knew years ago gave them to me," he explained. "I took care of some legal matters for her and she wanted to show her appreciation by giving me something that obviously meant a lot to her." I looked at the Bible for a few moments and then picked up the binoculars.

"These binoculars are really sharp." I focused on the cathedral quite some distance away. The intricate details on the town were brought up so clearly, looking close enough to be touched.

"Of course, Leica is, was, one of, if not the finest maker in the world of precision instruments like this. Pity, but they are in the east now."

I returned the binoculars.

Time passed quickly and pleasantly until I said my good-byes. I mounted my bicycle ready to go, leaving the Morris family standing on their front lawn waving me off amid admonitions to ride carefully.

Saturday morning, Phyllis and I were sitting across from each other in the express train going to London. I was returning from my vacation and she was going in search of a job.

"You know I will be visiting my aunt and uncle in Hastings tomorrow," she said, "but you are going with me. My father gave me the money for your fare to make sure you can come along."

I was speechless and I must have looked quite surprised. After all, Mr. Morris had been a perfect stranger to me until a few days ago.

"How very kind of your father," I finally managed to say.

Phyllis chuckled. "Well, I think it is okay for me to tell you now: when I came home last Saturday after having tea with you at Grace's house, I told my parents that I had invited you for tea. My father got really upset and kicked up a fuss. He said, 'No bloody German is going to set foot in my house.'"

Ach du lieber! (Oh boy!) This time I was really shocked. I sat staring at her and then, suddenly and simultaneously, we burst into peals of laughter.

That was England, late spring 1948.

The first time I visited Germany after moving to England was in 1953. During this visit, I learned from Mama what had happened to my childhood friends. Guenter did not return from the war but she did not know what actually happened to him. Another boy who lived in Mama's apartment building and was my age was also lost.

Dieter, my gentle friend, with his blue eyes and beautiful blond wavy hair, who had never once been out of Berlin on a vacation or away from home, was called up five days after his 16th birthday in 1944. Dieter's mother told me that Dieter was sent to the eastern front. His unit was commanded by former HJ leaders who were promoted to officers in the field. They were fanatic and instead of retreating west they led their units into battle. Dieter was taken prisoner by the Soviets. He died of starvation in a Russian prisoner of war camp somewhere in Russia shortly before or shortly after his 17th birthday. The camp doctor (a woman) even gave him some of her food but it was too late for he was far too weak. One of his comrades survived and visited Dieter's mother.

When I think of him, I grieve and I remember a conversation we had one day when we were out on the street playing. He said, "I wonder if we will see the year two thousand?" I said, "Why not?" We figured out how old we would be by that time. I often think of this now.

582

A Year's Celebrations and Events

New Year's Day was, and still is, an official holiday in Germany. Many people slept late after celebrating well past midnight or into the early hours of the morning. In my day, it was a day of leisure, reflection on the preceding year, and for making plans and resolutions for the coming year. The afternoon and evening was spent with friends or relatives. Candles on the Christmas tree were lit one last time. Their soft glow created a mellow, relaxing atmosphere and mood.

Florists, open for a few hours in the morning as always on Sunday and holidays, sold tiny pots of four leaf clover wrapped in gold foil and decorated with good luck symbols: stick pins of pigs, golden horseshoes, chimney sweeps and *Fliegenpilze* (toadstools with a white stem and a red cap with small white dots). We presented these good luck tokens to friends, relatives and acquaintances when making New Year's calls. Other gifts were marzipan pigs with gold covered chocolate coins in their snouts, small nets filled with gold and silver covered chocolate coins, foil covered four leaf clovers and other chocolate novelties. If one could not call in person, New Year's cards were sent.

On January 2, it was back to business as usual.

Fasching, or carnival, was celebrated elaborately and vigorously in the predominantly Roman Catholic Rhineland, climaxing in huge fancy dress parades on Rose Monday and Shrove Tuesday. I listened to the live radio coverage of these events broadcast from Cologne and Mainz.

Appendix

Berlin had no such parades. We had Bock Beer Festivals and masked balls. The Bock Beer Festivals were big beer parties, Bavarian style, where people drank the dark, strong Bock beer brewed especially and only at this time of year. Masked balls were held at restaurants, hotels and dance halls prior to Ash Wednesday. These balls were great fun. Mama and my aunts discussed them excitedly. Groups of people, relatives and/or friends planned to attend a certain ball, all wearing fancy dress and masks, but arriving separately. Everyone kept his/her disguise a secret. The fun part and object was to mingle with the crowd, try to find and identify the other members of your party and unmask them before midnight. At midnight, all masks came off. If a guest managed to avoid recognition until then, they were proud.

Passion and Palm Sunday were traditionally the Sundays when the Rite of Confirmation took place in Protestant churches. Protestant boys and girls were confirmed at the age of 14 after attending confirmation instruction the preceding year.

Good Friday was, and still is, an official holiday in Germany. All the shops were closed, even the florists. Churches held special services. Only serious classical music was broadcast on the radio until 6 p.m. And cinemas programmed serious drama. People dressed in dark or black clothing and the day was spent very quietly. We always ate fish for dinner and no meat at other meals.

Easter Saturday saw crowds of shoppers buying traditional Easter candy, clothing and hats. Department stores decorated their windows with spring and Easter merchandise and symbols connected with this special time of the year. There were animated bunnies, ducks, dwarfs and flowers set in imaginary landscapes. The Easter Bunny was portrayed in his workshop painting Easter eggs, assisted by many little helpers, or hiding eggs in a garden. Spring fashions adorned by spring millinery graced other windows. Confectioners displayed gorgeous assortments of Easter confections, ranging from jelly bean eggs to large chocolate eggshells wrapped in gold, silver, purple, pink or pale blue foil decorated with satin bows, sprigs of silk spring flowers and catkins and filled with delectable chocolates. Easter bunnies came in all sizes, plain or milk chocolate, foil wrapped or plain. They wore bows and little bells around their necks. Some carried egg filled baskets on their backs. Easter eggs came in various sizes, solid or hollow, filled with or made of marzipan. There were baby chicks of yellow sugar crusted fondant or marshmallow, dipped partly in chocolate to represent a remnant of adhering eggshell. There were chocolate boats, cars, canoes and many more novelties to delight children and adults.

Easter Sunday brought early morning surprises and excitement because it was time to search for Easter eggs. Mine were hidden in our living room.

The two holidays, Easter Sunday and Easter Monday, were spent much the same each year. On Easter Sunday morning, I visited Oma, Opa and Papa. Oma and Opa did not hide my eggs but gave me a few to take home. On Easter afternoons, we went visiting or walked in the zoo and had coffee in one of the many cafes.

Flowers associated with and given at Easter were tulips, daffodils, primroses, violets, narcissus and twigs of cherry or

Appendix

peach blossoms. For Pentecost and Mother's Day, we gave lilacs, early roses and peonies.

After Hitler came to power, May 1st became an official paid holiday. For me, it was just another day off to be spent leisurely in the usual Sunday fashion. Nobody in my family attended any of the rallies that took place before or after Hitler came to power except Kurt, who was ordered to attend with his colleagues from Scherl.

Mother's Day, which had been observed on the second Sunday in May, was moved to the third Sunday in May after Hitler came to power. On that day, celebrations were arranged by the regime to present the Mother's Cross to women, usually at a Nazi party meeting hall.

On Mother's Day, I went to the florist first thing in the morning and purchased bouquets for Mother and Mama. Sometimes I also bought Mama a small gift of handkerchiefs, perfume, soap or a vase. We did not have greeting cards for Mother's Day. In fact, greeting cards for birthdays and holidays, like Easter, Pentecost, Christmas and New Year, came in the form of postcards.

Ascension Day, ten days before Pentecost, was traditionally "Men's Day" and was celebrated with "Men Only" parties. Early in the morning, groups of men gathered and departed together in open lorries or horse drawn wagons, decorated with garlands of green crepe paper streamers and signs reading "Away from Women!" Each conveyance had at least one musician on board, an accordion or violin player, because singing was an integral part of the fun and created the right mood for merrymaking and hilarities. More often than not, the truck or wagon carried a

Appendix

barrel of beer. The destination was usually a garden restaurant in the Grunewald or other suburban area, where the men spent the day singing, eating, drinking and playing cards. They returned at various times in the evening in various stages of inebriation. All was in good fun. Seldom did people exceed the limits of good behavior. Other people spent the day taking walks, visiting friends, going to cafes or to the zoo.

On the Saturday before Pentecost, small birch trees, in a pail of water, appeared outside all pubs and restaurants. It was also the season for the Maikaefer *(Melolontha vulgaris* or cockchafer.)* It is large European beetle and a cute bug. Actually, these bugs were a pest because the larva lived underground, feeding on the roots of crops. Every fourth year, in the so-called Maikaefer Year, they appeared in extremely large numbers. Mother and Father told me how, in the country many years ago, children went out early in the morning when it was still cool and damp and spread sacks under the trees. They then shook the trees so the bugs fell off. They wrapped them up and took them to be ground into fertilizer. Pet shops in Berlin sold cockchafers for 10 pfennig each. Some had black legs, others had reddish legs. I kept mine in a glass or in a cigar box with birch leaves until I set them free.

Confectioners produced a great variety of chocolate Maikaefer in all sizes, plain and fancy. Big ones with raised gold foil covered wings had assorted chocolates and pralines hidden away under them. Dainty transparent yellow and purple silk ribbons decorated these creations, together with sprigs of silk primroses, violets, catkins and birch leaves.

Appendix

We had two holidays, Pentecostal Sunday and Pentecostal Monday. Open air restaurants attracted customers with early morning band concerts, and an early happy hour. The zoo was famous for its traditional early morning Pentecost concert which hundreds of people made a point of attending every year.

Pentecost was the last long weekend before summer vacations began. Our summer vacations varied in length from year to year, lasting from four to seven weeks.

Sundays were sometimes dull. Like most children, I was not allowed to go out and play. I dressed in my Sunday clothes and whiled away the time by reading, going for walks with Mama or Father and Mother, or visiting relatives or friends, or going to the movies. Often, Mama's and Kurt's friends visited them. We had afternoon coffee at home or went to a café near the Charlottenburg Castle or at the Kurfuersten Damm. In the summer, we walked to a garden restaurant. Every spring, we went to Sanssouci in Potsdam when the pink magnolias were in bloom. This was a tradition, as was the annual trip to view the fruit tree blossoms in the suburb of Werder. Father and I walked in the Tiergarten on Sunday mornings, where we watched equestrians. We went to the Grunewald or the Wannsee, a large lake with a long bathing beach, or to the zoo.

Aunt Marga and I made many excursions into the Mark Brandenburg, sometimes taking a tiny railway train called "Little Hermann," which left from the Hermannstrasse station. I got to know and love many parts of the province surrounding Berlin as a result of these day trips. Brandenburg is an interesting place with a variety of landscapes, many historical places and stories about them.

Appendix

Beginning in May and throughout the summer, steamers began plying the Berlin waterways. Their destinations were the various lakes on the east side and west side of Berlin but most of them began their trips in the center of town. We took several trips every summer. It was very pleasant to glide along the canals and the river Spree on the way to the lakes. Passengers disembarked at the destination of their choice. Along the shore, beginning in Treptow, restaurants lined the water front. We picked a destination, mostly one of the lakes east of Berlin, and usually stayed in the restaurant where the steamer docked. Many people took long walks through the woods and countryside to reach another inn or restaurant. They returned to the landing stage in time to catch the steamer or returned to the city by rail.

The restaurant gardens were large and shaded by old, tall trees. The restaurants offered delicious sheet cakes, cut into large rectangular pieces and served with whipped cream, such as *Bienenstich*. *Bienenstich* is a sheet cake with a yeast base. For the topping, one melts butter, sugar, milk and vanilla. To this mixture, one adds chopped almonds, lets it get cold and then spreads it on the dough before baking. There were butter cakes, streusel and cheese cakes or, in season, fresh apple, plum, cherry and blueberry cakes. A peculiarity in those days was that restaurants advertised: "Here families can brew coffee." In fact, that is what many families and groups did. They brought their own coffee and simply paid for boiling water and rented the coffee pots, cups, saucers and plates. We never took anything and we did not make our own coffee. We found a table along the waterfront or under a nice tree and ordered what we wanted. Almost all restaurants had an orchestra that played all afternoon

Appendix

and in the evenings. It was relaxing and enjoyable to sit by the water, watch boats and steamers glide by, listen to the music, and chat with family and friends.

Children were catered to by Uncle Pelle, a kind of clown whose job it was to keep the children amused. When evening came, the gardens were illuminated with small lanterns strung from tree to tree. Each child was handed a candle lantern on a stick. The candles were lit and, while the orchestra played a lively march, Uncle Pelle led the children on a march weaving between and around the tables. At certain times, the steamers called on their way back to Berlin. We embarked and enjoyed the trip back through the warm starlit night.

Occasionally, Mama, Kurt and I visited the huge Treptow fairground, which attracted thousands of people. Rows upon rows of tents, carousels, shooting galleries, side shows, animal tamers, magicians and wheels of fortune attracted scores of Berliners. Every Wednesday, Saturday and Sunday night, Treptow was "in flames", as the ad stated, because hour long spectacular fireworks illuminated the sky. I was even able to see them from Mama's balcony. Before I went on my first visit to Treptow, I remember Mama telling me about this wonderful place and a wonderful train ride through fairyland. My imagination ran away with me and I imagined something magical. When I finally saw it, my disappointment was immense. The train was a small carousel and all it had was paintings of some fairy-tale characters on the inside, which we passed again and again while riding around and around.

The Berlin Zoological Gardens were officially opened on August 1, 1844 and was Germany's first and the world's ninth

Appendix

zoo. By 1939, the Berlin Zoo was the most outstanding one in the world with approximately 4,000 mammals and birds. The equally famous aquarium housed 8,300 reptiles, amphibians, fish and invertebrates, with more than 750 species.

Berliners loved their zoo and visited it frequently. Many people had season tickets and had "pet" animals they visited regularly. Bands on several band stands provided musical entertainment for visitors who wanted to sit, rest, listen, take refreshments or promenade to the sound of familiar and popular tunes. A number of restaurants offered anything from snacks to full course meals. I visited the zoo at least two or three times a year and once on a school field trip. The Aquarium was great. I particularly liked the large tropical forest in a hot house with a bridge leading over some muddy water where crocodiles and alligators lay in the mud. I also loved the huge fish tanks lining the walls of the first floor, with many colorful tropical species. Reptiles were exhibited on the second and insects on the third floor.

After summer vacation was over, we celebrated Harvest Home Sunday in September. Decorations for this day were stalks of rye or wheat, poppies, cornflowers (bachelor buttons) and white daisies.

Protestants observed Reformation Day on October 30, the Eve of All Saints' Day. Reformation Day was an official holiday in Berlin and churches held special services.

Two solemn days took place in November: Repentance and Penitence Day, an official holiday in Berlin, and a Memorial Sunday for the Dead. The radio played only serious music and cinemas showed dramas. Many theaters and other places of

Appendix

entertainment were closed. There was no dancing. People dressed in black or other dark colors and visited the cemeteries to decorate the graves of loved ones with sprays, pillows and blankets made from all natural plant materials, like grey and green mosses, berries, pine cones and catkins. These would remain on the graves throughout the winter. Remembrance services were held in the churches.

Immediately thereafter, Advent wreaths appeared in the florists' shop windows. They hung on wires strung across the window and came in all sizes. They were tied with long gold or silver ribbons that ended in a bow and a hanger so they could be suspended from the ceiling light over a living room or over a dining room table. Candles were white, golden yellow or red. People added other decorations, if they so desired. Our wreath was suspended from the ceiling light in the living room or simply placed on the table. On Advent Sundays, we took our afternoon coffee by candlelight.

Most children were given Advent calendars before December 1 and I would fasten mine to the kitchen window. Every morning, I opened a little window in the calendar revealing a transparent picture of some Christmas related item, such as a toy, a candle or an angel, until finally only one, the biggest, most important, remained: December 24, the Nativity Scene. In later years, I received more elaborate Advent Calendars made of cloth and embroidered. They had little rings or pockets containing a candy or a miniature chocolate bar for each day.

The evening of December 5, or the eve of St. Nicolas Day, held a special meaning for children. Before going to bed, children put one shoe outside the door (in the case of apartment living, like in Berlin, they put their shoe just inside the apartment door). During the night, St. Nicolas made his rounds and filled the shoe with a foretaste of Christmas. I was always eager to rush to the door in the morning to see what the good Saint had left. Mostly I found a chocolate St. Nicolas, some foil covered chocolate Christmas tree ornaments, candy, cookies and, on several occasions, a red ceramic boot filled with chocolate novelties.

The Christmas season was enchanting. All the department stores decorated their windows elaborately and offered special shows in their toy departments. Everything was different each year. Scenes were from different fairy tales or one particular fairy tale, winter outdoor activities, Santa's workshop, Dr. Doolittle and a visit to a zoo with stuffed and animated wild animals. Visitors followed along a rope from one showcase to the next and the only illumination came from the display, thus creating a greater impact. Evening comes early in December. When there was a low cloud ceiling, which was the case most of the time, it would begin to get dark soon after four in the afternoon and the window displays were especially attractive after dark.

In Berlin, the sale of fresh Christmas trees began traditionally on December 11. The dealers roped off streets at main intersections and in city squares to display rows upon rows of trees. It was like walking through a pine forest and I deeply inhaled the scented air. Choosing a tree was a serious matter. It could take quite some time with the dealer bringing out and turning several trees for the customer's inspection. He praised his merchandise and pointed out the tree's good features. The chosen tree was carried home and placed on the balcony to keep fresh.

Simultaneously with the Christmas trees, the Christmas markets made their appearance. Vendors put up trestle tables at the edge of the sidewalk bordering the road, which were covered over with tarpaulin creating an alley between them and the house fronts. Christmas markets only came to life at dusk. Kerosene lamps hissed, shedding their strange cold bluish light. The vendors huddled behind their counters dressed in big felt boots, thick layers of jackets, coats, scarves, hoods and gloves with cut off fingers. Kerosene heaters provided extra comfort. It was an enchanting and magical little world to wander through where unusual sounds and aromas filled the air.

Only Christmas related items, such as Christmas tree decorations, hand blown glass ornaments, tinsel and candles, were sold at some stands. Gingerbread men and gingerbread hearts, decorated and inscribed with "I love you" in white, pastel pink, blue or red icing, were at others. Names could be inscribed on them and the hearts had red ribbons so they could be hung around the neck. Candy makers plied their trade, watched by an admiring crowd of adults and children. Other stands offered noisemakers, wooden rattles and simple toys dyed in bright shades of pink, yellow and green. The wonderful aroma of sugar burned almonds, roasted chestnuts and *Gluehwein,* red wine heated with spices, made one's mouth water.

The ever popular long Vienna sausages were available. A man called *Wurst Maxe* (Hot Dog Max), attired in his traditional garb of black and white checkered pants, white chef's jacket, hat

Appendix

and apron, plied his trade. He carried a large shiny stainless steel container around his neck. It was filled with hot water and a small kerosene flame kept it hot. A tall metal spike attached to it held the hot dogs, which he put into the water as needed. Hot dogs were served on an oblong paper plate with a dab of mustard and a small piece of crisp roll. A *Wurst Maxe* could be found plying his trade any evening along the main streets and in city squares.

Stores always remained closed on Sunday. However, on the two Sundays preceding Christmas Eve, called Silver Sunday and Golden Sunday, stores opened at 8 or 9 a.m. and remained open until 5 p.m. I believe there might have been a third Sunday when the shops were open, the Bronze Sunday. I only ever heard about the Silver and Gold Sundays. On Christmas Eve, businesses closed at 2 or 3 p.m. to give everybody a chance to get ready for the Christmas Eve celebrations.

On Christmas Eve, Father and Mother were busy. The Christmas tree was brought into the living room, tried out for size, and trimmed, if necessary, put into its stand and set up in the corner near one of the living room windows. Before decorating the tree, Father screwed long-stemmed iron candle holders into the tree trunk at strategic places so as to prevent branches above the lighted candles catching fire. The tree was decorated with white candles and single strands of tinsel, carefully hung on the branches to look like a veil of silver. Next came Mother's old hand blown glass ornaments, which had decorated their trees over the decades. In addition, there were foil covered chocolate ornaments.

Appendix

Our tree always stood on a low table. On the table were cardboard Christmas plates, fluted or star shaped, filled with ginger breads, chocolate pretzels, mixed nuts, apples, oranges, mandarin oranges and chocolates. Everyone had his or her own plate and ate its contents whenever he or she felt like it. I mention this because normally we did not eat between meals. We kept strictly to mealtimes. I was not allowed to go into the kitchen and help myself to food any time I felt like it.

At about 7 p.m., the family gathered at Father and Mother's apartment. We stood outside the living room until Mother opened the door revealing the Christmas tree in all its glory. Until I was 6 years old, we waited for the *Weihnachtsmann*. I was always nervous, pacing up and down, listening for the sound of the doorbell which heralded the arrival of this important personage. Soon enough, it happened.

When I was very small, I learned a simple verse that I had to recite when the *Weihnachtsmann* (Also called *Knecht Ruprecht. Knecht Ruprecht* is the faithful servant of the Christ Child. It is actually the Christ Child who gives gifts and he is accompanied by *Knecht Ruprecht*, who carries the sack containing the presents.) came to call. I dressed in my best velvet dress and my patent leather shoes. The family was gathered in the living room. I was fidgety and on edge because, any moment now, the door bell would ring and *Knecht Ruprecht* would come in, dressed in his brown hooded cowl belted with a rope. His hood hid his face except for part of his grey beard. He carried the two traditional items: a *Rute*, which is a bunch of birch twigs, to chastise naughty and unrepentant children, if necessary, and a sack that, I hoped, contained gifts and toys.

Appendix

When the apartment door was opened and before *Knecht Ruprecht* entered the apartment, I could hear his deep voice asking, "Are there any children here?" Then he came into the living room, spotted me and remarked, "Ah, yes, there you are! What is your name?" Now was the time for me to say my little verse, "Dear *Weihnachtsmann*, don't look at me so sternly, put away your *Rute*, I promise to be always good," which in German rhymes. I had to submit to questions and admonitions from the Christ Child's faithful servant. "Have you been a good and obedient girl this year?" he asked. "Have you caused your grandparents heartaches. Have you been polite to everybody? I heard you did not always eat your dinner and you answered back when Mother told you to do something. Are you sorry you misbehaved? Well, go and apologize and promise not to be naughty again." I had to go to Father and Mother and apologize for any and all misbehavior. Then *Knecht Ruprecht* admonished, "Behave yourself at all times so I need not chide you next year." He grumbled into his beard but, nevertheless, he relented and one by one he began taking gifts from his sack. I thanked him and curtsied. Blessing one and all and wishing all of us a "Very Merry Christmas and a Happy New Year," the *Weihnachtsmann* departed.

When I was older and *Knecht Ruprecht* stopped calling, I had to memorize a longer Christmas poem and recite it on Christmas Eve. I was always glad when I had finished.

My ordeal was over and now the fun could begin. First, we sang several Christmas carols including my favorite at the time, "The candles burn on the Christmas tree." I liked this song because it told of two invisible angels entering the room. They

Appendix

go to the tree and pray, then, facing the people, they pronounce a blessing upon them, turn and depart. It appealed to me. After singing "Silent Night," I could finally look at my presents, which had been hidden by a cloth under the tree. The adults exchanged presents and there was much excitement as gifts were unwrapped and admired. I played with my new toys until it was time to gather once again around the tree to sing carols. A repast of coffee and Mother's wonderful butter streusel cake followed before everybody went home.

Years later, I found out that it was Uncle Gustav who impersonated *Knecht Ruprecht*. I never noticed his absence from the assembled company, simply because he was in the habit of taking a nap after work and often arrived late for family gatherings.

Christmas school holidays began a few days before December 24 so I spent that day as much as possible outside, especially if there was already snow on the ground and I could go sledding or skating. Snow fell often well before Christmas and I remember that it also snowed many times on Christmas Eve.

Our traditional Christmas Eve dinner was a simple one and was eaten earlier than usual. It consisted of pork, kale and boiled potatoes.

We observed two holidays, the First Christmas Day and the Second Christmas Day. The morning of the First Christmas Day was busy indeed. The Christmas goose was prepared and roasted in Mother's oven. I visited Oma, Opa, Papa and my aunts Frieda and Trudchen but I did not eat my dinner with them. Oma and Opa's tree was inevitably decorated with tinsel, candles, sugar

Appendix

and chocolate ornaments. I was allowed to eat a few of the ornaments off the tree. They usually made up a Christmas plate for me, which I packed up and took home with me. As far as presents were concerned, I do not recall receiving any except once when Aunt Frieda gave me a box with three handkerchiefs.

The afternoon and evening found the family at Aunt Martha's apartment enjoying afternoon coffee. Aunt Martha's tree was always a blue spruce, reaching from the floor to the ceiling, and decorated with tinsel, white candles and blue and silver Christmas balls. Afterwards, the grown-ups sat around, talked and occasionally played a game of cards while I played by myself. Sometimes I was allowed to help Aunt Martha prepare supper.

After supper, we sat around the table and played games like "I am a musician and come from Swabia." One person sang, "I am a musician from Swabia." Everybody answered, "We are musicians from Swabia." It went on, "I can play," "We can play," "On the piano," "On the piano" "Play on the right, play on the left, and in the middle, too." This way we went through a number of instruments, such as violin, trumpet or drums, and so on, each time making appropriate sounds and adding them the previous ones so the song got longer and longer. "A Song Goes Around About," was sung and ended with one person being picked to sing a solo. While they thought about what to sing, we sang, "(name of person) prepares herself or himself," and if they did not begin their solo quickly enough or did not do it at all, they had to forfeit some personal item that had to be redeemed later by performing some action decided upon by the other participants. We sang and used sign language for "My hat, it has three corners." When someone was caught making a mistake, they had to sing a solo or had to give a pawn and redeem it later by singing, telling a story or doing some other funny thing. It was fun, especially when I was allowed to join in.

As time went on, many people began using electric candles instead of real ones to minimize the fire hazard. I did not like them. There is nothing like a live tree with real candles. We were always very careful and had no problems. Naturally, one would only light the tree while people were in the room and it was never left unattended while the candles burned.

After Mama and Kurt married, afternoon coffee and supper on the Second Christmas Day were served at their apartment. Here we did not play games and the grown-ups just talked. Often friends joined us. The gathering broke up earlier than on the previous evening because everybody had to go to work the following day.

I did not have school between Christmas and New Year's. I was free to play, go sledding, skate and visit my friends to look at their trees and presents.

For Sylvester, or New Year's Eve, restaurants advertised dinner dances and New Year's Eve parties long in advance. Many people went to private parties or entertained at home. We spent New Year's Eve at Aunt Martha's. Our good friends, the Muellers, joined us for the celebration on this and many other occasions. One time, they arrived dressed as Bavarians, complete with lederhosen.

The festivities began with dinner, served at 6 p.m. After dinner, we donned fancy paper hats, pulled crackers, sang and played games. At about 10 p.m., coffee was served by the light

Appendix

of the Christmas tree accompanied by the famous Berliner doughnuts, which was the traditional New Year's Eve pastry. On New Year's Eve, all the bakeries produced enormous numbers of Berliner doughnuts, iced or sugared and filled with raspberry, strawberry, pineapple or plum preserves.

One year, we found a particularly delectable looking sugared doughnut on our cake plate. When we were about to eat it, we were astonished. It was a fake! It was so well made we did not suspect anything until we tried to eat it. Instead of a raspberry preserve, each doughnut contained either a fancy handkerchief for the ladies or a fine linen one for the gentlemen. We had boxes of pretty and fancy crackers with cute party favors, noisemakers and whistles inside. They were fun but when I was small I was nervous about the bang they made when pulled.

Champagne was ready to be served when the hands of the clock had moved to almost midnight. We watched the clock and listened for the church bells, signaling the beginning of the New Year.

Champagne corks popped, glasses were filled and the adults toasted and wished each other a "Happy New Year." I was included and was given a mouthful of champagne in a small glass. My uncle and I went out onto the balcony while the church bells were still ringing. As soon as they stopped, we heard people shouting *"Prosit Neujahr!"* ("Happy New Year,") blowing noisemakers, rattling rattles, waving sparklers and red and green Bengali lights. We did the same. We shouted, lit sparklers and Bengali lights. After a few minutes, we felt cold and returned to the warm living room.

Appendix

On New Year's Eve, we observed another custom. We bought boxes of lead pieces shaped like flowers, clover leaves and such. After midnight, we each selected a piece, heated it in a special ladle over the flame of a candle. When it melted, we poured the liquid lead into a bowl of ice cold water where it instantly turned into a bizarre shaped nugget. "Reading" the nugget told something about the future. It was carefully inspected, held up to a strong light to throw a shadow on the wall and it was interpreted. It was just for fun and nobody took it seriously. After the champagne had been consumed and perhaps a few glasses of wine, the party broke up and we walked home through the cold night, meeting revelers, greeting each other with a jolly *"Prosit Neujahr!"*

The traditional New Year's dinner was carp bleu, carp cooked in beer. We had fish stores where live fish was sold. Many a time on this particular day, a carp swam in our bath. I did not like it and never developed a taste for it. The scales of the carps were quite big and after cleaning the fish, they were washed and dried. A few scales, carried around in your change purse, ensured that you would not run out of money in the coming year. Everybody was given three or four as good luck tokens.

The circle of the year was complete and another one began.

Appendix

Games and Birthday Celebrations

As soon as the snow melted and the sidewalks were clean and dry, we played with hoops, jump ropes and tops and played hide-and-seek and tag. When it was a little warmer, we scooped out small round dents in the earth by one of the linden trees that lined our street and played marbles. Ball games included "Emperor, king, nobleman, farmer, beggarman," for which we drew chalk circles some distance apart and wrote the designation inside them. Everybody chose a place and we threw the ball to each other. If a player did not catch it, he or she had to run and get it. Meanwhile, everybody else tried to get to a circle denoting a higher standing than the one he or she occupied, in order to eventually end up emperor. Another ball game was "The most disliked animal." For this game, we wrote names of animals on a wall or fence and each player picked the animal he or she wanted to be. A ball was placed on the ground by the wall or fence. A line was drawn some distance from the wall or fence and players crouched behind it, ready to run. One person started the game by calling, "The animal I most dislike is..." and mentioned one of the animals. As soon as the players heard the name of the animal, all of them except the one mentioned, ran as far away from the fence or wall as possible. The animal called ran to the fence, picked up the ball and shouted, "Halt." All other animals stopped and the one with the ball threw it at one of them, trying to hit him or her. If he or she was successful, the animal hit was given a mark beside his animal name. Whoever had the most marks, lost. The ball thrower was the person who called the next name. We played charades, hopscotch and various singing games such as "The Golden Bridge," and "Make me cry, make me laugh."

We rode scooters and self-propelled four wheelers, if we owned them.

My life was fairly quiet when I was young and very few exciting things happened. The highlights of the year, apart from the holidays described, were summer vacation, visitors and birthdays.

Birthdays were generally celebrated with an open house in the afternoon and evening. Family and friends were expected to call. If someone sent a birthday card, it meant that they could not come in person. The birthday person was ready to receive guests after 2:30 p.m. The kettle was softly humming and the coffeepot stood ready. The table, covered with a fine cloth, was set with *Sammeltassen* (bone china sets of matching medium size plate, cup and saucer, each set in a different pattern) and a large platter of assorted, fancy pastries and/or a gateaux. Guests arrived and stayed however long they wanted, many of them until evening. For supper, open garnished sandwiches, long Vienna sausages, potato or herring salad, smoked shrimp in aspic and other dishes were served.

Special birthdays warranted special celebrations. Special birthdays were the 30th, 40th, 50th and 60th. After the 60th birthday, people celebrated every fifth birthday in an even more special way.

Our family celebrated all special birthdays at Aunt Martha's apartment, usually with a five course sit down meal, followed later by coffee, pastries and a special birthday gateaux.

When people went to somebody's birthday and open house, they took flowers and a small gift. Popular gifts for women were perfumed soap, chocolates, *Sammeltassen*, colognes, vases,

Appendix

boxes of fancy embroidered or lace handkerchiefs and books. Men received flowers and books, cigars, cigarettes, cologne, handkerchiefs and ties. The gifts were never extravagant.

As far as children's birthdays went, we had no parties like we have in the United States. My birthday, so close to Christmas, was a problem because everybody was so busy. Nevertheless, it was made to be a special day. I wore my Sunday dress to school and it was the custom for classmates and teachers to recognize and congratulate the birthday child. The flowers I received and which were sold in the stores at this time of year were white paper narcissus, yellow mimosa, some type of red flower in the anemone family and poinsettias. I always received birthday gifts and Christmas gifts. Nobody combined them into one.

I was invited to many of my friends' birthday celebrations. I dressed in one of my Sunday dresses and took flowers, as well as a small gift, such as a book, a game or candy. Before or after the refreshments were served, we played games, like pin the tail on the donkey, word games or throwing dice for chocolates.

Throughout the years of my early childhood, the observance of these holidays and special occasions remained unchanged. They even continued to be observed in the same manner after the Nazis came to power.

Appendix

ABOUT THE AUTHOR

Gisela R. McBride was born in Berlin where she lived and was educated. At the end of World War II, she went to London where she worked for a number of firms, lastly for Lloyds Bank. Ms. McBride received a certificate for conference interpreting as well as a British Red Cross certificate in first aid and home nursing. She sang in Lloyds Bank's Amateur Operatic Society. In 1957, Ms. McBride emigrated to Canada and worked for the Canadian Broadcasting Corporation in Toronto until she moved to the United States. She has resided in California, New York, New Jersey and Pennsylvania, with a short intercal in Bermuda.

Ms. McBride translated a copy of a commentary on the Book of Revelation by Landesbishof Edouard Lohse of Hanover, Germany, into English and self-published a volume of Estonian Folk Tales which she translated also from German into English.

At the age of 62, Ms. McBride graduated with a liberal arts degree from the Pennsylvania State University. She audits university and college courses in subjects of interest including religion, Japanese civilization, German history, and art. An avid reader, she reads biographies, art history, German poetry and novels, and mysteries.

Ms. McBride studied oil, pastel, and watercolor painting and has exhibited throughout Pennsylvania and in Washington, DC. While living in Washington, she was a foreign language docent at the National Gallery of Art. Ms. McBride uses the profits from sales of her paintings towards the spaying and neutering of homeless cats.

Her many activities presently include singing both solos and chorus, traveling, baking, needlework and growing indoor and outdoor plants.

Ms. McBride currently lives in Carlisle, PA.